Redefining Autobiography in Twentieth-Century Women's Fiction

Gender & Genre in Literature

VOLUME 3
Garland Reference Library of the Humanities
Volume 1386

Gender & Genre in Literature

Carol L. Snyder, General Editor

TITLES INCLUDE

Mothers in the English Novel: From Stereotype to Archetype
MARJORIE McCORMICK

Female Heroism in the Pastoral
GAIL DAVID

Redefining Autobiography in Twentieth-Century Women's Fiction: An Essay Collection
JANICE MORGAN AND COLETTE T. HALL

Shakespeare's Theater of Desire: Troilus and Cressida
BARBARA BOWEN

Redefining Autobiography in Twentieth-Century Women's Fiction
An Essay Collection

EDITED BY
Janice Morgan and Colette T. Hall

Garland Publishing, Inc.
New York & London 1991

© 1991 Janice Morgan and Colette T. Hall
All rights reserved

Library of Congress Cataloging-in-Publication Data

Redefining autobiography in twentieth-century women's fiction : an essay collection / edited by Janice Morgan and Colette T. Hall.
    p. cm. — (Gender & genre in literature ; v. 3) (Garland reference library of the humanities ; vol. 1386)
    Includes bibliographical references.
    ISBN 0-8240-7392-4
    1. Fiction—20th century—History and criticism. 2. Fiction—Women authors—History and criticism. 3. Autobiography—Women authors. 4. Self in literature. 5. Identity (Psychology) in literature. 6. Women authors—Biography. I. Morgan, Janice. II. Hall, Colette Trout. III. Series. IV. Series: Garland reference library of the humanities ; vol. 1386.
PN3426.W65R4   1991
809'.89287'0904—dc20   90-49120
                                                                                     CIP

Printed on acid-free, 250-year-life paper
MANUFACTURED IN THE UNITED STATES OF AMERICA

Contents

SERIES EDITOR'S PREFACE
Carol L. Snyder   ix

ACKNOWLEDGMENTS   xi

FOREWORD
Molly Hite   xiii

INTRODUCTION

Subject to Subject/Voice to Voice: Twentieth-Century Autobiographical Fiction by Women Writers
Janice Morgan   3

REDEFINING AUTOBIOGRAPHY: STRATEGIES OF THE SELF FROM COLETTE TO CLARICE LISPECTOR

Lies, Half-truths, Considerable Secrets: Colette and Re-Writing the Self
Catherine Slawy-Sutton   23

Breaking from the Cage of Identity: Doris Lessing and *The Diaries of Jane Somers*
Cora Agatucci   45

"'She' is me more than 'I'": Writing and the Search for Identity in the Works of Marie Cardinal
    Colette T. Hall   57

Fiction and Autobiography/Language and Silence: *The Lover* by Marguerite Duras
    Janice Morgan   73

H.D.'s *The Gift:* "Hide and Seek" with the "Skeleton-Hand of Death"
    Miriam Fuchs   85

Two Modes of Writing the Female Self: Isabel Allende's *The House of the Spirits* and Clarice Lispector's *The Stream of Life*
    Flora H. Schiminovich   103

WRITING THE SELF FROM THE OUTSIDE-IN

Father Land and/or Mother Tongue: The Divided Female Subject in Kogawa's *Obasan* and Hong Kingston's *The Woman Warrior*
    Donald C. Goellnicht   119

Gender, Culture, and Identity in Paule Marshall's *Brown Girl, Brownstones*
    Keith E. Byerman   135

Self-Representation as Art in the Novels of Nella Larsen
    Jacquelyn Y. McLendon   149

The Question of Lesbian Identity in Marie-Claire Blais's Work
    Janine Ricouart   169

CONTENTS vii

FEMINIST REVISIONS OF FEMININE TEXTS

Katherine Anne Porter's Miranda: The Agrarian Myth
and Southern Womanhood
 Mary Titus — 193

Gabrielle Roy's *Children of My Heart* or Portrait of
the Artist as a Young Woman
 Agnès Whitfield — 209

PERSONAL TEXTS AND HISTORICAL CONTEXTS

The Kaleidoscopic Vision: Autobiographical
Inscription in the Works of Tatyana Mamonova
 Sharon Hileman and Ann K. Johnson — 229

A Never-Ending Autobiography: The Fiction of
Carmen Martín Gaite
 Concha Alborg — 243

The Difficulty of Saying "I": Reassembling a Self in
Christa Wolf's Autobiographical Fiction
 Kathleen L. Komar — 261

Ideology and Self-Representation: The Case of Israeli
Women Writers
 Yael S. Feldman — 281

NOTES ON CONTRIBUTORS — 303

Series Editor's Preface

If genre is a particularly suspect term in post-modernist criticism, that is in good part because feminist theorists have exposed some of the ways in which supposedly value-free literary classifications actually privilege male discourse. They have allowed us to see genre as the authorizing and valorizing instrument of the male canon, a grillwork barring women entrance, or a ladder on which women's writing occupies the lower rungs of the sub-genres. The literary types, we have seen, inscribe an economy of representation that profits male expression at the expense of women's experience; the "law" of genre imposes a regularity against which women's writing must, if it appears at all, appear deviant.

These broad attacks on genre as a sex-inflected system lay the groundwork for this series, an array of particular studies of the gender-genre linkage. There is much to be done. The past decade has given us explorations of such forms as the *Bildungsroman*, the *Künstlerroman*, the utopian and Gothic novel as women have written them; studies are even now emerging of the female-authored elegy, sonnet sequence and other pure and mixed poetic modes. Women's work in non-fiction prose and in the dramatic genres is being resurrected and reassessed. At the same time, feminist critics continue to deconstruct women as signs in patriarchal literary forms, explaining the effect of male gender on structures of signification, the narrative and stylistic codes of genre. This series welcomes such studies, encouraging as well accounts of sexuality and textual inheritance, the influence of female authorship on the evolution of a genre or the creation of a new genre, and challenges to genre theory from a gender perspective.

Such a project should reinvigorate a practical criticism which has long proceeded unquestioningly along lines laid down by genre. A gain for literary theory can also be predicted, if not yet precisely delineated: as we accumulate a corpus of texts and submit them to analyses which include the variables of sex, race, and nationality, our premises about the patterns of literary construction, authority, and interpretation are bound to evolve. The ultimate aim of this series, however, as of all feminist endeavors, is no less than the revision of culture, a remaking of the reality we create and construe through symbolic action.

The present volume, *Redefining Autobiography in Twentieth-Century Women's Fiction*, enters the critical discourse on gender and genre at a particularly advantageous moment. Key works by Carol Gilligan (*In a Different Voice*), Nancy Chodorow (*The Reproduction of Mothering*), and French feminist theorists Cixous and Kristeva have supplied a base for reconsidering female subjectivity by tracing a different developmental model for women than men, an identity formation leading to a sense of self at once fluid and attached and a language of the self described by the semiotic challenge to the symbolic. While autobiography has recently gained status as a genre, feminist critics have worked to recuperate value for women's contributions to the mode and to dismantle androcentric notions of the autobiographical paradigm. At the same time, there has been a dramatic outpouring of works by women in diverse cultures that cross the boundary between autobiography and fiction. These texts raise the host of questions about women's writing of the self addressed in the essays Colette Hall and Janice Morgan bring together here.

Carol Snyder
University of Houston-Clear Lake

Acknowledgments

This has been a truly collaborative project bringing together scholars from a variety of different cultures and literary backgrounds. We would particularly like to thank our many contributors for their trust, their patience, for their willingness to rethink and revise their work and, very often, for their sense of humor. Working with each of them has genuinely been a rewarding and pleasant experience.

We wish to thank Molly Hite for graciously accepting to critique our manuscript and to write a foreword; Carol Snyder, the series editor, for her speedy and thoughtful response to our essays; and Kennie Lyman, the general editor, for her supportive comments when the project threatened to become overwhelming.

We also wish to acknowledge the support we have received from both Murray State University and Ursinus College, our respective institutions. They have equally contributed to the completion of our manuscript.

Many thanks go to our families and friends, especially to David Slawson and Derk Visser, for their confidence in us and for their valuable advice.

Last, but not least, our heartfelt thanks go to Lilli Mueller, the secretary, and to Linda Jessup, the user support specialist at Ursinus College, for their tireless efforts in preparing the manuscript for publication. Without their expertise and perseverance, this major task could never have been carried through.

The publishers and editors wish to thank *The French Review* (AATF, 57 East Armory Avenue, Champaign, Illinois 61820) for permission to reprint the article on Marguerite Duras by Janice Morgan. This article is reprinted with translations from *The French Review* 63:2 (1989), 271-79.

A brief note on format: The translation of most foreign book titles is given in parentheses with the date of the original publication and the date of its translation. If no published translation exists, then the book title in English will not be italicized in the main text.

Foreword

Margaret Atwood tells about how some time ago she did a series of readings from the first part of her novel *Lady Oracle,* in which the protagonist is an obese teenage girl. She describes beginning each performance by explaining carefully that although the work she was about to read had a first-person narrator, it was fiction, made up, a product of the imagination. And, she reports, invariably the first question after she finished was "How did you lose all that weight?"

This seems to me to be a story not only about how readers are prone to conflate the narratorial with the authorial "I," but about how readings that identify protagonist with author are nearly inevitable when the author is a woman. Female writers of fiction find it difficult to evade the imputation that they are "writing themselves," in the sense of transcribing in narrative form their own experiences, emotions, attitudes, and ideas. Evasion is an issue because the attendant implication is that little or no artistry is involved: for women, to "write oneself" is a procedure analogous to rubber stamping, in which a preexisting self is simply inked and then imprinted on the page. From the standpoint of this model, self-inscription is something women do because they cannot help it. Mimesis requires little mediation; at most, only the simplest and most clerical act of transliteration suffices to turn world into word.

This is a remarkably undertheorized account of what, and how, women write, but it continues to permeate critical approaches, feminist as well as non- or antifeminist, that regard women's writing primarily as a *manifestation*, whether of the author's nature, culture, social situation, political situation, or personal situation. The tacit premise of such approaches is that the author is somehow present in her work, not in any secondary sense, as in the relation of producer to product, but in some wholly accessible and unmediated manner. The critic construes the text as a vehicle for the presentation of the author, who is there exposed to readers who have the advantage of seeing her without being seen. One depressingly familiar consequence is that the critic will discern flaws or deficiencies in textual resistance to the most obvious strategies of reading, and will go on to interpret these alleged shortcomings as evidence of the author's anxiety or ambivalence about her subject matter. In these ways, "autobiographical" becomes a term of dismissal, relegating women's fiction to secondary status. Serious fiction, it seems, is more . . . well, fictional.

At the same time, however, there has been an enormous amount of interest in the genre of autobiography itself, and this interest has served to establish autobiography *as* a genre, a kind of writing with its own conventions that are transformed and transcended by successive practitioners. Contemporary autobiographical theory has complicated the "self" posited as origin and subject-matter of self-writing by focusing attention on the ways it is constructed *by* that writing, as well as by the surrounding social and cultural discourses. Moreover, this kind of theory necessarily emphasizes nonfictionality as one of the genre's defining characteristics, and thus raises the uneasy specter of discursive correspondence—to a "real" world, to the "truth" of experience—and the means by which assurances of veracity are conveyed to readers. Such concerns effectively strip the veneer of obviousness or naturalness from the idea of self-writing.

In the context of this recent work on autobiography, the category of "autobiographical fiction" emerges as less self-evident—indeed, as mysterious to the point of being an oxymoron. In particular, the stress on the nonfictionality of autobiography brings contemporary literary theory up against a question it has generally preferred to bracket, that of the relation of representation to truth. What does it mean to designate an account as nonfictional? What sorts of assent does such a designation compel? And how does that assent differ from the assent required of a reader of fiction? After all, if there is nonfiction there is also fiction, its other, counter, and opposite. In this relation, fiction begins to take on the connotations that have given it a bad reputation with philosophers from Plato to John Searle, connotations of duplicity, dissimulation, veiling, and perhaps outright lying. Of course, these connotations also attach, in a surprisingly wide range of cultural contexts, to women. And women write not only fiction but autobiographical fiction, a category that now appears doubly problematic inasmuch as it takes deception to another level, blurring the distinction between confession and fabrication, between laying bare and cunningly draping. What sort of assent can this kind of writing demand of the reader? And what of the woman who "writes herself" in this manner—in what sort of act is she engaged? Clearly, "writing oneself" does not occur by reflex or through inadvertency, nor is it necessarily done by those short on creativity, for lack of an alternative. Self-writing is, in fact, a *kind* of creativity, a peculiarly momentous kind. To the earliest of the (predominantly male) contemporary autobiographical theorists, the poststructuralist insistence on the constructed nature of identity arrived with the force of revelation: this insight informed and on occasion transformed their readings of the (predominantly male) autobiographers they took as cases in point. Subsequent female autobiographical theorists noted that female autobiographers are often motivated to write by their *awareness* of the ways their identities have been constructed. They are aware these identities have been constructed because these identities are correspondingly narrower and more constricting than the identities acknowledged as belonging to privileged men. To be marginal to a dominant culture is to have been denominated its other, which means to carry its least prized attributes. To be marginal to a dominant culture is also to have had little or no say in the construction of one's own socially acknowledged identity. All this suggests that for the marginal subject, the act of "writing oneself" is unlikely to be perceived as a process of simple transcription, the faithful replication of a "self" presumed to exist prior to all discourse. For such a subject, self-writing tends to be participation in the multiple discourses that establish and reestablish this "self." It is by definition a revisionary activity, inasmuch as it reinscribes a prescribed subjectivity in another register, intervening in the social construction of identity to bring a somewhat different self into being.

The notion of *fictional* self-writing seems in ways even more congenial to the marginal subject, in that it implies an acknowledgment that the self is always to some extent (and in some senses) a fiction and a correlative freedom to engage in self-invention without regard for external standards of truth or authenticity. Such freedom is not by definition revolutionary: it could entail constructing a self more consonant with the values of the dominant culture, as Mary Titus has shown to be the case with Katherine Anne Porter. But it does suggest that the writing of fictional autobiography involves more, rather than less, artistry and artifice than the writing of other kinds of fiction.

The works considered in this collection tend to confirm this inference. To a striking degree—and in striking contrast to writing in the predominantly male modernist and postmodernist canons—the most formally and stylistically innovative fiction by women in the twentieth-century is also autobiographical fiction. But the "autobiographical" component does not in itself dictate any particular style or structure. "Autobiographical fiction" can designate very different kinds of narrative, from first-person confessions to historical realist novels to the syntactical experiments of H.D. or Clarice Lispector.

Although all the writers under consideration here could be called established, they are established in a variety of cultural contexts. If autobiographical fiction is a way of both acknowledging and revising cultural determinants of identity, this collection emphasizes that cultural determinants vary considerably: "culture" is not a monolithic entity. Nor does it shape a monolithic "woman." Differences in class, race, and sexual preference among women ostensibly inhabiting the same national culture entail different degrees of marginality, and commensurately different relations to the project of fictional self-writing—to what autobiographical fiction involves and what it is for.

The central concern shared by all the critics in this volume is precisely this question of what "autobiographical fiction" means in the writing of an author or authors, in particular how autobiography is related to fiction in concrete instances of literary practice. Predictably, the answers to this question are as diverse as the writers treated. It is worth noting, however, that no one in the anthology is inclined to view autobiography as the uncontrolled or unintended other of women's fiction, the inadvertent mark of authorial presence, representation as symptom. In regarding autobiographical elements as positive aspects of an overall fictive strategy, these critics have arrived at some of the strongest readings of twentieth-century women's fiction that I have yet seen. I regard this book as something of a landmark and trust that it will also be a precedent.

Molly Hite
Cornell University

Introduction

Subject to Subject/Voice to Voice: Twentieth-Century Autobiographical Fiction by Women Writers

Janice Morgan

> And this tale was really about being allowed to invent us, all of us, all over again, finding our several voices through our metaphors, and with enough time to stay.
>
> Mary Ann Caws, speaking of *The Quest for Christa T.* by Christa Wolf[1]

It was not too long ago that literary critics, when discussing the works of well-known modernist authors, were—like county coroners—frequently compelled to pronounce, with great solemnity, "the death of the subject." This recent post-structuralist rejection of the author as a unified, originating subject has striking—if presumably unintended—affinities with the critical doctrine it proposed to supplant. New Critics, in response, no doubt, to the excesses of their romantic, less disciplined predecessors, were highly concerned about what they called "the intentional fallacy": it was, in their view, necessary to separate literary works from their authors' subjectivity precisely in order to respect the integrity of meanings generated by the works themselves. Yet this critical correction, in turn, eventually produced its own excesses. For one of the tenets of New Criticism was to consider the text alone as a quasi-sacred edifice, a sort of aesthetic temple where the "happy few" would come to worship. The text was a closed system, a highly self-contained world, perfect in its own unity; and the critic's role was to admire the harmony of its parts. It was irrelevant (indeed, one suspects, downright embarrassing) to ask questions about the identity of the author, or about the cultural, social, and economic circumstances surrounding that authorship. These kinds of issues were dismissed to the remote province of some other discipline (history, political science, sociology) or, in the case of the identity of the I-writing, to the subordinate (and vastly inferior) genres of biography and autobiography. The texts themselves stood alone and, "the Moving Finger (of God? of genius?) having writ, move[d] on," and that was that.

In our own time, however, the arrogance of this attitude toward literature with its accompanying world view has been significantly challenged. For, historically, we have witnessed the emergence of the civil rights movement, the feminist movement, the struggle for greater political and economic liberties on the part of peoples who once lived in the shadow of vast colonial empires, and—with these movements— the rise of new critical discourses that explore the bases and strategies of political power and social change. Far from being irrelevant, it now appears necessary to ask the question "Who is speaking? Who is writing?" For couched in the prior disregard of the I-writing, recent critics have detected a hidden but unmistakable ideology and a hidden, perhaps unconscious agenda: the establishment of a literary canon that effectively excludes and silences all other alternative voices and visions, the establishment of a tradition where those experiences that have been lived and written from a perspective other than white, male, upper-middle class, Western are not fully represented.

Along with this expanded view of the body politic has come a more active role for the individual reader, an awareness that readers' experiences, their own particular cultural baggage and assumptions, their desires and interpretive strategies all contribute to the meaning of a literary work. Clearly, then, the companion question to "Who is speaking?" is "Who is listening?"—and even beyond that—"Who will respond?" For isn't our relationship to literature more alive, more vital than the notion of absent authors or "dead subjects" would seem to imply? And for literature to remain alive, it must be approached by each new generation of readers in a direct way, subject to subject, voice to voice.

It is within the framework of these larger developments that we observe the growing interest in autobiography, for the whole subject of I-writing has come into its own in the latter part of the twentieth-century, attracting ever greater attention on the part of writers and readers alike. So much so, in fact, that far from being considered a minor subset of literature as it certainly was in the not-so-distant past, certain contemporary critics (notably Georges Gusdorf, James Olney, and Paul John Eakin) have boldly asserted that all literature—whether poetry, fiction, drama, or philosophical essay, even literary criticism itself—may be considered to be, at heart, some aspect of autobiography. That is to say, each of these literary genres participates in one larger, central endeavor—the writing of the self.

It is James Olney, perhaps, who offers the clearest representation of how the autobiographic paradigm has shifted historically. Examining the etymology of the word itself, he reminds us that in the pre-modern past, writers and readers were primarily concerned with the "bios" or factual life as depicted in the work; later in modernist times (late nineteenth-early twentieth centuries), the center of interest shifted to "autos" or the exploration of the self; still later, in our own postmodern era, much of autobiographic focus is centered on "graphe"—that is, on writing, on textuality—all the rich congeries of sensuous and metaphysical associations evoked by the word *écriture* in French deconstructionist commentary.

At the same time as this last shift has occurred, we witness a related phenomenon, the gradual breakdown in the notion of autobiography as a separate genre to be distinguished, in particular, from fiction. For as the paradigm has shifted to privilege the relationship between "autos" and "graphe," a new kind of autobiographical writing has come into being—a writing neither wholly autobiographic nor wholly fictional, but rather a provocative blend of both—hence, the use of the term autobiographical fiction.[2] Hardly a year goes by without yet another contribution to this distinctive hybrid form, one often highly self-conscious in its expression, and one which alters our expectations—indeed, our very definition—of what constitutes the "autobiographic."

We no longer expect to receive, as eighteenth century readers would have, a full, factual account of the author's public self, nor do we anticipate a linear, chronological exposition of events, nor do we expect the autobiographical enterprise to be contained, necessarily, within a single work. In the eighteenth century, as Patricia Spacks points out, autobiographies and novels, however similar may have been their central concerns (the integration of the self into society), always carefully preserved their *separateness* as each genre maintained a "different rhetoric and a different narrative atmosphere" (313).

Accordingly, each elicited a very different response from readers as one purported to be a "real" account of actual events while the other offered itself as being a special kind of neither-true-nor-false illusion. Furthermore, the distinction between the two was reinforced by two, interlocking assumptions about self and writing: first, a confidence in the fixed, identifiable reality of the self; secondly, a confidence in the referential power of language to name and hold that reality in a written text.

Since then, both of these assumptions have been cast into doubt and with them, the belief they supported that autobiographical writing—unlike fiction—is easy, factual, and transparent. Accordingly, contemporary writers have brought the domains of life and literature, experience and textuality, into a much more complex, more mutually creative, and in fact, complicitous relationship. To read such works as *Speak, Memory* by Nabokov or *The Woman Warrior* by Maxine Hong Kingston is to be made aware of the evolving self as an endless negotiation between event and illusion, the actual and the imaginary, where myth, allegory, and lived experience combine in complex, interdependent patterns to form what Michel Leiris calls the "authenticity" of the self.[3]

For certain twentieth-century writers, the mutually supportive tension between "autos" and "graphe" becomes almost a source of anxiety. In reading *Roland Barthes by Roland Barthes*, for example, or "Borges and Myself" by Borges, one senses beneath the playful, reflexive surface of the text a fascinating suspicion that the self may be so essentially elusive, so insubstantial that it requires the sheer materiality of the text (with its familiar narrative tropes and characterizations) to attach itself to. Then, too, for critics like Michael Sprinker, the self's relationship to language is inherently problematic and even mutually reductive: "the inquiry of the self into its origin and history is always circumscribed by the limiting conditions of writing, of the production of a text" (Sprinker 432 in Olney). Carried to its extreme, from this perspective the whole project of I-writing itself takes on a shadowy, shimmering, mirage-like unreality. The "I" is caught, if at all, only in the refracting prism of language: literary subjectivity becomes, then, a mere ghost reflected—ever more vertiginously—in textuality's hall of mirrors. Taking stock of this scene, no wonder some have announced the inevitable disappearance of the self altogether and with it, "the end of autobiography!" (321).

All of these issues take on a compelling "other" dimension if one looks specifically, as we do, into the case of women writers. For, as Nancy K. Miller has observed, it is "in the face of the current trend toward the massive deconstruction of subjectivity" that the whole question of female subjectivity arises (103). That is to say, at the very same time that the (male) tradition was chronicling the death, disappearance, or absence of the author (see Barthes and Foucault), feminist critics have been busy introducing the body of women's writing as an unmistakable *presence*.

Domna Stanton, in noting this phenomenon, offers a possible (indeed, probable) explanation for this differing agenda: "[Perhaps] Professor Y [the liberal male critic] was feeling paralysed by the identity that the symbolic order bestowed (or imposed) upon him, whereas F.S. [the corresponding feminist scholar] was still struggling, in that recently constructed room of her own, to assert an identity that was denied her" (15). The search for more genuine concepts of female identity—other than those projected through male fantasy—certainly constitutes one of the major motives behind feminist criticism today. This search, in the work of critics such as Mary Mason and Sidonie Smith, for example, has led to the recovery of a lost tradition of women's autobiographical writing and to an argument for the specificity of this writing, for what we might call a poetics of women's selfhood. Subjectivity, as it turns out, (playing on a phrase from Nancy K. Miller) is not only "headier" than we had thought, but "sexier" as well (17).

Furthermore, these scholars have recently pointed out that the by-now canonical features of contemporary self-representational writing—fragmentation, discontinuity, duality, and above all, a pervasive textual self-consciousness—have, in fact, frequently been present in women's autobiographical writing all along. These "innovations," usually credited to enterprising, iconoclastic male authors such as Roland Barthes, for example, have consistently played a key role in the elaboration of an alternate, "feminine" poetics. It is as if, from our current perspective, the status of women as "outsiders," writing at the margins of public discourse, has bestowed (or imposed) on them a peculiar prescience; that is, the "otherness" intrinsic to their experience as outsiders looking in on an "androcentric genre" (Smith 101) has necessitated alternate and, to some extent, oppositional strategies of self-representation.

Turning on the work of sociologist Nancy Chodorow, who was one of the first theorists to explore the culturally-determined role patterns that shape, differently, the development of ego boundaries in young boys and girls, critics such as Sidonie Smith, for example, have postulated that female selfhood is far more concerned with various levels and intensities of connection *to* (rather than separation *from*) significant others. Rather than being unitary, monumental, and posited as either extraordinarily unique (à la Rousseau) or else thoroughly exemplary (à la Henry Adams), women's sense of self as portrayed in autobiographic texts has been much more locally-bound, tied to the exigencies of a particular place and time, tied especially to the key individuals who marked their development.[4] Basing her conclusions on a study of several major autobiographical texts by British and American women from the fifteenth to the twentieth centuries, Mary Mason finds a common theme and structuring principle: "the self-discovery of female identity seems to acknowledge the real presence and recognition of another consciousness" (22). This gradual, informing process she describes as the "evolution and delineation of an identity by way of alterity" (41).

Perhaps because of this primal connection to significant others, one also finds in these writers a sense of the self as plural; from at least as early as the Renaissance these women have been aware of their roles/identities as multiple—and, given societal constraints on women's aspirations, frequently in conflict with one another. Informing Margery Kempe's fifteenth century narrative, for example, is her dual, conflicted sense of vocation: first, as worldly bourgeois wife and mother, secondly, as otherworldly Christian pilgrim and mystic.[5] Kempe's narrative, colorful and eccentric as it is, articulates a conflict that becomes paradigmatic in later autobiographic texts/lives by women: the conflict between the private role specifically reserved for her by society and the more public, authoritative or adventurous role she aspired to exercise. Her entry into discourse, then, bears the peculiar, conflicting stresses of this dual experience.

Another related characteristic of women's autobiographical writing is its particular brand of textual self-consciousness. As Brodzki and Schenck point out in their introduction to the collection of essays in *Life/Lines*, women in particular—long associated (both in admiration and in scorn) with the mirror of Venus—have also maintained a profoundly ambivalent relationship with the "mirror" of self-reflecting literary creation. "Why hath this lady writ her own life?" This question, posed rhetorically toward the end of her own life history by Margaret Cavendish, duchess of Newcastle (1624-1674), reverberates through the centuries in many a woman's autobiography. Women, traditionally, have felt a particularly urgent need to justify their entry into the realm of public (thus, male) discourse. Cavendish's own history, for all its fire and spirit as the record of a remarkable woman of her time, yet reveals in its self-deprecating disclaimers and in its disjunctive forms that she is posturing uncomfortably before the audience of male readers she knows to be watching and judging her. Fully anticipating the raised eyebrows her audacity will invite, she replies to those "censuring Readers": "I answer that it is true, that 'tis to no purpose to the reader, but it is to the Authoress, because I write it for my own sake, not theirs" (quoted in Smith 100). In the disarming candor of this assertion lies a key insight that, in the intervening centuries, has become commonplace; the representation of the self in a written text responds as much if not more to the inner needs and desires of the author than it does to the expectations of that author's public. And finally, even the signing of her name to the final document bears touching witness to the anxieties of authorship that she, as a woman, experiences. Cavendish gives us her full signature, carefully including her father's name and town of origin, "lest after-ages should mistake" who she was, "for my Lord having had two Wives, I might easily have been mistaken, especially if I should dye and my Lord Marry again" (quoted in Smith 100). In this one phrase, one senses the fear underlying the energy of her ambition; clearly, she is "writing for her very life" (Smith 100)—to rescue an identity, already precarious and effaced by the legal practices of a patriarchal culture, from the complete oblivion caused by death.

Though later writers have not felt compelled to resort to such extreme postures of self-conscious defense, one still finds in the writing of Colette (1873-1954), for example, an on-going debate with a (male) reader and a supreme discomfort within the confines of the autobiographic enterprise as it had been defined by the literary establishment. The case of Colette is, indeed, an emblematic one in several respects and deserves further attention. A writer who first began her career penning popular novels under her older husband's watchful eye (*and* under his legal name and property rights), she eventually left him to venture out on her own, only signing her name (actually, her father's surname) to her works when she was nearly forty. Furthermore, as a writer of fiction she was during her lifetime, like many another woman writer both before and since, constantly chastised for being "too autobiographical"; yet Philippe Lejeune, a highly influential critic of autobiography as genre, strikingly leaves Colette out in the cold when he addresses the subject of *Autobiography in France* (1975).[6] Colette, being a fiction writer, does not fulfill Lejeune's contractual obligations; she does not, as "true" autobiographers do, conclude an "autobiographical pact" with her readers (25-26). What does not interest Lejeune, however, is why that should be the case, why Colette—who is so evidently sensitive to the demands of her readers, should have preferred *not* to conclude such a pact with them while at the same time, she also so evidently wanted to write about her own life experiences. As in the case of Margaret Cavendish, rhetorical questions addressed to an imagined reader provide some revealing answers. Colette's most pointed question/retort is justly famous: "Man, my friend, you willingly make fun of the works of woman, because they are fatally autobiographical. On whom did you rely to paint her . . . On yourself?" (*La Naissance du jour; Break of Day* 452). Elsewhere, as Catherine Slawy-Sutton's essay shows, she goes beyond the seemingly obvious to probe issues relating to writing and gender, the public versus the private, as well as to everything surrounding the thin, tenuous line between revelation and disguise. "The instinct of dissimulation has not had a terribly large place in my different lives. But it was important for me, as well as for many other women, to escape the judgement of some people, who, I knew, were subject to be mistaken, yet inclined to proclaim certitudes with affected indulgence. Such treatment pushes us women to steer away from the simple truth as from a flat melody without modulations, and to content ourselves with half-lies, half-silences, and half-evasions" ("La Dame du photographe" 26, quoted in Slawy-Sutton). For Colette, whose multiple careers as vaudeville dancer, journalist, and cosmetics entrepreneur not only lent her unconventional life a great deal of color, but—more importantly—gave her also a keen awareness of the powers and uses of artifice, there was no such thing as telling the truth of her experiences in a simple, straightforward way. Instead, Colette's musings in the above passages, and indeed, the whole body of her work, radically question the public domain of autobiographical writing as it was then understood and acknowledge what must necessarily be an essentially ambiguous process of self-discovery. Curiously, the French word *découvrir* (to discover; to un-cover) conveys part of this ambiguity. Colette's autobiographical fiction begins to outline a strategy for self-discovery/disclosure as a negotiation between self and other that necessarily engages with acts of disguise, artifice, and creative invention. No wonder, then, that her first signed novel, *The Vagabond*, shows a marked affinity for masks and mirrors, or that the central character's point of view should be that divided one of "seeing herself being seen"—the dual perspective, clearly articulated by critics John Berger and Laura Mulvey, that remains so absolutely intrinsic to women's experiences. Furthermore, long before it became commonplace to assert the plurality or the "fictionality" of the self, Colette, rich with the knowledge gleaned—not without pain—from her "other" lives, playfully mocks authorial assertions of definitive self-knowledge. "How can this man know that I am me, since I have such a hard time to know it myself?" (*Etoile vesper* 324). Finally, we begin to see in this writer's life-long dialogue between fiction and autobiography an awareness that later writers (both men and women) would make, in Sidonie Smith's words, "the matter and medium of their texts" (62)—an awareness of writing as a continuous process of self-integration, one that can never be fully completed. "Why stop the course of hand on paper which has been collecting, for so many years, what I know of myself, what I try to hide, what I invent, and what I guess?" (*La Naissance du jour; Break of Day* 451).

We have pursued this record of what certain women have set out to do and what they have accomplished because we believe that before moving forward into the future, it is important to know where we have come from. In the light of this history, we read Barthes's and Foucault's essays on dead or absent authors with changed eyes. That is to say, we fully appreciate Barthes's caveat that fiction certainly is *not* a "more or less transparent allegory" of an author's life or personality ("Death" 143). The abuses of this false assumption are well known, particularly with regard to women writers. Nonetheless, it is difficult for us to accept his counter-proposition that "the author is never more than the instance writing" (145) or that the modern *scriptor's* hand (in Barthes's terminology) "traces a field without origin—or which, at least, has no other origin than language itself" (146). By insisting so exclusively on the eternal present of the text as it is being read, Barthes effectively de-historicizes both writer *and* reader; both alike are unmoored from the very contingencies of place and time that shape their identities. True, literature is *not* merely the receptacle for an author's life, but neither is it entirely disembodied or "empty outside the very enunciation which defines it" (145). Rather, like Arachne's spidery web (to borrow a mythological metaphor developed by Nancy K. Miller), textuality is always *already* attached to the material structures of its production.[7] Textuality, like selfhood, is formed—either by or against—the shaping contingencies of historical moment, place, gender, race, class.

Similarly, Foucault, in the essay "What is an Author?" has done much to debunk—very usefully—the notion of "an originating subject" (137) who, master of his own speech, creates a world of meaning entire unto itself. Foucault, by analyzing what he calls the "author function" in the separate domains of literary and scientific discourse, goes far toward clarifying the wider cultural context and "system of dependencies" (137) in which ideas with their various modes of expression take shape. Yet, we might ask, does he not go too far at the end of his essay by attempting to sweep us all into a presumably transcendental—but, in fact, strangely disembodied—future where "discourses, whatever their status, form, or value, and regardless of our manner of handling them, would unfold in a pervasive anonymity" (138)? The alienating potentialities of this very phenomenon have, in fact, already been traced with hallucinatory lyricism by Jean Baudrillard in response to the all-pervasive rhetoric and iconography of advertising, political marketing, and the mass media.[8]

Undoubtedly, both Barthes and Foucault are protesting the inherited nineteenth century deification of the Author, whose "I" had been elevated and reified by critical custom into a sort of Romantic monstrosity, a *monument historique*.[9] Indeed, to those writing from a privileged centrist position, as both of these authors clearly are, the deconstruction of authorial subjectivity must, at least in the short term, represent a welcome, liberating prospect—a lifting of the heavy burdens of the past. To those writing from the margins, however, to those long familiar with the anonymity that the power hierarchy has assigned to them, the supposed advantages to be derived from such absence must remain dubious at best. Furthermore, doesn't this deconstructionist emphasis on the autonomy of language, on the sovereignty of discourse, work to promote precisely those metaphysical anxieties of detachment we discussed earlier, anxieties that effectively disenfranchise the independent psychic or spiritual life of the individual? And without the active engagement of that life, isn't there a danger that our response to "Who is speaking?" may well be *limited to* the "murmur of indifference" Foucault imagines hearing on the not-so-distant horizon?

However much the anxiety about self and writing may, indeed, be symptomatic of our age, so, too, is a powerful, countervailing force—an expanded awareness of the social, political, and moral dimensions in which selves and texts are produced. It is from within this wider context, with its strong sense of connection to a specific place and time and in the resulting play—not of indifference—but of *differences*, that we bring together this particular collection of essays on autobiographical fiction by women writers. Accordingly, one of our goals has been to invite discussion of writers from as wide a range of cultural formations as possible. As editors, we especially wanted to extend the map of women's experience and textuality beyond the usual, well-charted Anglo-American or European boundaries. In so doing, we cannot conceal our reconstructionist intent to affirm—rather than deny—the mutually productive relationship between self and place, self and other, self and writing.

In order to feature some of the major themes presented in the collection, we have elected to group our essays into four categories. Like many categories, however, these are somewhat artificial in that certain characteristics of one category often overlap the boundaries of another. Nonetheless, we hope that this particular presentation will help orient the reader as key issues are addressed and elaborated by juxtaposed essays.

In "Redefining Autobiography: Strategies of the Self from Colette to Clarice Lispector," we present studies of texts which are among the boldest and most innovative of our time. Here, specific aesthetic choices reveal personal visions by writers who—like those before them—continue to express the shape of their own quests by playing both with and against the conventions of their craft. These authors exemplify what Molly Hite has recently discussed in *The Other Side of the Story*, that women's choice to "write other-wise" (6) is not an accident, nor is it "an unavoidable effect of a pre-existing limit called femininity" (8), but that this writing constitutes a deliberate challenge to the prevailing social and literary constructions of gendered selfhood. Colette seems to provide a good point of departure, since many of the issues she first addressed in the earlier part of the century have been taken up and further developed by later, more contemporary writers. Our relatively small selection of authors studied here is certainly not meant to be exclusive; furthermore, we acknowledge that many fine autobiographical studies have already been produced on well-known American or English writers such as Gertrude Stein, Virginia Woolf, or Lillian Hellman.[10] We, therefore, wanted to feature other authors who, though equally important, are less known to the English-speaking public.

Our second subtitle "Writing the Self from the Outside-In" refers to authors who—because of race, ethnicity, or sexual persuasion—have had to work through a kind of dual oppression. Doubly marginalized, twice silenced, these writers (Maxine Hong Kingston, Joy Kogawa, Paule Marshall, Nella Larsen, and Marie-Claire Blais) have had to negotiate a particularly complex relationship to their cultural positioning in order to establish a valid identity and to discover a speech that would serve them. If it is true that—in the words of the poet—we are living at a time when "the centre cannot hold," then perhaps new sources of energy and revitalization may be found along the margins. Certainly it has been one of the insights of postmodern critique that marginality has much to tell us about what the central discourses in a culture repress or deny.

In "Feminist Revisions of Feminine Texts," we present essays on two women writers—one, American (Katherine Anne Porter); the other, French Canadian (Gabrielle Roy)—each of whom has acquired a reputation for upholding a particular kind of femininity. Both critical essays challenge these stereotypical assumptions as they explore two different women's responses to the accepted myths of womanhood in a patriarchal society.

Our last heading "Personal Texts and Historical Contexts" might well serve as a thematic umbrella for the entire collection since any writer's concept of self is shaped in close response to a specific cultural era. In these essays, issues of subjectivity and gender intersect with certain historical moments and political realities. In the case of Mamonova, a recently defected writer from the Soviet Union, we see this played out in her desire to practice an inclusive, globally-oriented feminism against the strictures of a repressive, ethnically-divided totalitarian state. For Martín Gaite, self-discovery occurs in the context of Franco's Spain. Focussing on the aspirations of women as they confront the particular socio-political repressions of that period, her fiction encompasses both a personal and a generational autobiography. Writing from East Germany, Christa Wolf looks back through the prism of fiction to the impact of Naziism on her generation in an effort to discern how individuals might better respond to the pressures of political instability and ideological conflict. In an age of continuing nuclear threat and growing environmental destruction, Wolf establishes the moral imperative to reconcile the demands of individual selfhood with those of responsible community. Shulamit Lapid of Israel feels compelled to disguise a feminist autobiography in the clothes of an epic pioneer romance. Through this mythical projection, she—like other contemporary Israeli writers—attempts to satisfy the conflicting demands of both individual fulfillment and a nationalist ideology that condones only collective, defense-related interests. We have decided to conclude with Feldman's study of Lapid, for through its specific example, this essay provocatively re-articulates the central issues of our collection, thereby setting the stage for further discussion.

A cross-cultural study such as this offers a unique interplay of both commonalities and differences. It is in the spirit of this interplay and with a sense of the resulting possibility for dialogue that we have entitled our introduction "subject to subject/voice to voice." We hope this dialogue will work on at least two levels: first, in the way each author/text might engage with others in the collection and secondly, in the way each will eventually engage with different readers. We particularly stress the latter, for in the end, we acknowledge that autobiographical writing—however private or intimist its concerns may be—is also a gesture toward others; however self-oriented, it is addressed to a community of readers. This idea is central, for as readers, the writing of the self has much to do with our primary interest in literature, and fictional identifications of various kinds are certainly among the many ways we use (however mysteriously) to construct our own identities. Ultimately, it is this reciprocal dynamics of identity through alterity that we wish our collection to convey: a sense of difference-in-connection based—as we believe things usually are—on complex, interwoven patterns of exchange. Perhaps, then (to echo Sidonie Smith's words), these essays will contribute toward providing a richer and more diverse set of voices through which and against which we may each be able to find our own.

NOTES

1. This evocative citation occurs toward the end of Caw's essay entitled "The Conception of Engendering: The Erotics of Editing," 61.
2. Here, one might note also the use of the terms "poetic autobiography" (see Smith) or "fictional autobiography," the differences between these three terms being related to the perceived balance of fact/reportage and fiction.
3. Michel Leiris is often regarded as one of the classic postmodern autobiographers. Germaine Brée, in her essay, "Michel Leiris: Mazemaker" seeks to define the code and the ethic this writer gradually evolved in his approach to the autobiographic mode.
4. This important thematic and structuring feature of women's lives has often led to their obfuscation by the lives of their partners. That is to say, the lives of famous women have very often been led in the shadow of famous men. Even to this day, for example, so important a writer as Simone de Beauvoir has been anthologized almost as a footnote to the career of Jean-Paul Sartre. As a notable exception to this practice, in a perceptive chapter on

Beauvoir by Martha Noel Evans, the name of her life-long companion appears only once.

5. On a light note, we observe in passing that Kempe may well qualify as the first modern superwoman. Not only did she manage to produce fourteen children, but she also travelled across Europe on an arduous spiritual mission. Essentially self-taught through an oral tradition of religious teachings related by women, she later recounted the story of her long quest (via male scribes, since as a woman she had not been taught to read or write) in a complex, layered narrative.

6. Miller notes: "It is a nice paradox that Colette is always read biographically, and at the same time excluded from the corpus of autobiographical writing. Perhaps this is a useful way to think about the place of women's writing" (62).

7. In the essay "Arachnologies: The Woman, The Text, and the Critic," Miller advocates a specific strategy for interpreting literary texts written by women, one that she calls "over-reading": "To overread [to read for the signature of a gendered, historical self] is also to wonder, as Woolf puts it famously in *A Room of One's Own*, about the conditions for the production of literature: 'fiction,' she writes, 'is like a spider's web, attached ever so lightly perhaps, but still attached to life at all four corners . . . [W]hen the web is pulled askew, hooked up at the edge, torn in the middle, one remembers that these webs are not spun in mid air by incorporeal creatures, but are the work of suffering human beings, and are attached to grossly material things, like health and the houses we live in'" (43-44, quoted in Miller, *Subject to Change* 83).

8. See, for example, his essay "The Ecstasy of Communication" in Hal Foster's *The Anti-Aesthetic: Essays on Postmodern Culture*. "I pick up my telephone receiver and it's all there; the whole marginal network catches and harasses me with the unsupportable good faith of everything that wants and claims to communicate. Free radio: it speaks, it sings, it expresses itself. Very well, *it* is the sympathetic obscenity of its content. In terms a little different for each medium, this is the result: a space, that of the FM band, is found to be saturated, the stations overlap and mix together (to the point that it no longer communicates at all). Something that was free by virtue of space is no longer. Speech is free perhaps, but I am less free than before: I no longer succeed in knowing what I want, the space is so saturated, the

pressure so great from all who want to make themselves heard. I fall into the negative ecstasy of the radio" (131-32).
9. In "Mapping the Postmodern" Andreas Huyssens comments: "Isn't the 'death of the subject/author' position tied by mere reversal to the very ideology that invariably glorifies the artist as genius, whether for marketing purposes or out of conviction or habit? Hasn't capitalist modernization itself fragmented and dissolved bourgeois subjectivity and authorship, thus making attacks on such notions somewhat quixotic?" (44). Nancy K. Miller also takes on this argument in her essay "Changing the Subject: Authorship, Writing, and the Reader" in *Subject to Change* 106.
10. Here, it is appropriate to mention the pioneer collection edited by Estelle C. Jelinek, *Women's Autobiography: Essays in Criticism (1980)*. A later study by the same author is *The Tradition of Women's Autobiography from Antiquity to the Present* (1986).

WORKS CITED

Barthes, Roland. "The Death of the Author." In *Image, Music, Text*. Trans. Stephen Heath. New York: Hill and Wang, 1977.
———. *Roland Barthes by Roland Barthes*. Trans. Richard Howard. New York: Hill and Wang, 1977.
Baudrillard, Jean. "The Ecstasy of Communication." In *The Anti-Aesthetic: Essays on Postmodern Culture*, ed. Hal Foster. Port Townsend: Bay Press, 1983.
Berger, John. *Ways of Seeing*. New York: Viking, 1973.
Borges, Jorge Luis. "Borges and Myself." In *The Aleph and Other Stories 1933-69*. Trans. Norman Thomas di Giovanni. New York: E.P. Dutton, 1970.
Brée, Germaine. "Michel Leiris: Mazemaker." In *Autobiography: Essays Theoretical and Critical*, ed. James Olney. Princeton: Princeton UP, 1980.
Brodzki, Bella and Celeste Schenck, eds. *Life/Lines: Theorizing Women's Autobiography*. Ithaca: Cornell UP, 1988.
Caws, Mary Ann. "The Conception of Engendering: The Erotics of Editing." In *The Poetics of Gender*, ed. Nancy K. Miller. New York: Columbia UP, 1986.
Chodorow, Nancy. *The Reproduction of Mothering: Psychoanalysis and the Sociology of Gender*. Berkeley: U of California P, 1978.

Colette, Sidonie Gabrielle. "La Dame du photographe" (The Photographer's Wife) 1944. Vol. X. In *Oeuvres complètes*. 16 vols. Paris: Flammarion, 1973.

———. *Etoile vesper*. (*Evening Star*) 1946. Vol. X. In *Oeuvres complètes*.

———. *La Naissance du jour*. (*Break of Day*) 1928. Vol. VI. In *Oeuvres complètes*.

Eakin, Paul John. *Fictions in Autobiography: Studies in the Art of Self-Invention*. Princeton: Princeton UP, 1985.

Evans, Martha Noel. *Masks of Tradition: Women and the Politics of Writing*. Ithaca: Cornell UP, 1987.

Foucault, Michel. "What is an Author?" In *Language, Counter-Memory, Practice*. ed. Donald Bouchard. Ithaca: Cornell UP, 1977.

Gusdorf, Georges. "Conditions and Limits of Autobiography." In *Autobiography: Essays Theoretical and Critical*, ed. James Olney. Princeton: Princeton UP, 1980.

Hite, Molly. *The Other Side of the Story: Structures of Contemporary Feminist Narrative*. Ithaca: Cornell UP, 1989.

Huyssens, Andreas. "Mapping the Postmodern." *New German Critique* (1984), 33: 5-52.

Jelinek, Estelle C. *The Tradition of Women's Autobiography from Antiquity to the Present*. Boston: Twayne, 1986.

———, ed. *Women's Autobiography: Essays in Criticism*. Bloomington: Indiana UP, 1980.

Kingston, Maxine Hong. *The Woman Warrior: Memoirs of a Girlhood Among Ghosts*. New York: Knopf, 1976.

Lejeune, Philippe. *L'Autobiographie en France*. Paris: Armand Colin, 1971.

Mason, Mary G. "The Other Voice: Autobiographies of Women Writers." In *Life/Lines: Theorizing Women's Autobiography*, eds. Bella Brodzki and Celeste Schenck. Ithaca: Cornell UP, 1988.

Miller, Nancy K. *Subject to Change: Reading Feminist Writing*. New York: Columbia UP, 1988.

Mulvey, Laura. "Visual Pleasure and Narrative Cinema." *Screen* (1975), 16: 6-18.

Nabokov, Vladimir. *Speak, Memory: An Autobiography Revisited*. New York: Putnam, 1966.

Olney, James. "Autobiography and the Cultural Moment: A Thematic, Historical, and Bibliographic Introduction." in *Autobiography: Essays Theoretical and Critical*, ed. James Olney. Princeton: Princeton UP, 1980.

Smith, Sidonie. *A Poetics of Women's Autobiography: Marginality and the Fictions of Self-Representation*. Bloomington: Indiana UP, 1987.

Spacks, Patricia. *Imagining a Self: Autobiography and the Novel in Eighteenth-Century England*. Cambridge: Harvard UP, 1976.

Sprinker, Michael. "Fictions of the Self: The End of Autobiography." In *Autobiography: Essays Theoretical and Critical*, ed. James Olney. Princeton: Princeton UP, 1980.

Stanton, Domna C. "Autogynography: Is the Subject Different?" In *The Female Autograph: Theory and Practice of Autobiography from the Tenth to the Twentieth Century*, ed. Domna C. Stanton 1984. Chicago: U of Chicago P, 1987.

Redefining Autobiography: Strategies of the Self from Colette to Clarice Lispector

Lies, Half-truths, Considerable Secrets: Colette and Re-Writing the Self

Catherine Slawy-Sutton

Sidonie Gabrielle Colette was born in 1873 and brought up at Saint-Sauveur-en-Puisaye, in the Bourgogne region. At the age of eighteen, she was brought to Paris by her first husband, Henri Gauthier-Villars, "Willy," who introduced her to literary and musical milieux. After discovering his wife's writing talents, Willy published, under his pen name, a series of novels written by Colette, the Claudine series, which brought fame through scandal to the couple. After her first divorce, Colette became a music-hall artist and continued writing under the name Colette Willy. While working as a journalist for Le Matin, *she married Henri de Jouvenel and, at thirty-nine, had her daughter, Colette de Jouvenel. In the twenties and thirties, she wrote her most famous works under the name of Colette:* Chéri, Le Blé en herbe, La Maison de Claudine, La Naissance du jour, Sido, La Chatte. *In 1936, she married Maurice Goudeket, the "best friend" of her later works. A very popular figure at the end of her life, she kept on writing, and became the first woman to be President of the Académie Goncourt, and a member of the Belgian Académie Royale de Langue et de Littérature Françaises. Yet, significantly, when she died in 1954, the Church denied her religious burial.*

Decades before literary critics became interested in questions of *genre* and gender, it is with a twist of irony that Colette called her male readers' attention to a possible difference between male and female approaches to writing: "Man, my friend, you willingly make fun of the works of woman, because they are fatally autobiographical. On whom did you rely to paint her? . . . On yourself?" (*La Naissance du jour [NJ]* 452). Probably because of the generic use of "woman," this statement has, recently, caused Colette to be seen as the participating victim of an ideology that devalued female writings (Stanton 4), or as conforming to expectations about women and women writers (Relyea 159).[1]

In order to suggest that Colette may have been, instead, a *brouilleuse de piste*—one who chose to deliberately confuse/provoke her readers—I will here attempt to define Colette's particular strategies of self-revelation and disguise. Moving from defensive self-consciousness to confident "self-authorization,"[2] these strategies in writing will be related to an oft-used motif in her texts, needlepoint. But, since Colette's strategies have to do with her place in the definition of *genres*, I shall first briefly examine the question of the history of literary *genres* in France. My purpose is not to enter the domain of theory, but rather to show how Colette presents an intriguing case in the gender/*genre* controversy surrounding autobiographical writing, as both earlier and contemporary criticism of her texts exemplify.

On the one hand, her writings used to be read as strongly autobiographical when this idea had a rather negative connotation (see Larnac). Henri Peyre called Colette "antediluvian," because she "is best when she harks back to her childhood"(49). Trahard, while praising her art, reproached her for being unable to go beyond personal concerns or to be interested in metaphysical questions. Thus aware of being "relegated . . . to the ranks of light reading" (Relyea 151), Colette herself probably knew she was a curiosity for not bringing her own answers to moral, metaphysical or philosophical problems, as the above apostrophe to "Man, my friend" suggests.

In light of this, Colette's works were therefore not taken seriously because they could not "help" being autobiographical. Yet, if we now turn to the French theoreticians of autobiography, we find that in his earlier studies on autobiography in France, Philippe Lejeune, while giving this genre its *lettres de noblesse*, *excluded* Colette from the canon on several counts: first on the grounds that she had not written a "continuous" (linear) autobiography; secondly because she claimed that she disliked to talk about the self and refused to write her Memoirs; finally, and more importantly for Lejeune, because she did not establish a "pact" with the readers (1971: 25-26). Lejeune's earlier definitions of autobiography insist on the author's "central project" to give "a meaning" to a personality, and on an attempt to order the genesis of a person in his/her totality, so as to understand his/her life. In that sense he sees autobiography as akin to a "scientific or historical discourse" (1975: 36).³ Beaujour has nuanced Lejeune's definitions by drawing a distinction between the more logical, chronological narration of *autobiographies*, and the discontinuous, "interminable" presentation, in the present tense, of the *autoportrait*. Lejeune's and Beaujour's studies, as well as Gusdorf's emphasis on "isolated being" (separate selfhood), have recurringly been criticized by such critics as Susan Friedman, Elaine Marks, and Nancy Miller, as male centered, indifferent in their analysis to the "gender of genre" (Miller 1981: 165, 172). This preoccupation reflects the theoretical debate in the Anglo-American branch of criticism, about gender and the *genre* of autobiography.⁴ For example, Miller sees *La Naissance du jour* more as an autoportrait than an autobiography but with "a twist, a feminine orientation" (1981: 167). I especially question, with this critic, Lejeune's earlier, recurring insistence on ordering and "making sense" of a life: "to the extent that autobiography, like any narrative, requires a shaping of the past, a making *sense* of a life, it tends to cast out the parts that don't add up, or what we might think of as the flipside of the official *reconstructed* personality" (Miller 1980: 268). Indeed, if, as Gusdorf suggests, justification is an important element of autobiographies, it is hard to reconcile Lejeune's notion of "making sense" with an author's intention to be glorified or justified, unless one suspects that a certain falsification is a large part of the process of "making sense." I believe, as we shall see later, that it is precisely in the awareness of this factor that we meet Colette's resistance to writing her memoirs.

However, my purpose here is not to go further into the controversial definitions of *genres*. I simply want to deal with the case of Colette, while supporting Smith's general call for the need of a new perspective on women's autobiography (7), as well as Miller's more specific approach to Colette from an "angle of sexual difference" (1980: 267, 1981: 167). For, if I do not agree, as I argue here, either with the notion of victimization of Colette, nor with Lejeune's radical rejection of this writer from a canon of autobiography (in formation), I see her case as a most intriguing example of the current theoretical debate raised by feminist critics. Indeed, she raises a most pertinent question, asked by Stanton about women's writings in general: "How could [the absence of women's texts in discussions of autobiography] be reconciled with the age-old, pervasive decoding of all female writing as autobiographical?" (4).⁵

Finally, let us examine recent literary criticism of Colette's texts. Such criticism has rightly pointed out that, although there may be a close relationship between the sequence of her life and that of her subject-matters and interests, one must beware of a literal reading of Colette's chronicles or of an autobiographical reading of her novels. The written memories of her childhood and family, of her mother Sido in particular, should be seen not so much as "scientific" discourse (as Lejeune would have it), but as the various constructions of a writer in search of an identity. This last conception has given rise to a host of different (and sometimes contradictory) responses to Colette. Critics have shown the difficulty in identifying author, narrator and the real Colette in texts using the personal pronoun "I" (Marks). This ambiguous use of "I," as well as the manipulation of point of view and the mixing of *genres* in *La Naissance du jour* (use of letters, essay, memoirs, love story) are viewed as technical innovations (Raaphorst-Rousseau). Colette's writing is "true-lying" (Gouaux-Coutrix). It is also seen as assertion and preservation of the mother (Brée, Courtivron), as conjuring up the maternal presence and body (Milner, Tinter); or, on the contrary, it is seen as sublimation of a repressing mother (Bal, Dupont). Her texts are considered as the literary bearing of the mother by the daughter (Lastinger); her prolific works are viewed as the expression of an incestual desire for Sido (Jouve). The film that Yannick Bellon shot of Colette in 1951 may be her "real" self-portrait because "the verbal discourse constitutes the major system of self-mythification, while bodily language, images and props make up a deconstructive, demystifying system" (Makward 185).

Interestingly enough, Colette may have been the most severe critic of her own writings. At a time when she had long reached fame for her third person narratives—what we usually refer to as "novels" and "short stories"—[6] , as well as the earlier, beautiful evocations based on recollections of her privileged childhood, and of her mother,[7] Colette questions the very *genres* based on autobiographical memory (what she calls in *L'Etoile Vesper [EV]* "the warm pell-mell of crinkled souvenirs"–377), the validity of childhood souvenirs written by adults: "I mistrust even [my own recollections]. With old age we become imaginative, at the same time as optimistic, in order to deform [our memories] while painting them" (*Belles Saisons [BS]* 36).

So, we may ask in the end, if Colette is too autobiographical for her fiction to be taken seriously, but not enough to be included in a canon in formation, if her "I" is ambiguous and constantly put in question, is that because she did not know any better? I don't think so. I believe that there are elements of subversion in her conscious disregard for the classification of *genres*. If we exclude the texts which were specifically written for the theater (often rewrites of previous texts[8]), I would suggest that, rather than classify Colette's texts in categories according to *genre*, one should consider that most fall under the more general rubric of "autobiographical fiction," with all the nuances and shades of the third to the fifth colors of the spectrum, as suggested by Georges May,[9] because I believe with Jouve that "a version of self is at stake in every single text she wrote" (186). Although this may seem at first to be oversimplifying, it takes the collected works more or less as a whole, as complementary inscriptions of an autoportrait in an "interminable écriture" (Beaujour), an inescapable inscription of a changing self; it also calls for a reading across "the body of her writing" (Miller 1980); finally it has the advantage of being more fluid, and of fitting Colette's avowed repulsion for hierarchies and categorizations.[10] The third person narratives shed new light on the first person narratives, and vice-versa, one filling the gaps of the other, one being a rewrite of the other, each calling attention to the ambiguity of the terms author, narrator, protagonist.[11]

There are several reasons why I choose to refer to Colette's body of works as "autobiographical fiction": I shall now briefly talk about *what* in her thematic contents leads me to lump autobiography and fiction together. Then I shall try to show *why*, due to her own awareness about her position as a female writer and about her authority—or lack thereof—as writer, Colette may have come to deliberately confuse/provoke her readers. And thirdly, I will address more directly the question of *how* she proceeds in revealing and disguising herself.

First, the body of Colette's writings can be read as autobiographical fiction because of the recurrent subject matter. Whether overtly talking about the self and her personal past, or about imaginary protagonists, her texts tirelessly explore the sphere of domesticity and intimacy,[12] offering the most personal insights into human and inter-species relationships. Indeed, one cannot talk about Colette's texts without considering her biography and appreciating her unusual life as a woman (writer, dancer, mime, journalist, critic, beautician, lover, etc . . .), nor is it possible to neatly classify her texts according to fiction, non-fiction and/or autobiography. From the early *Claudines* to the later recordings of the forties, they deal again and again with the same themes, based on personal history and found in the intimacy of the self: amorous relationships, jealousy, dissimulation and duplicity; "half-truths" and "half-evasions"; female dependency and fear of solitude, independence and appetite for survival;

mother/child relationships and the imaginary and creative world of children; communication or lack thereof between sexes, generations, and even species.

When talking about the content of her texts, we can certainly relate, for example, her first signed work *La Vagabonde [V]*, as well as *L'Envers du Music-Hall* to Colette's own apprenticeship of independence, and to her career in the theater;[13] or novellas like "Le Képi" and "Le Tendron" to young Colette's seduction by an older man, and to her forced beginnings as a writer.[14] We can observe how her most objective first and third person narratives are rooted in autobiographical elements:[15] "I called myself Renée Néré or else, prophetically, I introduced a Léa" (*NJ* 420). We are able to shed light on a work like *La Chatte*[16] by listening to Colette identify her protagonist's strange dreams with her own: "I have lent to my heroes my most faithful phantoms" (*Journal à Rebours [JR]* 270); and on both *La Chatte* and *Duo*[17] by reading an anecdote in "Nudité": it tells the story of a young married couple "met" by the narrator (89-92). Besides jealousy, all three stories evoke a pessimistic view of gender relationships through the recurring motives of female natural easiness and male modesty, or prudishness, in sexuality; they underline how by exposing their nude body, females may only reveal a fraction of their real intimacy.[18] Or again, we can explore how several texts evoke the maturing writer's own curiosity about relationships between older women and younger men, by connecting the male characters of *Chéri* and *Le Blé en herbe* to the younger men in Colette's life, as well as comparing them to Charlotte's young lovers in *Le Pur et l'impur*.[19]

But one must equally allow room for fiction in a more personal inscription like *La Naissance du jour*, which also uses the last theme mentioned but sends critics to wild speculations as to *who* the young Vial might have been.[20] And along the same lines, we must recall the free play between author, narrator and protagonist, between the real Colette and the persona of "Madame Colette" appearing throughout the works from the late twenties to the forties. More precisely we must recall on the one hand the ambiguities between the real self and the constructed self, between the real mother and the mythic Sido; and, on the other hand the free use of personal but *rewritten* letters from her mother in *La Naissance du jour*, the liberal use of "*rearranged* fragments of her emotional life."[21]

What comes through, in the final analysis, is Colette's blurring of autobiographical and fictional elements. The body of her writings relies on a shift, back and forth, between personal anecdotes and construction, expansion of fiction. So why such deliberate confusion between autobiography and fiction? Why does she seem to cast a shadow of doubt on the very veracity of her drawn portrait? Why is it that, each work being in some way a nuance of autobiographical fiction, we are constantly brought back to her most famous epigraph: "Do you imagine, in reading my works, that I draw my portrait? Patience, it's only my model" (*NJ* 411). I believe that Colette was tirelessly, albeit unsystematically, commenting on the illusions of her trade (the illusion of self-knowledge and of the ultimate power of the written word[22]) and on her own position and authority as a female writer.

"I would not dare be satisfied with a temporary word and tell [to my piece of paper]: 'Wait for me here, I am coming back, and I'll dress you up in your Sunday best clothes'," she comments on the ability of writers to *invent* the self (*JR* 271). Or again, about one of her visitors: "But how can this man know that I am me, since I have such a hard time to know it myself?" (*EV* 324). Just a few years before her death, shaken by the recent experience of the Second World War, immobilized by old age and arthritis, Colette pokes again at the optimistic, humanist aspiration that through old age one reaches self-knowledge: while *L'Etoile Vesper* discloses new aspects of a personality still being made and still faced with new challenges (sickness, war, confinement), it reasserts Colette's distrust in intellectualism, her disregard for the rigidity of classified *genres*, her disdain for the belief in the ultimate truth of self-portrayals:

> Do I have anything better to note today? I doubt it. Who keeps me from putting here a full stop [to writing]? No part of this book is geared towards a praising conclusion or an apotheosis. "When will you decide to give us your Memoirs?" Dear editor, I shall write them no longer, nor better, nor less than today. . . . I believe that [the younger editors] have a confused, but highly colorful image of my life. (452)

So why keep on writing at the ripe old age of seventy-three? Quite simply, because everything has not been said yet, nor can it be said: what if she were responsible for this "highly colorful image of [her] life"? Quite simply too, because "one gets tired of everything, even of keeping silent" (*EV* 344). Quite simply, finally, because of an acute awareness of the deliberate falsifications contained in inscriptions of the self.[23] If Colette claims that she had never had, as a child, a vocation for writing and was really meant *not* to write but did it out of necessity (*JR* 311-314), she also underlines the paradox of her prolific career. Once writing becomes a habit you can no longer escape it: "How difficult it is to put an end to oneself" (*EV* 455), for "writing only leads to writing" (*Le Fanal bleu [FB]* 207). The later works just quoted therefore resort to the recording of an unstructured series of meditations that became typical of her signature: on the recent past, the war, her visitors, food, graphology, the arts of writing and needlepoint. In that sense, they, too, are inscriptions of a self, both truthful and fictitious, which record the impossible challenge to put an end to writing. Here again we come close to Beaujour's definition of the autoportrait as an endless task: "I am surprised to give a written form to the memories brought about by the ringing of the bell" (*EV* 344).[24]

The excerpt from *L'Etoile Vesper* quoted above ("Do I have anything better to note today?") would seem to point towards a certain self-consciousness about her authority as writer. As Colette had argued elsewhere, what is public is not necessarily the most revealing aspect of the self:

> If I do not see any problem with putting in print, into the hands of the public, rearranged fragments of my emotional life, let me knot tightly into the same bag, everything that concerns a *preference* for animals, and—it's also a question of predilection—the child that I have borne. (*NJ* 439)

For, in the woman living off her marketable skills, there constantly conflict the tendencies to preserve the private self while revealing a public self. Montaigne preserved his "arrière boutique" *by* and *in* writing about himself.[25] Colette suggests that in her case, and perhaps in most women's writing the "arrière boutique" is what is left *unsaid*. "You talk about a lover and you keep quiet about *the rest*" (*EV* 378—emphasis added). Isn't it fascinating that the specific marks of the female gender in autobiographical writings (fragmentation, silence, intimacy, self-consciousness), now suggested by some current theoreticians, were so very acutely perceived by Colette?:

> An amorous catastrophe, its sequels, its phases, have never, ever, been part of the real intimacy of a woman. How is it that men—men writers, or so-called men writers—are still astonished that a woman should give so freely to the public love secrets, lies, half-truths? By divulging these, she manages to save from publicity other *obscure and considerable*

secrets that she herself does not understand very well. (*NJ* 452—emphasis added)

"The rest," then, is something more intimate and confusing than the autograph's expected love life and/or association with famous people. Here, it is a "preference" that the writer desires to reveal, and does at times, but that she knows will be judged, and discarded by her readers as "frivolous," or even "monstrous": "From the perspective of humans, monstrosity starts at a connivance with animals" says the perceptive narrator, as she comments on "the logical defiance of a very humanized man" (439). Incidently, the very "humanized" man in this passage of *La Naissance du jour* happens to be Colette's second husband, De Jouvenel. But it might as well be an intransigent reader, for husband and reader alike come through as the "adversaries," rather than the "friends," for whom she writes. Or this "very humanized man" might be a critic looking for grandiose answers to moral or metaphysical codes in her texts, only to find that she would rather talk about pets, flowers, a banal encounter, "the frivolous taste for life." Hence, we find an awareness of the vulnerability of her authorship under the scrutiny of her husband's gaze (quoted as saying: "'But can't you write a book that is not about love, adultery, incest or breaking-up?'" (*NJ* 420); or under the scrutiny of the reader's gaze:

> When I return [from exploring the world of cats] I sometimes happen to be welcomed like a somewhat suspicious explorer. Haven't I, over there, eaten my fellowman? Or made some criminal pact? It is high time that the strictly-called human race be worried about it . . . Actually, it is worried. On my table I have a newspaper article, seriously entitled: "Does Madame Colette have a soul?" (*JR* 321)

> —What has come over you, my dear, one [male] reader said to me, to want to attract attention to such an exceptional type as your Chéri, and that's not to use the word unbelievable. And that world, that world of prostitutes, of . . .
>
> Instead of reacting . . . , I kept silent. I accepted that a virtuous and male incompetence could call a lover devastated by his unique love, a "pale gigolo" and a "fag." For the first time in my life, I felt intimately sure that I had written a

novel about which I would neither have to blush nor doubt. (*EV* 411)

These ironic passages would seem to border on a fear of judgment from an hypothetical Other (husband, reader) about the seriousness of her own texts: they constitute an awareness of lacking authority in the eyes of more assertive judges of "good" literature.

Self-consciousness, then? This very notion somehow clashes with my response to reading Colette. Beaujour considers autoportraits as guilt-ridden by definition because, deep down, writers see their project as basically useless (448). Marks thinks the woman narrator "tends to see herself as if she were being seen or looked at" (1975: 4). Miller, Smith, and Evans suggest that female autobiographers are self-conscious because they are outside of the language of patriarchy and have to achieve a male-like discourse. These critics therefore underline, in female inscriptions of the self, the awareness of writing mostly for male readers.[26]

Although there exists, in Colette, this awareness of "being looked at" by "male readers," it is hard, however, to completely support the notion of self-consciousness, for self-consciousness in Colette is counter-balanced by humor, irony, the ultimate pleasure of writing *per se*: it does not lead to any kind of justification. Strikingly, Colette may stand out as one being particularly cheerful and disdainful of imposed hierarchies, as one particularly intent to keep on being "frivolous"[27]: "Haven't I too much, and too often spoken about cats? Too bad for my reader, for I have not yet finished to sing the Cat" ("chanter le chat," *JR* 318). The initial self-consciousness of the young provincial woman brought to Paris by her older husband (see note 14) has been transformed, through the habit-forming practice of writing, into this assertion of the maturing writer: "Too bad for my reader . . . " (my male reader perhaps?). From a perceived lack of authority, then, we thus gradually arrive at deliberate "self-authorization": "Why stop the course of a hand on this paper which has been collecting, for so many years, what I know of myself, what I try to hide, what I invent and what I guess?" (*NJ* 451). Rather than self-conscious, the narrator has become quite aware that, since neither she, nor her texts, fit in any expected "norm," she might as well keep on "doing her own thing":

> I wanted this book to be a journal. But I do not know how to write a real journal, that is to say how to give shape, grain after grain, day after day, to one of those rosaries that

> become priceless and take on the color of a jewel, merely through the writer's precision, his self-esteem, his consideration for his period. . . . After promising myself not to write anything after *L'Etoile Vesper*, here I am, covering two hundred pages, neither Memoirs, nor journal. Let my reader resign himself to it: . . . my lantern does not shed light on events large enough to surprise him. (*FB* 98)

If her writings show a keen awareness that her "preferences," her literary objects of predilection, may be outside the norm, perhaps we can now define further what became the mark of Colette's specific strategies of self-revelation.

Sometimes the narrator *affects* to denigrate herself, saying for example, after awkwardly questioning an empress of feminine fashion: "Mme Misia S . . . laughed at me, and sent me back, heartily, to my dear studies, which, as everybody knows, deal with animals, gardens and cooking recipes" (*BS* 67). At other times, she *pretends* that she will keep quiet: "But I no longer like to write the portrait, the story of animals. . . . I will end up hiding mine, except to a few friends whom they will choose. . . . I shall now keep quiet" (*NJ* 438-439). Or: "Instead of reacting . . . I kept silent" (*EV* 409). But does she keep quiet? *"Too bad for my reader. . . ."* And she continues to reveal only "rearranged fragments" of her intimacy; or she fills in the fake silence by writing her intimate conviction about the value of her works. And she throws her critics into puzzlement as to *where* she stands exactly (as she had done in *La Chatte*—see note 16). And she goes on writing about what are thought of as "culturally inferior" topics, thus offering for example, in the poetic mode, one of the most precursory—yet overlooked—aspects of her work: namely an anticipation of current theories of animal communication, and of the now fast-growing movement for animal rights.

A third strategy consists of condemning her own writings. For example, in one of her more overtly autobiographical texts about her first husband Willy and her forced beginnings as a writer, *Mes Apprentissages*, Colette came close to actual confession about "the hidden woman" in her[28]:

> My most certain art . . . is not writing, but the domestic art of knowing how to wait, dissimulate, pick up the pieces, stick back together, gild again, change the worst into the best, lose and gain back in the same instant the frivolous taste for life . . . . (216)

But she later criticized this work as "bordering on slander" and, supposedly, did not attempt to be so directly autobiographical again (*EV* 378). Yet through her fiction, the same sort of revelation about the self often seeped through. For example, in the middle of "La Dame du photographe" *[DP]*, a lesser known, short narrative casually introduced as the story of one of the "passing persons of a long-gone past,"[29] the narrator, while avoiding gossiping about her personal life with Willy, reverts to brief inscriptions of the self. After mentioning the "rectangular and inflexible attitude" of her first husband, she thus explains women's (and her own) attraction to secrecy:

> The instinct of dissimulation has not had a terribly large place in my different lives. But it was important for me, as well as for many other women, to escape the judgement of some people, who, I knew, were subject to be mistaken, yet inclined to proclaim certitudes with affected indulgence. Such treatment pushes us women to steer away from the simple truth as from a flat melody without modulations, and to content ourselves with half-lies, half-silences, and half-evasions. (*DP* 269)

Half-lies, half-silences, half evasions, considerable secrets. . . . These words best describe not only a reaction, perceived as female, to harsh judgment from males, but perhaps also Colette's manner of speech, an esthetics of "Mentir-Vrai" ("True-Lying"—Gouaux-Coutrix). As Evans best states it in her study of *La Vagabonde*, "By equating the dynamics of marriage with her situation as a woman writing in a male tradition, Colette sets up an ultimate and essential conflict between female authenticity and male power"(43). In this sense, just like answering "indiscreet" personal questions (see note 23), writing itself *has become* for Colette a role to play, a paradoxical means of survival which, in turn, must reveal or dissimulate aspects of the intimate self.

In the final analysis, Colette's particular strategies are defined by a play between revelation through fiction and disguise through autoportrait. A specific mark of Colette's signature is to reveal the portrayed female characters in their entirety (showing their "lies," "half-truths," "considerable secrets," the unconscious movements of revelation in their relationships to others—as shown in the stories of *La Femme cachée*), while *preserving* the intimacy of the writing female (Colette, as "hidden woman," who revels in ambiguity). Just as the blurring of narrator and author in *La Vagabonde* produces a discourse in which "blatant self-revelation of the one makes a perfect hiding place for the other"(Evans 47), there is a definite relationship between dissimulation in behavior and ambiguity in writing: both being aspects of disguise, *ambiguity* in writing the self may thus be but a synonym for the *dissimulation* pointed out in the female protagonists. Rather than bringing her readers to any type of unified, indiscreet voyeurism on her life, rather than intentionally presenting memoirs with a meaningful center, Colette points towards the inevitable plurality of one's inscriptions of the self, factual or fictive alike.

Colette's strategies in autobiographical fiction are perhaps best illustrated by her use of the leitmotiv of needlepoint, which recurs intermittently in her texts, and always seems contrasted and compared to reading and writing.[30] At times the narrator considers needlepoint rather negatively. In this case, like reading, embroidery is viewed as romanesque escapism (a kind of bovarism). It is not only synonymous with a task which will inevitably separate mother and daughter, but it is also presented as alienating, because, somewhat like writing, it encourages a reconstruction of the truth and of the self (*La Maison de Claudine* 81, 144-147). However, when needlepoint *becomes* the very metaphor of writing and evokes a movement towards confident self-authorization, it then shows assertion and pleasure. Colette confesses to having long liked the art of tapestry:

> After roughly fifty years occupied by the duty to write black on white, I think of needlepoint as soothing. . . . Ten, twenty years passed. I scribbled on paper with docility. Then, more daringly, I reached this multi-colored haven . . . : needlepoint . . . For a while—a long while—I thought that . . . cross-stitching would prevent the access to . . . writing. (*BS* 41-45)

Thus contrasting the seemingly exclusive activities conventionally associated with gender, the text suggests that needlepoint used to conflict with writing, a "superior" access to inscribing the self. When the two types of production become equally pleasurable, they define an androgynous self who has integrated its two sides by coming to terms with both activities. As a sequel to writing, needlepoint means reaching a "haven": "My Memoirs are inscribed in green grass, pink lilac, multi-colored anthemis. I shall begin the portrait of my star Vesper from nature" (*EV* 455, *BS* 42).[31]

Yet, what remains in the end is the ambiguity of both inscriptions. Needlepoint also reveals a feminine self "content with half-lies, half-silences, half-evasions":

> I have said and cursed enough; back to the needle. . . . An amount of daily resignation, of memories, of leisure, answers my call and *traces with cross-stitches some words that are readable only to myself*: 'Once upon a time, there was, in my life . . . '" (*BS* 49—emphasis added)

The "words" or messages produced by cross-stitching are, too, at best enigmatic, "cabalistic" (*EV* 454), or, as Miller has stated, an equally "perverted" form of inscription as that of the autoportrait, because they are not "strictly speaking communicative" (1981: 170-171).[32]

Throughout her texts, "Colette does not engrave the "I" so much as . . . embroider it" (Fraiman 52). She thus unfolds self-inscriptions which are deliberately different from "the forward drive of logocentric certitude and individuality" (Smith 13). The use of embroidery as metaphor for writing evokes a writer who was most likely a deliberate *brouilleuse de pistes,* one who refused to be bound and limited by genre, and who set out to do it her way. Writing and needlepoint alike evoke a patient weaving and reweaving of the needle, of the pen, a personal way of ultimately finding self-esteem through coming back, dutifully, to the same task/text, that is to say to "a notebook with smooth paper that needs to be *embroidered with my writing.*"[33]

NOTES

1. Such interpretations could be supported by yet another of Colette's statements in one of her more overtly autobiographical works: "In my youth, I did happen to wish to become 'someone important.' If I had had the courage to formulate my real hope, I would have said 'someone else'." Personally I see this line as indication of a certain self-consciousness in the *beginning* female writer evolving in the literary circles of her already famous first husband Willy. For the more established, mature narrator comments with assurance: "But I quickly renounced that. I have never been able to become someone else" (*Mes Apprentissages* 168-169).

2. I borrow the word from Nancy Miller (1988).
3. As noted by Miller (1980) and Smith, Lejeune somewhat nuanced "his earlier normative or essentialist definitions" (Smith 6). Indeed, in *Je est un autre*, Lejeune attempts to "deconstruct the illusion of unity of the subject encouraged by the *genre* of autobiography" (136—translation mine). Although he devotes a little more attention to Colette in this book (135-137), he concentrates on André Parinaud's radio interviews of Madame Colette (Oct.-Nov. 1950). Lejeune acknowledges here that her work inscribes itself in the "autobiographical space," but his interest in the radio interviews is used to support his earlier remark about Colette's "refusal of autobiography, in its double dimension of confession and totalisation" (137—translation mine). I have not found other references to Colette in "Le Pacte autobiographique (bis)," nor in *Moi aussi*.
4. See for example Friedman, Stanton and Smith. One difference that seems to recur among the theoreticians, is that the account by the "andrograph I" is chronological, logical, linear, for purposes of justification (Gusdorf), given as an example of the human condition; whereas the account by the "gynograph I" is fragmented, contradictory, it has no total conception of the self. Stanton says that there are also counter-examples, and Felski argues that the theoreticians of *écriture féminine* have not been able to prove the relationship between femaleness and non-linear, fluid writing.
5. It may be, as Smith argues, that the "norms" of the canon of autobiography needed to exclude women's writings in order to define more easily the *genre* as a public contract between a (male) author and his readers, especially within a patriarchal system which considers "contingent responsiveness to others . . . [as characterizing] the *life* of woman but not *autobiography*. From that point of view, woman has no 'autobiographical self' in the same sense that man does" (50—emphasis added).
6. *La Vagabonde, Le Blé en herbe, Chéri, La Chatte*, etc.
7. *La Maison de Claudine, La Naissance du jour, Sido*.
8. As in the case of *Chéri* and *La Vagabonde*, for instance.
9. Although he suggests in the end that it is impossible to rigorously separate the two *genres*, Georges May has proposed seven categories in a spectrum ranging from pure novel to pure autobiography (188-194).

10. For example, about the numerous young reporters who wish to interview her, Colette says: "Since the war, I do not know anything about *him*, about *her*, while *they have an old*, stereotyped image of me. . . . They think that I could not do without claiming to the world an opinion about the right of women to vote, about epuration, about the role of young women in *l'ordre nouveau*, about the reform of the theater, about the closing of restaurants, about the issues of paper and housing. He asks me for, she demands, the enumeration of my literary projects. *They think that I have general ideas*. (*EV* 406-407—emphasis added).
11. For a precise illustration of this point, see for example Jouve's brilliant analysis of Colette's novella "La Lune de pluie" (Jouve 186-199).
12. Jouve has rightly pointed out how literary criticism has traditionally, but mistakenly, associated these themes with women's writings, and how Colette does stand out as original (16).
13. *L'Envers du Music-Hall* is a series of moving anecdotes on the personal life of performers. *La Vagabonde* is the first person narrative of Renée Néré, an actress who chooses to keep on with her independent way of life (and therefore to face her fear of aging and of solitude) over a more comfortable, protected life with the well-off Max. For detailed analysis of *La Vagabonde*, see Eisinger (95-103), Evans (36-740), Miller (1988: 229-261), Stewart (36-45).
14. "Le Képi" is the story of Marco, a young writer paid by the line (like Madame Willy herself at the beginning of her career when Willy had discovered the exploitable talents of his wife), who has a brief affair with a soldier. "Le Tendron" tells the story of an older "friend" of Colette who likes adolescent girls, and of his involvement with a fifteen-year-old peasant when he was fifty. The male narrator says to his interlocutor, Colette: "If I remember correctly, weren't you yourself sixteen when you claimed that you were in love with a balding man who, at forty, looked twice his age? The words are yours, I believe" (414). For an analysis of this novella, see McCarty in "Charting Colette" 367-374.
15. By "elements" I do not mean true-to-life events, but rather feelings, emotions, reactions to arranged "fragments" of personal, or heard, stories.
16. *La Chatte* is the story of Alain and Camille, a young couple, whose marriage ends in failure. Some critics argue that Saha, Alain's cat, is the cause of the break up. I prefer to think that,

rather than the cause of the marital failure, their individual relationships to (and understanding of) Saha, exacerbate their differences and basic lack of communication. For longer analysis of *La Chatte*, see Bal, Forde and Sanchez.
17. *Duo* is the story of Michel's discovery of his wife Alice's former adulterous relationship, and his subsequent suicide.
18. For more on this aspect of nudity, mask, and make-up, see Evans's analysis of the character of Renée Néré in *La Vagabonde* (36-74).
19. *Chéri* is the story of a young man involved with forty-nine year-old Léa, who nurtures him as well as loves him. The character of Chéri may have been inspired by Auguste Hériot (Dormann 130). Colette also had a brief affair with her stepson Bertrand de Jouvenel, but this was only *after* she had written *Chéri*. *Le Blé en herbe* tells the story of the adolescent Phil and Vinca's sexual initiation. The first section of Colette's essay on sexual "impurities," *Le Pur et l'impur*, describes Charlotte, a middle-aged woman, who fakes orgasm to please her young lovers. For analysis of *Chéri* see for example Bal (1986), Olken and Relyea; for studies of different aspects of *Le Blé* see for instance Fischler and Offord; and for interpretations of the complex *Le Pur*, see for example Cothran and Whatley.
20. Loved by the character of Hélène, Vial is a young man in love with the older "Colette."
21. Emphasis added. For a more precise analysis of *[NJ]*, see for example Raaphorst-Rousseau, Jouve 146-149, Miller (1980).
22. "Between what is real and what is imagined, there is always room for the word, the magnificent word, bigger than the object it designates" (*JR* 348).
23. Even about the interviews of her conducted by young reporters, Colette writes: "Do I have projects, young man? But of course. At quarter to seventy-three, you always have projects. I have plenty of them. I project to live a little longer, to continue to suffer in an honorable way. . . . But these projects are not for you. And I answer gravely to you, such a young man, so early responsible for the investigation: 'My projects . . . Well, eh . . . I won't be able to tell you for a few months . . . No, no . . . Perhaps a volume of souvenirs . . . As for a novel . . . Oh! no, I could not tell you anything about my method of working . . .'
I keep a straight face. . . .
He seemed to think that it was quite natural for me to have a method of working, and even that I should want to keep it secret.

Surely, *he* has one . . . I should have interviewed *him* . . ." (*EV* 407-408—emphasis added).
24. The first part of *[EV]* is a kind of meditation on the recent past and the war. It casts the narrator in the process of recording her thoughts, but the train of thoughts is constantly interrupted by incoming visitors ringing the bell. This ringing brings back the awful memory of her third husband's arrest at their home in 1942, as well as the sequel of conflicting emotions that then invaded the aging woman.
25. For a brief comparison between Montaigne's and Colette's self-portraits, see N. Miller (1981). For an analysis of Montaigne's constant additions to his own portrait and writing, see C. Blum's essay.
26. Miller 1981: 166; Smith 49-50; Evans 19-20, 70.
27. Nancy Miller, noting that Colette's writing is linked to the maternal body, also agrees that Colette's "self-portraying enterprise betrays the absence of a *certain* self-consciousness" and that this particular female writer seems unafraid of seeming frivolous (1981, 173).
28. My choice of words refers to her collection of stories entitled *La Femme cachée*.
29. Colette frames the story somewhat like Maupassant does his, i.e. by positing herself as a witness and relating the story of Mme Armand to her personal, but here rather insignificant, history: it is when she had her pearl necklace restrung that she met Mme Armand on several occasions, and then heard the story of her failed suicide. For an analysis of this story, see Dehon.
30. My study somewhat intersects here with more theoretical essays about quilting and writing (Showalter), and about female textuality (Miller: 1986). Miller proposes to read the story of Arachne (the spider artist, weaver of texts) "both as a figuration of woman's relation of production to the dominant culture, and as a possible parable (or critical modeling) of a feminist poetics" (272). But Showalter's approach to the poetics of gender in "Piecing and Writing" shows ambivalent reactions to the use of this metaphor of female artistic composition.
31. Some of the pages collected under the title of *Belles Saisons* were rewritten and included in *L'Etoile Vesper*.
32. These messages remind us of Sido's last letter to Colette, from her death-bed, which carried mostly penciled signs, "readable only" to her hesitant daughter: "interweavings, vegetal convolutions, all messages from a hand that was trying to transmit to me

a new alphabet" and "no longer felt obliged to use our language" (*NJ* 509-510).
33. *NJ* 144 (emphasis added).

WORKS CITED

"L'Autobiographie." *Poétique* 56 (Nov. 1983).
Bal, Mieke. *La Complexité d'un roman populaire: Ambiguïté dans "La Chatte."* Paris: La Pensée Universelle, 1974.
———. "Inconsciences de *Chéri*: Chéri existe-t-il?" Bray 1986: 15-23.
Beaujour, Michel. "Autobiographie et autoportrait." *Poétique* 32 (1977): 442-458.
Benstock, Shari, ed. *The Private Self.* Chapel Hill: U. of North Carolina P, 1988.
Blum, Claude. "La peinture du moi et l'écriture inachevée. Sur la pratique de l'addition dans 'Les essais' de Montaigne." *Poétique* 53 (Feb. 1983): 60-71.
Bray, Bernard, ed. *Colette: Nouvelles approches critiques.* Paris: Nizet, 1986.
Brée, Germaine. "Le mythe des origines de l'autoportrait chez George Sand et Colette." In *Symbolism and Modern Literature: Studies in Honor of Wallace Fowlie.* Marcel Tetel ed. Durham: Duke UP, 1978.
Colette, Sidonie Gabrielle. *Oeuvres Complètes.* 16 vols. Paris: Flammarion, 1973.
All pages refer to this edition. Translations of quotes are mine. For purposes of clarity, I list here, by chronological order, the works to which I refer in this essay, their abbreviations, their English titles if they have been translated, as well as their dates of publication, and the volumes of the *Oeuvres Complètes* in which they were included. For editions of available translations, see the bibliography by Joan Hinde Stewart in *Colette*, 1983.
Claudine series, 1900-1903. I and II.
La Vagabonde [V], (*The Vagabond*), 1911. III
L'Envers du music-hall (*Music-Hall Sidelights*), 1913. IV.
Chéri (Chéri), 1920. V.
La Maison de Claudine (*My Mother's House*), 1922. VI.
Le Blé en herbe (*Ripening Seed*), 1923. VI.

La Femme cachée (*The Other Woman*), 1924. VI.
La Naissance du jour [NJ], (*The Break of Day*), 1928. VI.
Sido (Sido), 1929. VII.
La Chatte (*The Cat*), 1933. VII.
Le Pur et l'impur (*The Pure and the Impure*), 1941. VII. (New title for *Ces Plaisirs*, 1932).
Duo (Duo), 1934. VIII.
Mes Apprentissages (*My Apprenticeships*), 1936. VIII.
"La Lune de pluie" ("The Rainy Moon"), 1940, IX.
Journal à Rebours [JR], (*Looking Backwards*), 1941. IX.
Le Képi (*The Kepi*), 1943. IX.
"Nudité" (not translated), 1943. XI.
"Le Tendron" ("The Tender Shoot"), 1943. IX
"La Dame du photographe" [DP], ("The Photographer's Wife"), 1944. X.
L'Etoile Vesper [EV], (*The Evening Star*), 1946, X.
Belles Saisons [BS] (not translated), 1945. XI.
Le Fanal bleu [FB], (*The Blue Lantern*), 1949, XI.
"Colette." *Europe* 631-632 (Nov-Dec 1981).
Cothran, Ann. "*The Pure and the Impure*: Codes and Constructs." *Women's Studies* 8 (3) (1981): 335-357.
Courtivron, Marie Françoise de. "La mère comme dynamique de l'écriture: distanciation et identification." Paper delivered at the Colette Colloquium, Cerisy-la-salle: Aug. 13-19, 1988.
Dehon, Claire. " 'La Dame du photographe': sa structure, son sens." *Revue du pacifique* 4 (Spring 1978): 59-67.
Dormann, Geneviève. *Amoureuse Colette*. Paris: Herscher, 1984.
Dupont, Jacques. "Identités et Identifications dans l'oeuvre de Colette." Bray 27-36.
Eisinger and McCarty, eds. "Charting Colette." Special issue of *Women's Studies* 8 (3) 255-378 (1981).
———. *Colette, the Woman, the Writer*. University Park: Penn State UP, 1981.
Evans, Martha Noel. *Masks of Tradition: Women and the Politics of Writing in Twentieth Century France*. Ithaca: Cornell UP, 1987.
Felski, Rita. *Beyond Feminist Aesthetics*. Cambridge: Harvard UP, 1989.
Fishler, Alexander. "Unity in Colette's *Le Blé en herbe*." *Modern Language Quarterly* 30 (2) (June 1969): 248-264.
Forde, Marianna. "Spatial Structures in *La Chatte*." *French Review* 58 (1985): 360-367.

Fraiman, Susan. "Shadows in the Garden: the Double Aspect of Motherhood in Colette." *Perspectives on Contemporary Literature* 11 (1985): 46-53.
Friedman, Susan Stanford. "Women's Autobiographical Selves. Theory and Practise." In Benstock 34-61.
Gouaux-Coutrix, Mireille. "Fiction et Autobiographie: le 'mentir-vrai' chez Colette." *Europe* 631-632: 13-20.
Gusdorf, Georges. "Conditions and Limits of Autobiography." 1956. Trans. James Olney. In Olney 28-48.
Jouve, Nicole Ward. *Colette*. Bloomington: Indiana UP, 1987.
Larnac, Jean. *Colette: sa vie, son oeuvre*. Paris: Krâ, 1927.
———. *Histoire de la littérature féminine*. Paris: Krâ, 1929.
Lastinger, Valérie. "*La Naissance du jour*: la désintégration du 'moi' dans un roman de Colette." *French Review* 61 (March 1988): 542-551.
Lejeune, Philippe. *L'Autobiographie en France*. Paris: Armand Colin, 1971.
———. *Je est un autre: l'autobiographie de la littérature aux médias*. Paris: Seuil, 1980.
———. *Moi aussi*. Paris: Seuil, 1986.
———. *Le Pacte autobiographique*. Paris: Seuil, 1975.
———. "Le Pacte autobiographique (bis) (relecture)." *Poétique* 56 (Nov.1983): 416-434.
———. "Women and Autobiography at Author's Expense." In Stanton 205-218.
Makward, Christiane. "Colette and Signs: A Partial Reading of a writer 'Born *Not* to Write'." In Eisinger 185-192.
Marks, Elaine. *Colette*. New Brunswick: Rutgers UP, 1960.
———. "'I Am My Own Heroine': Some Thoughts About Women and Autobiography in France." *Female Studies IX—Teaching About Women in the Foreign Languages*. New York: Old Westbury, 1975.
May, Georges. *L'Autobiographie*. Paris: PUF, 1979.
McCarty, Mary. "Possessing Female Space: 'The Tender Shoot'." *Women's Studies* 8 (3) (1981): 367-374.
McConnell-Ginet, et al. eds. *Women and language in Literature and Society*. New York: Praeger, 1980.
Miller, Nancy. "The Anamnesis of a Female "I": in the Margins of Self-Portrayal." In Eisinger 1981: 164-175.
———. "Arachnologies: the Woman, the Text and the Critic." *The Poetics of Gender*. Ed. Nancy Miller. New York: Columbia UP, 1986. 270-295.

———. "Woman of Letters: The Return to Writing in Colette's *The Vagabond*." *Subject to Change: Reading Feminist Writing*. Ed. Nancy Miller. New York: Columbia UP, 1988. 229-264.

———. "Women's Autobiography in France: for a Dialectics of Identification." McConnell-Ginet 1980: 258-273.

Milner, Christiane. "Le Corps de Sido." *Europe* 631-632: 71-84.

Offord, Malcolm. "Colours in Colette's *Le Blé en herbe*." *Nottingham French Studies* 22 (Oct. 1983): 32-52.

Olken, I.T. "Aspects of Imagery in Colette: Color and Light." *PMLA* 77 (1) (March 1962): 140-148.

Olney, James, ed. *Autobiography: Essays, Theoretical and Critical*. Princeton: Princeton UP, 1980.

Peyre, Henri. "Contemporary Feminine Literature in France." *Yale French Studies* 27 (1962-1963): 41-65.

"La question autobiographique." *Etudes littéraires* 1984: 209-427.

Raaphorst-Rousseau, Madeleine. "Complexité de stucture et ambiguïté de *La Naissance du jour*." *Cahiers Colette 3/4* (Actes du Colloque de Dijon 1979). Saint-Sauveur-en-Puisaye: Société des amis de Colette, 1981. 56-67.

Relyea, Susan. "Polymorphic Perversity: Colette's Illusory 'Real'." In Eisinger 150-163.

Sanchez, J. Carrascal. "Les personnages et l'élément comparatif dans une oeuvre de Colette: *La Chatte*." *Revue du pacifique* 2 (Spring 1976): 50-60.

Showalter, Elaine. "Piecing and Writing." *The Poetics of Gender*. Ed. Nancy Miller. New York: Columbia UP, 1986: 222-245.

Smith, Sidonie. *A Poetics of Women's Autobiography. Marginality and the Fictions of Self-Representation*. Bloomington: Indiana UP, 1987.

Stanton, Domna C. *The Female Autograph*. 1984 Chicago: The U of Chicago P, 1987.

Stewart, Joan Hinde. *Colette*. Boston: Twayne, 1983.

Tinter, Sylvie. "Sidonie Colette ou le temps de la mère." *HUSL* (Spring 1987): 33-45.

Trahard, Pierre. *L'art de Colette*. 1941. Genève: Slatkine, 1971.

Whatley, Janet. "Colette's *Le Pur et l'impur*: On Real and Phony Mysteries." *Modern Language Studies* 13 (3) (Summer 1983): 16-26.

Breaking from the Cage of Identity: Doris Lessing and The Diaries of Jane Somers

Cora Agatucci

Doris Lessing was born October 22, 1919, of British parents in Persia. When she was six, her family moved to an isolated 3,000-acre farm in Southern Rhodesia. There she expended what she called a "hellishly lonely" childhood. Growing up, she read the European and American literary classics and was educated at a Catholic convent school for girls until age fourteen, when she left the school to work as nursemaid and secretary. After two failed marriages and three children, Lessing concluded that she hadn't "the virtues marriage requires." She left Africa for England in 1949 committed to a career in writing. She briefly joined the Communist Party, then began earning her living as a professional writer. 1956 marked her last visit to Africa; Southern Rhodesian authorities had earlier declared Lessing a prohibited alien because of her activism against apartheid. Today she continues to live and work in England.

Doris Lessing has forged a remarkably productive and influential writing career, beginning with her first novel The Grass Is Singing (1950) of white Africa, and continuing through her most recent The Fifth Child (1988), a sociological novel with disturbing political implications. Her fiction has developed through several major shifts, from the autobiographical Children of Violence series (1950-1969), which culminated in the critically acclaimed The Four-Gated City, to her multi-volume space fiction Canopus in Argos, a social history of all humankind, to her return in the 1980s to realistic novels like The Diaries of Jane Somers (1984) and The Good Terrorist (1985). These shifts illustrate the range and diversity of an extraordinarily gifted writer who continually resists labels and limitations readers and reviewers would impose on her work. Lessing established her lasting claim as one *of the most distinguished novelists writing in English today with her most important novel* The Golden Notebook *(1962). Its experimental form challenges traditional literary realism in an attempt to find new and truer ways to render modern realities, and the novel asserts the validity of the female voice and experience in shaping the record of our age. Both these projects are advanced in important ways in* The Diaries of Jane Somers, *originally published pseudonymously as two separate works* The Diary of a Good Neighbour *and* If the Old Could. . . .

When, in 1984, Doris Lessing revealed that she had published two novels under the pseudonym Jane Somers, a furor arose in the publishing world surrounding her critique of the publishing and selling of new works by authors without established names. Few of her critics and reviewers gave adequate weight to the most compelling of the reasons Lessing acknowledged for the double deception of presenting novels as diaries and Lessing as the fictional Somers: her desire "to get free of that cage of associations and labels that every established writer has to learn to live inside" (Pref. to *The Diaries* vii). Ellen Goodman was one who recognized the pseudonymous publication and the subsequent revelation of Lessing's authorship as a "real life experiment" in identity by an author who has spent her life writing about "questions of who-am-I." Goodman suggests in her 1984 *Washington Post* article that Lessing was addressing "in public a theme that haunts her writing: life is too fragile if your identity is solely defined by others; it is a hard, a life-long task to go on defining and redefining yourself" (213, 214). In their introduction to *Critical Essays on Doris Lessing,* Claire Sprague and Virginia Tiger see this ongoing task as integral to Lessing's authorial history: as *The Golden Notebook* was an escape from the "cage of the Children of Violence series," and the Canopus space fiction was "a liberation from the cage of realistic writing," so was the publication of Somers's *The Diary of a Good Neighbour* and *If the Old Could* . . . a release from the unacknowledged "constrictions of Canopus" (3). Sprague and Tiger welcome this last shift in Lessing's work for they are reluctant to grant Lessing release from the feminist identity working in the realist mode they favor. One cannot help but feel this is just the kind of pressure of which Lessing complains in the preface to the *Diaries*: "most reviewers and readers want you to go on writing the same book" (xi). Yet Sprague and Tiger wisely recognize in these shifts in Lessing's corpus an author seeking "to unsettle our fondest notions of her" (23).

The preface to the *Diaries* supports this interpretation. There Lessing wryly observes that reviewers and publishers have assigned her many labels, each serving "for a few years" (vii), each felt as an attempt to constrain her authorial identity and artistic choice.

> [W]hen I began writing my Canopus series I was surprised to find I had been set free to write in ways I had not used before. I wondered if there would be a similar liberation if I were to write in the first person as a different character.
> ... And it did turn out that as Jane Somers I wrote in ways that Doris Lessing could not. (vii-viii)

The authorship of the *Diaries* having been found out, its author having been labeled once again, Lessing admits elsewhere to a panic, for "psychological reasons ... that I don't know much about": "'Oh God! I must write a book under another name, I simply cannot *stand* this, I'm going to!'" ("Doris Lessing Talks" 3). In fact, the temporary freedom from reviewers' labels and readers' expectations afforded by the pseudonymous publication was precious to her. It was another means to challenge fixed notions of her identity and to reopen the question of who Doris Lessing is.

This is the challenge offered by and the question presented by *The Diaries of Jane Somers*. Identity—the processes of its construction and deconstruction, the role of others in its definition, the necessity of growth through continual redefinition, its enabling and crippling properties—is a major theme of the two novels, and a major issue implied by the circumstances of their publication and by Doris Lessing's discussions of her relationship to Jane Somers.

The *Diaries* and their implied author may be conceptualized in Bakhtinian terms as a new entry in the ongoing conversation represented by Lessing's corpus, a confrontation with previous authorial identities readers have constructed from her works, an attempt to dialogize those constructions and reopen the debate. Thus, the *Diaries* require critics to reconsider conclusions such as Ellen Friedman's that Lessing has transcended the limitations of the "Female and the 'Great Tradition,'" or Elaine Showalter's that Lessing has moved away from concern for the "anguish of female imagination," developed an aversion to the "feminine sensibility," and condemned "lady authors" like Jane Somers through parody (*A Literature of Their Own* 309, 310). In fact, Jane Somers, a romantic novelist and journalist for the women's magazine *Lilith*, can be read as a reconsideration and full sympathetic treatment of the character Ella from Anna's Yellow Notebook in *The Golden Notebook*, whom many feminist critics have interpreted as "a more stereotypical fictionalized version" of the protagonist, outlined through the conventions of popular romance and the "agony column" of her magazine *Hearth and Home* (Waugh 76). Somers, the genuine "good neighbour" who visits, cares for, and befriends the elderly, offers a personal, if meager, solution to the growing problem of industrialized nations. Jane's response to the needs of her aged friends is similar to the solution represented by "matrimonial social work" adopted by Anna of "Free Women" in *The Golden Notebook*. And such solutions have been scorned by one feminist critic of the latter novel as acts of "social affirmation" that merely help things "limp along as usual" rather than move them toward genuine change (DuPlessis 101). Yet in the *Diaries* Doris Lessing has chosen to reimagine a character type parodied and trivialized in *The Golden Notebook* and generally ignored by feminists, she charges, because of their "political bigotry." Through Jane Somers, Lessing pays "tribute" to active, efficient working women who often held conservative political views and paid a high price trying to meet the demands of career, family, and social work in periods before women's liberation offered encouragement or support ("Doris Lessing Talks" 5).

As Claire Sprague has reminded us most recently in *Rereading Doris Lessing*, Lessing continually reworks and transforms characters, themes, and situations from earlier fiction in subsequent novels. Kate Brown of *The Summer Before the Dark* can be read as "To Room Nineteen"'s Susan Rawlings "positively reimagined" (Sprague 109). Having treated midlife crises through these characters, Lessing moved on to the subject of old age and dying in *The Making of the Representative for Planet 8* (1982) and in *The Diary of a Good Neighbour* (1983) to very different effect. In the latter, Sprague argues, Lessing "confronts more directly than she could in earlier novels or in the Canopus novels her own guilt and her own fears about aging and dying" (111). The aging process itself requires the redefinition of attitudes and identity. In the Canopus Archive, Representative Doeg transcends the death of Planet 8; for Maudie Fowler, death is simply and terribly the end. In Doeg a population coexists; in the Canopus chronicles, multiple first-person perspectives represented in collections of documents, letters, and reports shape the narratives; in the *Diaries*, Lessing chooses immersion in a single character's restricted perspective. Lessing's practice of varying and transforming character, theme, and narrative forms acts to resist closure: to reject, delay, debate once again conclusions about the meaning of her work and definitions of her authorial identity.

In the same year Lessing acknowledged authorship of the *Diaries*, she publicly reiterated her refusal to be identified as a woman writer. As Elaine Showalter observes, Lessing's April appearance at the 92nd Street Y Poetry Center provided yet another opportunity for the author "to dissociate herself from her devoted female reading public and from the women's movement, which regards her as the Cassandra of sexual politics" ("Women Who Write" 1). Understandably Showalter is alarmed by "[t]he phenomenon of successful women artists refusing to be identified or associated with women"; it bespeaks the degree to which the term "woman writer" has been denigrated and identification with a female tradition is considered injurious ("Women Who Write" 1, 31). To be sure, as Showalter charges, Lessing is impatient with expectations that she must speak for women even as she is denied authority to speak on other human questions; yet Lessing is not among those who have internalized contempt for "women's writing," excluded the female experience in efforts to depict the universal or ordinary human condition, or rejected female narrators and subjects—as is made clear in the *Diaries*. Whatever Lessing may say publicly to challenge restrictive, including feminist, definitions of her authorial identity, the fact that she does challenge restrictions, most demonstrably in the works themselves, serves important goals Showalter argues feminist critics and women writers must share: to counter damaging stereotypes of women artists that limit esthetic freedom, and that deny recognition both of the capacity and diversity of their tradition, and of the power, originality, and profundity which they may rightfully claim ("Women Who Write" 33). *The Diaries* strike at the heart of such a stereotype, the lady author and journalist, by forcing us to look beneath the glamorous, well-groomed, seemingly trivial surface of beautiful "Janna" Somers. Such an examination shatters the stereotype and requires the meaning constructed for Lessing's work and for the work of women writers like Jane Somers to be reconstructed.

Lessing must, of course, engage in this reconstruction and, inescapably, challenge herself as well as her publishers and readers. To set herself the task of becoming Jane Somers, a character she confesses admirable but very different from herself ("Doris Lessing Talks" 5), is to set in motion a paradoxical process that initiates dialogical opposition even as it requires imaginative merging.

Of course all writers become different characters all the time, as we write about them: all our characters are inside us somewhere. (This can be a terrifying thought.) . . . [The process requires] activating one of the gallery of people who inhabit every one of us, strengthening him or her, setting her (or him) free to develop. (Pref. to The Diaries viii)

In a woman like Jane, "efficient, practical, obsessively tidy, orderly, rather conservative, . . . to whom the darker sides of life come as a continual surprise," "a romantic" who "has protected herself against being married emotionally"—a woman whom "untidy, disorderly, indecisive" Doris Lessing would make very "uneasy," as does niece Kate—the author becomes a new identity ("Doris Lessing Talks" 5). Bakhtin calls this process a kind of "hybridization": in the utterance conjoin the representing and the represented consciousness, simultaneously speaking from *without*—and able to see, and allow the reader to see, the character's limitations, sophistries, insufficiencies, and falsenesses—and from *within*, inside the character, using her voice, as perhaps the author can use no other, to express values that must be brought before the reader in dialogic exchange (361, 45). As Doris Lessing attests, while living "inside the skin of Jane Somers" is to inhabit a "very narrow" world, it is nevertheless a "liberation," a release from labels, a chance to reshape reader expectations, a choice to reimagine a character earlier parodied and dismissed. And these choices initiate a dialogic conversation from which one cannot emerge unchanged.

Lessing requires of her protagonist this same kind of imaginative merging and confrontation with others very different from her; Jane must write—and in so doing become—Maudie Fowler and Eliza Bates and niece Kate, characters who initially, and in the case of Kate finally, repel and confound her. Because of this exchange, these characters succeed in breaking down Jane's emotional isolation and sterility. Jane changes a great deal, and for the better Lessing concludes, through these dialogic contacts "with the old, and . . . with this very unfortunate niece of hers who is a disaster area" ("Doris Lessing Talks" 5). The *Diaries* enact the process of open-ended change, of coming not to know oneself, of continually and radically reconsidering the question of one's identity—or, more accurately, identities.

Jane begins *The Diary of a Good Neighbour* by asserting, "I see everything differently now from how I did while I was living it" (5). She thinks of how "I had let Freddie down and let my mother down *and that was what I was like*," then begins to challenge the belief that her past identity has circumscribed her future. She is not doomed to repeat, to "let down," to behave like a little girl rather than a human being (11). The process of reopening the question of who she was—is, will be—begins with Jane's imaginative effort to understand others' viewpoints, to see herself as others see her. And she learns to see much through Maudie Fowler, who embodies Jane's fears of age and death, her guilt for denying the needs and the emotional claims of her mother and her husband. Gradually, Jane accepts the dirt, decay, and death for the sake of love. Maudie comes to care fiercely for and to rely solely on "pretty Janna." Jane, in her turn, feels emotionally entrapped by the relationship, yet allows Maudie to break down the protective barriers against caring for others and to open Jane up to new relationships and experiences. Finally, Jane must come to see and accept her future self in the decaying, dying Maudie Fowler, one of the many selves peopling Jane's diaries that she must acknowledge and confront.

Jane's shifting identities present themselves formally as other characters; Jane multiplies and fragments before the reader into past, present, and future selves, each a voice in the dialogic conversation shaping the diaries. Jane's master narrative is only apparently univocal. Multiple perspectives and identities vie for ascendency within Jane. Such a multiplicity of perspectives, Molly Hite argues, is for Lessing closer to the truth of personal experience and identity (487).

Through her friend Joyce, Jane must confront her former refusal to know the aged and dying; she must resist the pressures Joyce and others bring to bear on her to limit her to former, familiar identities if she is to change, to go on becoming. In Hermione Whitfield and Phyllis, whom Jane dislikes because they make "me think of how I was" (41, 63), she faces her former—now distressing—concern for superficial images and appearances, her previous evasion of inner being and unpleasant realities. Jane Somers was not someone to ask for help, not someone then who could respond to her mother or Freddie dying and in need of her. With her niece Jill, Jane becomes most closely involved with a past self, her young self, in whom she sees her own initial aversion to Maudie, the early construction of her emotional barriers against others, especially her husband, her gradual adoption of a "controlled . . . overcontrolled" personality: "I sat there looking at—myself, at her age" (195). In her belated relationship with Richard, she learns to appreciate the possibilities of a deeply affectionate and reciprocal attachment to a man, and to regret all she had lost when her younger persona barricaded herself against her husband's love. The second niece Kate, who comes to live with her after Jill moves out, stretches to the limits Jane's new capacity for imaginative empathy but delivers the final blows against her reluctance to involve herself too closely with others. In her relationship with Kate, Jane must confront her inadequacy to deal with the younger girl's deep dislocation and insecurity, and realize that to Kate she must ever appear "a challenge, a burden," an "unreachable accomplishment" that grinds her niece down (285-286). Seeing this, Jane cries out: "My heart hurt me. And what of it? I am now expert in this world of the heart, that recalcitrant, obstinate, self-determining organ" (304).

Played out in Jane Somers's *Diaries* through confrontations and identifications with her multiple selves is a narrative battleground with no neutral ideological space, as Bakhtin conceived the novel, a heteroglossia that once introduced is difficult to control: thus, Bakhtin defines the novel by its resistance to the unified, authoritative, and absolute. Yet the hypothesis of heterogeneity in the *Diaries* is inimical neither to artistic value nor to constructive identity. Lessing's treatment of identity within the novels and her stance outside them argue against the need to fix or unify disparate selves, to label or reduce and thus stop the dialogic conversation centering in her own or Jane Somers's identities. Sprague notes that in *The Making of the Representative for Planet 8*, the novel preceding the publication and probably overlapping the writing of *The Diary of a Good Neighbour*, "shifting, multiple selves have become totally positive" (123). In the *Diaries*, too, multiplication or fragmentation of selves is a regenerative process needed to transform Jane; it serves a healing, redemptive function enabling her to break down her emotional sterility, expiate the sins against her mother and husband, and find more satisfying ways of being-becoming. So, too, do *The Diaries of Jane Somers* serve their author in helping to break once again the cage of labels and expectations imposed by those who would fix her authorial identity.

Lessing's choice of the diary, a "feminine" autobiographical genre, as the form of the novels of Jane Somers, her "woman journalist"—a phrase that put off many potential male reviewers, Lessing observes in the preface (ix)—advances the identity themes elaborated here. The appearance in print of the supposed diaries with no author to promote them is certainly a form of protest against the cult of personality Lessing deplores. Lessing's previous disclaimers against the referentiality of what Sprague and Tiger call "patently autobiographical" works such as *The Golden Notebook* and the Martha Quest series (24), are consistent with Lessing's battle against the constriction of labels and the public's tendency to read the author's life into the work rather than to read the work itself. "We have reached the point where a novel is not enough, the book is not enough, you have to have the photograph and the biography and the whole personality thing. . . ." This Lessing calls a major "feature of publishing in our time," and it is not a glamorous, but rather a "cold," "mechanical, very predictable," and "extremely commercial" business. Some of its readers indeed were not ashamed to reject *The Diary of a Good Neighbour* because it was "too depressing to publish" ("Doris Lessing Talks" 4-5, 3).

Of equal importance, the two novels that comprise *The Diaries of Jane Somers* remain multiple; they are not forged into a unified narrative, although the second reintroduces characters and reopens themes from the first. Nor does Lessing silence the polyphony of voices that speak through Jane's diaries. The forms of autobiography have become increasingly experimental and various in this century, and the legitimization of multiple forms, multiple autobiographies offered by a single author, and multicultural authors claiming value for their lives through autobiography challenge the hegemony of the Augustinian paradigm, of a single version of a life, of dominant theories of individual significance. Lessing's statements about the autobiographical dimension of her previous works suggest that she rejects narrowly prescriptive notions of life writing as well. In Bakhtinian terms, Lessing chooses for Jane Somers a mode of discourse already overpopulated with others' intentions and past usages. The Diaries would traditionally speak from the margins of mainstream paternalistic society, the literary form as well as the authorial identity muted and constrained further by dominant androcentric valuations. Yet Lessing rejects what Sidonie Smith calls the "normative" androcentric form of autobiography that offers a fixed unity of self (6). This paradigm is best suited to express a clear sense of identity and a coherent life perceived as a purposeful, linear progression. When such certainties, and the privileged cultural assumptions about personality and significance underlying them, cannot or will not be claimed, other forms must be adopted or created for self-expression and self-invention.

Lessing took as her protagonist a stereotypical figure in order to challenge the reader's preconception of a "woman journalist" and romance writer; so too does Lessing force us to reassess an autobiographical genre often dismissed as subliterary and inartistic, not least because it is closely associated with female expression. In the *Diaries*, Lessing redefines the mode of discourse and empowers a formerly muted voice—muted even by her peers in the women's movement, Lessing charges—to speak, though it is not Jane's voice alone that we hear in the novels. Central to Jane's discourse are her frequent questionings and re-visions of her identities. As Molly Hite has argued of *The Golden Notebook*, to possess a "clear identity is damning evidence of limitation" (485). Jane's multiple identities embodied in other characters become a strategy to resist stultifying enclosure and constraint. For Jane to resist this fragmentation would mean to accept as whole but a fragment of what she had been and is capable of becoming. Hite locates *The Golden Notebook* in the tradition of "mimesis of personal experience": the novel is a formal experiment arising out of Lessing's "dissatisfaction with realism as a means of representation" (484). While divergent experimental forms of representation may also prove inadequate, a writer like Lessing cannot cease trying them out it seems (and glad her readers are): "It's a funny thing," Jane muses, "this need to write things down, as if they had no existence until they are recorded.... As if it is not valid until in print" (64). And Lessing is concerned in the *Diaries* to create and adapt an appropriate, if inevitably flawed, form to refract and reinvent Jane Somers's identities.

Jane enacts the rejection of the androcentric model of autobiography in presenting Maudie Fowler's life stories. At first Jane struggles with Maudie to pin down dates and sequence, to construct a traditional linear unity out of Maudie's disjunctive and often invented narratives; "None of it adds up," Jane complains (29). But Maudie "doesn't like to have a progression made, her mind has bright pictures in it that she has painted for herself and has been dwelling on for all those decades" (29). From shared stories, Jane and Maudie build their relationship. Jane revises her own initially constraining view of making stories out of life, realizing imposed unity and linear order are neither authentic nor desirable. She freely interposes Maudie's and others' stories into her own, a dialogizing procedure which acts to challenge, engage, decenter her own narrative. To condense, reduce, sum up is to falsify the "reality," she decides at one point, is to leave out all the "grit and grind" of her meetings with Maudie and the others (31). Jane comes to see the diary as "a builder's yard, bits and odds stacked up, lying about, nothing in place, one thing not more important than another. You wander through ... and see a heap of sand there, a pile of glass here, ... That is the point of the diary, the bits and pieces of events, all muddled together" (137). She may revisit the diary looking for clues to explain, for example, the unsuccessful relationship she is developing with Kate. Seen through a particular need or a momentarily dominant theory of meaning, one may "look back through the year and begin to know what was important" (137). But this is a process requiring transient single vision, reducing experience to a fragment, that the main impetus of the *Diaries* resists.

Jane Somers's diaries are open, often disjunctive, if roughly chronological, fluid records of her becoming and un-becoming, writing that itself enacts a liberation in refusing to fix identity or be fixed by the identities made of the past and of others' expectations. The unfinished process, the lack of resolution in the end as the "[h]ouse lights" dim and "the curtain goes up" once again on her empty room (502)—these are not threats to integrity. Rather they empower possibilities that would otherwise be closed to Jane Somers—and to Doris Lessing.

WORKS CITED

Bakhtin, Mikhail Mikhailovich. *The Dialogic Imagination: Four Essays*. Trans. Caryl Emerson and Michael Holquist. Ed. Michael Holquist. U of Texas P Slavic Press Series No. 1. Austin: U of Texas P, 1981.

DuPlessis, Rachel Blau. *Writing Beyond the Ending: Narrative Strategies of Twentieth-Century Women Writers*. Bloomington: Indiana UP, 1985.

Friedman, Ellen G. "Doris Lessing: Fusion and Transcendence of the Female in the 'Great Tradition.'" *The Centennial Review* 30 (Fall 1986): 452-470.

Goodman, Ellen. "The Doris Lessing Hoax." *Washington Post* 27 Sep 1984, 31. Rpt. in Sprague and Tiger 213-214.

Hite, Molly. "(En)Gendering Metafiction: Doris Lessing's Rehearsals for *The Golden Notebook*." *Modern Fiction Studies* 34 (Autumn 1988): 481-500.

Lessing, Doris. *The Diaries of Jane Somers: The Diary of a Good Neighbour and If the Old Could.* . . . New York: Vintage-Random House, 1984.

———. "Doris Lessing Talks about Jane Somers." *Doris Lessing Newsletter* 10 (1986): 3-5, 14.
———. *The Golden Notebook.* 1962. Toronto: Bantam, 1981.
———. *The Making of the Representative for Planet 8. Canopus in Argos: Archives, V. 4.* New York: Knopf, 1982.
———. *The Summer Before the Dark.* 1973. New York: Vintage-Random House, 1983.
———. "To Room Nineteen." 1963. *Stories.* New York: Vintage-Random House, 1983. 396-428.
Showalter, Elaine. *A Literature of Their Own: British Women Novelists from Bronte to Lessing.* Princeton: Princeton UP, 1977.
———. "Women Who Write Are Women." *New York Times Book Review* 16 Dec 1984: 1+.
Smith, Sidonie. *A Poetics of Women's Autobiography: Marginality and the Fictions of Self-Representation.* Bloomington: Indiana UP, 1987.
Sprague, Claire. *Rereading Doris Lessing: Narrative Patterns of Doubling and Repetition.* Chapel Hill: U of North Carolina P, 1987.
Sprague, Claire, and Virginia Tiger, ed. *Critical Essays on Doris Lessing.* Boston: G. K. Hall, 1986.
Waugh, Patricia. *Metafiction: The Theory and Practice of Self-Conscious Fiction.* London: Methuen, 1984.

"'She' is me more than 'I'": Writing and the Search for Identity in the Works of Marie Cardinal

Colette T. Hall

Born in 1929 in Algeria, Marie Cardinal has become a very popular author in France since her much acclaimed book Les Mots pour le dire *(1975)*, which was translated into English in 1983 under the title The Words to Say It.
To this date she has published eleven volumes of fiction and nonfiction, all of them using an autobiographical experience as a point of departure: for example the troubled relationship with her mother in Les Mots pour le dire *as revealed through her psychoanalytical cure; the relationship with her children in* La Clé sur la porte *(The Key in the Door 1972); with her husband in* Une Vie pour deux *(A Life for Two 1979) with her father in* Le Passé empiété *(1983). Her latest book* Les Grands Désordres *(The Great Disorders 1987) deals with her daughter's drug addiction.*
Deeply personal as well as political, her work is a critique of the mechanisms of oppression, namely the Catholic church and the sexist and paternalistic values of the bourgeois class in collusion with the colonial system, all of which fetter the lives of women and of the powerless. Her work has to be read against the social and political background of French society; the emergence, after May 1968, of the Women's movement; and the post-colonial era. She has had a unique experience as a woman caught in the individual and collective oppression in Algeria before and during the war of independence.
Cardinal's writing is also a good representative of l'écriture féminine *though not as much in Hélène Cixous's sense of experimental writing as in her choices of topics. Cardinal gives voice to those experiences which hitherto have been repressed, for instance women's relationship to their bodies and to their sexuality.*

When I write, I always start with something I know, something I have lived and then it transforms itself. It opens itself up, it wanders around; the "I" could become a "she," but "she" is more me than "I." The "I" is a mask.

(*Autrement dit*, Marie Cardinal)[1]

When Marie Cardinal's book *Les Mots pour le dire* (The Words to Say It) was first reviewed in the press, it was received as an autobiographical—even psychoanalytic—document but not as a novel. This perception was quite distressing to the author who wrote in *Autrement dit* (In Other Words):

> As if all novels are not autobiographical. As if the fact of hiding oneself behind the third person to write or of changing sex . . . is not as revealing, not as close to confession or intimacy, not ultimately as autobiographical as writing a story in the first person. I do not know how nor do I want to write any longer in another fashion. I want to be the woman of each of my books. I have been the six women of my six books (some of which are written in the third person) and since I hope to write at least twenty books, one will be able to say that I wrote twenty autobiographies. (85)

Cardinal's forceful reaction to the critical reception of her book is quite revealing of the critics' commonly held belief that autobiographical writing is not fiction and by implication not "a real work of art." This criticism is particularly damaging to women writers whose creative productions are often read as autobiographical accounts and are considered thus more spontaneous and less consciously crafted than those of their male counterparts.[2] This notion, however, of the inferior status of autobiographical writings has recently come under vehement attack by such scholars as James Olney and before him Georges Gusdorf who see "two versions of autobiography: on the one hand that which is properly called confession, on the other hand the artist's entire work which takes the same material in complete freedom and under the protection of a hidden identity" (46). Likewise, Cardinal claims the autobiographical nature of all fiction—

whether the author hides behind a third or first person narrator—and implies conversely the fictional aspect of all autobiographical writings. Cardinal's second point—that she needs to identify with the female protagonist (even, as we shall see, with several protagonists) of each of her books—is quite congruent with recent feminist scholarship which has pointed to the search for self-definition as one of the main themes of nineteenth and twentieth century women writers.[3] Using writing as a means to gain insights into the self applies equally to male writers, but the task seems even more urgent for women writers whose self-definitions are caught up in a web of male expectations which the act of writing puts into question.

In her recent book *Beyond Feminist Aesthetics*, Rita Felski argues that many women writers, among whom she places Cardinal, have chosen to write autobiographical woman-centered narratives because they serve as "a medium for working through contradictions in women's lives and as a source of powerful symbolic fictions of female identity" (78). Furthermore, as she points out, this writing should be seen "as a social practice which creates meaning rather than merely communicating it; feminist literature [which she defines as 'texts that reveal a critical awareness of women's subordinate position and of gender as a problematic category' (14)], does not reveal an already given female identity, but is itself involved in the construction of this self as a cultural reality" (78).

Cardinal's works are good examples of this construction of the self through the practice of writing. All her texts concern themselves with the process of writing and with its meaning for the female subject. Writing and self-writing are consubstantial as the author chooses narrative strategies shaped by her quest for self-definition as much as her self is shaped by her writing. And though Cardinal's autobiographical fiction does not exhibit the more traditional features of an autobiography such as the chronological retelling of one's life or an explicit pact with the reader, I suggest that we read her works not as a place to find her "toute vive entre les pages," to use one of Colette's vivid expressions, but as the ongoing autobiography of the writer as a woman (140).

Les Mots pour le dire, the novel that brought fame to Cardinal, is emblematic of the construction of the female self in writing. In this text, the narrator—the author's alter-ego—undergoes a long psychoanalysis in order to cure a crippling psychosis. In therapy the narrator finds the words to talk about herself and free her from her madness; at the same time, she discovers the words she needs to write about her old and new self in a secret diary. At the center of her alienation, she finds her mother, a malefic but ultimately tragic figure who poured her own despair and frustration on her daughter. Yet, when the daughter goes deeper into the relationship, she discovers that her mother is not just an "executioner" who has warped her, trying to fit her daughter in the mold of femininity prescribed by their class, but that the mother herself has been a victim of those very values. Belonging to a rich, land-owning family in Algeria, the mother has perpetuated the paternalistic and racist system that had earlier enslaved her. The narrator thus uncovers her personal oppression as well as the collective oppression of women exacerbated by the colonial situation. Through the words spoken during her analysis and written in her diary, the narrator reveals all the mechanisms of oppression which have fettered her life. She gives birth to herself as a woman and as a writer since the diary becomes also her first book to be published.

Cardinal's subsequent novels, two of which—*Une Vie pour deux* (A Life for Two) and *Le Passé empiété*—I will analyze in more detail, offer variations on this theme.[4] Specifically, these two works share a narrative structure which presents a fiction embedded in another fiction as the narrator becomes involved in writing a story—her own or that of another (usually) female character—which helps her construct her own identity as a woman and writer.

This "need," as Cardinal puts it, to identify with her narrator and other female protagonists of her novels, may reflect—as theorists like Nancy Chodorow suggest—the lack of ego boundaries between mothers and daughters that produces a female identity defined in relation to others.[5] And, indeed, if one looks at the twelve books Cardinal has published since 1962, one is struck by the deep unity of her works centered on an important relationship in the life of her narrator. Be they fiction or essays, in each of Cardinal's books, the narrator—the author's double—searches for her identity in connection to others: her mother in *Les Mots pour le dire*, her children in *La Clé sur la porte* (The Key in the Door), her husband in *Une Vie pour deux*, her father in *Le Passé empiété* or her daughter in *Les Grands Désordres* (The Great Disorders).

But I think that Cardinal's use of the specific narrative structure involving the narrator's identification with the experiences of other female protagonists is also a deliberate attempt to show the commonalities between women's experiences. Thus the narrator's experiences transcend her individual existence and become emblematic of the experiences of all women as Mother, Daughter and Wife. This narrative technique allows Cardinal to bring to light the constraints imposed on all women as her narrator realizes her own alienation but also her own creative power while she constructs the fiction of another woman's life.

This narrative strategy, as I intend to show, is successfully used in *Une Vie pour deux*, the story of Simone and Jean-François, who have been married for twenty years but have lived separately off and on for the last several years. They are now taking a vacation in Ireland. For Simone, her relationship with Jean-François depends on the outcome of this time spent together: will they both be able to bridge the gap between them, a gap made up of years of silence, half-truths and misunderstandings? Will Ireland be the land where Jean-François's northern reserve—he came from the French coal region—can unite itself with Simone's Mediterranean exuberance? This alliance of "their geographies" is at the core of Simone's wish as she wants to rebuild a strong, unified couple (12). However, Jean-François's discovery of a drowned woman on the beach starts a slow process of reappraisal of their life together during which the romantic notion of the couple as a fixed-forever unit will be dismantled and replaced by that of a couple made up of two individuals, each one separate, and constantly renegotiating the terms of their relationship. "I went from 'We' to we, from what does not move to something which is forever evolving" (16) says Simone at the beginning of her story, thus setting the stage for the unfolding of the process which took her and Jean-François on the road of the fleeting and the transitory like an old "Charlie Chaplin movie whose image quivers" (10).

It starts with Simone's realization that despite all those years, she does not know her husband. She thought she was speaking for him, for she enclosed him in the "We" of the couple, but in fact knew little of his deep feelings. Even worse, she does not know who she is behind the mask of "Mother" and "Wife" as dictated by the male expectations of her social class. The drowned woman whom Jean-François had discovered on the beach becomes an obsession for both Simone and her husband because she embodies their lack of communication. Each of them is deeply intrigued by the woman's body but incapable of or unwilling to share the emotions that it stirs in them. A first breakthrough occurs for Simone under the guise of an uneasy memory involving another woman. Several years ago, she once witnessed a love-making scene between her then-employer and a young woman named Angèle as she entered the man's study to work. Simone is at first the repulsed spectator of their union since the man insists upon dictating his letters as usual. Little by little, however, Simone is mesmerized by the beauty and power of the young woman's body which is not the mere receptacle of the man's desire but an active participant in the act of love. "I had never seen a sight as beautiful as Angèle's body. She makes love, she fabricates it, she constructs it, she structures it" (107). Simone moves from the position of *voyeuse* to that of vicarious participant as she becomes one with Angèle. In this revealing scene, she discovers her own beauty and power through another woman's experience. She also discovers another facet of woman's sexuality as she feels the urge to take Angèle in her arms and to cover her body with kisses.

Sister and lover, Angèle shatters Simone's assumptions about her own sexuality which she had never dared to consider outside the heterosexual plot. This memory, which she finally shares with Jean-François, unsettles her universe, forcing her to question her identity: "What woman would she be? what mother? what wife?" (111) if she were to accept her desire for another woman? Angèle opens the door to Simone's self-exploration during which a different woman will slowly unfold at first in the secret of her mind and finally in the open.

This journey becomes possible through the mediation of another woman, (another woman's "body," the one found on the beach) since Simone and Jean-François decide to invent the life of Mary MacLaughlin—as they call her—to exorcise themselves of her presence. They both project on Mary's fictitious life their own frustrations and regrets. "Mary MacLaughlin's story that they were inventing together united them at the same time as it created deep conflicts between them" (292).

Because Mary is a woman, Simone feels that she can better imagine her story than Jean-François. From the beginning, she identifies with Mary and gives her her own experiences—her pregnancies, her struggle to be a good mother and to hold a job at the same time, her worries about money, her needs for love and intimacy—all that constitutes the everyday life of a woman raising children on her own. Through Mary's story, Simone attempts to explain to her husband what it means to be a mother and a woman. Soon, however, they reach a dead-end: their story cannot go on, for they radically disagree on Mary's death. Simone sees it as a suicide, for Mary has no choices left to her in a society which punishes women who are outside the norm: Mary has a good job, a child but no husband. Jean-François, on the contrary, interprets her death as an accident. He cannot accept Simone's pessimistic version.

The crisis will be resolved ultimately with the help of another story, Simone's second version of Mary's life, which she had been writing in secret at the same time that she and Jean-François were inventing Mary's story together. This "other" version of Mary's story is "intertwined with her own [Simone's life]. Not about events or facts of her life but about impulses, unhappiness, yearnings, whims, laughters, tears and desires" (299). Writing transforms Simone's existence and self-image because it reveals a more independent and more subversive self that both attracts and frightens her as she is able to break away from the traditional images assigned to women. Writing Mary's story was "taking her away from the woman she was. It was destroying her reality" at the same time as it was helping her dream of freedom, of "adventures, of long journeys, of streams of words" (312). In the process she creates a new story, which Carolyn Heilbrun calls "another possibility of female destiny" (110).

Writing is thus a liberating experience for Simone because it is linked to the discovery of an identity which has been hidden through the years under the "Wife/Mother" role she had to play. Simone's new awareness is connected, however, to the writing of the fiction of another woman's life on whom the narrator can project freely her own frustrations and also her aspirations. As she gives birth to Mary, Simone gives birth to herself and establishes a community of selves. "Mary is your sister" says her husband after reading her manuscript, a manuscript which reveals a woman he had never suspected and who forces his admiration.[6] "Mary is me" replies Simone (313) and the chapter ends in a dream-like sequence in which Mary, Angèle and Simone hold hands and go swimming in the sea naked while Jean-François looks on.

Each of these women thus become part of Simone's identity as she engenders herself through the fiction of their lives. Likewise, Cardinal, who uses her own life experiences as a starting point for her creation, establishes her own identity when she projects on her female protagonists her possible selves. Like Mary and Simone she is this woman whose identity is caught in her role of mother and wife as well as this more independent woman, the author of fiction who, like Simone, questions by her very act of writing the order in which she lives and in which all women live. *Une Vie pour deux* can be read as an allegory of writing, an allegory which brings to light Cardinal's narrative strategies and becomes the stage on which are enacted the tensions between Cardinal's several selves, as a woman and as a writer in a patriarchal society.

In *Le Passé empiété*, the search for the self and writing becomes even more complex as the narrator chooses a male figure—her father—and a female mythological figure— Clytemnestra—

through whom she attempts to understand her own family history, past and present. This book is a further meditation on the problems women writers confront as they search for "a room of their own."

The narrator is a fifty-year-old woman whose life has been shattered recently by her children's nearly fatal motorcycle accident. In addition to the anguish of fearing for their lives, she feels totally responsible for their accident—the motorcycle was bought with the money she made through the sale of her embroidery, an occupation she had taken up recently despite her family's disapproval. She interprets her children's accident as a punishment for having transgressed her role of wife and mother. She had dared to engage in a creative and lucrative activity apart from her family and had even been successful at it.

> I am guilty of having disobeyed people, their rules, their laws, the culture, the morals, what they call "the feminine mystique," and the astronomical price for this transgression is the life of my two children. (47)

If we replace embroidery by writing, a common metaphor in women's texts emblematic of the marginality but also of the perseverance of their authors, *Le Passé empiété* can be read as a follow-up of *Une Vie pour deux* since it unveils the conflict between a woman writer's responsibility to her family and her responsibility to herself. The narrator's identity as an artist and a woman is doubly challenged in this text as she has just turned fifty and is aware of the received ideas surrounding the "mature woman." Her family expected her to dabble a bit in embroidery but not to focus her whole life around it. They see her artistic activity as inappropriate for a woman of her age. She should settle down and devote herself to her children and eventually her grandchildren. Yet, the narrator cannot resign herself to this destiny. She is looking for other avenues. Her body has lost its youthfulness but is full of vitality and energy. It has gained a balance and does not rule her life any longer: "I feel that I am in control of myself" she says, marvelling at the new found wisdom of her body and mind (80). Her children's near death, however, puts all of this new life in question by activating a sense of guilt which engulfs her. She has to understand what happened and decides to "give birth to [herself], to meet the other one, the woman [she] became when she turned fifty" (21).

Her father, whom she hardly knew, becomes the first mediator between the narrator and herself. It is the first book in which

Cardinal seeks to come to terms with the father figure of her past. In her other books, the father is seen through the eyes of the narrator's mother who pursued her husband with an implacable hate, making him responsible for their divorce. The narrator's task is to wrench her father away from her mother's interpretations and to meet him on his own ground. She thus starts to imagine her father's life in the same way that Simone invented Mary MacLaughlin's story. This time, however, the narrator has to penetrate a world with which she is unfamiliar. She has to "understand his world in which she does not know how to live, a world of which she is suspicious because it has harmed her," and which has rejected her when she became independent (52). If at first the narrator uses the third person to write about her father, she soon discovers that it is not enough and that she has to merge with him, body and soul.

> I have to become my father to express him. I have to become him. I, is him and me. I want to be my father, to live in his skin and in his head, feel his mustache grow under my nose, love like him. Let my breasts disappear, let my vagina close itself up, let my clitoris grow longer, thicker, harder in order to become the phallus of the man who fathered me. (81)

From here on the narration of her father's life continues in the first person, interrupted from time to time by the narrator's doubts about her ability to feel and think like him. "Who can tell anything but about one-self, about one's phantasms, one's memory, one's knowledge or one's desires?" (113). Again and again the narrator, Cardinal's alter-ego, stresses the lack of distance between herself and her characters, for they have to become part of herself as they help her explore the multiple facets of her identity. The birth metaphor comes often under Cardinal's pen to express this reciprocity: "I invent you," she writes about her father. "You are born of me as I am born of you" (89).

However, the narrator—like Simone and Jean-François in their telling of Mary's story—reaches an impasse. She cannot go on identifying with her father's feelings and actions when she puts together, through her mother's recollections, their disastrous wedding night as well as the role he played in the death of their first child.

> I can no longer think "he." Since the wedding night I can no longer do so. "I" cannot be "Him," he refuses to do so. "He"

cannot be "She;" "She" cannot be "He." "Madame Bovary is me" is impossible, it is a vain boast. (233)

The narrator's allusion to Flaubert puts into question both the ability and the truthfulness of the representation of one sex by the other. The allegiance to the mother and the maternal values which link the mother and the daughter across generations reappear and make it impossible for the daughter to reenter the world of the father. The shock for the narrator is so intense that she stops her embroidery. She cannot go on with her creative work since she is torn between a yearning to love her father and her incapacity to relate intimately to her father's feelings, particularly when they deal with his relationship to his children. "I cannot think about children the way a man would do it. How do men experience their children? For me, the experience is in my womb, it is visceral" (234).

It is the mythical figure of Clytemnestra who will guide the narrator through the maze of her conflicting feelings. As she remembers her mother's vengeful attitude towards her father, the narrator invokes the name of Clytemnestra, the queen who killed her husband, Agamemnon. The Clytemnestra she recalls from her highschool readings is an evil, blood-thirsty character who accepts her fate at the end when she is killed by her children to avenge their father's death. This legendary figure haunts the narrator, and she decides to discover more about her. In libraries, she learns about Clytemnestra as the daughter of a God, as the wife of a king, as the lover of a young courtier, but cannot find anything about Clytemnestra herself, separate from the roles she has to play. Yet, she is drawn to her because, though their stories are different, she feels that both their lives rest on "this mixture of love and anger, on this powerlessness . . ." (310).

When Clytemnestra starts appearing in her kitchen, the narrator engages in a dialogue with her, trying to reconstruct Clytemnestra's story from the queen's point of view as she had done with her father's life. At the same time as she records the queen's story, she embroiders it, attempting to capture the essence of her life and of her passions.

In the narrator's mind Clytemnestra is not an isolated figure of a cursed woman, but she blends with her mother, her sister, herself, with all the other women of her family. The narrator gives Clytemnestra a voice of her own which tells of her despair when her daughter Iphigenia is immolated to the Gods; this recalls her love, jealousy and finally hate for her husband. When she evokes her difficult relationship with her adolescent children, Electra and Orestes, the narrator relives her own ambiguous relationships with her children. The commonalities of their experiences as mothers—giving birth, caring, loving their children but also yearning to be freed from their demands—create a deep bond between the two: "There is no more distance between her and me, between the children and mine" (325). Though she is a queen of legendary status, Clytemnestra becomes a woman among others with whom, across the ages, the narrator can merge. As she mixes Clytemnestra's story with her own, the narrator is able to better understand the role of guilt in women's lives. Relying on history but also on Clytemnestra's story (her-story), the narrator draws the portrait of a woman, the queen, who despite her strength is incapable of escaping guilt for she has internalized society's dictates. Though Clytemnestra realizes that she has killed Agamemnon because she wanted to free herself of his yoke and of the power he embodied, and not, as the story has it, because she was a woman controlled by her lust, the queen accepts—even calls for—her death as a just punishment for her crime. She does not want the narrator to alter her story. At this point, as in her father's story, the narrator stops her narration. This time, however, she deliberately decides to "move away from her as I did from him" and to distance herself from her creation. The narrator refuses now to identify with Clytemnestra and to accept the guilt as women's inescapable lot. Clytemnestra's story represents the narrator's search for the self through identification but also through separation.

> Contrary to what it seems, my life with Clytemnestra was never a complete loss, nor an alienation. On the contrary, I always knew during that period that I was projecting on her the one I no longer wanted to be. . . . I am going to break away from myself, from the woman I was. (347)

The dead-end the narrator reached with her father's story does not seem as dramatic any more. The fiction of Clytemnestra has helped her make a break with her past and to exorcise the guilt that engulfs women's lives and stifles their creativity. Though the narrator feels connected to Clytemnestra, she is wary of her as a model just as she has been wary of her mother. If the narrator values solidarity between women, she refuses however to follow blindly the examples that her (fore)mothers have set:

I must, forever, refuse to be bewitched by role models. They must stay in my memory, but they should not determine my future. I must neither fear them nor depend on them. (360)

Clytemnestra's death, in the narrator's version, is desultory. The narrator is in a hurry now to do away with her character and with its symbolism: "I do think that this whole story has lasted long enough. It is over" (371).

However, the act itself of rewriting Clytemnestra's myth from a woman-centered perspective, even if as we have seen, the narrator does not espouse all of her character's values, has empowered the narrator to move on with her own future.[7] She will resume her creative work not as a furtive activity for which she has to apologize but as a full-fledged one upon which her life is centered. In a move echoing Virginia Woolf's plea for a room of one's own, on the last page, the narrator decides to look for a studio and to move her embroidery from a small room in a corner of the house to the center of her house, in the living room.

In *Writing a Woman's Life*, Heilbrun explains that while she was creating her female character Kate Fansler and her guests, she was recreating herself. She believes that many women authors create female characters, "and sometimes male characters, who might openly enact the dangerous adventures of a woman's life, unconstrained by female propriety" (112). This act of self-creation as Heilbrun projected her possible selves onto her female characters seems to parallel Cardinal's self-discovery as she came to writing. Cardinal's protagonists are not engaged in adventures as bold as Kate Fansler's, but they are engaged in the perilous adventure of living a woman's life which dares to be different. Cardinal—like her narrators—is sustained by the fictions of other women's lives through which she can attain her identity as a woman and a writer.

This construction of the self within the context of an awareness of others and particularly of a community of women has been perceived by many scholars of women's autobiographical writings as a characteristic that sets women's texts apart from the male tradition.[8] This awareness, however, does not come only from the psychological needs of connectedness which women might possess to a greater degree than men, but should also be interpreted as Susan Friedman suggests from a political perspective where "the self constructed . . . is often based in, but not limited to, a group consciousness—an awareness of the meaning of the cultural category *woman* for the patterns of women's individual destiny" (41). Throughout her books,

Cardinal's narrators—like herself—have to face the consequences of this cultural construct for their lives. However, Cardinal chooses to present her female readers with fictions of women's lives which can empower women by refusing—as the Clytemnestra example shows—to follow a plot which repeats women's alienation. She succeeds, in my opinion, in offering new models of women's lives where the delicate balance between the connection with other women, both past and present, and the invention of new, bolder life stories for women is preserved. "Le passé empiété," an embroidery stitch that uses a previous stitch to move forward on the cloth, is an apt metaphor to describe Cardinal's writing which connects to the past and to the experiences of other women in order to construct the future.

NOTES

1. All translations are mine except for Pat Goodheart's translation of *The Words to Say It.*
2. In her new book *The Other Side of the Story* (1989), Molly Hite addresses this problem and shows how "two meanings of otherness—otherness as a deliberate project of writing other-wise, and otherness as an unavoidable effect of a preexisting limit called femininity—seem almost inextricably conflated" (8).
3. See Sandra M. Gilbert and Susan Gubar, *The Madwoman in the Attic: The Woman Writer and the Nineteenth-Century Literary Imagination* (1979); Elaine Showalter, *A Literature of Their Own* (1977); and more recently Domna Stanton, *The Female Autograph* (1987) and Rita Felski, *Beyond Feminist Aesthetics: Feminist Literature and Social Change* (1989).
4. I have chosen not to translate this title for lack of a word which would embody all the rich connotations of the French. "Le passé empiété" is an embroidery stitch—split stitching in English—which uses a previous stitch to move forward on the cloth. It literally "encroaches upon the past" and thus becomes a metaphor for Cardinal's writing which uses the past in order to construct the future.
5. Nancy Chodorow's *The Reproduction of Mothering* has been complemented by several studies such as Carol Gilligan's *In a Different Voice* and Judith Kegan Gardiner's "On Female Identity

and Writing by Women." This latter essay sees a direct connection between women's ego formation and the narrative structures they use.
6. In *Les Mots pour le dire*, a same scene occurs when the narrator gives her journal, which she had hidden under her bed, to her husband. After reading it, her husband sees her in a different light and admires the new person she has become or that she never revealed before.
7. See Rachel Blau DuPlessis's chapter on "'Perceiving the otherside of everything': Tactics of Revisionary Mythopoesis" in *Writing Beyond the Ending* for a discussion of twentieth century women writers' revision of myths.
8. See in particular Mary Mason's article "The Other Voice: Autobiographies of Women Writers" in *Autobiography: Essays Theoretical and Critical*, ed. by James Olney (1980) and Julia Watson's "Shadowed Presence: Modern Women Writers' Autobiographies and the Other" in James Olney, *Studies in Autobiography* (1988).

WORKS CITED

Cardinal, Marie. *La Clé sur la porte*. Paris: Grasset, 1972.
———. *Les Mots pour le dire*. Paris: Grasset, 1975. *The Words to Say It*. Trans. Pat Goodheart. Cambridge: Van Vactor & Goodheart, 1983.
———. *Autrement dit*. Paris: Grasset, 1977.
———. *Une Vie pour deux*. Paris: Grasset, 1978.
———. *Le Passé empiété*. Paris: Grasset, 1983.
———. *Les Grands Désordres*. Paris: Grasset, 1987.
Chodorow, Nancy. *The Reproduction of Mothering: Psychoanalysis and the Sociology of Gender*. Berkeley: U of California P, 1979.
Colette. *La Naissance du jour*. (1928) Paris: Garnier-Flammarion, 1969.
DuPlessis, Rachel Blau. *Writing Beyond the Ending: Narrative Strategies of Twentieth-Century Women Writers*. Bloomington: Indiana UP, 1985.
Felski, Rita. *Beyond Feminist Aesthetics: Feminist Literature and Social Change*. Cambridge: Harvard UP, 1989.

Friedman, Susan Stanford. "Women Autobiographical Selves: Theory and Practice" in *The Private Self: Theory and Practice of Women's Autobiographical Writings*, ed. by Shari Benstock.
Gardiner, Judith Kegan. "On Female Identity and Writing by Women." *Critical Inquiry* (Winter 1981). 347-361.
Gilbert, Sandra and Gubar, Susan. *The Madwoman in the Attic: The Woman Writer and the Nineteenth-Century Literary Imagination*. New Haven: Yale UP, 1979.
Gilligan, Carol. *In a Different Voice*. Cambridge: Harvard UP, 1982.
Gusdorf, Georges. "Conditions and Limits of Autobiography," 1956. Trans. James Olney. In Olney, *Autobiography*. 20-48.
Heilbrun, Carolyn. *Writing a Woman's Life*. New York: Norton, 1988.
Hite, Molly. *The Other Side of the Story: Structures and Strategies of Contemporary Feminist Narratives*. Ithaca: Cornell UP, 1989.
Mason, Mary. "The Other Voice: Autobiographies of Women Writers" in Olney, *Autobiography*. 210-235.
Olney, James, ed. *Autobiography: Essays Theoretical and Critical*. Princeton: Princeton UP, 1980.
———. *Studies in Autobiography*. New York: NY UP, 1980.
Showalter, Elaine. *A Literature of Their Own: British Women Novelists from Brontë to Lessing*. Princeton: Princeton UP, 1977.
Stanton, Domna C., ed. *The Female Autograph*. 1984. Chicago: The U of Chicago P, 1987.
Watson, Julia. "Shadowed Presence: Modern Women Writers: Autobiographies and the Other." In Olney, *Studies in Autobiography*. 180-189.

Fiction and Autobiography/ Language and Silence: The Lover by Marguerite Duras

Janice Morgan

Always the same, always different, the paradoxical career of Marguerite Duras continues to stir critical comment. As early as the 1950s, and particularly after Moderato Cantabile *(1958)*, Duras was hailed as one of France's most interesting contemporary writers. Throughout the 1960s, as she moved freely between fiction, theatre, and eventually film—often transposing the same work from one medium to the other—her work became increasingly recognized for its haunting poetry and extreme spareness of form. Well-known titles from this period are the screenplay Hiroshima mon amour *(1960)*, and the two novels The Ravishing of Lol V. Stein *(1964)*—object of a stunningly obscure commentary-homage by Jacques Lacan—and The Vice-Consul *(1966)*. Later, in the wake of the feminist movement of the 1970s, Duras was embraced by a new generation of emerging women scholars as a prime exemplar of what became celebrated as écriture féminine, a writing style characterized by its fluidity, open-endedness, and intersubjectivity. Representative of this period is the film India Song *(1975)* which, according to legend, played every day for six or seven years at a theatre in Paris. Still later in the 1980s, Duras maintained her controversial status as the appearance of new works, among them The Malady of Death *(1982)* and The Lover *(Prix Goncourt, 1984)* compelled a re-reading and re-assessment of earlier ones. Julia Kristeva, in her book of essays Soleil noir: Mélancolie et dépression *(1987)*, singles out Duras, "an author who continually harbors an unhealthy secret within a textual plot that is ever more elusive," as being particularly emblematic of a repressed malaise and pain in the modern world. Romantic, melancholy, and subversive, it appears likely that the *signature of Marguerite Duras will provoke divergent responses from her readers for some time to come.*

> To write is not to comment on what one already knows but to look for what one doesn't know yet.
>
> Viviane Forrestier[1]

In 1984, Marguerite Duras surprised the French literary world by producing *L'Amant* (*The Lover*), a lyrical, darkly-candid autobiographical book about her adolescence in Indochina during the late 1920s. The book, which opens with the young Duras crossing the Mekong river on a ferry and closes one and a half years later with her departure on an ocean liner for France, traces the young woman's passage from childhood to adulthood. In many ways, *The Lover*—written toward the end of what has been a long, distinguished career as an author—is the retelling of events described earlier in a novel called *The Sea Wall* (1950). More than thirty years separate the two works, more than thirty years of relative silence on this evidently formative part of Duras's life. It is as if until just recently, Duras wished to forget—both publicly and privately—about this very different childhood she experienced in what remains for Westerners an alien land. Gradually, however, the past has re-surfaced in Duras's writing—first in fiction, as in the Indian cycle beginning with *The Vice-Consul* (1966), then later in the growing number of photographs, interviews, and frankly autobiographical texts the author has published during the last few years.

In re-reading *The Sea Wall*, it is clear what Duras would have wished to forget—the poverty, isolation, and the lack of opportunity endemic to the remote, tropical outpost where the family, a widowed mother and her two children, lives. Informing the whole is the legend of how the mother, in a heroic but doomed attempt to become a wealthy landowner for her children's benefit, suffers one legal defeat after another at the hands of a corrupt, colonial administration. With their mother living afterwards in despair and close to madness, the son and the daughter have no one to turn to for consolation but each other and their romantic fantasies of a better life. An erotic liaison with a wealthy lover becomes for both of them the preferred avenue of escape.

Though *The Sea Wall* is based on personal situations and events that actually occurred, the novel is nonetheless a very public narrative: the story is told in the third person (yet closely tied to the daughter Suzanne's point of view) and develops in a conventionally linear, chronological fashion. Throughout, its realistic settings and terse dialogue recall the American novel style à la Hemingway so fashionable in France during the 1950s.

The Lover, while covering the same brief period in the author's life, differs dramatically from the earlier version. Narrated largely in the first person, the text is composed of fragments taken from shifting time frames, fragments that are related not in an external, linear way, but in circular, associative patterns that convey the more intimate, psychological rhythms of that experience. At times etched with a sharp sense of realism (the strident sounds and exotic mixture of smells in the night streets of Cholon, for example), yet at other times, passing with a dream-like fluidity beyond any set boundaries of place and time, *The Lover* creates a distinctive style all its own.

It is clear that Duras assumes the two different texts to be complementary, for each provides a certain content that the other leaves out. In this way, the first text becomes a kind of narrative *repoussoir* for the second, a foil against which the new text, this new interpretation of events, will be played. "Before, I spoke of clear periods, those on which the light fell. Now I'm talking about the hidden stretches of that same youth, of certain facts, feelings, events that I buried"(8). In thus characterizing the interdependency of the two texts, Duras asserts her need to clarify what had been written before, to re-discover a remembered vision of her past life and self that had previously been disguised. The author tells her readers that she now feels free to tell the true story of how things happened, now that her mother and her brothers are dead, now that the moral strictures governing literary culture (and women's writing in particular) have been unbound.

Yet though Duras pursues the past with a relentless candor, it would be naive to conclude that she is writing the book merely to settle accounts or that she is uncovering the past in an effort to reveal all. Estelle Jelinek, in her introduction to *Women's Autobiography*, speaks of a dual or conflicting intention in the writing of autobiography. While on the one hand authors "wish to clarify, to affirm, and to authenticate their self-images" (15), a writer will also tend to camouflage or in some way distance herself from intimacy in the projection of that self-image. Certainly, the psychological tension between intimacy and distance, self-revelation and self-effacement accounts for much of the fascination and allure *The Lover* exerts upon its readers. Central to this issue is the enigma of Duras's feelings for the man who first became her lover and with that, the sense we have of how much the author reveals or conceals, first from the lover and secondly, from the reader. For perhaps the real subject of this autobiography, unlike the earlier version in *The Sea Wall*, is writing—that is, the origins of Duras's desire to write and with that, her means of access to that writing.

To begin, many readers are struck by her tendency to slip from a predominantly first-person narration to a more distant third-person narration and to do so precisely in those scenes with the man from Cholon, scenes which are among the most intimate in the book. The more obvious explanations for this are not at all satisfying. For example, the split between the first person (I) and the third person (she) does not seem to convey, as one might anticipate in an autobiographical work, the distinction between the young girl of then as she lived her experiences and the mature woman of today looking back on those experiences. For the narrative, rather than shifting back and forth from the present tense to the past, is written very dominantly in the present tense (regardless of the particular time period being evoked) and with a high degree of vividness and immediacy that effectively erases the very distinction between past and present. Rather, the appearance of the third person seems to mark the deliberate intrusion in autobiography of a fictional artifice; that is, Duras, the public figure and author *narrating*, becomes Duras, a literary character, *narrated*, in her own story.

For some critics, this fictional intrusion compromises the transparency of Duras's early statement that this book is one of self revelation. Sharon Willis, for example, views the narrative split consciousness in *The Lover* as a kind of literary smokescreen, one highly characteristic of Duras's tendency to *décevoir* (in the dual sense of the French word *to deceive*; *to disappoint*) her public (4). The author would seem to stand accused, then, of intentional duplicity, "given the text's strategy of veiling and unveiling, where 'I' veils herself as 'she', but where 'she' just as frequently masquerades as 'I'" (6). In other words, one may well gain the suspicion that Duras, the writer, is playing the same game of seduction and evasion with her readers that the young girl played, then, with her lover.

As compelling as this interpretation might seem, I would like to propose another—namely, that is precisely through a certain artifice and duality that Duras's narrative is able to achieve its authenticity. Moreover, the tension that exists in the written text between intimacy and distance, deception and sincerity, language and silence is, in fact, intrinsic to the experiences as she lived them.

From the outset, Duras describes her erotic adventure as "the experiment," revealing already not only a taste for pleasure but a taste for speculative distance on that pleasure. From her opening statement about what constitutes a woman's beauty, her seductiveness, Duras shows a keen awareness of women's iconic value, their particular quality of (in Laura Mulvey's words) "to-be-looked-at-ness" (Mulvey 11). Having identified that quality in herself (through a somewhat elaborately detailed description of her clothing and makeup), she goes on to describe the Chinese man's approach, his interest—but also his apprehension because of the racial difference, her youth. It is at the moment when he approaches her that Duras slips into third-person narration, and thereafter, a dual awareness infuses the narrative. From the moment she describes her gaze going out to the man on the ferry, there is another gaze, beyond the couple, looking back—Duras consciously watching herself being watched, being enchanted by the phenomenon, writing about it. When Duras slips into the third person, she effectively transposes the transparency of the first-person account of an individual experience into a more complex kind of theater, one which transcends the limits of the personal.

The rhythmic force of the prose carries events forward as relentlessly as the Mekong River current, the girl being embarked with the man in what she calls "everyone's story,"[2] the knowledge which she says she already possessed, "in advance of time and experience" (9). Clearly, the balance of passion is weighted on his side, while the balance of power (the passive power of a desired woman) is on hers. Far from stressing the uniqueness of her experience—as we might expect—the young girl insists instead on maintaining almost an enforced impersonality with her lover. Alone with him for the first time, she asks the man to do with her what he "usually does with the women he brings to his flat" (37, 38) and later confides to him that she enjoys the idea of being curiously "one of them, indistinguishable [from them]" (42). No names are mentioned in the narrative; Duras refers to the man and to herself through third-person epithets: "the child" (35), "the man from Cholon" (74), "the little white girl" (83), "the Chinese millionaire" (91)—terms which not only convey the way each is viewed by a certain segment of society, but also the way the lovers inevitably view each other; they are attracted to and defined for each other by their separateness, their difference.

The young girl never equates the undeniable pleasure she receives from him with love for the man she meets each night; part of her is always outside the room where they are, beyond the space their two bodies occupy. Their affair is characterized, from the first night they are together, by an unbridgeable solitude: "He says he's lonely, horribly lonely because of this love he feels for her. She says she's lonely too. She doesn't say why" (37). Because of this solitude, her intense physical pleasure with him seems abstract, austere—almost brutal. The first person narration resumes suddenly in the memory of her mother, then in the vivid evocation of the particular atmosphere of the room where they are—so open to the Chinese streets outside its windows. In the midst of their lovemaking, the young girl hears the sounds of wooden clogs on the crowded streets, the strident sounds of merchants mingled with the rich aroma of roasted peanuts, soups, the sudden mountain fragrance of woodsmoke, and it is as if all the individuality, the unforgettable particularity of the event lay there, strangely outside herself.

Between the ebb and flow of physical desire, the girl tells the Chinese about her family in Sadec; soon surrounding the lovers' bodies alone in the room grows the shadowy presence of the mother, the two brothers, and their familiar "inspired silence" (34). After their first evening together, the narrative flickers back and forth from the nights in Cholon to the remembered days in Sadec. Thus, at the same time that Cholon inaugurates her separation from the family in Sadec, it also curiously confirms that original experience; both Sadec and Cholon share the identity of "a place that's intolerable, bordering on death, a place of violence, pain, despair, dishonor" (75). Gradually, the nights in Cholon, with their distinctive mixture of pleasure-in-pain, in their essential ambivalence, seem to parallel with the lover the same silent relationships of desire and difference, pride and shame, power and fear that existed within her family. It is undoubtedly to the intensity of this ambivalence—in recognition of these silences—that Duras owes the uniqueness of her vision as a writer. About Sadec she writes, "It's in its aridity, its terrible harshness, its malignance, that I'm the most deeply sure of myself, at the heart of my essential certainty, the certainty that I'll be a writer" (75). Here, in the powerful comfort Duras takes in the knowledge of her destiny as a writer, one can only conclude, as does the critic Yvonne Guers-Villate, that writing performs a very important and specific function for this author: it is through the writing of books that she will be able to transpose—in an aesthetic form—the wealth of contradictions, the polarities and distances, the emotional intensities and ambiguities of life as she experienced them.³ Her desire here is not to *resolve* these conflicting tensions, but rather—as in death—to free herself from them, to transcend them.

All these elements participate in the distances established by the oscillations in the narrative, of which the shift between she and I is but one indication. Yet there is another facet to this layered consciousness in the story. For also intertwined with the nights in Cholon are the remembered images of certain women: Marie-Claude Carpenter, Betty Fernandez, Helen Lagonelle. *The Lover* is a hymn to these women—to the desire they evoked in those around them, their mystery, their beauty, and also their peculiar absence, their silence. Among these women, one reigns supreme in memory, referred to here as "the Lady" (89), the wife of the French ambassador in Vinh Long, the one whose young lover committed suicide in Savanna Khet when she left there to join her husband in Vinh Long. This particular woman, first encountered by Duras at the age of eight, seems to have incarnated for her an unforgettable model of femininity—one strongly implicated in a precocious obsession with death.⁴ The model also for a literary character, Anne-Marie Stretter, who dominates several of Duras's most well-known works—notably *The Vice-Consul* and *India Song*, embodies for the young Duras a dual power and possesses a dual identity: first, as a wealthy woman of society, wife and mother, an elegant sustainer of the status quo and then, underneath that identity, a woman who contained within the sensuality of her body "this power of death, to create death, to bring it on" (*Lieux* 65).⁵

Duras's use of the third person (she) to introduce and frame her own erotic initiation, that curious fusion of she/I, works to connect her own individual story to this other myth of passion. In fact, the author draws a clear parallel between that other woman, then almost forty, and the fifteen-year-old girl; both alike "doomed to discredit because of the kind of body they have, caressed by lovers, kissed by their lips, consigned to the infamy of a pleasure unto death, as they both call it, unto the mysterious death of lovers without love" (90). The nights spent with the lover in Cholon repeat, too, the litany of "a pleasure unto death" (43, 90), and one senses strongly that Duras's account of this experience represents, for her, a personal access to a legend; one senses that the narrative enacts her own entry into the necessarily impersonal myth of passion and desire.⁶ It is this quality of the relationship that accounts, no doubt, for the externality of its narration: in the text, for example, Duras refers to the man as "the" not as "my" lover; and further on, she writes about him using once more the definite article where the possessive would be more customary, "I can still see the face, and I do remember the name" (44).[7] This same externality, this implicit allusion to a legend of erotic passion that exists curiously *beyond* the two lovers also provides the essential dimension to the young girl's previously expressed wish with her lover to be among all the other women "he'd had," to be "'mixed in' with them, indistinguishable" (42). In this wish, the lover becomes her accomplice (and, to a certain extent, her victim): "He understands what I've just said. Our expressions are suddenly changed, false, caught in evil and death" (42). "It was as if he loved the pain, loved it as he'd loved me, intensely, unto death perhaps, and as if he preferred it now to me" (110).

Nowhere does the force of this myth seem more striking than in the closing pages of the book when, again, the fictional register resumes in the telling of her departure on the ocean liner and, with that departure, the young girl's sudden realization one night—after their separation—that perhaps she had loved him after all, "with a love she hadn't seen because it had lost itself in the affair (*l'histoire*, the story) like water in sand" (114; *L'Amant* 138). The distanced, fictional mode here, the story, becomes a way of revealing the depth of illusion behind the experience as she lived it—a way of unveiling the self-deception that informed (or perhaps better, de-formed, concealed) the emotion contained within that experience. Thus, as in Duras's novels, even as the narrative weaves its spell of fantasy or illusion, it also reveals a lucid awareness of the central delusion it depicts. The text's duality, its "duplicity"—far from compromising the validity of the fundamental experience—becomes, in fact, the hallmark of its genuineness. Ultimately, for the writer, it is the "story" that triumphs: years afterward, through the man's phone call, we hear once more in the book's final pages the echoing testimony of a mythic love undiminished by time, of a passion that would endure until death. Here, personal event has been fully transposed into literature: autobiography has passed into legend.

We began by observing that *The Lover* is a work of revelation. In Duras's avowed intentions in writing the book, to tell those parts of her experience that were not expressed before, the text assumes the role of a testimonial or a confession. Yet in comparing this later book to the earlier *Sea Wall*, we note a peculiar irony: it is the earlier novel that is filled with movement, character, event, and dialogue—speech that passes even into invective and diatribe—whereas the later autobiographical book remains largely a record of silences. In effect, the text is saturated with silence, silences that exist at the level of the experience itself: in speaking of the family in Sadec, for example, "Never a hello, a good evening, a happy New Year. Never a thank you. Never any talk. Never any need to talk. Everything always silent, distant. It's a family of stone, petrified so deeply it's impenetrable" (54); about the subject of marriage between herself and the Chinese, "They never speak of it any more" (97); about their nights together in Cholon, "He scarcely speaks to her any more. Perhaps he thinks she won't understand any longer what he'd say about her, about the love he never knew before and of which he can't speak" (99); or at the moment when the young girl nearly confides her story to her mother: "I almost told her about Cholon. But I didn't. I never did" (93).

But silences occur also in the gaps and fissures of the narration, in the fragmentation and dislocation of memory as the text slips from one time-place to another. One cannot avoid the impression—confirmed even on the printed page, punctuated as it is by blank spaces—that a mysterious content must have been left out. Curiously, however, in comparing *The Lover* to *The Sea Wall*, one discovers that this later book is, at once, more fragmented yet more thematically coherent than its fictional predecessor, more elusive, yet more complete. Clearly, there is something here that goes beyond the contingencies of youthful reticence, the accidents inherent in either willful or unwillful failures to communicate; for the silence at the heart of Duras's childhood experience lies also at the heart of her aesthetic practice. One need only compare the style and structure of the text to those of her mature, fictional works: *Moderato Cantabile*, *Hiroshima mon amour*, *The Ravishing of Lol V. Stein*, *The Vice-Consul*—to recognize that the writing of silence represents for this author a deliberate, aesthetic choice. Both the fiction and the autobiography are based on a central conviction deeply held by the author, that language (the spoken) exists precisely to suggest, to evoke that which remains unspoken in life; that writing serves, therefore, primarily to render the substance of things imagined, the evidence of things not said.

Duras's own comments on the complex, hidden filiations between desire, silence, and writing in this autobiographical work make this conviction evident (25, 75, 103). Furthermore, in an interview, the author states that the intense, youthful affair in Cholon about which she has written "has eclipsed the other loves of my life, those that were declared, married"[8] and has done so precisely because it was "unspoken, undeclared" (Apos). In its silence, then, Cholon and all that it represents rejoins the imaginary photograph that opens the book, the one of the seductive young girl on the ferry crossing the river, the one that was never taken. Because it was never taken, she says, never "detached or removed from all the rest" (10), the tenuous, remembered image holds a great power, that of representing an absolute: it is precisely because their content was never expressed, never acknowledged or fixed in either image or words that both the absent photograph and the silent nights in Cholon have come to hold—much later in the author's life—an inexhaustible richness.

Here, a certain suspicion of language prevails, one shared by other contemporary writers (notably Maurice Blanchot, whom Duras admires)—a belief that language, even as it calls into being and names our past experience, can also betray that experience, can contain and kill its sensuous strangeness, its unrepeatable magic. The goal of the writer, then, is to create a style that does not attempt to directly express its ever-elusive content but only to suggest the contours, the dimension, or the shadow of that content. It is this quality that gives a literary text (like a memory) the power to resonate beyond itself, to engender other texts, other forms.

And this can be true, it seems, of autobiography as well as of fiction. In this way, Duras would not have us view this particular book as an endpoint or a conclusion to the past but rather as another possible point of departure and re-discovery of that past.[9] In its elusiveness, its fluidity, its ritual imperative of looking again, of saying again, *The Lover* asserts the re-performing of a self in writing that ultimately cannot be fixed, seized, rendered captive or named in words and images. Paradoxically, then, it is through a certain artifice, through the use of fictional registers, and through the shaping of silence that the writer is able to evoke a composite portrait of herself, one that in its complex facets of event and illusion begins to attain the fullness of authenticity.

NOTES

1. This epigraph by Forrestier is borrowed from a book about writing by Suzanne Lamy entitled *Quand je lis je m'invente (When I Read, I Invent Myself)*. Translation my own.
2. This citation is from a special interview with Marguerite Duras conducted by Bernard Pivot on the French television program *Apostrophes*. This particular program, broadcast by Antenne 2 on

September 28, 1984, is available on video upon request from the French Cultural Services in New York (FACSEA), 972 Fifth Avenue, NY 10021. Further references to this particular interview will be indicated in the text by the abbreviated (Apos) in parentheses. Translations are my own.
3. For a sensitive and highly perceptive discussion of this subject, see the chapter "Ambivalence and sentiment de contradiction" in *Continuité/Discontinuité* by Guers-Villate: "Without a single doubt, literary creation was the means chosen very early by the novelist to permit her to exorcise her own conflicts through transposing them" (58). Translation my own.
4. Duras speaks at length about the influence of this mysterious red-haired woman in *Les Lieux de Marguerite Duras*, an interview with Michelle Porte (61-69).
5. Far from being merely an idiosyncratic obsession, the eight-year-old's fascination with this particular woman's story seems to connect with a primal reverence and fear of the power of women's bodies that reaches back into the mists of recorded time. The dual feminine identity that the young Duras found so compelling touches upon ancient myths and rituals where "woman became recognized as both benign goddess and mysterious power, both a life giver and life destroyer, to be feared and desired, loved and scorned" (Arms 11-12). Even today, a deep ambivalence regarding the myth of "Woman" is very much in evidence, taking many curious forms in popular culture: the role of women in advertising, in *film noir*, in the presence of cult personalities such as Madonna, for example.
6. Though Duras's affair (as well as her fiction) is steeped in the mystique of "Woman," she nonetheless reveals a sardonic awareness of how women are often betrayed by this mystique. She describes the not-to-be-envied plight of the upper-class colonial women she knew of, cloistered in their mansions, saving their fragile white beauty through the tropical seasons while waiting for some vague future romance to change their empty lives (26-28). Duras's own story in *The Lover*, though it participates fully in this romantic mystique, also asserts a much bolder, more controlling approach to the satisfaction of feminine desire within that mystique.
7. These observations are made by Duras herself in an interview with Marianne Alphant in *Libération*.
8. Citation from the interview with Marianne Alphant, op. cit.

9. In the above-cited interview with Alphant, Duras suggests that this same brief period of her youth may well give rise to two or three other autobiographical books, each of them different. Further on, she quotes Stendhal, saying that no other part of her life holds as much meaning for her as a writer: "interminably, childhood."

WORKS CITED

Arms, Suzanne. *Immaculate Deception: A New Look at Women and Childbirth*. New York: Bantam/Houghton-Mifflin, 1975.
Alphant, Marianne. "Duras à l'état sauvage" and interview with Marguerite Duras. *Libération* (4 September, 1984).
Duras, Marguerite. *L'Amant*. Paris: Minuit, 1984.
———. *Un Barrage contre le Pacifique*. Paris: Gallimard, 1950.
———. *Hiroshima mon amour*. Paris: Gallimard, 1960.
———. *India Song*. Paris: Gallimard, 1973.
———, et Michelle Porte. *Les Lieux de Marguerite Duras*. Paris: Minuit, 1977.
———. *The Lover*. Trans. Barbara Bray. New York: Perennial, 1986.
———. *La Maladie de la mort*. Paris: Minuit, 1982.
———. *Moderato Cantabile*. Paris: Minuit, 1958.
———. *Le Ravissement de Lol V. Stein*. Paris: Gallimard, 1964.
———. *The Sea Wall*. Trans. Herma Briffault. New York: Perennial, 1986. c. 1952.
———. *Le Vice-Consul*. Paris: Gallimard, 1966.
Guers-Villate, Yvonne. *Continuité/Discontinuité de l'oeuvre durassienne*. Brussels: Editions de l'Université de Bruxelles, 1985.
Jelinek, Estelle C. "Introduction: Women's Autobiography and the Male Tradition." *Women's Autobiography: Essays in Criticism*. Ed. Estelle Jelinek. Bloomington: Indiana UP, 1980.
Lamy, Suzanne. *Quand je lis je m'invente*. Montréal: L'Hexagone, 1984.
Mulvey, Laura. "Visual Pleasure and Narrative Cinema." *Screen* 16: (1975): 6-18.
Willis, Sharon. *Marguerite Duras: Writing on the Body*. Urbana: U of Illinois P, 1987.

H.D.'s The Gift: "Hide-and-Seek" With the "Skeleton-Hand of Death"

Miriam Fuchs

H.D. was born in 1886 in Bethlehem, Pennsylvania. Influenced by the Moravian heritage of her family and her community, H.D. explored her history, notions of revelation, mystery and later in her life, mysticism and spiritualism along with psychoanalysis and the unconscious. Leaving Bryn Mawr College before receiving a degree, H.D. left the United States in 1911 for Europe and settled in London. Ezra Pound, to whom she was briefly engaged, introduced her within literary circles, and soon H.D.'s "Imagist" poetry was appearing in anthologies and literary magazines such as Poetry, Little Review, and The Egoist.

Those with whom she formed her closest or most enduring ties—Bryher (Winifred Ellerman), who helped her to raise her daughter; Richard Aldington, whom she married in 1913, separated from in 1918, and divorced in 1938; Pound; Lawrence; Cecil Grey, who fathered her daughter; Freud, with whom she underwent analysis in the 1930s—are portrayed in H.D.'s large body of works. Hospitalized for a breakdown after World War II, H.D. lived primarily in Switzerland, where she wrote sections of Tribute to Freud, End to Torment, "The Mystery," Compassionate Friendship and the poetry of Helen in Egypt and Hermetic Definition.

Many of H.D.'s works were published years, sometimes decades after composition, and others that were published soon went out of print; still other works were in manuscript form when H.D. died in 1961. As her poetry and prose are posthumously published or re-issued, H.D.'s early association with Pound and Imagism is eclipsed by her literary efforts in a variety of genres. Of the early Imagists, H.D. is one of the few who experimented extensively in translation, poetry, prose fiction, film criticism and acting, journalistic memoirs, and autobio-

graphical narrative. Positioning herself within much of her writing, and thus disclaiming the early Modernist insistence on authorial impersonality, H.D. believed that textual dynamics should boldly reflect her own psychodynamics.

> But we fight for life,
> we fight, they say, for breath,
> so what good are your scribblings?
> this—we take them with us
> beyond death . . .
> from *The Walls Do Not Fall*[1]

It is January 17, 1943. German fighter planes blast London in a third wave of bomb attacks. Surviving the strike, H.D. looks to the future, but can only envision herself dying, "caught in the fall of bricks . . . pinned down under a great beam, helpless. . . . burned to death" (*The Gift* 136).[2] Working to recall a time in her past when "There was a promise and there was a gift," she fails, realizing that the promises of her childhood have been broken, and the gift somehow lost (134). H.D.'s memory fixes not on childhood but, in the final chapter of *The Gift*, on the one hundred days and nights of bombing since the Battle of Britain. And of her present conditions, H.D. is astonished to find that she is alive, in fact, "sitting in the hall in one of the little chairs. . . . we can breathe, we can talk" (138).

Trapped by historical and political forces, between the fear that she may be burnt to death and the relief that comes from periods without sirens and explosions, H.D. concentrates on survival. Personal freedom while she was writing *The Gift* seemed remote, for even the intermittent lulls brought unforeseeable and discomforting results. Writing from her Lowndes Square flat to May Sarton on July 26, 1941, H.D. observes that since her "terrible psychic wonderings and probing and exacerbated nerves . . . [have] calmed down," she has reacted to intervals between bomb attacks like a convalescent to a disease. But she diagnoses her improved condition as a remission that deceives and betrays. Although her anxiety has lessened she remains "really ill." "We are tragic and horribly battered, but so glad to be alive." With discernible sarcasm H.D. adds, "that is the gift, the 'reward' for having endured so much" (Sarton, "Letters from H.D." 53).

The Gift operates, in large measure, as meta-autobiographics. H.D.'s closing chapter "Morning Star" and the opening pages by Perdita Schaffner (H.D.'s daughter) frame the interior chapters by presenting H.D., an American living in wartime London, simultaneously engaged in two processes: anticipating her death and writing her life. H.D. makes this very clear in "Morning Star." In the draft that she intended for publication, this chapter is over one third longer than the version which was edited and published in 1982 by New Directions; although the shortened "Morning Star" retains passages that describe the air raids, H.D.'s exhaustion, and the effort required for her to continue her work, the original version offers more numerous references to the tortuous months of bombing. H.D. depicts herself crawling like a cat out of an "avalanche of ruins . . . of what had once been home," and Bryher, her longtime companion, explains that civilians have only "three minutes from the blast of the gun to the falling of the shrapnel or the shell-cases" to run for cover.[3] In a deadly game of "hide-and-seek," the primary players pursue each other through "the whirlwind, the tornado of enemy night-fighters" while the secondary players, H.D. included, must scramble for safety, for time, and thus for their lives (typed draft, "Morning Star" 9, 13-14).

Returning to her project at intervals, H.D. moves among her childhood memories, leaving individual episodes not quite finished, bringing others to abrupt conclusions. Occasionally H.D.'s anxiety perfuses an episode and adds significance which readers must discern from the conditions in which H.D. lived while working on *The Gift*. For example, in the chapter entitled "The Secret," H.D. describes her grandmother's trancelike evocation of rituals that were shared by a small group of Native American Indians and her ancestors who settled in Pennsylvania. H.D. recreates the intimacy between her and her grandmother on that evening half a century earlier and dramatizes her disappointment when her grandmother ("Mamalie") began to lose her memory: "Mamalie, Mamalie, Mamalie, what were you saying? Wait, Mamalie, there are a thousand questions that I want to ask you" (98). As the narrative voice continues to address Mamalie it maintains its childlike diction and the same entreating tone, but the encroaching references to World War II signify the voice as the adult H.D.:

> Mamalie, don't go away. Because the thing that will happen, will happen to me, this winter after Christmas or before Christmas begins, about November, but I won't remember.

I will forget, like you forgot . . . and I will be afraid too, there will be the *Storm of Death* that *roars sweeping by* that I sang to you in a hymn, and it was just words in a hymn but it will be the *Storm of Death* and it will roar, it will roar over my head and there will be children huddled in little shelters, and there will be fire . . . and I will remember the fear that you feared. . . . Mamalie, there will be savages and they will have ugly symbols like some of the bad Indians, to bring ugly and horrible things back to the world and the *Storm of Death* is storming in my ears now; Mamalie wait, there is so much I want to ask you" (typed draft, "The Secret" 66-67; a shorter version on 99 of New Directions edition).

Disparate time frames coalesce: the evening that Mamalie recalls the ritual; a subsequent time when Hilda has forgotten Mamalie's story; another time when Hilda sings the hymn; and the autobiographical present in which H.D., the adult writer, hears German planes and alludes to SS storm troopers and the Nazi swastika. The narrating voice springs from various sites and times, merging memories of the past with H.D.'s present experiences of war. Writing "during, before and after the worst days of the 1941 London Blitz" (Notes 56) and fearing sudden, violent death, H.D. inscribes that fear, creates a multiplex autobiographic voice, and thus heightens the drama of her childhood recollections.

Uncertain whether she has the strength to complete *The Gift*, H.D. draws her self-doubt into its narrative structure. Images from the past run "in luminous sequence" through her mind, but too dispirited to work them into words, she records her inhibitions instead. Caught between inertia and activity, she writes: ". . . I could not write [them] down, though I sketched the preliminary chapters. In the other room, my bed-room, were the chapters, but how could I see and be and live and endure these passionate and terrible hours of hovering between life and death, and at the same time, write about them?" (typed draft, "Morning Star" 8). In the published chapter "The Secret," Hilda asks Eric, her older half-brother, if a shooting star will "fall on us. . . . sometimes I wonder if they are able to tell if really a shooting star will not fall down and fall on us and fall on the house and burn us all to death" (75). She turns to Mamalie with the same question, "Why do they call a shooting star, a shooting star. . . . It might hit a house, mightn't it? I mean, it might shoot down and hit us?" (76). Exposing H.D.'s dread of and obsession with being bombed—when the autobiographic voice is ostensibly recalling H.D.'s childhood fear of stars—this passage and others like it suggest that the autobiographical process was not, for H.D., a linear recollection of events from her past. Not quite autobiography and not quite fiction, *The Gift* is a hybridized text. Precariously, it unfolds between the contours of the past, as H.D. intermittently and imperfectly recalls it, and the present, which is a state of continual imperilment. The extreme subjectivity of *The Gift*, an index to H.D.'s sense of vulnerability and powerlessness, situates her work outside the boundaries of classic American autobiography. As Robert F. Sayre explains in his essay "Autobiography and the Making of America," autobiography in America, traditionally written by men, has traditionally been written *for* men. John Adams, Henry Adams, and Ben Franklin intended their writings to serve as public documents for teaching their readers the prerogatives and responsibilities of democratization. Writing plainly of his achievements, Franklin hoped that readers would wish to imitate the way he had lived, and for John Adams, writes Sayre, emulation was "an instinct second only to self-preservation as a force in human life" (152, 157). Confident and accomplished, these men valued qualities that were appropriate to masculine behavior, and they encouraged activities that were available primarily to men: participation in government or the military and endeavors in private enterprise. Franklin, however, addressing his reader by "Dear Son," offers another, more personal reason for writing the *Autobiography*. Unable to relive his life from the beginning, he will settle for "the next Thing most like living one's Life over again . . . a *Recollection* of that Life; and to make that Recollection as durable as possible, the putting it down in Writing" (44). Franklin readily acknowledges the satisfaction, even the vanity of his project although he believes that the documentation of his life will serve as a paradigm for others. The drive behind H.D.'s *The Gift* is more urgent than the desire to offer models for imitation or emulation. For H.D., the autobiographical project is fragile, not durable; a process, not a product; a private, not public, gesture; impelled by an instinct more fundamental than edification or vanity—the desire to survive.

Writing *The Gift* was H.D.'s version of self-therapy.[4] Although she often thought that neither she nor her work could survive the attacks on London, she chose not to send her manuscripts to people living in the United States who had offered to keep her work until the war was over. In "Dream of a Book" (dated on its title page January 1941), which is one of the fourteen unpublished stories of *Within the Walls*, H.D. writes: "if I am blitzed, the house will go with me and the stack of papers will go, too. This, that I now write will go with it," and thus she asks herself why she continues to "type pages that only have the slightest chance of survival" (typed draft 2). She offers an answer in another story of *Within the Walls*, this one entitled "Blue Lights" (January 1941), where she compares the writer to a dying physician. "If we can be the doctor, alive, watching ourselves dying, we may come across some amazingly important and staggering discoveries . . . " (typed draft, 2-3). Diagnosing her own condition, H.D. concludes that writing is not a product to be sent to interested friends for safekeeping. It is a psychic fire that she wishes to perpetuate.

> People [who] write from America. . . . will not understand that this [my writing] is burning, that this is a flame in a skull, and that this flame must meet another flame. . . . I write because the little blue flame in my skull, needs me in order to burn. I write just anything as just now. . . and then let the words run along. What are the words? I do not stop to consider them. (typed draft, "Blue Lights" 3)

The "burning" in her brain, which H.D. believes works apart from her conscious will, is an internal, involuntary combustion of creative energies. After a "click" sparks the fire, the flames—which are H.D.'s flashbacks of memory and insight—burn themselves into existence. H.D. yields to the ongoing, external attacks that could burn her to death, but she also shapes her fear into psychic images of her own creative forces and stamina. Meticulous style, self-contained episodes, the fine thread of chronology—none of these weighs heavily on H.D., who explains that as she releases her critical faculties she opens a space in which the blue flame can ignite: "I feel simply a click, as it were, and that other-mind is burning in my mind" (typed draft, "Blue Lights" 3). H.D.'s "other-mind" is capable of recalling not just her own, but memories belonging to Mamalie and to other family members. As Adalaide Morris explains in her essay "A Relay of Power and Peace: H.D. and the Spirit of the Gift," what H.D. offers as memory reaches beyond the individual to myth, legend, and sacred history, knowledge accessible by a commingling of family (racial) memory and imagination (518).

H.D. is resigned to the knowledge that what ought to be impossible—that "the enemy now seem the only reality"—is indeed a fact of daily life. She turns to her writing as a means to "abracadabra-ize something" (typed draft, "Escape" 5), to reconstruct other "realities" that under ordinary circumstances would be just as improbable. In contrast to Franklin's untroubled tone and felicitous style in the *Autobiography*, H.D.'s tone ranges from sophisticated to innocent, her diction from complex to simple. Its aggregate of styles suits her purpose: ". . . I can not afford to criticize or re-consider these words. They are the words of the spell; no matter how haphazard, how apparently unrelated, how profuse, how illogical, they are the words that in a sense—this is what it is—*keep me alive*" (typed draft, "Dream of a Book" 3).

H.D.'s autobiographic voice is a voice-in-crisis. "There was a girl who was burnt to death at the seminary, as they called the old school where our grandfather was principal" is *The Gift*'s opening sentence.[5] H.D.'s father and grandfather, whom Hilda calls Papa and Papalie, are described briefly, but the initial memory breaks in after just a few lines, this time with more detail: "But the girl who was burnt to death, was burnt to death in a crinoline. The Christmas tree was lighted at the end of one of the long halls and the girl's ruffles or ribbons caught fire and she was in a great hoop"(1). Attempting to move on, the voice begins again, this time focusing on a photograph of H.D.'s mother, Helen Wolle Doolittle, and H.D.'s aunts. The memory interrupts the narrative line for a third time, adding to and intensifying the preceding references: "But the girl in the crinoline wasn't a relation, she was just one of the many girls at the seminary when Papalie was there and she screamed and Papalie rushed to her and . . ." The sentence continues, but it jolts the episode into the present tense: ". . . Papalie wrapped a rug around her, but *she is shrieking* and they can not tear off her clothes because of the hoop (italics added 2). H.D.'s knowledge of the student's death is indirect. Francis Wolle, her grandfather, had retired in 1881 from his position as principal of the "Young Ladies' Seminary" in Bethlehem, five years before his granddaughter was born.[6] Not an incident one's grandfather would readily share with children, it is more likely that someone else described the incident to Hilda—as it was described to that person and so on. H.D., in effect, recalls someone else's memory of perhaps someone else's memory of a transmitted *story*. But the present progressive (*she is shrieking*) has a strong, disconcerting effect. It pulls the tragedy out of the category of "remembered stories," extends its borders into the present and leaves it open-ended to reverberate into the future. If only in H.D.'s mind, the dying girl traverses her singular position in history and many decades later, she continues to shriek. This single, isolated, remote tragedy, which opens the narrative and seems to forestall its progress, suggests the force of H.D.'s obsessive fear of her own death by fire. H.D. states that at the height of an attack she is quite surprised that she has *not* screamed in panic, as if to distinguish herself from the dying student. Restraining herself, she insists ". . . if you keep your head and don't let the shriek that is caught in your throat get the better of you," chances of survival are increased (typed draft, "Morning Star" 4, 14).

Fear of death by burning, explicit and reiterated in the final chapter, shapes H.D.'s evocation of her Pennsylvania childhood in the preceding chapters of *The Gift*. H.D. recalls from those years what her present crisis allows her to recall, bringing back conversations, interrupting their articulation, conflating distant times, and entangling disparate events. She describes the evening that Mamalie revealed the secret of the gift, and in the midst of presenting what Mamalie told her had taken place, H.D. begins to doubt her own rendering of it. Perhaps, she thinks, the version that she is writing in *The Gift* is what she, as a child, made up when Mamalie did not recount all of the details. Or wondering if "a shooting star might swish out of the sky and fall on the house," perhaps she dreamed Mamalie's version: "Maybe, it was because I was afraid of being burnt up that I made Mamalie, in the dream, say she wasn't just afraid of being burnt up . . ." (94-95). Death, fire, shooting stars, burning stars, morning stars, flames and explosions: these rebound in memory—triggered when H.D. was a child frightened by the night sky, and still hurling about as H.D., in recalling events of her life, writes a symbolic narrative of both the tensions of war and her own tenuous existence.

If, as Brother Francis told Mamalie, who told Hilda, who years later writes in *The Gift* that "Nothing is lost" (95), then as the present determines one's sense of the past, the past lies just beneath the surface of the present. H.D. assents: "If we do not remember, it is nevertheless there" (62). In *Tribute to Freud*, the memoir in which H.D. juxtaposes memories of her analysis with Freud and other events of her life, H.D. describes the day when she, no more than five years old, discovered a large, rotting log. Turning it over, she was stunned at the mass of curled, white slugs flourishing on the underside, a living, swarming network. Learning as a child that "there were things under things, as well as things inside of things" (29), H.D. as an adult understands that her mind, moving back and forth in time, inlays one memory with another. For example, the dying student in her grandfather's seminary permeates and alters H.D.'s experience of World War II (as the war brings back the dying student). Compressing her contemporary experience to a distant memory, H.D. writes, "I could think in terms of one girl in a crinoline, I could not visualize civilization other than a Christmas tree that had caught fire" (*The Gift* 136). More than reciprocal, H.D.'s past and her present are interfusing contexts; it is through the present that H.D. recalls moments from childhood, and it is through the past that she interprets her present. These periods in her life invade, then occupy each other's space:

> Now Mamalie was speaking and there was a rattle of the curtain rings as the curtains blew a little inward. It wasn't a thunderstorm, no, it was a star. . . . It was a shooting star that was going to fall on the house and burn us all up and burn us all to death. Bryher is looking at me; she does not know why I am able to sit here. I am sitting here because there is a star, Mamalie told me about it. (*The Gift* 134)

The bridge from Mamalie speaking to Hilda to Bryher's inquisitive look (H.D. and Bryher shared the Lowdnes Street flat) is the shooting star, once a child's "boogeyman," now an adult's daily terror.

H.D. also explains in *Tribute to Freud* that by allowing her impressions to claim autonomy she circumvents "correct" or "stylized" language (19-20), whose constraints she believed would diminish the power of her work. Eluding the requisites of a fixed point of view, predictable sequence, consistent tense and narrative voice, all of which enforce linearity and continuity, H.D. in *The Gift* lets her memories, factual, fictive, accurate, erroneous—distinctions among them collapsing—flow by association.[7] Releasing individual pronouns as though they are projectiles, and rupturing time by strategically dropping just a single precipitous verb into her sentences, H.D. manipulates perspective and tense like narrative sling shots. For example, the first-person voice which uses the past tense to describe the Doolittle children at school ("We took lunch in a basket and did not get back until four" [34]) is thrown over by a discerning third-person voice ("Hilda felt Harold's pain and loneliness but could not translate it into words" [34]), which is thrown over by a first-person voice that shifts dramatically into the present tense. The voice becomes Hilda, a young girl, speaking out from childhood: "We go to a public school . . . It isn't that the room *smells* differently, it's the way the clock ticks on the wall" (*The Gift* 34). Flinging itself between enunciating sites, the narrating autobiographic voice catapults one way, then another, seems distant from Hilda the child, then proximate. Observing this pattern, Morris in "Autobiography and Prophecy" suggests that the lesson which "author, narrator, and protagonist reiterate is that the self is not limited by its temporal body, conscious brain, or spatial location" (230). Like the recollection of the girl in the crinoline, the evocation of the classroom jerks what *should be* a distant memory into present time as the processes of H.D.'s memory split the fine line between past and present, child and adult.

H.D. provides, both in *The Gift* and in her Notes to this work, perspicacious judgments of her project. On July 2, 1944, she explains that she intended for the story to "tell itself, or the child tell it for me." But in changing very little and letting "things stand as they were" (Notes 56), H.D. also leaves intact the numerous shifts away from a child's tone and point of view. In the chapter entitled "The Dream," for instance, H.D.'s adult voice comes forward, as though anticipating questions from readers: "You may wonder. . . . You, yourself may wonder at the mystery in this house . . . you may glance at the row of children on the horsehair sofa and at the plaque of mounted butterflies . . . [but] the children can not tell you for no one has been able to answer that question for them" (26). The autobiographic voice is also aware of Helen Doolittle's disappointment in her children: "We were not any of us 'gifted,' as if we had failed them somehow." "How could I know that [my mother's] apparent disappointment that her children were not 'gifted' was in itself her own sense of inadequacy and frustration, carried a step further?" (21). This is the judgment of an adult, expressed as H.D. draws back from the text and presents her material from a posterior perspective.

"I" and "she," as pronominal links between H.D. the adult writer and Hilda Doolittle, the child, are unreliable indicators of the distance or proximity—either psychological or chronological—between the writer and the child. "She" does not necessarily designate authorial distance and objectivity; nor does "I" necessarily designate intimacy and subjectivity. Often fractured, the narrating autobiographic voice will settle into first-person, split into third-person, even swerve into the vague referentiality of a second-person address. By splicing each other in the middle of paragraphs, even in mid-sentence, the first- and third-person sometimes create a series of incursive voices. These shifts are unsettling, calling attention to the voice that recalls each event, and to the person from whom the voice issues, rather than to the ostensible subject—H.D., her large family of siblings, parents, aunts, uncles, grandparents, and the influence of her Moravian heritage.

H.D.'s autobiographic voice is not simply a formal device that operates invisibly to present the subject of the text. In effect, it becomes a second subject, and because it is both elusive and mobile, H.D.'s subject becomes a configuration of various selves, from various times and places, particularly from the time and place that H.D. lived while writing her autobiographic narrative. Sidonie Smith explains in *A Poetics of Women's Autobiography* that as the correspondence between the narrating "I" and its points of identity widens, "the drift of the disappropriation . . . reveals more about the autobiographer's present experience of 'self' than about her past, although, of course, it tells us something about that as well" (47). The "disappropriation" between H.D.'s autobiographic voice and H.D.'s ostensible subject is sharp enough to constitute a break rather than a "drift." The voice severs, restores, then severs its affiliation to the text's apparent subject, denuding it of unitary semblance.

Using multiple modes of vision, memory, and narrative perspective, H.D. evades a "strictly historical sequence" (*Tribute to Freud* 19) which, by enforcing a continuous design, would suggest a sense of authority that she did not feel she had while writing *The Gift*. Like traditional prose fiction, traditional autobiography often depicts a singular subject. He overcomes significant obstacles, enacts significant deeds, reaches his goal and, in time, as Franklin concedes in the introduction of his *Autobiography*, completes the journey of his life. Powerless to have any significant impact on the course of a world war, but suffering its effects, H.D. pursues the goals immediately before her—to keep her family and herself alive and to complete her manuscript. Working in the lulls between attacks, H.D. releases her autobiographic voice to travel through the twists of memory, and the childhood she discovers is formed by the crises she experiences in her middle age. She reveals herself prismatically, from one angle, then another, from one enunciating site, then another. Events that flash before her are thus both shaped and altered by H.D.'s unremitting fear that "This . . . is my last place, my last little room; this hall-way . . . my last habitation" (typed draft, "Morning Star" 12).

H.D. was not alone in trying to work regularly on her manuscripts. Living primarily at Monk's House in Sussex before and during the daily raids in August and September 1940, Virginia Woolf was completing her biography of Roger Fry. Tired from the concentration that it required, she began to write "A Sketch of the Past," structuring her family memories by recording specific days on which she wrote from April 18, 1939 to November 17, 1940. The progressive though noncontinuous chronology, along with Woolf's frequent references to the present, functions meta-autobiographically, calling attention to the adult Virginia, author of *Night and Day*, *The Years*, and *To The Lighthouse* (works that she mentions), as well as to Virginia the child and young woman. For Woolf, the present accommodated the past, even on June 8, 1940 when: "The battle is at its crisis; every night the Germans fly over England . . . closer to this house daily" (100). On September 29, 1940, a bomb came very close to hitting the Woolfs' house.

With the confidence of a sustained and brilliant career behind her, Woolf writes with composure.[8] She confines her remarks on the air attacks and possible invasion by Germany to intermittent observations or parenthetical additions, thus neutralizing their effect at least temporarily on her work. Woolf not only uses the present (a "platform to stand upon") to contain her peripatetic recollections, she comments on her method and examines the process of writing one's memoirs. For H.D., wrestling with her recollections, the present is more intrusive. It fixes her imagery, and grades her perspective. Thus, Woolf's first memory in "A Sketch of the Past" is of her mother's flowered dress; H.D.'s first memory in *The Gift* is of the young girl, whose dress ignites into flames. Woolf's second memory is of herself as an infant in the nursery, listening to the ocean beyond the yellow blinds, her luxuriant "colour-and-sound memories" (66) reminiscent of *The Waves*; H.D. recalls the terrifying sounds of the young girl shrieking as her dress catches fire. Her earliest recollection of flowers is associated with death: the bouquet she places on the graves of the females in her family who died as infants.

The Gift was a crucial manuscript for H.D. She and Richard Aldington had finally divorced in 1938, she had suffered numerous personal tragedies, and was fighting a debilitating writing block that went back to the 1930s. Struggling with *The Gift*, H.D. was able to make progress in other genres as well, and she rapidly produced some of her finest poetry: *The Walls Do Not Fall* (1944), *Tribute to the Angels* (1945), and *The Flowering of the Rod* (1946), published collectively as *Trilogy*. She continued to write actively throughout the 1940s, producing sections of *Tribute to Freud* and *By Avon River*. In the 1950s she wrote the poetry of *Helen in Egypt*, "Sagesse" and "Winter Love," which are included in *Hermetic Definition*, and her memoir of Pound in *End to Torment*. Much of H.D.'s canon is autobiographical, from her early roman-à-clef *Bid Me to Live* to the unpublished stories of *Within the Walls* and the memories recounted in *Compassionate Friendship*. But it is in *The Gift*, whose time and place of composition induce, then interrupt its progress, that H.D. treats the autobiographical act as a personal, psychological war. From this perspective, the autobiographical text is neither a public document nor a model for emulation. It is a battle that H.D. finally wins.

Dorothy Richardson, whose thirteen volumes of autobiographical fiction became her life's project, remarked in *March Moonlight* that "the past does not stand 'being still'. It moves, growing with one's growth" (657), and thus it stops, dying with one's death. (When Richardson died in 1957 at the age of 84, she left *March Moonlight*, the last volume of *Pilgrimage*, unfinished). Reclaimed in *The Gift*, the past does not stand still, but neither does it unbreachingly "grow." It is, instead, erratically formed by events in H.D.'s adult life. Marked by breaks and ruptures, *The Gift* is less casual than many memoirs, more idiosyncratic than many autobiographies, and more urgent than most fictions. H.D. believed that the Lowndes Square flat would be her last. She was wrong, however. H.D. died in 1961 at the age of 75, having written over forty volumes of poetry and prose.[9]

NOTES

1. Quoted from *H.D.: Collected Poems 1912-1944* (518-19). *The Walls Do Not Fall* was initially published by Oxford University Press in 1944. According to Barbara Guest, writing *The Gift* enabled H.D. to concentrate on *The Walls Do Not Fall*, which became the first volume of *Trilogy* (269). The other two volumes, *Tribute to the Angels* (1945) and *The Flowering of the Rod* (1946), were also published by Oxford UP.
2. H.D.'s typed drafts of *The Gift*, written in the early 1940s, are housed in the Beinecke Rare Book and Manuscript Library at Yale University. The published version of *The Gift* which New Directions made available in 1982, is substantially different from H.D.'s text. One chapter, "Fortune Teller," and many other passages have been omitted without editorial commentary, along with a multitude of smaller changes. Despite this extensive editing, the discontinuous prose is also an effect of H.D.'s impressionistic style (evident in the original typed drafts) and of the extreme conditions in which H.D. lived as she worked on *The Gift*, which caused her to write between air raids. DuPlessis in "A Note on the State of H.D.'s *The Gift*" gives an excellent summary and examples of the changes made by New Directions. For the convenience of most readers who must rely on the published text, I quote whenever possible from the New Directions edition. When I quote from passages found only in the typed draft, page

numbers are preceded by "typed draft" and the title of the chapter. Pagination in the drafts of *The Gift* and *Within the Walls* is not continuous. Each chapter of *The Gift*, and each story of *Within the Walls*, starts with page 1. All quotations from H.D.'s unpublished work are used with the permission of Perdita Schaffner and the Collection of American Literature, the Beinecke Rare Book and Manuscript Library, Yale University.
3. See Susan Stanford Friedman's *Psyche Reborn* (5-6, 35-39, 131-34), Barbara Guest (105-115, 253-79), and Hanscombe and Smyers (33-46) on H.D. and Bryher's long relationship.
4. In her Introduction to *Psyche Reborn* Susan Stanford Friedman writes that World War II affected H.D. much as World War I had affected writers such as Pound, jolting "H.D. out of a decade of relative latency." DuPlessis also emphasizes the impact of the war on H.D.'s work. For other discussions of H.D., see Shari Benstock's *Women of the Left Bank* and Friedman's "Modernism of the 'Scattered Remnant'" and "Exile in the American Grain."
5. DuPlessis in *H.D.: The Career of That Struggle* cites burning as "the most ambiguous and potent recurrent image" of *The Gift*. Among the instances she cites are the girl in the crinoline, the fires of the Bethlehem steel mills, and the candle that burns in the room as Mamalie tells Hilda what she recalls of her ancestors' history (77). See 76-83 for DuPlessis's discussion of *The Gift*. Adalaide Morris also examines H.D.'s references to shooting stars in "A Relay of Power and of Peace: H.D. and the Spirit of The Gift."
6. H.D.'s maternal grandfather, Francis Wolle, was a Moravian minister and the principal of the Young Ladies' Seminary in Bethlehem, Pennsylvania. The seminary operated as a school before the Civil War, but afterwards was used as a medical facility. Retiring from his position as principal in 1881, five years before H.D. was born, Wolle pursued his interest in microbotany. In "Magical Lenses: Poet's Vision Beyond the Naked Eye," Charlotte Mandel analyzes H.D.'s writing in view of her early exposure to her grandfather's research. When he died, Wolle had published three books and was an "international authority on freshwater algae, desmids and diatoms, identifying thousands of species" (302). H.D.'s father, Charles Doolittle, was Professor of Astronomy and Mathematics at Lehigh University and Director of Flower Observatory at the University of Pennsylvania.

7. For discussions of H.D.'s fiction within the tradition of twentieth-century women's experimentalism, see Friedman and Fuchs, "Contexts and Continuities" (7, 17-18, 24-26) and Linda W. Wagner-Martin, "H.D.'s Fiction: Convolutions to Clarity (148-60), both in *Breaking the Sequence*. See also by Fuchs, "H.D.'s Self-Inscription."
8. Woolf's equanimity in "A Sketch" is a complex response to the events of the war and to her psychological condition. Examining her "imperturbability," Quentin Bell postulates that living through the air attacks was in some ways "therapeutic": "Shattering, nerve-racking though such experiences must have been, unfit though Virginia was to be at the periphery, let alone the centre of a battle . . . the effect may have been therapeutic. From the time when she came literally under fire, the talk of suicide ceased" (Vol. II, 217). Leonard and Virginia had discussed suicide in the event that the Germans invaded Great Britain. Although Woolf alludes to these discussions and although Paris was to fall a few days later, the June 8, 1940 entry of "A Sketch of the Past" turns quickly to the engagement of her sister Stella and Jack Hill forty years earlier.
9. Many works were published long after H.D. wrote them, some have been posthumously published, still others like *Within the Walls* and *Compassionate Friendship* remain unpublished. DuPlessis's bibliography in *H.D.: The Career of That Struggle* (150-54) provides dates of both composition and publication.

WORKS CITED

Bell, Quentin. *Virginia Woolf: A Biography*. Vols. I and II. New York: Harcourt, 1972.
Benstock, Shari, ed. *Feminist Issues in Literary Scholarship*. Bloomington: Indiana UP, 1987.
———. *Women of the Left Bank: Paris, 1900-1940*. Austin: U of Texas P, 1986.
Doolittle, Hilda (H.D.). *Bid Me to Live (A Madrigal)*. 1960. Redding Ridge, CT: Black Swan, 1983.
———. "Blue Lights" (typed draft). In *Within the Walls*.
———. *By Avon River*. 1949. Redding Ridge, CT: Black Swan, 1987.

———. *Collected Poems: 1912-1944*. Ed. Louis L. Martz. New York: New Directions, 1983.

———. *Compassionate Friendship*. The Collection of American Literature, Beinecke Rare Book and Manuscript Library, Yale University.

———. "Dream of a Book" (typed draft). In *Within the Walls*.

———. *End to Torment: A Memoir of Ezra Pound*. Ed. Norman Holmes Pearson and Michael King. New York: New Directions, 1979.

———. "Escape" (typed draft). In *Within the Walls*.

———. *The Flowering of the Rod*. London and New York: Oxford UP, 1946. In *Trilogy*.

———. *The Gift*. Introd. Perdita Schaffner. New York: New Directions, 1982.

———. *The Gift* (third typed draft). "Dark Room," "Fortune Teller," "The Dream," "Because One Is Happy," "The Secret," "What It Was," "Morning Star." The Collection of American Literature, Beinecke Rare Book and Manuscript Library, Yale University.

———. *Helen in Egypt*. 1961. New York: New Directions, 1974.

———. *Hermetic Definition*. New York: New Directions, 1972.

———. *Nights* (as "John Helforth"). 1935. New York: New Directions, 1986.

———. Notes to the third typed draft of *The Gift*. The Collection of American Literature, Beinecke Rare Book and Manuscript Library, Yale University.

———. *Tribute to Freud*. New York: Pantheon, 1956.

———. *Tribute to the Angels*. London and New York: Oxford UP, 1945. In *Trilogy*.

———. *Trilogy*. New York: New Directions, 1973.

———. *The Walls Do Not Fall*. London and New York: Oxford UP, 1944. In *Trilogy*. In *Collected Poems* 509-43.

———. *Within the Walls* (typed draft). "Within the Walls," "Bunny," "Pattern," "Dream of a Book," "Escape," "Blue Lights," "Tide-Line," "Warehouse," "The Last Day," "Nefert," "She Is Dead," "Saint Anthony," "The Ghost," "Before the Battle." The Collection of American Literature, The Beinecke Rare Book and Manuscript Library, Yale University.

DuPlessis, Rachel Blau. *H.D.: The Career of That Struggle*. Grt. Britain: Harvester, 1986.

———. "A Note on the State of H.D.'s *The Gift*." *Sulfur 9* (1984): 178-82.

Franklin, Benjamin. *The Autobiography of Benjamin Franklin.* Ed. Leonard W. Labaree, et al. New Haven: Yale UP, 1964.

Friedman, Ellen G. and Miriam Fuchs. "Contexts and Continuities: An Introduction to Women's Experimental Fiction in English." *Breaking the Sequence.* 3-51.

———, eds. *Breaking the Sequence: Women's Experimental Fiction.* Princeton: Princeton UP, 1989.

Friedman, Susan Stanford. "Exile in the American Grain." *Women's Writing in Exile.* Ed. Mary Lynn Broe and Angela Ingram. Chapel Hill: U of North Carolina P, 1989. 88-112.

———. "Modernism of the 'Scattered Remnant': Race and Politics in H.D.'s Development." *Feminist Issues in Literary Scholarship.* 208-32.

———. *Psyche Reborn: The Emergence of H.D.* Bloomington: Indiana UP, 1981.

Fuchs, Miriam. "H.D.'s Self-Inscription: Between Time and 'Out-of-Time' in *The Gift. Southern Review,* Summer 1990.

Guest, Barbara. *Herself Defined: The Poet H.D. and Her World.* Garden City, NY: Doubleday, 1984.

Hanscombe, Gillian and Virginia L. Smyers. *Writing For Their Lives: The Modernist Women 1910-1940.* London: Women's Press, 1987.

King, Michael, ed. *H.D.: Woman and Poet.* Orono, ME: National Poetry Foundation, 1986.

Mandel, Charlotte. "Magical Lenses: Poet's Vision Beyond the Naked Eye." In King 301-17.

Morris, Adalaide. "Autobiography and Prophecy: H.D.'s *The Gift.* " In King 227-236.

———. Introduction to "Fortune Teller." *Iowa Review* 16 (1986): 14-16.

———. "A Relay of Power and Peace: H.D. and the Spirit of the Gift." *Contemporary Literature* 4 (1986): 493-524.

Richardson, Dorothy. *Pilgrimage* (including *March Moonlight*). Introd. Gillian Hanscombe. 4 vols. London: Virago, 1979.

Sarton, May. "Letters From H.D." In King 49-57.

Sayre, Robert F. "Autobiography and the Making of America." *Autobiography: Essays Theoretical and Critical.* Ed. James Olney. Princeton: Princeton UP, 1980. 146-68.

Schaffner, Perdita. "Unless a Bomb Falls . . . " Introd. to H.D.'s *The Gift.* ix-xv.

Smith, Sidonie. *A Poetics of Women's Autobiography: Marginality and the Fictions of Self-Representation.* Bloomington: Indiana UP, 1987.

Wagner-Martin, Linda W. "H.D.'s Fiction: Convolutions to Clarity." In Friedman and Fuchs, *Breaking the Sequence*. 148-60.

Woolf, Virginia. *Night and Day*. London: Duckworth, 1919.

———. *Roger Fry: A Biography*. London: Hogarth, 1940.

———. "A Sketch of the Past." *Moments of Being: Unpublished Autobiographical Writings*. Ed. Jeanne Schulkind. New York: Harcourt, 1976. 64-137.

———. *To the Lighthouse*. London: Hogarth, 1927.

———. *The Waves*. London: Hogarth, 1931.

———. *The Years*. London: Hogarth, 1937.

Two Modes of Writing the Female Self: Isabel Allende's The House of the Spirits and Clarice Lispector's The Stream of Life

Flora H. Schiminovich

The Chilean writer Isabel Allende began her work as a journalist at the age of seventeen. After the military coup that overthrew the government of Salvador Allende (her uncle), Allende moved to Venezuela. She has recently taken permanent residence in the United States.

Her first novel, The House of the Spirits (1982), brought the author international stardom. Because of her tendency to transform human experiences through a fusion of reality and fantasy, a combination of story and magic much in the style of Gabriel García Márquez, Allende's work has often been compared with that of the Colombian writer.

Allende's second novel, Of Love and Shadows (1984), deals with the atrocities committed by the Pinochet government and is also a very moving love story. In her third novel, Eva Luna (1987), Allende has succeeded in creating a modern day picaresque tale with a feminist twist. Her last book, a volume of short stories, Cuentos de Eva Luna (Eva Luna's Tales 1990), serves to confirm once more Isabel Allende's extraordinary narrative gifts.

Foremost among Latin American women writers is the Brazilian Clarice Lispector. Her first novel, Perto do Coraçao Selvagem (Close to the Savage Heart 1944), already anticipates the dazzling poetic imagination she displays in The Stream of Life (1973). Her career was a long one and her recognition was slow in coming. By 1960 she had already published two more novels and two volumes of short stories. But it was not until her fourth novel, Apple in the Dark (1961), that Lispector achieved general recognition. The novel was written in a style similar to Virginia Woolf's lyricism.

103

A fifth novel by Lispector, The Passion According to G.H. *(1964) was even more successful in blending poetic imagination with subtle physical and metaphysical experiences.* The Hour of the Star *(1977), Lispector's last novel, was made into a film that received international recognition. French feminist critics, especially Hélène Cixous, use Lispector's writings as a model of* écriture féminine—*the inscription of the female body and female differences in language and writing.*

Were one to write a history of Latin American autobiographical works, this history would perhaps include many more than the ones we know today. From all the available information one thing is apparent: there are fewer autobiographies of Latin American women writers than there are of men, and the small number of critical studies about the subject do not reflect a concern for the idea of establishing separate literary traditions for men and women writers.[1]

Outside the Latin American world definitions of autobiography and fiction have followed closely changes in critical theory. Several books on criticism of women's autobiography have appeared in recent years that point toward a distinctive female tradition in that genre.[2] The most recent ones: *Life/Lines: Theorizing Women's Autobiography*, edited by Bella Brodzki and Celeste Schenck and *Beyond Feminist Aesthetics* by Rita Felski open an interesting theoretical dialogue among different perspectives in this postmodern age's deconstruction of the unified subject. When we read fictional autobiographies today we have to consider a complex range of conditions that govern textual reception, including the sex-gender system that constitutes the primary category of textual analysis for feminist criticism.

It is not my intention to engage here in the long standing debate over the question of referentiality in autobiographical projects.[3] I only want to focus this essay on the study of two works: *The House of the Spirits* by Isabel Allende and *The Stream of Life* by Clarice Lispector. My claim for these two novels is that besides the particular way in which they raise questions about autobiographical theory and fiction, they also pose important questions for feminist literary criticism in general and Latin American women's writing in particular.

Lispector's *The Stream of Life* and Allende's *The House of the Spirits* are two very different fictional works. It is not easy to talk about a shared Latin American experience by these two authors. While we can recognize in *The House of the Spirits* a particular social and historical Latin American reality, Lispector's novel escapes a visible space or context and concentrates in landscapes of the mind, exploring and recreating a person's inner reality. In spite of these differences, both novels benefit from being seen in the light of the autobiographical mode and tell us something about the thinking that this type of writing elicits among Latin American female writers. The act of writing or thinking a life seems for Allende and Lispector a claim to identity; we recognize in their works the desire to capture images of the self within the framework of a feminist ideology.

Allende's first novel, *The House of the Spirits*, is comparable to the work of Gabriel García Márquez, but with a significant difference. The Colombian writer is compelled to construct an encyclopedic narrative, which attempts to put in perspective the totality of knowledge and beliefs of Latin American culture; Allende's work centers on women's experiences and women's feelings toward particular historical events without pretension of global understanding. *The House of the Spirits* seems to be hiding its autobiographical tendencies within the fictional world in order to reaffirm more freely a matrilineal consciousness of life and history. The author has stated: "I have written the history of a family like mine or like that of many other families in Latin America, during a period of time that covers almost a century. I began at the beginning, with the most ancient and with what they told me, transformed by magic and emotion and I continued writing without stopping till the end."[4]

An important aspect of this novel centers around autobiographical elements. In a review of the novel the critic Alexander Coleman claims that: "Isabel Allende combines the central theme of Latin American fiction with autobiography in complex ways. She is the niece of Salvador Allende, the President of Chile, last seen alive on September 11, 1973 . . . She was close to her uncle—he stood in for her father at her wedding . . . She avoids mentioning her connection to the late President, but the family name, which she has kept, carries tremendous emotional weight as a symbol not only for the Chilean cataclysm, but also for the struggle over the definition of social justice in Latin America. *The House of the Spirits* draws on this experience, though always in veiled terms"(22).

Even though her own signature commits the Chilean writer to autobiography, her position toward this subject is ambivalent. We know, for example, that Isabel Allende's grandfather is the model for Esteban Trueba, the book's tormented patriarch; and her grandmother, like the novel's Clara, really did chat with ghosts. The author grew up in her grandfather's house, which was like the house in the novel—an ornate mansion peopled with shadows as well as men and women of indestructible substance, where magical beings come and go with unnerving regularity, and where time is a convenient illusion. Allende both affirms and negates the autobiographical tendencies of her work: "It was easy to write the book, you see, because I had nothing to invent,"[5] says the author. On another occasion, however, Allende offered a disclaimer: "People say that every first novel, specially the ones written by women are autobiographical. This is not my case. I am not part of *The House of the Spirits*, I am not one of the novel's characters."[6]

I think that it is easy to understand why the Chilean female author rejects the autobiographical link to her narrative, since traditional definitions of autobiography as a genre have usually limited it to "a cohesive, chronological and retrospective account of an author's life, centered around a unifying vision of self-identity."[7] The critic Rita Felski observes that prescriptive definitions of autobiography as a genre are no longer valid today, conventional "rules" having been broken and interpretations having clearly changed: "Theorists of autobiography have moved away from prescriptive definitions to an examination of the more fundamental problems involved in establishing a satisfactory distinction between autobiography and fiction"(89). Nonetheless, we cannot always assume that authors and readers are consciously aware of these changes, and even if they were, there is always a tendency to see and interpret the symbolic world of literature following a familiar tradition. For instance, we recognize a poem printed on the page because of its form. The problem arises when we want to define what a "prose-poem" is. The same is true for autobiography and fiction when we want to cast them into separate molds ignoring the existence of works that blur the distinction.

The House of the Spirits tells the story of one family's deep and violent loves, their deaths and transfigurations over many years. The adventures of the several generations of the Trueba family remind us of the Buendía family in García Márquez's *One Hundred Years of Solitude*, but in Allende's novel lineage is transmitted through the females. It is in fact the narration of the matriarchal lineage of the del Valle and Trueba families. The main events of Esteban Trueba's life run parallel to that of his mother-in-law, Nivea, his wife Clara, his daughter Blanca and his granddaughter Alba. There are several first person narrators in the novel: Clara, Alba and Esteban Trueba. Together with the authorial voice they converge in the writing of the story and of history.

One of the most distinctive characteristics of the novel has to do with the writing of Clara's journal. It is essentially Clara's story that is being told: it is her journal, later discovered by her granddaughter Alba, which constitutes the narrative of the book we are reading. Says Alba:

> My grandmother wrote in her notebooks that bore witness to life for fifty years. Smuggled out by certain friendly spirits, they miraculously escaped the infamous pyre in which so many other family papers perished. I have them here at my feet, bound with colored ribbons, divided according to events and not to chronological order, just as she arranged them before she left. Clara wrote them so they would help me now reclaim the past and overcome terrors of my own. (368)

What does this narrative strategy signify within the context of the work? The journal, the diary, have been traditionally ideal forms for feminist confession because they lend themselves to recording details of daily events as they occur. The journal is an open-ended structure that permits a critical exploration of female experiences. Suzanne Juhasz observes: "The diary provides the sense of factualness (of the documentary, of non fiction), the sense of process, the sense of dailiness, the sense of immersion rather than conclusion or analysis or patterning"(237).

It is therefore not surprising that Allende has chosen the diary as a principal form of expression for the novel's narrative. As critic Nora Glickman notes: "The experiences of the novel's four heroines are intrinsically linked. Nivea's stories are imprinted in Clara's journals. Blanca's letters mold Alba's character, the latter's life testimony reaches the reader in episodic segments that Alba announces, elaborates, orders and revises to offer that reader the most sensible way to rescue the past"(59).

Clara's diary inspires a process of involvement and identification by the reader;[8] while dramatizing female bonding and textual production it makes claim to historical veracity. The matriarchal lineage, the life experiences of the women that have preceded Alba form, together with this character's own story, the narrative texture of the novel. The journal emphasizes the stages common to women's experiences, like the stage of moving from adolescence to the coming of age:

Around the age of eighteen Alba left childhood behind for good. At the exact moment when she felt like a woman, she locked herself in her old room, where she still held the mural she had started so many years before. Next she rummaged through her paint jars until she found a little red and a little white that were still fresh. Then she carefully mixed them together and painted a large pink heart in the last empty space on the wall. She was in love . . . she sat down to contemplate her drawings, which is to say, the history of her joys and sorrows. She decided that the balance had been happy and with a sigh said goodbye to the first stage of her life. (270)

The main female characters of *The House of the Spirits* inscribe themselves into a text. By reading, writing and rewriting they attempt to develop a trajectory of female experiences that allows the articulation of a feminist vision. Alba's relationship to the material she narrates replicates the psychological dynamics of intimacy and mirroring theorized by Chodorow to be an intrinsic aspect of female bonds.[9] Alba's participation, only apparently limited to the book's last chapters, becomes a central one, allowing her presence to merge almost completely with the others. Clara's journal acts like a kaleidoscopic mirror of events and also reflects women's changing perceptions of the self within a particular historical context.[10]

Paralleling the saga of the Trueba family, *The House of the Spirits* narrates the history of Chile in the twentieth century —particularly that country's internal struggle for political power and democracy. Within this historical and social framework Allende's novel emphasizes the ways in which conceptions of identity have been shaped by socially accepted constructions of gender and class and—moving beyond that—provides alternative models.

Though rebellion against existing power takes many forms in Allende's novel and is not limited to female characters, women are the ones predominantly defiant of institutions, laws, class structures, and sexual morality. With the exception of Nivea, the women refuse to define themselves in terms of men and marriage. Most of their emotional satisfaction comes from their desire to break away from traditional domestic structures. Aware of social inequalities, they engage in political and social action. The great-grandmother Nivea actively works for women's right to vote, her daughter Clara has supernatural and magical powers and enough imagination to become a writer. She rejects her husband's ideology and decides to live a life independent from him. Blanca resents the restrictions her femininity imposes upon her; she causes her father's despair when she falls in love with a man from a lower social class and gives birth to a daughter. Alba, the youngest, has to endure the most difficult trials: she is jailed and tortured by the military police who take over the government after Salvador Allende's overthrow.

The novel's female characters lead different and exceptional lives, but they are united in their challenge of patriarchal structures and in their quest for freedom and individuality. They demand to be subjects of their own discourse and want to be recognized for their ability and right to create a society free of socio-cultural inequalities. Rita Felski's observations about emancipation narratives in feminist literature apply to *The House of the Spirits*:" Both feminist literature and feminist politics organize discursive meaning around the projected liberation of an individual or collective female subject generating a number of narrative models of emancipation grounded in different conceptions of history and truth" (127). Allende's characters challenge cultural formations; moreover, her female protagonists discover that identity—like history—is a process always in the making, multiform and open to a variety of experiences and events.

Allende's choice of autobiography and fiction within the historical perspective of her country can be seen as a form of struggle, a political action upon her culture and herself. In reconstructing history—and in defining herself through female bonding which occurs in the primal relations of the family—she committed herself to resist and denounce the patriarchal and dominant power structures of her country. Her novel effectively exemplifies one of the directions that feminist writing has taken in our century showing a woman inserting herself into history, making a place for herself in the cultural and political life of her time.

The Brazilian writer Clarice Lispector has been considered one of a small number of true innovators of her country's literature. When her first novel, *Perto do Coraçao Selvagem* (Close to the Savage Heart) first appeared in 1944, perceptive critics recognized at a glance the strong individuality of this promising young writer (she was only nineteen years old). But recognition of Lispector's worth on any large scale was slow in coming and her literary reputation only began to crystallize with the publication of a collection of short stories, *Family Ties*, published in 1960, and a major novel, *The Passion According to G.H.*

One could classify Lispector either as an avant-garde writer or as one of the most representative practitioners of "feminine writing" in Latin America. The two traditions seem remarkably alike but they have remained separate and invisible to each other mainly because of critical (and also political) interpretations. The critic Marianne De Koven argues that: "The invisibility of the avant-garde tradition to most exponents of *écriture féminine*/female aesthetic/women's writing is superseded only by the monumental male exclusivity of the avant-garde, particularly in American postmodernism. . . . To the male avant-garde, however, *écriture féminine*, women's writing as a category, and, in the vast majority of cases, women writers altogether, simply do not exist" (78).

Lispector's fiction has suggested some interesting comparisons with works by James Joyce and Virginia Woolf but before her discovery by Hélène Cixous and other French feminist writers, Lispector had never been associated with a feminist tradition or considered as a practitioner of feminine writing. Lispector's style evinces the desire to break conventional structures of meaning, the willingness to subvert logic or fixed authoritarian points of view and to undermine patriarchal forms.

Are we then supposed to read Lispector within the discourse of modernity or from the perspective of *écriture féminine*? In her work *Gynesis: Configurations of Women and Modernity*, Alice Jardine confronts modernity and feminism and relates the valorization of the feminine, of "woman," to new and necessary modes of thinking, writing, and speaking. Jardine poses an interesting question: "What happens when 'women' take over the discourse (of modernity) in the name of 'woman'" (263)?

I would attempt some answers by referring to one of Clarice Lispector's finest novels, *The Stream of Life*. It is a significant work in which the question of the relationship between modernity and feminism also encompasses questions of the relationship between autobiography and fiction or between life and creation, relevant to my present analysis. A flowing verbal monologue, in which discourse on the creative process is closely intertwined with the unfolding of the first person subjectivity, constitutes the narrative of *The Stream of Life*. It is a novel made of fragments, of impulses, a series of displacements and disseminations that reflect life as a dynamic and constant process. The narrative form of the novel undoes itself in the form of instants, of the division and fragmentation of the instant, a time that resists a linear and orderly chronology (in opposition to the apparent order in traditional autobiography):

I want to possess the atoms of time. And I want to capture the present which, by its very nature, is forbidden me: the present flees from me, the moment escapes me, the present is myself forever in the now.
Is my theme the instant? my life theme. I try to keep up with it, I divide myself thousands of times, into as many times as the seconds that pass, fragmentary as I am and precarious the moments—I pledge myself only to a life that is born with the time and grows with it: only in time is there space for me. (4)

The Stream of Life proposes a reflection on the construction of a female self and a critical exploration of the relationship between living and writing. In her introduction to the American translation, Cixous says:

If there is a subject of this text, or an object, it is on the question of writing. *Agua viva*[11] is about writing, as a verbal activity. I write you. This is something active. The circulation of blood in this text, the vital theme of this text is writing, all the questions of writing. Everything is organized around the mystery of writing. This mystery has to be read at the level of: why I write, how I write, from where I write, to whom I write, with what I write, of what I write, about what, toward what. (XV-XVI)

Lispector wants her writing to remain in close contact with life but is aware of the difficult task this project entails. In *The Stream of Life* the materiality of a woman's existence struggles to become the material of the text itself: "I am not going to be autobiographical. I want to be bio" (26), says the first person narrator. Can writing make one live? Why is the "bio" so important in the inscription of a personal trajectory? How are we forced in the reading of this novel to acknowledge some relationship between the text and its author and more, between the text and its author's experience of life as a series of fragmentary instants?

I have to confess that I owe the pleasure of having discovered Clarice Lispector to Hélène Cixous and not to my Latin American background. In my studies Lispector did not appear among the canon of twentieth century innovators like Borges, Cortázar or Carlos Fuentes. While I am thankful to Cixous for the "gift" of Lispector I recognize that I am almost unable to dissociate my readings of the

Brazilian writer from Cixous's interpretations. This poses an interesting point for contemporary criticism: there is no textual reading which is not implicated in the problems of theory and no theory which is not implicated in the problems of literature. Cixous and also Irigaray have greatly contributed to our approaching *The Stream of Life* as a specifically identifiable feminine form of experimentation.

Lispector's novel presents a narrative erotics—a *jouissance*—that replicates the nature of experience in a non-linear, non-hierarchical and decentering form associated with the writing of the feminine. The "woman" in the text is, then, an effect of the textual practice of breaking patriarchal fictional forms. Says Cixous:

> Pleasure is all *Agua viva* is talking about. It is caught between two prohibitions which are not the same. . . . It is that to say and to have pleasure are not simultaneous. To say something always betrays something. That is the very theme of *Agua viva*. What is tragic is that the word separates. There is a difference in language between the subject who has pleasure and the one who writes it. (XI)

Cixous observes that "Clarice tries to be as essentialist as possible, even if there is of course no essence" (XIX). Lispector's project, thus viewed through Cixous's eyes, becomes an essentialist one, because it accentuates female differences and the vision of an autonomous women's language and aesthetics. It also reiterates the long-standing symbolization of "woman" in western society, as Felski points out (37). However, *The Stream of Life*'s presentation of the struggle between living and writing lends itself to the identification and recognition of a distinctive female *jouissance* that echoes Cixous's call to write the body: "I write you completely whole and I feel a pleasure in being"(4). The novel's narrator aims to articulate bodily rhythms: "And if here I have to use words for you, they must create an almost exclusively bodily meaning. I am battling with the ultimate vibration"(5). The narrator affirms life by putting herself into the text, by writing herself.[12] For Lispector, "a woman in the text" is the creation of a woman's inner life, her inner rhythms, in the very moment and movements of the urge to write. In *The Stream of Life* modernity meets French feminist critics to expose the vitality of a woman's practice. The present of writing becomes in the novel a process of inscription, of female self-assertion and self-celebration:

It's with such intense joy. It's such an hallelujah. "Hallelujah." I shout, an hallelujah that fuses with the darkest human howl of the pain of separation but is a shout of diabolical happiness. Because nobody holds me back anymore. (3)

Thus Allende's *House of Spirits* and Lispector's *The Stream of Life* exemplify, each in its own way, the dialectic in feminist writing between the personal and the political. The importance of Allende lies in the particular way she inserts Latin American women and herself into history. The central subject of the text is 'woman', woman as mother or daughter, woman as historian, woman as writer, woman as lover. If Latin American history has been marked by the marginality of women as writers and readers, Allende's novel challenges this condition and exposes the danger of patriarchal hegemony.

In a different voice, Lispector presents a more metaphysical version of the problematics of the relationship between life and art. Can a woman write "her self" within the context of modernity? Can poetic avant-garde language fully reproduce the essentialist female desire for presence? These are some of the questions that Lispector's text addresses. And, even if it is debatable that the works of modernity can be identified with modes and processes characterized as "feminine," *The Stream of Life* presents a particular challenge to accepted conceptual dualisms. We can feel with Cixous that Lispector's text explores contradictory relations with "traditional patriarchal structures" of meaning while exposing an unceasing exploration of its own writerly project.

At the threshold of autobiography and fiction, *The House of the Spirits* and *The Stream of Life* seem to articulate different directions in the contemporary female quest. Between subjectivity on the one hand and community on the other, these works influence the ways in which we understand the construction (or deconstruction) of "woman in the text" and shed light on the questions of thematics and form in the fictional autobiographical mode. Finally, in crossing generic boundaries, these two works by Allende and Lispector emerge as important markers of a collective enterprise that suggests how far-reachingly intertwined the dictates of genre and gender, history and fiction, art and life really are.

NOTES

1. Silvia Molloy suggests that in Latin America the lack of interest in autobiography is due to the fact that this mode of writing always appears in a hybrid form. Molloy (177) also notes that women's autobiographies in Latin America are rare.
2. Relevant texts are *Women's Autobiography*, edited by Estelle C. Jelinek and *The Female Autograph*, edited by Domna C. Stanton.
3. See for example Paul John Eakin, *Fiction in Autobiography*.
4. Isabel Allende "Sobre *La casa de los espíritus*," *Discurso Literario*, Vol. 2, No. 1 (otoño, 1984), 71-72.
5. See Cathleen Medwick's interview with Isabel Allende.
6. See Isabel Allende's own remarks in *Discurso Literario*.
7. Rita Felski bases the definition on early critical surveys such as Roy Pascal's *Design and Truth in Autobiography*.
8. Nancy Miller's theory of "gender-bound reading" could apply here. See Miller, 267-268.
9. See Nancy Chodorow's *The Reproduction of Mothering: Psychoanalysis and the Sociology of Gender*.
10. See Mario Rojas's analysis.
11. Cixous uses in the foreword the original title of Lispector's novel: *Agua viva*.
12. In "The Laugh of the Medusa" says Cixous: "Woman must write her self: must write about women and bring women to writing. Woman must put herself into the text—as into the world and into history—by her own movement."(876)

WORKS CITED

Allende, Isabel. "Sobre *La casa de los espíritus*." *Discurso Literario*, Vol. 2, No. 1 (otoño 1984): 71.

Allende, Isabel. *The House of the Spirits*. Transl. Magda Bogin. New York: Alfred A. Knopf, 1985.

Brodzki, Bella and Celeste Schenck, eds. *Life/Lines. Theorizing Women's Autobiography*. Ithaca: Cornell UP, 1988.

Chodorow, Nancy. *The Reproduction of Mothering: Psychoanalysis and the Sociology of Gender*. Berkeley: U of California P, 1978.

Cixous, Hélène. *La Jeune Née*. Paris: Union Générale d'Editions, 1975.

———. "The Laugh of the Medusa." Transl. Keith and Paula Cohen, *Signs*, Vol. 1 (Summer 1976): 876.

Coleman, Alexander. "Reconciliation Among the Ruins." *The New York Times Book Review* (May 12, 1985): 22.

De Koven, Marianne. "Male Signature, Female Aesthetic. The Gender Politics of Experimental Writing." *Breaking the Sequence. Women's Experimental Fiction*. Ed. Ellen G. Friedman and Miriam Fuchs. Princeton: Princeton UP, 1989.

Eakin, Paul John. *Fictions in Autobiography*. Princeton: Princeton UP, 1985.

Felski, Rita. *Beyond Feminist Aesthetics*. Cambridge: Harvard UP, 1989.

García Márquez, Gabriel. *One Hundred Years of Solitude*. Transl. Gregory Rabassa. New York: Harper, 1970.

———. *El General en su laberinto*. Bogotá: Editorial Oveja Negra, 1989.

Glickman, Nora. "Los personajes femeninos en *La casa de los espíritus*." *Los libros tienen sus propios espíritus*. Ed. Marcelo Coddou. México: Universidad Veracruzana, 1987.

Irigaray, Luce. *This Sex Which is Not One*. Transl. Catherine Porter. Ithaca: Cornell UP, 1985.

Jardine, Alice. *Gynesis: Configurations of Woman and Modernity*. Ithaca: Cornell UP, 1985.

Jelinek, Estelle C., ed. *Women's Autobiography*. Bloomington: Indiana UP, 1980.

Juhasz, Suzanne. "Towards a Theory of Form in Feminist Autobiography: Kate Millet's *Flying* and *Sita;* Maxine Hong Kingston's *The Woman Warrior*." *Women's Autobiography*. Ed. Estelle C. Jelinek. Bloomington: Indiana UP, 1980.

Lispector, Clarice. *Perto do Coraçao Selvagem*. Río de Janeiro: Vozes Ltda., 10th ed., 1984.

———. *The Stream of Life*. Foreword by Hélène Cixous. Transl. Elizabeth Lowe and Earl Fitz. Minneapolis: U of Minnesota P, 1989.

Medwick, Cathleen. "Interview with Isabel Allende," *Vogue*, (March 1985): 606.

Miller, Nancy. "Women's Autobiography in France: For a dialectics of Identification." *Women and Language in Literature and Society*. Eds. Sally Mc Connell, Ruth Borker and Nelly Furman. New York: Praeger, 1980.

Molloy, Silvia. "Dos proyectos de vida: cuadernos de infancia de Norah Lange y el archipiélago de Victoria Ocampo." *Femme des Amériques*. Ed. Claire Pailler. Toulouse: Université de Toulouse, 1986.

Ortega, Julio. *Poetics of Change. The New Spanish American Narrative*. Austin: U of Texas P, 1984.

Pascal, Roy. *Design and Truth in Autobiography*. London: Routledge and Kegan Paul, 1960.

Rojas, Mario. "*La casa de los espíritus* de Isabel Allende. Un caleidoscopio de espejos desordenados." *Los libros tienen sus propios espíritus*. Ed. Marcelo Coddou. México: Universidad Veracruzana, 1987.

Stanton, Domna C., ed. *The Female Autograph*. 1984. Chicago: U of Chicago P, 1987.

Writing the Self from the Outside-In

Father Land and/or Mother Tongue: The Divided Female Subject in Kogawa's Obasan and Hong Kingston's The Woman Warrior

Donald C. Goellnicht

Joy Kogawa was born in Vancouver, British Columbia in 1935. As part of the Japanese Canadian community on the West Coast, she and her family were evacuated and interned during the Second World War. She has worked as a schoolteacher and as a writer for the office of the Prime Minister of Canada; she now lives in Toronto. An accomplished writer in different fields, she is the author of four volumes of poetry — The Splintered Moon (1967), A Choice of Dreams (1974), Jericho Road (1977), and Woman in the Woods (1985) — and a book for children, Naomi's Road (1986). Obasan (1981), based in part on her own experiences, is her first novel and the winner of the 1981 Books in Canada First Novel Award, the Canadian Authors' Association 1982 Book of the Year Award, and the American Book Award (1982).

Maxine Hong Kingston was born and raised in Stockton, California. She graduated from the University of California at Berkeley in 1962 and has taught high school and college English in California and in Hawaii, where she lived in Honolulu for many years. She has been visiting professor at the University of Hawaii and Eastern Michigan University; she now lives in Oakland, California. She is the author of two celebrated (auto)biographical fictions: The Woman Warrior (1976), winner of the National Book Critics Circle Award for non-fiction, and China Men (1980), winner of the National Book Award for non-fiction. She has also published Hawai'i One Summer (1987), a series of prose sketches with woodblock prints and calligraphy, and recently published her first novel, Tripmaster Monkey: His Fake Book (1989).

> An all-purpose feminist frame of reference does not exist, nor should it ever come prepackaged and ready-made. We need to keep building one, absolutely flexible and readjustable, from women's own experience of difference, of our difference from Woman and of the differences among women; differences which . . . are perceived as having as much (or more) to do with race, class, or ethnicity as with gender or sexuality per se.
>
> Teresa de Lauretis *Feminist Studies/Critical Studies* 14

In the last ten years French feminist theory has proved a tremendously liberating and revolutionary force in North America. Its articulation of *écriture féminine*, or "writing the body," has provided us valuable new insights into women's writing, as has its stress on glossolalia/polyphony/heteroglossia, what Cixous calls speaking "the language of 1,000 tongues which knows neither enclosure nor death," in a play of various discourses against a phallocratic monism (889). But now that the revolutionary wind has blown for some time, we must examine it more closely; we find it, I think, despite all the talk of trans-Atlantic feminism, fraught with problems for our North American context. Most significant for my paper, this writing—for all its stress on diversity—strikes me as primarily Eurocentric—or at least academic and white—and "writerly" rather than "speakerly." The models it establishes are designed for a society that still regards itself as much more monolithic than ours, one that has not begun to come to terms with the *voices* of its minority and/or immigrant cultures. The question I am asking is: "Are the models and doctrines of Western academic feminism sufficient to explain a different social, political, and cultural specificity, in this case Asian American women's writing?"

I am by no means the first to raise this issue, as a look at the work of critics like Alice Jardine, Gayatri Spivak, and Sondra O'Neale will indicate.[1] Within the American context, black women have long been in the vanguard of those challenging the dangerous totalizing tendencies of academic feminism that has often paid too little attention to race and class,[2] feminism which, in its attempt to isolate Woman within patriarchy, has run the risk of becoming centered. One of the most problematic—some might say imperialistic—approaches that has been embraced by recent feminism is, I think, psychoanalysis in its Lacanian guise. While engaging many strategies to avoid the liberal humanist label of "universalist"—in particular, the denial of a fixed identity—Lacanian psychoanalysis has still succumbed to totalizing tendencies inherited from Freud.[3] Of course, feminists like Juliet Mitchell argue that the study of Freud continues to be valuable as a means of uncovering patriarchal structures (see *Psychoanalysis and Feminism*), but the fact remains that Freudian psychoanalysis posits a universal, ahistorical theory of the psychic construction of gender; Lacan's revisions of Freud in terms of language pretend to the same universal mythologizing.

French feminists like Cixous, Irigaray, and Kristeva have led the movement to revise Lacan in order to establish a female discourse—based on the plurality and autoeroticism of female sexuality—which differs from male discourse's focus on the phallus. The otherness of female libido produces the otherness of female language—illogical, incoherent, non-linear. The result is linguistic play that manages to escape binary male/female oppositions by discovering points in discourse at which the semiotic transgresses the law of the symbolic or acts as a "supplement to the symbolic order" (Paul Smith 121).[4] But while these theorists are successful in countering Lacan's sexist model, they—especially Kristeva who stresses "feminine" and "masculine" modes of language rather than men and women, and to some extent Cixous—remain reluctant to let go of his entirely figurative tropes for fear of being labelled essentialist. As one group of critics asks, however, "[i]f woman is nothing but a category within language, constructed by male desire, where and what are women?" (Garner, Kahane, Sprengnether 22). Concomitant questions can be posed regarding racial difference, to which I will return. The point to be stressed is that such primarily psycholinguistic theory does not allow sufficient room for the social and material construction of gender to be fully discussed. The emphasis on the abstract "subject" tends to elide the social and material consequences of, and beyond, language.[5]

The American Nancy Chodorow has also focused on female sexuality, and especially on the preoedipal mother-daughter relationship, in an attempt to correct Freud, but unlike her French counterparts, she has been willing to link psychoanalysis with sociology to arrive at a theory that situates the acquisition of gender within a social and cultural specificity. She has used clinical studies of real women instead of purely abstract subject positions to form her argument about mothering; to some extent, her literal approach subverts the very figurative theories of male discourse and thus becomes boldly feminist. Her findings are too detailed to summarize here, but she concludes that "[t]he girl's preoedipal mother-love and preoccupation with preoedipal issues are prolonged in a way that they are not for the boy" (108). The mother's "[p]rimary identification and symbiosis with daughters tend to be stronger" (109), while a girl's preoedipal attachment to her mother "often [extends] well into her fourth or fifth year" (96), after she has acquired representational language; "Finally, the resurfacing and prevalence of preoedipal mother-daughter issues in adolescence . . . provide clinical evidence of the claim that elements of the preoedipal mother-daughter relationship are maintained and prolonged in both maternal and filial psyche" (110).

Building on Chodorow's study, literary critics like Chris Weedon point out that, unlike the son, the daughter does not recognize any difference between herself and her mother, nor is the Law of the Father against incest as applicable to her as to a son. "[B]ecause difference does not open up between her and her mother in the same way that it does between mother and son, the daughter does not experience desire in the Lacanian sense, that is, as differentiated from a preoedipal merging with the mother" (11). The daughter continues to identify with her mother, whom she does not see as lost, and so does not experience a complete break with the preoedipal, literal language as she moves, more reluctantly, into the symbolic order of the Father. According to Margaret Homans, "the daughter therefore speaks two languages at once" (13), the symbolic and the literal, and traces of the literal surface in women's writing.

Studies like Chodorow's, then, point the way forward for feminist critics like Homans and Weedon to recuperate—and to valorize—the traces of literal, preoedipal language in the writings of women; however, while historically and socially specific, Chodorow's study does not take race into account. What I want to hypothesize here, very tentatively, is that for a girl from an immigrant Asian minority, the achievement of mature psychological adjustment does not simply involve negotiation between the subjective space of silent communication inherited from the mother and the symbolic language inherited from the figurative father, a movement from preoedipal to oedipal development;[6] it also involves an attempt at balance between the old "mother tongue/culture" (in the case of Kogawa's *Obasan*, Japan, and of Hong Kingston's *The Woman Warrior*, China) and the new "father land" (Canada and the United States respectively). This is an aspect of splitting or division not usually addressed by psycholinguistic theories. While being careful to avoid any simple equation between literal and literary parents—a proposition fraught with danger: I find myself in the bind of those trying to move beyond a transparency theory of language, but who end up reading in what Jardine describes as "a schizophrenic manner, . . . adopting a kind of 'yes, I know characters are not real but . . .' approach to the literary text" (*Gynesis* 39)[7]–I would speculate, on the evidence of autobiographical fictions like these, that the girl from an immigrant racial minority experiences not a single, but a double subject split: first, when she takes on the gendered position constructed for her by the symbolic language of patriarchy; and second, when she falls under the influence of discursively and socially constructed positions of racial difference. This situation of potential double powerlessness—of being woman and minority—is brought home to her with the recognition that the "fathers" of her racial and cultural group are silenced and degraded by the Laws of the Ruling Fathers (the white majority): in *Obasan*, Naomi's father is interned and her uncle rarely speaks, engulfed in memories of his own loss; in *The Woman Warrior*, Maxine's father and uncles rarely break their silence except to utter curses against women (54-55), and throughout there is a sense that their powerlessness—both linguistic and political—in the new society intensifies their silence and their patriarchal domination of Chinese American women. Discriminatory laws of exclusion against Asians in both Canada and the United States entrenched the relative weakness of Asian patriarchy within the context of the new culture.

In fact, Hong Kingston's second work, *China Men*, is hugely dependent—much more so than *The Woman Warrior*—on the *daughter's* fiction-making to create voices for men who say little, for a father who salutes his family with a touch of his hat rather than with words, so that his children do not even recognize another man's voice as not their father's (*China Men* 6-7). Significantly, the opening section traces the crossing of a man, Tang Ao, from China to the Land of Women, where he is feminized, becoming an object of painful beauty, and where the women joke about "Sewing [his] lips together" (4), silence being seen as a condition of womanhood within patriarchy. Scholars believe this Women's Land, we are told, "was in North America" (5), a suggestion that Chinese men are forced into female subject positions in the new land. Thus, Hong Kingston continues to blur binary distinctions between masculine and feminine, symbolic and semiotic, a practice started in *The Woman Warrior*.

Ironically, however, in the face of the emasculation of minority "fathers," the task of preserving the "mother tongue/culture" (of Japan and China) seems to fall to the oral traditions of minority "mothers." In *Obasan* it is the Katos, the mother's family, who are still in Japan, and the mother who maintains the connection with the "mother culture," returning to Japan where she dies in the atomic attack on Nagasaki; in *The Woman Warrior*, it is Maxine's mother who transmits the "mother tongue" through "talk-stories" of China, daring even to narrate stories, like "No Name Woman," that her husband has forbidden, excised, unnamed because they challenge patriarchal lineage and authority: "Whenever she had to warn us about life, my mother told stories that ran like this one ["No Name Woman"], a story to grow up on. . . . Night after night my mother would talk-story until we fell asleep. I couldn't tell where the stories left off and the dreams began. . . . At last I saw too that I had been in the presence of great power, my mother talking-story" (*Woman Warrior* 5, 24). Elsewhere, Hong Kingston states that even "[m]any of the men's stories were ones I originally heard from women" (quoted in Kim 208).

In such cases of cultural and linguistic dislocation based on racial difference—a psychic and social dislocation rather than a physical one in that both Naomi and Maxine are born in North America—the daughter appears to face a number of difficult choices: does she turn back to the literal, preoedipal language she once shared with her mother, thus retreating into a world of silence in an attempt to dissolve all mature subject positions by refusing figurative language; or does she adopt the oral tradition of the "mother culture" which is the domain of women, and which challenges some Western feminists' stress on writing/*écriture*; or does she elide and repress both mother *and* father as representative of the "mother tongue/culture" and embrace the figurative language of the new "father land"? These choices involve more than a single transference of identification from one parental presence to another, from Mother to Father, from literal to symbolic language; they also complicate the rather unproblematic privileging of preoedipal/semiotic mother-daughter language, or its traces, that much Western feminism has valorized.

Kogawa does celebrate the preoedipal mother-daughter relationship of silent communication as a period of absolute security and trust, symbolically depicted as an umbilical cord. Naomi describes how, as a four-year-old "Speech hides within me, watchful and afraid" (58), yet in moments of crisis her mother acts "Without a word and without alarm. . . . All the while she acts, there is calm efficiency in her face and she does not speak" (59). This kind of meaningful silence, which Naomi believes to be especially Japanese, continues to haunt her into adulthood in the figure of Obasan, her substitute mother, within whose small body "silence . . . has grown large and powerful" (14). Unfortunately, the umbilical cord between Naomi and her mother is soon severed not only by her mother's departure for Japan but by the sexual abuse Naomi suffers by Old Man Gower, a white neighbor, the racial implications of domination by the powerful majority being quite clear. She refuses to tell her mother of this abuse, thus causing a rift between them: "If I tell my mother about Mr. Gower, the alarm will send a tremor through our bodies and I will be torn from her. But the secret has already separated us. The secret is this: I go to seek Old Man Gower in his hideaway" (65). Here Kogawa effectively links a particularly female condition of sexual silence to her more general concern with the condition of minority silence. The sense of Japanese propriety Naomi has been taught to uphold defies articulation of this abuse, so that the "mother tongue"—symbolized by her mother—fails her for the first time; simultaneously, her confusion is compounded by her perverse attraction to the sex and race that abuses her, perhaps because that race holds, while denying through an injunction to silence, access to the very language that would allow her to utter her abuse. In either case, uncommunicative silence leads to powerlessness, as the Indian, Rough Lock Bill, who acts as a foil to Old Man Gower the silencer, tells the child Naomi at Slocan: "Can't read. Can't talk. What's the good of you eh?" (145). It appears that without the discursive power of language there can be no communication, no knowing, no identity, no self as a linguistically constituted subject. We must narrate ourselves into history or be doomed to extinction.

A parallel situation and idea arise in *The Woman Warrior* when the young Maxine, trying to force a silent Chinese American girl—who substitutes for Maxine's own silent self—to speak by pulling her hair, tells her: "If you don't talk, you can't have a personality. You'll have no personality and no hair" (210). The minority child is left in a double bind of psychic and linguistic dislocation where the once-communicative silence of absolute trust with the mother and mother culture provides a false sense of security as this silence constitutes an unconscious complicity in the acts of abuse inflicted on the minority by the majority, on the weak by the powerful.

Hong Kingston treats more directly and brutally the issues between minority mother and daughter that Kogawa tries to ameliorate. Maxine never simply celebrates a preoedipal sense of direct communication between her mother and herself; instead, she problematizes the mother-daughter relationship in a story like "No Name Woman" by presenting the literal, preoedipal communication between mother and daughter as intimate—"Carrying the baby to the well shows loving. Otherwise abandon it. . . . It was probably a girl" (*Woman Warrior* 18)—but at the same time demonstrating a link between inarticulateness and doom for women: "No one would give her a family hall name. She had taken the child with her into the wastes. At its birth the two of them had felt the same raw pain of separation, a wound that only the family pressing tight could close" (17). But patrilinear family denies the very existence of this mother who has transgressed its rules, punishing her by withholding her name, opening rather than healing the wound, casting her into a vast hole in which she drowns, dooming her to what Maxine sees as the void of silence by refusing to utter the words that would grant her a linguistically constituted identity. Ironically, Maxine's own mother reinforces this doom on motherhood: "'Don't tell anyone you had an aunt. Your father does not want to hear her name. She has never been born'" (18). There is, however, a second, liminal irony by which the maternal oral tradition disrupts and subverts patriarchal power to silence women: in telling Maxine this story, her mother breaks the silence, thus providing an example for Maxine, whose written text, alive with the vocal cadences of oral Cantonese (a dialect, not a written language),[8] continues that breach, a breach that becomes both an act of vengeance—revenge in Chinese is "report a crime" (63)—and of healing for violated women.

But the use of maternal language, inherited "talk-stories," is double-edged for Hong Kingston, different from itself; a long time is needed for Maxine to come to terms with it and for it to help empower her. As children she and her siblings tried to escape their mother's stories of war, violence, bombing raids, shrinking babies, insane women stoned to death (113). Further, the "mother tongue" reifies the patrilineage of Chinese patriarchy, inscribing for the young Maxine a space that offers two equated—and equally unacceptable—subject positions: girl and slave (56). As Sidonie Smith points out, even the woman warrior Fa Mu Lan, who takes her father's place in battle, thus embodying a gender cross-over that might delineate liberation for women, also distances herself from the band of female avengers in China, instead insisting that she avenges the wrongs perpetrated on her *brother*; and once these filial duties are fulfilled, she returns to the *female* tasks of childbearing and nurturing her husband and his parents (Sidonie Smith 158-59). Fa Mu Lan subverts and enshrines patriarchal culture at one and the same time.

In Kogawa's fiction, Naomi remembers her mother's oral tradition of "milk and Momotaro" (57)—Japanese stories—with affection, but like Hong Kingston she recognizes that these patriarchal stories of male warriors prescribe a filial respect which for women, and for Japanese Canadians generally, dictate roles of obedience and passivity that made them easy victims for the racial attacks—the internment, evacuation and dispersal—that took place during the War. She sees a return to such a tradition as impossible and instead attempts to embrace the "father land" by becoming a good Canadian teacher, by assimilating into the mainstream, her situation when the novel opens. In contrast, Maxine remembers her mother's Chinese stories with pain, confusion, humiliation, but her reaction is similar: she tries consciously to reject them, to unpack the heritage that her mother has crammed into her head, to cut off her "mother tongue" in an attempt to become "American feminine." Ironically, she projects this cutting of her tongue onto her mother, whom she portrays as the locus of blockage on her route to the acquisition of language: she claims her mother cut her fremun so that she could not speak: "The Chinese say 'a ready tongue is an evil'" (119). Naomi too blames her mother for imposed silence: "Gentle Mother, we were lost together in our silences. Our wordlessness was our mutual destruction" (243). Obasan has tried to keep Naomi in that state of childhood, to protect her through silence, but in adulthood that silence has turned to stone, becoming a burden Naomi must carry through her life because she has repressed all the questions about her past, her heritage, her mother (culture). For these questions no answers have been forthcoming: "This is the way it is whenever I ask questions. The answers are not answers at all" (135). Maxine, too, feels that she was refused initiation into the genuinely empowering "secrets" of Chinese culture: "'It's nothing,' [her mother] said. She never explained anything that was really important. [Her children] no longer asked" (141). For these minority girls the mother and the "mother tongue" emerge as both desirable and terrifying, empowering and debilitating; silence is at once escape and doom.

For minority boys the transference from "mother tongue" to "father land" *seems* simpler—I offer this view tentatively in light of the fact that the texts I am looking at are written by women; but it is perhaps significant that these types of minority texts have been written by *women*. Chodorow claims that:

> From the retention of pre-Oedipal attachments to their mother, growing girls come to define themselves as continuous with others; their experience of self contains more flexible and permeable ego boundaries. Boys come to define

themselves as more separate and distinct, with a greater sense of rigid ego boundaries and differentiations. The basic feminine sense of self is connected to the world, the basic masculine sense of self is separate. (169; see also Gilligan 8)

In *Obasan*, Naomi's brother Stephen separates from his heritage, flies from Obasan and Uncle, from everything Japanese, into the arms of the dominant white culture, the "father land" of the English language and of European music (14), where he succeeds with a vengeance; in *The Woman Warrior*, Maxine's brothers will have nothing to do with their mother's talk-stories nor with her elaborate plans for her sister's return to her husband ("At the Western Palace"). In each case, men of the second generation manage no play of linguistic, social, and cultural differences, but set up binary hierarchies in which the "mother tongue/culture" occupies a position of inferiority and must be repressed so that they can smoothly enter the "father land."

The task of negotiating between parental presences, and between "mother tongue" and "father land," falls to the female narrators, who are left in confusion, symbolized by initially weak voices. I would suggest, though, that once the daughter has negotiated a successful balance within this play of differences, her liability becomes an asset, that of being able to juggle the positions of a multiple, shifting identity, and to utilize a multiplicity of discourses so as to critique the Law of patriarchy and the totalizing voice of dominant history. Paradoxically, but significantly, Naomi discovers this empowered voice for the breaking of silence in the very "amniotic deep" of prefigurative, literal mother-child communication, so that her culminating epiphany of "water and stone dancing" (247) brings together, and holds in harmoniously negotiated tension, the "stone" of silence and the "stream" of language that have run through the novel, and brings us full circle to the opening prose poem:

There is a silence that cannot speak.
There is a silence that will not speak.
Beneath the grass the speaking dreams and beneath the dreams is a sensate sea. The speech that frees comes forth from that amniotic deep. To attend its voice, I can hear it say, is to embrace its absence. But I fail the task. The word is stone. (vi)

Maxine, too, negotiates a balance between her Chinese mother and her American self in her final episode, "a story my mother told me, not when I was young, but recently, when I told her I also talk-story. The beginning is hers, the ending, mine" (240). The "ending" story is of Ts'ai Yen, the captured bride of a "barbarian" chief who returns to her Han people with songs she developed among the "barbarians," songs that "translated well" (243) between cultures.

For both Hong Kingston and Kogawa, however, translation is never easy integration and assimilation. Instead, on a generic level, both replace simple mimetic and humanistic realism with complex works of metafictional life writing that, in their very self-conscious rejections of univocality, their contorted and problematizing mixtures of history and fiction, biography and fiction, lyrics and diaries, legends and prosaic dailiness, challenge the dominant discourse of the "father land." They refuse to seek identity through homogeneity, and instead exploit the difference of multifarious subject positions so as to create junctures where radical agency becomes possible. They enter the dialogical fray surrounding the "silenced" subject of race in North America as forces of disruptive excess, as powerful, but self-conscious, "word warriors."

> There are two gates in the north wall, three in the south, two in the east and two in the west. Winds blow from all sides. In the center is stillness. Winds blow from all sides. The gates are open. The center shifts. (Chuang Hua: *Crossings*)

NOTES

1. See, for example,
    Alice Jardine:
    > [W]omen, who have historically filled in as translators of culture, are today, as "international feminists," running the danger of simply translating "woman as concept" from one culture to another. There is, after all, a difference between really attempting to think differently and thinking the Same through the manipulation of difference. (*Gynesis* 17)

    Gayatri Spivak:
    > The point I am trying to make is that, in order to learn enough about Third World women and to develop a differ-

ent readership, the immense heterogeneity of the field must be appreciated, and the First World feminist must learn to stop feeling privileged *as a woman*. . . . [T]here has to be another focus: not merely who am I? but who is the other woman? How am I naming her? How does she name me? Is this part of the problematic I discuss? (136, 150)

Sondra O'Neale:
White feminism is one of the "sexy" issues in academia in the eighties. In most of the literature, regardless of the discipline involved, the white feminist defines "female" from the assumption that the experience of white females is the "standard" female experience, from which all others must (negatively) deviate. (145)

See also Barbara Smith and Trinh T. Minh-ha for further discussions of difference based on race.

2. I should point out that, in its focus on race, the present study does not deal with class as a factor in the construction of gender, although Hong Kingston's text might certainly be examined from that perspective. Hong Kingston herself has said: "I'm also writing about poor people in another subculture" (Islas 12). As an example of a study that does consider race and class in relation to gender, see Angela Davis, *Women, Race and Class*.

3. For example, the acquisition of gender and language is rather different for the daughter, a fact that Lacan does not take much into account, but which has been stressed by many feminists. Lacan argues that his use of "phallus," "masculine," "feminine," etc. are figurative tropes or subject positions not dependent on the biological sex of the individual, so that his theory is equally applicable to men and women; but as Margaret Homans and Chris Weedon, among others, point out, "Lacanian theory employs an anatomically grounded elision between the phallus and the penis which implies the necessary patriarchal organization of desire and sexuality. . . . Men, by virtue of their penis, can aspire to a position of power and control within the symbolic order. Women, on the other hand, have no position in the symbolic order, except in relation to men" (Weedon 54). Homans observes that only those who believe they can lack the phallus (men) can embrace symbolic language as a substitute; "daughters lack this lack" (9). Lacan's stress on the figurative attempts to overcome Freudian dependence on biology, but itself betrays a dependence on anatomical difference.

4. Here Paul Smith is discussing two of Kristeva's major texts: *The Revolution in Poetic Language* (1974) and *Desire in Language* (1980).
5. Kristeva's earlier, more Marxist, work *On Chinese Women* does concern itself with cultural differences between East and West; but, as Paul Smith observes, Kristeva's later work "begins to expand the psychoanalytical basis for the semiotic/symbolic coupling and locates the semiotic much more determinedly in the pre-oedipal where it is assigned logical and ontological priority over the oedipal symbolic. This move . . . 'individualizes' [the semiotic], makes it transhistorical and largely removes it from the closely worked historical and material dialectic of the earlier work" (126-27). Monique Wittig, another French feminist, reminds us, however: "Our refusal of the totalizing interpretation of psychoanalysis makes the theoreticians say that we neglect the symbolic dimension. These discourses deny us the very possibility of creating our own categories. But their most ferocious action is the unrelenting tyranny that they exert upon our physical and mental selves. . . . [W]e forget the material (physical) violence that they [discourses] do to the oppressed people, a violence produced by the abstract and 'scientific' discourses as well as by the discourses of the mass media. I would like to insist on the material oppression of individuals by discourses" (105-06). These quotations also make clear that "French feminism" is by no means as unified or homogeneous a set of theories as my too-brief summary—and those of many others—might imply.
6. I recognize the irony involved in my use of the very Freudian/Lacanian binary terms which I am calling into question; as Audre Lorde has reminded us, "*the master's tools will never dismantle the master's house*. They may allow us temporarily to beat him at his own game, but they will never enable us to bring about genuine change" (112). But until we develop a new vocabulary and a new economy, less patriarchal and Eurocentric, all the critic can do is gesture towards cracks in the existing structure that might become passages to new light and space. Feminists like Irigaray have already begun to move in that direction, although I think Irigaray runs the risk of installing a female economy that cannot take into account other constructs of difference.
7. A compounding danger lies in the question of how "representative" of its group a minority text can be. In an interview with Arturo Islas and in her article "Cultural Mis-readings by Ameri-

can Reviewers," Hong Kingston denies that her fictions "represent the race" (Islas 11); yet, in a parenthetical statement, she reveals: "(For the record, most of my mail is from Chinese American women, who tell me how similar their childhoods were to the one in the book [*The Woman Warrior*], or they say their lives are not like that at all, but they understand the feelings. . . .)" ("Cultural Mis-readings" 63). This rejection of the representativeness of her work may amount to Hong Kingston's refusal to assume the position of authorizing center of her minority group.

8. Hong Kingston is aware of the problems of trying to *write* an oral language: "I write about illiterate people. . . . So it's a matter of starting with a language that has no writing and yet writing about people who talk-story in that language" (Islas 13).

WORKS CITED

Chodorow, Nancy. *The Reproduction of Mothering: Psychoanalysis and the Sociology of Gender*. Berkeley and Los Angeles: U of California P, 1978.
Chuang, Hua. *Crossings* (1968). Foreword by Amy Ling. Boston: Northeastern UP, 1986.
Cixous, Hélène. "The Laugh of the Medusa." Trans. Keith Cohen and Paula Cohen. *Signs* 1 (Summer 1976): 875-93.
Davis, Angela Y. *Women, Race and Class*. New York: Vintage, 1981.
de Lauretis, Teresa. "Feminist Studies/Critical Studies: Issues, Terms, and Contexts." *Feminist Studies/Critical Studies*. Ed. Teresa de Lauretis. Bloomington: Indiana UP, 1986. 1-19.
Garner, Shirley Nelson, Claire Kahane, and Madelon Sprengnether, eds., *The (M)other Tongue: Essays in Feminist Psychoanalytic Interpretations*. Ithaca, N.Y.: Cornell UP, 1985.
Gilligan, Carol. *In a Different Voice: Psychological Theory and Women's Development*. Cambridge, Mass.: Harvard UP, 1982.
Homans, Margaret. *Bearing the Word: Language and Female Experience in Nineteenth-Century Women's Writing*. Chicago and London: U of Chicago P, 1986.
Irigaray, Luce. *This Sex Which Is Not One*. Trans. Catherine Porter and Carolyn Burke. Ithaca, N.Y.: Cornell UP, 1985.

Islas, Arturo. "Maxine Hong Kingston." *Women Writers of the West Coast: Speaking of Their Lives and Careers.* Ed. Marilyn Yalom. Santa Barbara: Capra, 1983. 11-19.
Jardine, Alice. *Gynesis: Configurations of Woman and Modernity.* Ithaca, N.Y.: Cornell UP, 1985.
——. "Pre-Texts for a Trans-Atlantic Feminist." *Yale French Studies* 62 (1981): 220-36.
Kim, Elaine H. *Asian American Literature: An Introduction to the Writings and Their Social Context.* Philadelphia: Temple UP,1982.
Kingston, Maxine Hong. *China Men.* New York: Knopf, 1980.
——. "Cultural Mis-readings by American Reviewers." *Asian and Western Writers in Dialogue: New Cultural Identities.* Ed. Guy Amirthanayagam. London: Macmillan, 1982. 55-65.
——. *The Woman Warrior: Memoirs of a Girlhood Among Ghosts* (1976). New York: Vintage, 1977.
Kogawa, Joy. *Obasan* (1981). Markham, Ontario: Penguin, 1983.
Kristeva, Julia. *Desire in Language.* Ed. Leon S. Roudiez. New York: Columbia UP, 1980.
——. "On the Women of China." Trans. Ellen Conroy Kennedy. *Signs* 1 (Autumn 1975): 57-81.
Lacan, Jacques. *Feminine Sexuality.* Ed. Juliet Mitchell and Jacqueline Rose. Trans. Jacqueline Rose. New York: Norton, 1982.
Lorde, Audre. "The Master's Tools Will Never Dismantle the Master's House." *Sister Outsider.* Trumansburg, N.Y.: Crossing P, 1984. 110-13.
Mitchell, Juliet. *Psychoanalysis and Feminism.* New York: Random House, 1974.
O'Neale, Sondra. "Inhibiting Midwives, Usurping Creators: The Struggling Emergence of Black Women in American Fiction." *Feminist Studies/Critical Studies.* Ed. Teresa de Lauretis. Bloomington: Indiana UP, 1986. 139-56.
Smith, Barbara. "Toward a Black Feminist Criticism." *The New Feminist Criticism.* Ed. Elaine Showalter. New York: Pantheon, 1985. 168-85.
Smith, Paul. *Discerning the Subject.* Minneapolis: U of Minnesota P, 1988.
Smith, Sidonie. *A Poetics of Women's Autobiography.* Bloomington: Indiana UP, 1987.
Spivak, Gayatri Chakravorty. *In Other Worlds: Essays in Cultural Politics.* New York and London: Routledge, 1988.

Trinh, T. Minh-ha. *Woman, Native, Other*. Bloomington: Indiana UP, 1989.

Weedon, Chris. *Feminist Practice and Poststructuralist Theory*. Oxford: Basil Blackwell, 1987.

Wittig, Monique. "The Straight Mind." *Feminist Issues* 1 (Summer 1980): 103-111.

Gender, Culture, and Identity in Paule Marshall's Brown Girl, Brownstones

Keith E. Byerman

Paule Marshall was born in Brooklyn in 1929 to Samuel and Ada Burke, who had emigrated from Barbados after World War I to take advantage of American economic opportunities. With other island immigrants, they formed a cohesive community that valued hard work, property acquisition, and education. Paule (pronounced Paul) has described growing up in an environment of strong-willed, eloquent women who were powerful storytellers. She attended Brooklyn College, from which she graduated Phi Beta Kappa in 1953. She then worked for a small black magazine, Our World, *which gave her assignments in Brazil and the Caribbean. At the same time she worked on her first novel, which was published as* Brown Girl, Brownstones *in 1959. Since then, she has concentrated on writing fiction, though she has taught creative writing at Yale, Columbia, and the University of Iowa's Writers' Workshop. In 1961, she published* Soul Clap Hands and Sing, *a collection of novellas, and, in 1969,* The Chosen Place, The Timeless People, *a novel focusing on racial and cultural conflict in the Caribbean.* Praisesong for the Widow *(1983) shows an American black woman in search of her African roots through Caribbean experiences. She currently divides her residence between New York and the West Indies.*

Paule Marshall, in her long fiction, consistently concerns herself with the movement from one cultural context to another. In *Brown Girl, Brownstones* (1959) it is the Barbadian community of Marshall's parents' generation transplanting itself in New York; in *The Chosen Place, The Timeless People* (1969), it is the Americans and British-

135

trained blacks in the Caribbean; in *Praisesong for the Widow* (1983), it is the American black woman seeking her racial identity in the West Indies. As in all immigrant fiction, a strong emphasis is given to the cultural conflicts generated by strangers in a strange land. But Marshall, like all good writers in the genre, focuses on the psychological implications of such conflict. She is most interested in what uprooting and re-rooting do to the attitudes and perceptions of her characters. More specifically, she addresses, especially in *Brown Girl, Brownstones*, the ways in which cultural adjustments are manifested in gender conflict and sexual identity.

This first novel is autobiographical in its treatment of the generation which moved from Barbados to the United States in the early twentieth century. Marshall's parents were part of this first group, having immigrated to Brooklyn during World War I. It is the general meaning and consequences of such cultural change for the first two generations, rather than her personal history, that interests Marshall. She has said specifically that the characters are composites rather than allusions to individuals and, significantly, that Selina, the "brown girl" of the title, is an "idealized image of myself" (DeVeaux 123). In the same interview, however, she notes that, as a child, she was overwhelmed by the power of the voices of the older Bajan women: "I was always so intimidated by the awesome verbal power of these women. That might be one of the reasons I started writing. To see if, on paper, I couldn't have some of that power" (DeVeaux 71). It is precisely this female power in the immigrant generation and its relationship to expressiveness in their children that is crucial to the meaning of the novel.

Immigrant fiction generally deals with two levels of disruptions: the difficulties of the new group in its relationships with established groups and problems within the group—symbolized most often by its synecdoche, the family—as it tries simultaneously to preserve the old values and to live with the new ones. Often this latter drama is represented as a struggle between generations. The immigrants themselves keep the old language, old customs, and ties to the homeland, while their children seek as quickly as possible to develop new language skills and to adopt the behavior patterns of the new home. They often, in fact, display shame at the traditionalism of their parents.[1]

In *Brown Girl, Brownstones*, Marshall modifies this pattern. While there is conflict between generations, a fundamental battle takes place within the group of immigrants and, in this novel, within marriage itself. Moreover, the author reverses another pattern in the assigning of gender roles. Here it is not the mother-wife but the husband-father who is the bearer of the old culture, while it is the woman who aggressively explores the possibilities of the new world. A dialectic of difference is thus created as these two necessarily contend for dominance within the family. The synthesis that is brought about in the end—the daughter Selina—combines a need for understanding the homeland of Barbados with a need to act in the new home of the United States.

The polarities of the novel are defined through the characters of Deighton and Silla Boyce. Deighton is consistently associated with sensuous experience: the warmth of the sun, the feel of silk, the taste of rum. He dreams of returning to Barbados, which he sees as a space of relief from life's pointless struggles: "I going home and breathe good Bimshire air 'cause a man got a right to take his ease in this life and not always be scuffling" (85). The house that he plans to build there will not be a dark New York brownstone, but a house of light: "'I gon build it out of good Bajan coral stone, and paint it white. Everything gon be white! A gallery with tall white columns at the front like some temple or the other. . . . And upstairs 'nough bedrooms with their own bathroom—and every bathroom with a stained-glass window like in a church'" (86). He is rooted in a native Barbadian image of the good life, and he refuses, as we shall see, to modify this vision to fit the conditions of life in New York.

The religious imagery of temples and stained-glass in the quotation above suggests another traditional aspect of his character—a belief in magic. While he is not explicitly connected with obeah, the voodoo-like native religion of the island, he does seem to believe that goals are achieved through conjuration rather than hard work. While his wife works constantly to earn a down payment for a brownstone, he is given land back in Barbados when his sister dies. He believes that one masters accounting or music not by learning the fundamentals but by intuitively grasping the most complex levels: "'I ain got time to be practicing no scales or learning those foolish little pieces the teacher give me. I looking to play real songs—and fast'" (84).

Marshall locates Deighton's attitude in his complicated island past.[2] He was, we are told by other characters, spoiled by his mother, who worked very hard to provide him with everything, even a good education. Her protectiveness encouraged in him irresponsibility. In this sense, the island was for him a place of pleasure, of desires fulfilled. But, paradoxically, a very different kind of treatment reinforced his view of life. The white masters of the island repeatedly humiliated him despite his education and intelligence. This encouraged in him a belief that there was no purpose in hard work, since, in a white-dominated world, black skin automatically meant inferiority. Only by chance or magic could one overcome such racism. Deighton's motive for coming to the United States then is backward looking; he seeks that magic or chance that will enable him to return to Barbados on something like equal terms with the whites. He has no interest then in American values or property; he is only in the States awaiting an opportunity to return to his real home.

But his experience in this country is similar; after half-heartedly studying accounting for two years, he seeks employment at "the three places offering the best salary" (82). When Silla points out that such unfounded ambition is doomed to failure, he articulates his philosophy:

"I ain looking for nothing small. I ain been studying this course off and on for near two years to take no small job. Tha's the trouble with wunna colored people. Wunna is satisfy with next skin to nothing. Please Mr. White-man, gimme little bit. Please Mr. White-man, le' the boy go to Harrison College [in Barbados] so he can be a schoolmaster making $10.00 a month. Please Mr. White-man, lemma buy one these old house you don want no more. No, I ain with wunna. It got to be something big for me 'cause I got big plans or nothing a-tall. That's the way a man does things!" (82-83)

Thus, he seeks to transcend rather than overcome the hard facts of both the old and the new worlds. He leaves Barbados when racial domination threatens his manhood. In the United States, rather than risk similar humiliation, he guarantees his own material failure through inadequate preparation; he then blames the failure on racism. Even the choices he makes—accounting, music, and, later, religion—are abstract rather than concrete and thus permit him the temporary illusion that he can intuitively grasp their mysteries. But such illusion is essentially an evasion of reality; Deighton's claim of self-expression through them is paradoxically a means of escape from the truth of self. The refusal to beg and accept second-best—a refusal he sees as one aspect of manhood—leads to impotence because he rejects any realistic alternatives to Silla and the Barbadian community's quest for a place in America. His desire for return to his "real home" in Barbados is illusory; it is no real home, but an imaginary space free from conflict and need. It suggests the irony of his values.

His proud claim of manhood through magic and transcendence demonstrates how thoroughly he has come to believe in the real-world omnipotence of whites. Status and wealth cannot be earned by a black man in a white-dominated world. Therefore, self-preservation requires the creation of a mythic self located in its hilltop Barbadian temple.

His wife Silla, in stark contrast, is obsessed with having a home in her new land. For her, Barbados was a place of suffering: "'School, ha!' Her sardonic laugh twisted the air. 'Yes, you might call it a school, but it ain the kind you thinking of, soul. The Third Class is a set of little children picking grass in a cane field from the time God sun rise in his heaven till it set. With some woman called a Driver to wash yuh tail in licks if yuh dare look up. Yes, working harder than a man at the age of ten . . .'" (45). For her, too, the world is a place of white domination, but the key issue is not whether one works hard, but for whom. New York becomes a place where one can begin to labor for oneself and one's children. It is not a stopover on the circular path back to Barbados, but a new beginning, a way of forgetting the past.

Marshall is careful, however, to make it clear that Silla's past also contained pleasure. At a wedding reception, she initially refuses the invitation of an old man to dance. He then reminds her of moments of enjoyment in the past:

> "But what wrong with you, Silla, that you change up so since you come to these people New York? You don does dance! You must think I forget how you used to be wucking yourself every Sat'day night when the Brumlee Band played on the pasture. You must think I forget how I see you dance once till you fall out for dead right there on the grass. You must think I forget, but, girl, I ain forget." (144)

The crucial element here is not the old man's forgetting, but Silla's. Such joyful abandon is not possible if one is to stay focused on the goals of status and property.

Given her perspective, it is appropriate that she is associated with winter, with darkness, with machinery, and with language used not for magic but for ideological manipulation. These are the conditions and tools of the new life of hard work and property accumulation. Sunlight, dancing, even sexual passion must be repressed so that all one's attention and energy can be focused on the task. And if those who have other values get in the way, then they must be evicted and, if necessary, destroyed.

One implication of these differences is a conflicting set of definitions of success.[3] This conflict is in some sense at the heart of the book's dialectic. For Deighton, success means the realm of freedom; for Silla, the realm of necessity. Success for Deighton is a transcendence of the petty concerns of life, of the constant "scuffling." Self-expression, unrestricted by racial or economic considerations, becomes the ideal. To be forced into accepting these limits is to allow oneself to be defined by others. Success is pleasure, dreams, freedom.

For Silla, it is very different: "'But c'dear, if you got a piece of man you want to see him make out like the rest. You want to see yourself improve. Isn't that why people does come to this place?'" (174). Success is defined as the acceptance of responsibility, of limitation. One is valued in terms of a standard of improvement, of achievement, not in terms of an absolute freedom. And this standard is precisely one defined by others, by the whole community of achievers. It is not individuality but conformity that is the measure of success. The ideal here is not Deighton but Percy Challenor, a neighbor: "The husband, Percy, worked in the same mattress factory with Selina's father and sold stockings at night to meet the two mortgages. Silla always said with grudging respect, 'But look at Percy. He's nothing but a work horse'" (54). To work constantly and to demand much of oneself and one's children, are the marks of success in the American context.

These differences are truly dialectical in that the interaction of them creates the attraction and repulsion that is the central drama of the novel. Deighton requires the reality principle that Silla represents in order to give nurture and substance to his being while he dreams. Someone must make provision so that he can dream of freedom. The very envisioning of a realm of freedom is premised on control of the realm of necessity. Alone, he becomes passive and childish; after his final humiliation, he turns to Father Peace, a patriarch who finally frees him from responsibility but only by stripping him of his humanity. Silla brought structure to his existence; without it, he ceased to be.

On the other hand, Silla is dehumanized by her rejection of Deighton. She becomes one with the machines she operates in the factory: "the mother was like the machines, some larger form of life with an awesome beauty all her own" (101). She devotes herself so fully to money-making and property accumulation that she represses her own womanhood. Repeatedly, the text describes moments of tenderness that she holds back from. It is only Deighton's passion that humanizes her, only his joy in life that brings laughter into her house. And it is her tragedy that she recognizes the value of his kind of dream, even while she works to destroy it. For while the two definitions of success are symbiotic, they are also mutually destructive. For Silla, to accept Deighton means to question the self-reification necessary to achieve her own ends; it means to step outside the security of community values; it means to renounce the positive identity and power gained through struggle. For Deighton, acceptance of Silla's definition of success means death, since it would require entrance into that realm where his failure is guaranteed. Also, there is no freedom or pleasure for those who devote themselves to accumulation; they are consciously sacrificing themselves for future generations. One of the spokesmen of the Barbadian Association makes this point explicit:

> "But tell me why we start this Association now when most of us gon soon be giving business to the undertaker? I gon tell you. It's because of the young people! Most of us did come to this man country with only the strength in we hand and a little learning in we head and had to make our way, but the young people have the opportunity to be professional and get out there and give these people big word for big word. Thus, they are our hope. They make all the sacrifice, all the struggle worth while." (221)

For Deighton, sacrifice and struggle are meaningless. They only confirm the values of the white masters. Thus, in order to survive, either Deighton or Silla must destroy the other, which means, of course, destroying a vital part of the self.

Appropriately, the cause of the battle to the death is the land Deighton inherits in Barbados. For him this represents the ideal of return, the means of enacting his island dream. It is the landscape on which his freedom and manhood can be realized. It marks in this sense an end in itself, a fulfillment of his potential. For Silla, it is valuable only as a commodity; it can be sold for money to buy a brownstone, which itself would be a springboard to even greater possessions. For her, there is no end, only endless improvement.

The struggle is necessarily an uneven one. By entering the world of possession, Deighton becomes enmeshed in the net of language and manipulation that Silla has made her own. The very land which symbolizes his freedom is conditioned by the deeds, contracts, and testaments that can defeat him. Silla consciously chooses to defeat him on these grounds. Significantly, she defines her action as sacrifice of both herself and him: "'Even if I got to see my soul fall howling into hell I gon do it,'" (75) and "'He's Christ to you. But wait. Wait till I finish with him. He gon be Christ crucified'" (77). She writes letters to Barbados, forging Deighton's signature, which eventually produce the sale of the land. Her deceit gains her enough money to make a down payment on her house. Her purpose seems to have been, not the destruction of Deighton's manhood, but the transformation of his values. She wanted the move from his land to hers, from his reality to hers. But matters are not so simple, since his identity is tied to those values. His final act of self-assertion is a ritual of excess in which he spends all the money from the sale on gifts for himself, his children, and even Silla. It is his ultimate refusal to turn dreams into objects of exchange. But this is also a ceremony of death, for it is apparent that the dreamer cannot survive in this world. He can deny Silla the fruits of her Faustian contract, but he cannot change the conditions in which he lives. Shortly after his largesse, he is injured in a factory accident, then joins Father Peace's church, where he can completely lose his identity. His deportation, based on Silla's betrayal of him to the authorities, and his suicide within sight of Barbados are only the physical manifestations of a destruction that has already taken place.

Thus, symbolically the new culture has overcome the old; the concentrated forward-looking energy of Silla has uprooted the pleasurable but backward-looking dreaming of Deighton. But what remains is a kind of emptiness. Silla haunts the halls of the house she now owns, constantly watching the boarders. She seldom sleeps in her bed, but rather spends the nights cleaning the house. Without Deighton, there is no passion, only work. Without any alternative values available, she becomes machine-like in her efforts for her children. She, too, has in a sense died.

But dialectically this is necessary for the emergence of the synthesis, which is the daughter Selina. She is repeatedly identified with both parents; the neighborhood consistently calls her "Deighton Selina," but they also see her mother's features and attitudes in her. Even as a child, she has the dreaminess of her father along with Silla's assertiveness. At this early stage, she deeply loves Deighton and spends time with him while she fears the woman she calls "the mother": "It was as though the mother knew all that had transpired in the house since morning—her father's idleness, her quarrel with Ina, the news of the land—and was coming to chastise them all" (16).

Like her father, Selina is open to a wide range of experiences, though in her case these tend to be the experiences important to the development of a girl into a woman. She listens to the dying white woman living upstairs who recalls her own early romances; from her friend Beryl she learns about the physiological changes taking place in her body; Miss Thompson gives her advice about being a black woman in a white man's country; and Suggie, who also lives in the house, shows her the value of enjoyment of her body. Thus, the coming-of-age aspect of the novel, which in women's literature is often associated with the body,[4] here reinforces one side of the cultural-sexual conflict. In the father's expression rather than the mother's repression, Selina finds encouragement in trying to understand her own biology, an understanding brought about through the assistance of female figures that the mother considers disreputable.

Geta Leseur has suggested that Suggie and Miss Thompson serve as developmental mentors for Selina in her emergence into womanhood (119-29). Suggie is the female version of Deighton in her love of pleasure and her nostalgia for Barbados. Though she works hard at menial labor, her real life involves maintaining connections with the past through food, dress, and memory and in finding physical enjoyment through her various lovers. She specifically rejects the values of the Barbadian Association and sees herself as a life-affirming alternative to them. And it is she who urges Selina, after Deighton's death, to give up her obsession with mourning and replace it with love. If Suggie represents female passion, Miss Thompson is a literal embodiment of female suffering. Her story of victimization at the hands of white men teaches Selina important lessons about the double jeopardy of being black and a woman. But she is also an example of the ability of such women to endure suffering. Thus, both Suggie and Miss Thompson provide Selina with a sense of womanhood that neither parent can provide.

Nonetheless, Selina recognizes and respects Silla's strength. Even when the mother rages against her husband and children, even when Selina feels she must resist in self-protection, she still sees Silla as the center of being:

> Outwardly she was unyielding still, still uninvolved. But inside she was frightened by the thought of those memories always clashing within the mother. She was afraid that they would rend the mother soon and kill her finally, and she

would be left without her. The world would collapse then, for wasn't the mother, despite all, its only prop? (46)

This imagery, along with later associations Selina makes between her mother and the machines, contrasts nicely with the image of Deighton as a "dark god" fallen to earth. For the daughter, one parent provides the structure and daily working of the world, while the other gives it its vitality and its glory. In the conflict over the land, Selina sides with her father, though in the manner of her mother she urges him to active resistance.

After his death, Silla seeks to reshape her daughter to fit her values, but Selina has her own ideas. While she goes to college to please her mother, she also finds herself a boyfriend and an art form—dancing—which are unacceptable to the mother. The boyfriend Clive is a world-weary version of Deighton. He has the same passivity and an artistic sensibility, but he does not believe in anything, including his painting. Selina seems to select him precisely because of his similarity to her father and therefore because he signifies rebellion against the mother.

But Clive is no "dark god." He is world-weary rather than worldly. All the passion has gone out of him, and he is left only with a strong but cynical power of language. Selina, in her innocence, believes that her love can join with his intelligence and aestheticism to fully empower both of them. In this sense, her rebellion carries positive connotations. Her passionate womanhood can help to create a relationship and a self that transcend the limitations of her parents.

But, in her more explicit act of rebellion, her plot to get money from the Association so that she and Clive can go away together, she ironically re-enacts her mother's betrayal of her father. But her fraudulence is an affirmation of love, not a betrayal of it. And again, the man's passivity is crucial to the event. Clive lacks the strength of character to leave his mother and risk an encounter with the world. Faced with this situation, Selina reverses her mother's behavior and refuses to take the money, even for its intended purpose. She rejects the world of the mother, but she will not take unfair advantage of it.

What enables her to establish true independence is her discovery of a form of self-expression, dance, which reconciles the principles of father and mother. Consistent with the dialectical pattern of the novel, Selina discovers modern dance at the college her mother wished her to attend in order to enter a money-making profession. Thus, it gives her the opportunity to generate her own meaning out of the experience dictated by her mother. Unlike her father, she has mastered the mysteries of her expressive form through hard work and discipline. Unlike her mother, she takes Suggie-like pleasure in what her body can do. Her self begins to take shape through a process of differentiation from her parents that is also an absorption of their identities. As Sabine Brock has suggested, dance for Selina is the mechanism by which she creates her own place/space (83).

Moreover, it produces the circumstance in which she directly and personally encounters racism. Appropriately, the confrontation occurs after she has danced the birth-to-death cycle at her recital; the performance, the content of the dance, and the confrontation form a complex initiatory moment. The triumph of her artistry is juxtaposed to the meeting with the white woman as a way of revealing simultaneously the possibilities and limitations of Selina's emerging black womanhood. Margaret's mother assaults Selina's identity not so much by direct racist attack as by her assumption that blackness excludes individual identity. Thus, the woman equates Selina with her former West Indian maid and cannot see her as the young Brooklyn-born dancer, but only as another "specimen" of blackness: "Those eyes were a well-lighted mirror in which, for the first time, Selina truly saw—with a sharp and shattering clarity—the full meaning of her black skin" (289).

Selina's response to this insight is complex. Her initial anger and desire to escape are quickly replaced by the recognition that she herself has internalized some dislike for blackness, a view evident from the beginning of the book, where she identifies with the white family that once owned her family's brownstone. But she now also makes her own Miss Thompson's earlier advice:

> Exhausted, she fell against the glass [of a store window], her feverish face striking the cold one there, crying suddenly because their idea of her was only an illusion, yet so powerful that it would stalk her down the years, confront her in each mirror and from the safe circle of her eyes, surprise her even in the gleaming surface of a table. It would intrude in every corner of her life, tainting her small triumphs—as it had tonight—and exulting at her defeats. She cried because, like all her kinsmen, she must somehow prevent it from destroying her inside and find a way for her real face to emerge. (291)

Her solution to this problem is neither that of Deighton, who evades reality, nor that of Silla, who denies her self in the quest for security through acquisition. Rather, Selina joins their positive elements through art. She rejects the values of the Barbadian Association, but accepts the need for hard work to perfect her self-expression. She affirms the past, not through Deighton's nostalgia, but through a proposed return to the islands to learn traditional dance, which she will join to the modern techniques she has gained through practice in New York. Thus, her art can transcend cultural limitations by joining tradition and modernity, old and new worlds, Western and Afro-Caribbean expressive forms. Barbados can be a place of education, that value of her mother's, but education in the imagination. At the same time, the intended return is an affirmation of her blackness, a way of gaining strength for the endless struggle against those who would deny her black female identity. Consistent with the openendedness of struggle is the unspecified character of the dance that will emerge from Selina's experience. It, like her self, is in process of articulation rather than a completed form.

Finally, then, Paule Marshall defines selfhood as the joining of self-expression to self-control, of style to substance, of abstraction to materiality, of dream to reality, and of suffering to joy. The self is itself a dialectical process, constantly negotiating its many polarities; any attempt to structure a monolithic identity is destructive and life-denying. She is also asserting that art is the ideal means by which self can be empowered. To bring the story full circle, she herself finds an empowering voice in recreating those Bajan voices of her childhood. By constructing a narrative in standard American English that incorporates the oral patterns of those women, she gives them voice and at the same time shapes them to her ends. By constructing a narrative that explores the costs of restricted visions, she allows her own dialectical perception to emerge. Thus, Selina's dance becomes the metaphor of her author's own literary identity. The telling of the story of developing black womanhood in this first novel makes evident the power of Paule Marshall's own black female voice.

NOTES

1. See Fine, 102-117, for a discussion of the characteristics of immigrant fiction.

2. Here and elsewhere in her fiction, Marshall views the Barbadian experience as one in which, under the conditions of colonialism, all blacks, female and male, are usually made to work at menial labor. Deighton's past in this sense is deliberately made very different so as to foreground the dialectic of the narrative.
3. It is not insignificant that "manhood" is the term Marshall uses most often as a synonym for "success." Despite the power of women in her narrative, she recognizes that both the native and the immigrant societies are patriarchal in character. Silla's initial task, in this sense, is not to supplant Deighton but to force him to accept his role as patriarch.
4. See Gubar.

WORKS CITED

Brock, Sabine. "Transcending the 'Loophole of Retreat': Paule Marshall's Placing of Female Generations." *Callaloo* 10.1 (1987): 79-90.
DeVeaux, Alexis. "Paule Marshall—In Celebration of Our Triumphs." *Essence* May 1979: 70+.
Fine, David M. *The City, The Immigrant and American Fiction, 1880-1920*. Metuchen: Scarecrow, 1977.
Gubar, Susan. "'The Blank Page' and the Issues of Female Creativity." *Writing and Sexual Difference*. Ed. Elizabeth Abel. Chicago: U of Chicago P, 1982. 73-93.
Leseur, Geta J. "*Brown Girl, Brownstones* as Novel of Development." *Obsidian II* 1.3 (1986): 119-29.
Marshall, Paule. *Brown Girl, Brownstones*. 1959. London: Virago, 1982.
———. *The Chosen Place, The Timeless People*. New York: Harcourt, 1969.
———. *Praisesong for the Widow*. New York: Putnam's, 1983.

Self-Representation as Art in the Novels of Nella Larsen

Jacquelyn Y. McLendon

Nella Marian Larsen was born Nellie Marie on April 13, 1891. She was the daughter of a Danish mother and a Black West Indian father. Her father died when she was two years old and shortly afterward her mother married a Danish man by whom she had a second daughter. Thus, Larsen was raised in an all white family and in predominantly white surroundings. She attended schools in Chicago, Illinois, including a small private elementary school with children of primarily German and Scandinavian backgrounds.

At age sixteen, Larsen entered the predominantly black Fisk University Normal School (a high school) and remained for one year, 1907-08. A few years later she traveled to Denmark, where she visited with relatives and audited courses at the University of Copenhagen for three years. On her return to America, she entered a three-year nursing course at Lincoln Hospital in New York, graduating in 1915 and beginning a short career as a nurse. She left nursing in 1921 and worked as a librarian before embarking on her brief literary career.

In the meantime, on May 3, 1919, Larsen married Elmer Samuel Imes, a black physicist who later became chairman of the Physics Department at Fisk University. The marriage was unsuccessful, ending in divorce in 1933. A short time later, Larsen disappeared from the literary scene altogether, returned to her former career of nursing and worked at it until her death on March 30, 1964.

Larsen published one short story, "Sanctuary," in The Forum in 1930 and was accused by a reader of having plagiarized a story printed eight years earlier in Century magazine. The editors investigated the matter and exonerated Larsen, but scholars believe the incident was at least partially responsible for her subsequent literary silence. While her *personal correspondence indicates that she began several projects, including the one for which she won a Guggenheim Fellowship, nothing more was published; therefore, Larsen's literary career rests on the two novels,* Quicksand *(1928) and* Passing *(1929).*

> We have always been imagining ourselves....
> We are the subjects of our own narrative,
> witnesses to and participants in our own
> experience, and, in no way coincidentally,
> in the experience of those with whom we have come
> in contact. We are not, in fact,
> "other." We are choices. And to read imaginative
> literature by and about us is to choose to
> examine centers of the self....
> -Tony Morrison
> "Unspeakable Things Unspoken: The Afro-American Presence in American Literature"

> So detached and cool she is
> No motion e'er betrays
> The secret life within her soul
> The anguish of her days.
> -Clarissa Scott Delaney, "The Mask"

> I'm white, I'm white inside
> But that don't help my case,
> Cause I can't hide
> What is on my face.
> -Fats Waller
> "What Did I Do To Be So Black and Blue?"

Nella Larsen, black woman writer of the Harlem Renaissance, wrote only two novels, *Quicksand* (1928) and *Passing* (1929), during her brief literary career, both of which feature light-skinned middle and upper-middle-class black women protagonists and their struggles to move from margin to center. In an often quoted letter to Carl Van Vechten, white author, critic, and a patron of black arts, Larsen wrote of her first novel *Quicksand*, "It's the awful truth. But, who knows if I'll get through the damned thing. Certainly not I."[1] Although the facts known about her life are sketchy, enough details are known to substantiate what this comment suggests, that the book is, indeed, autobiographical. Yet, while there is value in reading it as such, a subject to which I will return momentarily, a primary interest of this text, as well as of *Passing*, lies in its critique of conventional narrative forms and subjects. That is to say, in both *Quicksand* and *Passing*, Larsen explores the metaphorical cogency of the figure of the mulatto (and of passing in the latter text) as an image of wider, or at least different, matters than simplistic dualism.

To claim a particular artistic value is not to argue against reading the texts as autobiographical, for they clearly are, as a brief recitation of the facts known about Larsen's life will reveal. Like her protagonist Helga Crane in *Quicksand*, Larsen was born of mixed parentage—a Danish mother and a black West Indian father. Her father died when she was two, and soon after his death her mother married a Danish man by whom she had a second daughter. Thus, Larsen grew up in an all white family and in predominantly white surroundings.

At age sixteen, however, she was plunged into the predominantly black environment of Fisk University's Normal School (a high school). Since she had lived all her life among whites and attended white schools, critics speculate that she was lonely and uncomfortable at Fisk and that this may have led her to travel to Denmark, where she visited with relatives and audited courses at the University of Copenhagen for three years. On her return to the United States, Larsen re-entered a black environment, and it is probably safe to say that she had felt no more comfortable in Copenhagen, among whites, than at Fisk. Perhaps like Helga Crane she grew "tired of being stared at," of feeling she did not belong but rather that she was "a curiosity, a stunt, at which people came and gazed."[2] She does make specific reference to having such feelings in her later life, and it is a certainty that she felt, like Helga, that she was an embarrassment to her white relations, even to her mother and sister. As she stated in an interview with Thelma E. Berlack of the *Amsterdam News* after the publication of *Quicksand*, "I don't see my family much now. It might make it awkward for them, particularly my half-sister."[3] Other details of the author's life follow closely events and situations in the book but these are perhaps the most salient.

Less apparent is the autobiographical nature of *Passing*, but it is equally influenced by the fact that Larsen was herself a mulatto and felt deeply the injustices of racism and sexism. The alienation, the unhappy marriages, and passing, among other themes she explores in the book, all reflect a world with which Larsen was indeed familiar.

For example, like Irene Redfield, Larsen was curious about and experimented with passing. In a letter to Van Vechten, she describes one such escapade in the "deep south" in which she and Grace Johnson "walked into the best restaurant in a rather conservative town ... and demanded lunch and got it, plus all the service in the world and an invitation to return."[4] Further, the depiction of Irene's pain and suffering brought on by her belief that her husband and Clare are having an affair is possibly all the more real for Larsen's having suffered through the discovery of her own husband's affair, through their divorce and his remarriage—all of which are written of in her personal correspondence. Finally, her correspondence also reveals her feelings of alienation both from her immediate family, as mentioned previously, and from the black race.[5]

Certainly there are advantages and disadvantages in reading the texts through the framework of "fictions of the self."[6] One advantage is that at this crucial moment in literary history when we are attempting to define and forge a space for (black) women's texts within that history, a reading of Larsen's texts as autobiographical situates them within—at the same time helping to (re)construct—a literary tradition that is both black and female. Her presentation of the "awful truth," even fictionalized, recalls antecedent black texts such as *Incidents in the Life of a Slave Girl* in which the author, Harriet Jacobs, was constrained to tell her story under a pseudonym and in which she "concealed the names of places, and [gave] persons fictitious names." Another such text is Harriet Wilson's *Our Nig; or, Sketches from the Life of a Free Black*, which fuses, as Henry Louis Gates, Jr. argues in his Introduction to the book, "parallel discursive universes," fiction and autobiography, resulting in a "transformation of the black-as-object into the black-as-subject" (lv). That Larsen's novels are intertexts of these and other works by black women argues, too, for Barbara Smith's notion that "Black women writers manifest common approaches to the act of creating literature as a direct result of the specific political, social, and economic experience they have been obliged to share."[7]

Unfortunately, the moment one chooses to view the texts in this way, one runs the risk of unwittingly marginalizing them. That is to say, while critics and scholars of African-American literature approve and even praise, for example, Langston Hughes's writing out of his own milieu, they often view Larsen's writing out of hers as a limitation—indeed, a failure—of her novels. To be more specific, Robert Bone argues that Larsen "wished to orient Negro art toward white opinion" (97). Feminist critic Barbara Christian, in *Black*

Women Novelists, unfortunately echoes past male critics (especially Nathan Huggins) by arguing that "the uninhibited female was too reminiscent of the loose-woman image" and so Larsen chose instead "to make [her] heroines light-complexioned, upper-middle-class black women with taste and refinement" (41-42). These comments are reductionist and presuppose the very concepts for which Larsen is often attacked. Such criticism also minimizes the importance of her contribution to the Harlem Renaissance by keeping her outside so-called "mainstream" Renaissance literature.

For Larsen, writing about the self was an enabling strategy. Because she was a mulatto, she felt "more qualified than any white" to write about the mulatto experience. She, along with several other writers of the Harlem Renaissance, was "affected" by the portraits of mulattoes in precursory American fiction by white writers, especially the portrait of Peter Siner in T. S. Stribling's *Birthright*. As Jessie Fauset pointed out in an interview, they all felt that Stribling's protagonist was not a "successful study of Negro life" (Starkey 217-20). In fact, in almost every instance, including Stribling's book, the mulatto is depicted as the victim of persistent longing and unattainable desires aroused by his mixed blood. Larsen, on the other hand, moves beyond the stereotype in providing non-biological motivations for her characters' behavior based on many of her own real life experiences.[8]

Besides a desire to render a more accurate portrayal of the mulatto, Larsen recognized the possibilities of revising this figure to explore the concept of doubleness as it inheres in the experience of African-Americans generally, not just in the mulatto's experience, to satirize the bourgeois class, and to explore the Eros/celibacy dilemma in regard to female sexuality. Moreover, Larsen "writes herself" in order to rewrite history, to reinterpret certain cultural signs, to redefine tradition, and to move from margin to center in her own life. Valerie Smith addresses several of these issues in *Self-Discovery and Authority in Afro-American Narrative*. She argues that "the protagonist-narrators of certain twentieth century novels by Afro-American writers affirm and legitimize their psychological autonomy by telling the stories of their own lives. . . ." Smith argues further not only that "the process of authorship" gives these writers a "measure of authority" but also, and more importantly, that "in their manipulation of received literary conventions they also engage with and challenge the dominant ideology" (2). This latter impulse in Larsen's writing defines the focus of this essay.

In *Quicksand*, Larsen's "manipulation of received literary conventions" may be seen in her use of the trope of the tragic mulatto as organizing metaphor. Appearance vs. reality, marginality, and entrapment, all intrinsic to the figure of the mulatto, are consonant with the strategies she employs in structuring the text and with its content. For example, a recurring pattern of enclosure and escape is manifested in the protagonist's frantic movement back and forth between the various geographic locations that provide the book's settings. She moves from Naxos to Chicago, from Chicago to New York, from there to Copenhagen, back to New York, and finally to the "tiny Alabama Town" from which she does not escape, movement indicative of the "restlessness" associated with the stereotype but here involving profoundly more—especially the protagonist's inner conflicts about her sexuality.

Imagery evocative of sexual desire and orgasmic release is present from the very beginning of the novel, at first vague and indefinite but increasingly explicit as Helga moves closer to actual sexual fulfillment in the later chapters. The frustration and yearning, followed by frantic, nervous energy, and then by peace and contentment—"transformation"—correspond to her intense movement from city to city. Thus, Helga's dilemma, her inability to "belong anywhere," cannot be seen simply in black and white terms. Larsen's depiction of the causes of Helga's restlessness shows a profound understanding of the intimate association of race, sex, and personal identity.

Helga Crane's actions admit of numerous explanations, not the least of which is her "unloved, unloving, and unhappy childhood" (63). Larsen gives us glimpses of that childhood through Helga's sporadic recollections, prompted most often by some hurt or longing she is experiencing as an adult. Helga's tragedy is caused by the non-biological and realistic experience, indeed, the double alienation, of a child "living among hostile white folks" or trying to fit in with blacks with whom "you [had to] prove your ancestry and connections," otherwise "you didn't belong" (34).

Larsen's treatment of Helga's childhood unhappiness is one of the significant ways in which she revises the figure of the tragic mulatto. That is, she inverts the pseudo-scientific correlation between the tragic mulatto and the blood theory by showing the influence of childhood environment and relationships (or non-relationships) on the formation of the adult. This same inversion has the effect, too, of dispelling the myth of the innate frigidity of light-skinned women. As a child, Helga witnessed the destruction of her own mother, who had been "flung into poverty, sordidness, and dissipation" for "forgetting all but love" (54-55). As a result, Helga grew up believing that society punishes passion. She, therefore, ignores her love for and sexual attraction to Dr. Robert Anderson, principal of Naxos College because she is afraid—not frigid.

The inhibitions of the male characters are also explored in the book. For example, Robert Anderson is unable to face his sexuality and his feelings for Helga. His marriage to her friend Anne is a manifestation of "his ascetic protest against the sensuous, the physical," and a denial of "that nameless and to him shameful impulse, that sheer delight, which ran through his nerves at mere proximity to Helga" (161). Larsen explores the inhibitions of males as varied as Robert Anderson and James Vayle, members of the black middle-class; the white Axel Olsen, an artist who lives in Copenhagen; and the Reverend Mr. Pleasant Green, a small town preacher and lower-class black. These portraits reinforce Larsen's negation of the myth regarding the innate frigidity of the light-skinned female, the alleged opposite of the dark-skinned loose woman, and thereby inveigh against the correlation of values with color or "blood." She provides, instead, a satiric commentary on middle-class mentality and on what it means to be "civilized" by suggesting that people may be as much imprisoned by their over-dependence on rationality as by an overdependence on emotion.

Helga's seduction of the Reverend Mr. Pleasant Green carries further Larsen's rejection of the frigidity myth, and the scene of the church revival at which Helga meets Green is a grotesque mosaic of all the themes and metaphors which converge on the central motif of entrapment. Larsen depicts the inextricability of gender and sexual oppression in this scene in which the women behave like crazed animals, crawling around on their hands and knees while the men watch. The women shout accusingly at Helga to "repent," calling her "a scarlet 'oman," and a "pore los' Jezebel" even as they themselves behave in ways that cause the scene to take on a "Bacchic vehemence," which Helga likens to a "weird orgy": "Behind her, before her, beside her, frenzied women gesticulated, screamed, wept, and tottered to the praying of the preacher, which had gradually become a cadenced shout" (188). Inevitably, Helga, too, becomes "Maddened . . . and with no previous intention began to yell like one insane" (189).

The contradiction between the holier-than-thou accusations the women direct at Helga and their own behavior, the embodiment of elements of the grotesque which shock us into recognition of the unnaturalness of their actions, imply a symbolic repudiation of women's subjugation and the suppression of their natural emotions. They are allowed to express their feelings only under the guise of religious fervor. Significantly, when Helga seduces a man whose name she can't even remember, she is "half-hypnotized" by her religious experience, and this begins Larsen's critique of religion and what Helga calls a "fatuous belief in the white man's God" (219), conflated here with her critique of culturally prescribed roles for women.

More importantly, though, with this encounter between Green and Helga, Larsen explores a subject that hardly fits in with the notion that she chose to depict only refined characters. What Helga feels for Green is lust, a feeling that has been the exclusive privilege of men, and Larsen explores it as a very real feeling women experience. In her wish to continue to fulfill her sexual desires, Helga ignores "her first disgust at the odor of sweat and stale garments," ignores the "atmosphere of self-satisfaction which poured from [Green] like gas from a leaking pipe" and waits eagerly for "night . . . at the end of every day. Emotional, palpitating, amorous, all that was living in her sprang like rank weeds at the tingling thought of night, with a vitality so strong that it devoured all shoots of reason" (202).

Helga is not subsequently defeated by this eroticism, as Robert Bone argues she is, but by society's condemnation of it, which weighs heavily in her choosing the wrong man. Her one regret in terms of her sexuality is that she did not recognize it earlier, that she did not respond to the feelings she had always experienced with Robert Anderson. Instead, she is destined to live, or die, with a husband she comes to hate, who uses her for his sexual gratification without regard for her feelings. In exploring this aspect of Helga's life, Larsen raises serious questions not only about female eroticism but also about the institution of marriage: "This sacred thing of which parsons and other Christian folk ranted so sanctimoniously, how immoral—according to their own standards—it could be" (220)!

The novel ends "And hardly had she left her bed and become able to walk again without pain . . . when she began to have her fifth child." For the sake of her children, Helga remains in the "bog into which she had strayed"—"she couldn't desert them" (221). Complaints about this ending abound because critics feel it is unconvincing, that Larsen creates a strong, rebellious character in Helga Crane only to have her recapitulate. Deborah McDowell argues, in her Introduction to the book, that "While Larsen criticizes the cover of marriage, as well as other social scripts for women, she is unable in the end to extend that critique to its furthest reaches" (xxx). It seems to me that the ending does not involve the issue of Larsen's ability but of narrative intent. Larsen titled the book *Quicksand*, a self-revelatory metaphor, one that captures the essence of Helga's struggle and foretells her fate.

While it is true that Helga rebels, the text tells us that she could not be "happy in her nonconformity" (33). Her own untenable position in society is precisely that which makes it possible for her to see through the myths that condone racism and sexism. But that she has insight, that she questions and even condemns, does not mean she has solutions to the problems. To return to the central metaphor, the entire book shows her slowly being pulled into the quicksand against which she struggles but against which she is powerless. I would argue, then, that the ending is part of the larger design of the book, that, in fact, Helga's sacrifice does not weaken it; rather, it forces "internal dialogue into the open,"[9] forces us to face the questions Larsen raises about marriage, motherhood, gender/sexual oppression, and, generally, about the unresolved tension between personal desire and societal expectation.

These very questions become central themes in Larsen's second and last book, *Passing*. Yet, as with *Quicksand*, analyses which focus on strictly thematic concerns will run the risk of missing Larsen's several points. Indeed, her narrative strategies provide ways to engage the text in more rigorous analyses. More particularly, the novel's parodic nature shapes and defines content, privileging not only its intertextuality but also a wide range of reading possibilities.

The simple title *Passing* suggests that what is to follow is the classic tale of the mulatto who tries to escape the miseries of black life by passing for white. Clare Kendry, one of Larsen's two women protagonists, to some extent embodies the stereotype. She physically abandons the race, marries a white man, eventually becomes dissatisfied with her "pale existence," and dies at the novel's end while allegedly trying to reestablish racial ties. However, Larsen again inverts the pseudo-scientific correlation between the tragic mulatto and the blood theory, this time by portraying a woman who makes a conscious decision to pass based on her desire for economical security and comfort as opposed to one who simply falls victim to the unfolding of inevitable biological events.

More significantly, Larsen revises this narrative form by presenting another character, Irene Redfield, who rarely passes but resorts to other kinds of disguise and erasure to escape the difficulties of being black and female, thereby experiencing, as completely as Clare, a loss of racial and cultural ties. With the characterization of Irene,

Larsen postulates the notion that passing is as much a state of mind as a physical act, imparting a parodic thrust to the received social meaning. The title, then, is ambiguous in that it refers both to Clare's actions, retaining the usual meaning of the word, and to Irene's actions, implying psychological passing or escapism. In short, passing may be regarded as any form of pretense or disguise that results in a loss or surrender of, or a failure to satisfy a desire for, identity—whether racial, cultural, social, or sexual.

The text comments on this concept of passing in a number of ways that provide a framework through which to examine its parodic nature. In one instance the text tells us that "Appearances . . . had a way of sometimes not fitting the facts,"[10] which is demonstrated not only through Larsen's use of the trope of passing but also through her satiric portrayal of the black bourgeois class. At another point, in response to a white character's admission that he found it impossible to distinguish blacks like Clare from whites, Irene says,"Nobody can. Not by looking" (132), which is another way of suggesting that there is a discrepancy between appearance and reality. Further, this scene and the scene in which Clare's white husband proclaims his hatred for blacks while unknowingly in the company of three black women and married to one of them are both ironic inversions of the concept that "blood tells,"[11] a *donnée* of conventional treatments of passing and the tragic mulatto.

Finally, the text provides a definition of passing that shares the ambiguity of the title. Passing is described as the "breaking away from all that was familiar and friendly to take one's chance in another environment, not entirely strange perhaps, but certainly not entirely friendly" (53). Irene uses this definition to describe Clare's passing, but it might just as easily describe her own. Irene Redfield, in her strict adherence to bourgeois ideological codes, strives to mask any feelings or behavior that appears to be uncivilized or unladylike, measures herself by white standards, and lives in constant imitation of whites.

It is this ironic similarity in their situations that Larsen emphasizes by juxtaposing the lives of her two women protagonists. She uses similar language to describe them and draws parallels between Clare's lack of security and sense of permanence in passing for white and Irene's in imitating whites. Clare's "longing" and Irene's "futile searching," Clare's "dark secret" and Irene's "fear" reveal the complexity of their shared experience, that they are, in fact, psychological doubles—not only in ways tied to race but also in their feelings about their roles as women, as mothers and wives.

This notion that Clare and Irene are psychological doubles has structural as well as thematic significance, revealed primarily through the text's narrative point of view. For reasons I will discuss in more detail later, it is helpful here to appropriate Roland Barthes's method of establishing a text's point of view as he outlines it in *Image-Music-Text*. He argues that narration "knows only two systems of signs: personal and apersonal" and they "do not necessarily present the linguistic marks attached to person (I) and non-person (he)" (112). To make the distinction, Barthes suggests rewriting passages of the text using a first-person pronoun to replace the third. If the only change is a change of grammatical pronouns, we can identify a "personal system." In *Passing*, the text that reads, for example, "But she looked, boldly this time, back into the eyes still frankly intent upon her" (41) might easily read, "But I [Irene Redfield] looked, boldly this time, back into the eyes still frankly intent upon me." This substitution of grammatical pronouns may be made easily for Irene's discourse throughout the text but not for Clare's. It is clear that this is Irene's narrative since much of the text surfaces in her mind through these "narrative episodes . . . which though written in the third person nevertheless have as their true instance the first person" (Barthes 112). This narrational mode creates a disguised "I," as it were, emphasizing Irene's repression and the use of passing as structure.[12]

Barthes's method is useful here for several reasons. First, by identifying the "personal system," we identify the dominant point of view as that of a character and not of the author, which is especially crucial in reading Larsen's text because critics often curiously confuse the two, forgetting that while the impetus for Larsen's novels might be autobiographical, they are still and foremost fictional. Identifying the "personal system," that is to say, establishing the point of view as predominantly Irene's, helps to negate the postulates of critics who see the characters' flaws merely as extensions of Larsen's own because it affirms that "Who writes (in real life) is not who speaks (in the narrative) and who speaks is not who is" (Barthes 111-112). In Larsen's text there is no single, ultimately authoritative voice; therefore, we can conclude that what the text represses is an indication of what Irene, the character, represses.

Second, it becomes clear that while Clare has an important function in the narrative, again, it is not her narrative, and therefore we must reconsider conclusions drawn about the text that minimize the significance of Irene's role.[13] For example, the way in which Clare's death is interpreted depends upon whether or not we recognize that Irene's complicity in that death is as important as, if not more important than, the death itself. Further, by directing our attention to Irene, to her perception of Clare and her denial of any similarities between them, the narrative point of view subverts the pathos usually associated with the tragic mulatto and conveys instead irony in its revelation of the two as psychological doubles.

Third and more significant is that identifying the "personal system" enables us to deepen our analysis by examining the ways in which the disguised "I" corresponds generally with disguise or masking as it figures in the concept of passing and specifically with Irene's need to disguise (repress) her true feelings. I am not suggesting that Larsen consciously effects the kind of distinction Barthes makes, but rather that examining the ways in which the narrative point of view operates in the text may be facilitated by such an approach. We may be sure, however, that making the dominant point of view that of a woman who represses all her feelings and, to borrow from Deborah McDowell, "deludes herself"[14] is a strategy Larsen consciously uses to explore the psychological dimensions of passing—its causes and effects.

Larsen explores the ways in which Irene, as much as Clare, is to some extent responsible for her own dilemma: as Clare disguises her heritage, Irene chooses to mask certain feelings and behavior in order to live up to societal expectations. Yet, the text supports even more the idea of external coercion for her actions and therefore the disguised "I" might itself function as a trope for the figures of silence, invisibility, and consequent powerlessness. A telling example is a scene in which Irene visits Clare at her apartment in Chicago and is constrained to keep silent while Clare's white husband, John Bellew, denigrates blacks. Irene's impulse to defend blacks is met by a "start from the uncomfortable Gertrude, and, for all her appearance of serenity, a quick apprehensive look from Clare" (77-78). The outcome is that "The impulse passed, obliterated by her [Irene's] consciousness of the danger in which such rashness would involve Clare . . . " (78).

In reality, the danger is as palpable for one as for the other, a fact we learn in the opening scene when the arrival of a letter from Clare sends Irene into a state of panic that totally paralyzes her. Significantly, for the entire first section, almost one-half of the book, Irene sits frozen at her desk. Further, when the narrative does move forward again, Bellew is physically absent and does not reappear until very near the end when his wife dies. Thus, while Irene's fear stems in part from her belief that Clare's tendency to risk danger might in some way impinge upon her own safety, at the beginning of section two, the text tells us that her fear is also stimulated by the letter's being a strong reminder of Bellew and his hatred for blacks. Her effort to convince herself that her fear and consequently her silence, indeed, her paralysis, stem from her need to protect Clare is an example of Irene's tendency to deny reality and also an indication that the fear goes much deeper: "She couldn't betray Clare, couldn't even run the risk of appearing to defend a people that were being maligned, for fear that that deference might in some infinitesimal degree lead the way to the final discovery of her secret" (93). Is it Clare's secret or her own that needs to be protected? The ambiguous pronoun in the phrase "her secret" could signify either, or both, in the same way that the title of the book and the definition of passing signify both Irene's and Clare's forms of passing.

This idea is repeated more explicitly in a passage that comes late in the text but is central to it, a passage in which Irene is brooding about the possible consequences of exposing Clare to Bellew. She feels "caught between two allegiances, different, yet the same," caught between "Herself" and "Her race." The concept of the divided self is implicit in this text, but Larsen invests it with greater significance by conflating race and sex, as evidenced by the phrase "different, yet the same."[15] Too, Irene's silence and paralysis are indicative of her feelings of powerlessness as a black and as a female against a force such as Bellew and what he represents: "It was, she [Irene] cried silently, enough to suffer as a woman, an individual, on one's own account, without having to suffer for the race as well" (164). Clearly, the three—race, sex, and personal identity—are intimately associated, but the complexities do not end here. These passages also reveal Irene's inability to separate herself from Clare—"her [Clare's] secret" is indeed Irene's and therefore Clare's silence is also Irene's. That is, Clare does not act as narrator of a narrative ostensibly about passing, and Irene's "presence" as narrator is subverted by the disguise. In short, the title, the language, and the narrative strategy all function to call into question the concept of "presence" that these women associate with assimilating into the dominant culture.

Larsen's conflation of race and sex reinforces, in part, the "double jeopardy" of the black female in a white male hegemonic society, but she reveals as well that sexist attitudes inhibit Irene's relationship with her own black husband. Her conversations with her husband clearly reveal her discomfort in broaching the subject of sexuality. After an attempted conversation with Brian about sex, she feels "the sense of having been wilfully misunderstood and reproved [which] drove her to fury" (105), an emotion which, of course, she represses. For while the text suggests that for males sex is "necessary education" (105), it also suggests that for females it is a taboo subject. Thus, Irene "passes" as a lady by keeping silent about topics deemed unladylike. Here and elsewhere the text formulates the idea that (male) society punishes women for their sexuality, and the stereotypical idea of the frigidity of light-skinned black women is again, as it is in *Quicksand,* inverted to suggest that fear, and not genetics, is a possible cause.

Critics are right, then, to say that the text is reticent about sexuality, but it is so because of Irene's reticence. Deborah McDowell's exploration of a possible sexual attraction between Irene and Clare is a clear indication that in making the dominant point of view that of a woman who represses all her true feelings, Larsen invites us to explore the very emotions Irene seeks to hide. However, I do not share McDowell's opinion that "the idea of bringing a sexual attraction between two women to full narrative expression is . . . too dangerous a move [for Larsen], which helps to explain why critics have missed this aspect of the novel" (xxx). First of all, the ability to face an issue such as lesbianism, to confront the emotions it involves, would be completely out of character for Irene. Nor would a head-on confrontation have been historically feasible as a rhetorical choice for Larsen. Second, Larsen's use of passing as structure suggests that the most compelling and pertinent aspects of her characters' lives are to be found in imaginative constructs, in the subtext rather than in subplots. Her narrative strategies intensify rather than obscure meaning because readers are invited to examine the text more closely. I would argue that critics miss certain aspects of the text when they approach it from a position that treats thematic concerns as separate and distinct from rhetorical concerns or when they presuppose knowledge of the author's values based on those assigned her characters.

As suggested earlier, Larsen demonstrates through both a revision of the tropes of passing and the mulatto and through a satiric portrayal of the bourgeois class that her characters' values are misdirected and self-defeating. Irene worries constantly about being humiliated, about "losing face," as it were, which is characteristic of her social class. As she sits in the restaurant of an elegant white hotel, she tells herself that she isn't "ashamed of being a Negro" but that her fear of being discovered is a fear of the humiliation she would experience being "ejected from any place" (41). She tells herself, too, that her anger at and fear of Bellew had been caused by the "galling and outrageous" humiliation to which she had been subjected during that visit to his and Clare's apartment and therefore she had "concealed her own origin" (92-93). There is always a close association between her fear of being humiliated and her fear of acknowledging her origin which implies negative attributes connected with being black. Ironically, then, by denying her origin in her effort not to be humiliated, Irene experiences in a more profound way exactly what she hopes to avoid—a loss of face. Clare's decision to become white is, of course, partly based on a similar need not to be humiliated, her need "to be a person and not a charity or a problem or even a daughter of the indiscreet Ham" (56).

In this way, Larsen satirizes the bourgeois class and finds in it a correlation with the concept of passing, for characteristic of the members of such a class is their propensity for behaving in ways designed to disguise the truth. This notion of appearance vs. reality is forcefully presented by Larsen's attention to the trivial details of society life. Clare is described at one moment as a woman who "wept attractively" and at another as one who might someday kill her husband if he gets in her way. Irene, too, sits "pouring tea properly and nicely" (152), all the while feeling the "impulse to laugh, to scream, to hurl things about. She wanted, suddenly, to shock people, to hurt them, to make them notice her, to be aware of her suffering" (153). These contrasting images, emphasizing the ramifications derived from the idea of appearance vs. reality, are apparent from the outset of the book: the descriptions of Irene's attention to her "little pile of morning mail" (29); of her having tea on the roof of an elegant white hotel; of the three women—Irene, Clare, and Gertrude—sipping tea from "tall amber glasses" (71), under the "illusion of general conversation" (73); and so on, are all subverted by intruding images of fear and repressed rage. Because of the narrative point of view, it is Irene's fear and repressed rage to which we are drawn as she becomes more and more like Clare, wishing first for the death of Clare's child and then for the death of Clare herself.

Clare's death and Irene's complicity in it should, therefore, come as no surprise. Not only have we been prepared for it by the fear and repressed rage that have been stressed throughout the novel but also Clare's death is foreshadowed by a number of subtle destructive acts performed by Irene. On the occasion that Irene, as she is leaving Chicago, receives a note from Clare, she becomes frightened and annoyed by Clare's attempted intrusion into her life. She tears "the offending letter into tiny ragged squares" and "drop[s] them over the railing" of the train (88). A few sentences later the text reads: "She dropped Clare out of her mind and turned her thoughts to her own affairs." On another occasion, frightened by the sight of Brian and Clare together because she believes they are having an affair, "Rage boiled up in her," and in the next moment "There was a slight crash. On the floor at her feet lay the shattered cup. Dark stains dotted the bright rug. . . . Before her, Zulena gathered up the white fragments" (156-57). In the last scene, too, moments before Clare's actual death, Irene is the one who opens the window from which Clare falls, after which she "finished her cigarette and threw it out, watching the tiny sparks drop slowly down to the white ground below" (183).

These acts are all described in ways that parallel the description of Clare's fall and are proleptic of her death and Irene's complicity in it. In the final scene, when Bellew enters the room accusing his wife of being "a damned dirty nigger," Irene is annoyed because Clare seems too "composed"; she is even smiling, "as if the whole structure of her life were not lying in fragments before her" (184). Irene feels that it is in fact the whole structure of her own life that Bellew's discovery threatens. Therefore, "maddened" by Clare's smile, she "ran across the room, her terror tinged with ferocity, and laid a hand on Clare's bare arm. One thought possessed her. She couldn't have Clare Kendry cast aside by Bellew. She couldn't have her free" (184). The description of the actual fall reveals only that "One moment Clare had been there, a vital glowing thing, like a flame of red and gold. The next she was gone" (184-85). Yet, the attention given to Irene's actions and reactions is evidence that the possibility of her complicity in Clare's death is of primary importance.

Claudia Tate argues rightly, in her essay "Nella Larsen's *Passing*: A Problem of Interpretation," that Clare's death is surrounded by ambiguity (145). Yet, again we must remember from whose point of view it is being related. After Irene "laid a hand on Clare's bare arm," the text itself tells us that "What happened next, Irene Redfield never afterwards allowed herself to remember. Never clearly" (184). We can, however, speculate because both the fore-shadowing and the descriptions of Irene's repressed fury, bordering on insanity, are strong suggestions of murder. Other compelling facts are offered as well: Irene tries desperately to convince herself that "It was an accident, a terrible accident. . . . It was" (186), but she is at the same time panic stricken at the thought that Clare might not be dead; and to Felice's announcement that Clare had died "Instantly," a "sob of thankfulness . . . rose in [Irene's] throat" (188).

The ending of Larsen's novel revises conventional endings of tragic mulatto and passing tales in its very strong suggestion of murder. Significantly, Irene is cast as both victim and victimizer so that at the same time there is textual evidence to support the possibility of murder, there is also implicit in the text the notion that death finds its symbolic correlative in passing. That is to say, it signifies the ultimate "crossing over," to borrow from Henry Louis Gates, Jr., "in that ironic double sense of 'passing' and 'dying'" (Figures 202). Irene's complicity in Clare's death may also be, then, symbolic of her need to destroy the Clare within.[16]

Had Larsen merely wanted to portray the conventional passing story, there would have been no need to present the character of Irene, to draw so painstakingly the parallels between her life and Clare's. Had she wanted to portray the plight of only "certain women," as Cheryl Wall argues in "Passing for What? Aspects of Identity in Nella Larsen's Novels," she probably would not have used the excerpt from Countee Cullen's poem "Heritage" as epigraph. "Passing," as Larsen defines it, certainly signifies upon Cullen's theme of the Black American's inability to relate to his African past. Yet, Larsen's other rhetorical strategies—especially the disguised "I" of her narrative point of view and a play on the doubleness of language— function to show that the phenomenon of passing is multifaceted (as also illustrated by my second and third epigraphs), and therefore readings need not be centered on race and class to the exclusion or minimization of other readings.

The demand during the twenties for black fiction that depicted "Harlem dives, race riots, and abject poverty" suggests that writing about the mulatto and bourgeois society was certainly not the "surest way for a black woman fiction writer to gain a hearing," as Wall argues it was, and therefore her argument that Larsen "chose to 'pass' as a novelist" is misleading, implying as it does that Larsen's narrative strategies were used more as a "protective cover" than to maintain integrity of plot and character.[17] Larsen stood firm against popular demand and wrote about what she knew, at the same time addressing many of the concerns that inform most writings of the period.

Further, although Larsen's characters are constrained to be silent, Larsen is not, and it is through her critique of narrative forms and conventions that Larsen articulates a distinction between herself and her characters. Despite the fact that she wrote only two novels, Larsen's legacy is not slight, for it is in her revision of narrative strategies that are white and male, in her ability to create art out of personal experience, that Larsen achieves and expresses her own voice.

NOTES

1. Letter to Carl Van Vechten, July 1, 1926, in the James Weldon Johnson Collection, Beinecke Rare Book and Manuscript Library, Yale University, New Haven, Connecticut. Hereafter referred to as JWJC.
2. Nella Larsen, *Quicksand* (New York: Collier, 1971). Subsequent references to this novel will be marked by page numbers in parentheses in the text.
3. Interview with Thelma E. Berlack, the *Amsterdam News*, 1928.
4. Letter to Carl Van Vechten, May 14, 1932, JWJC.
5. Letter to Carl Van Vechten, June 4, 1931; letters to Dorothy Peterson, July, 1933; September 6, 1933. Re: isolation and alienation: letter to Carl Van Vechten, March 5, 1930; letter to Dorothy Peterson, Tuesday 19th [1927], JWJC.
6. Henry Louis Gates, Jr. uses the term to describe the fusion of autobiography and fiction. See *Figures in Black: Words, Signs and the 'Racial' Self* (New York: Oxford UP, 1987).
7. Barbara Smith, "Towards a Black Feminist Criticism," *The New Feminist Criticism*, Elaine Showalter, ed. (New York: Pantheon, 1985), 174.
8. See Amritjit Singh's *The Novels of the Harlem Renaissance* (University Park: Penna. State UP, 1976).
9. Dale M. Bauer, *Feminist Dialogics: A Theory of Failed Community* (New York: State U of New York P, 1988), 4.
10. Nella Larsen, *Passing* (New York: Collier, 1971). Subsequent references to this novel will be marked by page numbers in parentheses in the text.
11. For a full discussion of the "blood theory," see Nancy Tischler's *Black Masks: Negro Characters in Modern Southern Fiction* (University Park: The Penna. State UP, 1969), 96.
12. My reading owes much to Robert Scholes's "Decoding Papa: 'A Very Short Story' as Work and Text," in *Literary Theories in Praxis* (Philadelphia: The U of Pennsylvania P, 1987). Scholes refers to this narrational mode as a "covert, first-person narration" and demonstrates its use as a "disguise, a mask of pseudo-objectivity worn by the text for its own rhetorical purposes" (176).
13. Sterling Brown sees Irene's role simply as that of Clare's "friend" and clearly misconstrues Larsen's purpose, as evidenced by his statement that Irene "lives in contrast [to Clare] a happy, respectable life" (143). Amritjit Singh feels it is "unfortunate that

Larsen . . . does not choose to deal with passing from Clare's point of view," adding that had she done so, *Passing* would have been "a very different book" (100). While Singh recognizes Larsen's skills as a novelist and her movement beyond the tragic mulatto stereotype, he, like Brown, minimizes Irene's role.
14. While I agree that Irene "deludes herself," I do not share McDowell's view that Irene "mislead[s] the reader" (xxiv). The highly manipulative narrative point of view intensifies meaning by enabling readers to see through Irene's denials.
15. See Gates's "The Same Difference: Reading Jean Toomer, 1923-1982," in *Figures*.
16. Wall discusses Clare's death as psychological murder or suicide in "Passing for What?" However, my own interpretation, first presented in a chapter of my dissertation, owes much to a reading of Gubar and Gilbert's *The Madwoman in the Attic* and, more recently, to Bauer's discussion of literary suicide and sacrifice in *Feminist Dialogics*, 4.
17. See Wall, 110 and McDowell, xxx.

WORKS CITED

Barthes, Roland, *Image-Music-Text*. New York: Hill and Wang, 1977.
Bauer, Dale M. *Feminist Dialogics: A Theory of Failed Community*. New York: State U of New York P, 1988.
Brown, Sterling. *The Negro in American Fiction*. Albany: The J. B. Lyon Press, 1937.
Christian, Barbara. *Black Women Novelists: The Development of a Tradition, 1892-1976*. Westport, Connecticut: Greenwood, 1980.
Gates, Henry Louis, Jr. *Figures in Black: Words, Signs, and the 'Racial' Self*. New York: Oxford UP, 1987.
Gilbert, Sandra M. and Susan Gubar. *The Madwoman in the Attic: The Woman Writer and the Nineteenth-Century Literary Imagination*. New Haven: Yale UP, 1979.
Larsen, Nella. *Passing*. New York: Collier, 1971.
———. Personal Correspondence, in the James Weldon Johnson Collection, Beinecke Rare Book and Manuscript Library, Yale University, New Haven, Connecticut.
———. *Quicksand*. New York: Collier, 1971.

McDowell, Deborah. "Introduction." *Quicksand and Passing.* New Jersey: Rutgers UP, 1986.

Scholes, Robert. "Decoding Papa: 'A Very Short Story' as Work and Text," in *Literary Theories in Praxis,* ed. Shirley Staton. Philadelphia: The U of Penna. P, 1987.

Singh, Amritjit. *The Novels of the Harlem Renaissance.* Univ. Park: Penna. State UP, 1976.

Smith, Barbara. "Towards a Black Feminist Criticism," *The New Feminist Criticism,* Elaine Showalter, ed. New York: Pantheon, 1985.

Smith, Valerie. *Self-Discovery and Authority in Afro-American Narrative.* Cambridge: Harvard UP, 1987.

Starkey, Marion L. "Jessie Fauset." *Southern Workman.* May 1932:217-20.

Tate, Claudia. "Nella Larsen's *Passing*: A Problem of Interpretation." Black American Literature Forum 14 (Winter 1980):142-46.

Tischler, Nancy. *Black Masks: Negro Characters in Modern Southern Fiction.* Univ. Park: The Penna. State UP, 1969.

Wall, Cheryl. "Passing for What? Aspects of Identity in Nella Larsen's Novels." *Black American Literature Forum* (1980):97-111.

The Question of Lesbian Identity in Marie-Claire Blais's Work

Janine Ricouart

Marie-Claire Blais was born in Québec City in 1939. She has pursued a brilliant writing career since her first novel, La Belle bête *(1959;* Mad Shadows *1960). She lives partly in Québec, and partly in France.*

Her fiction includes the famous Une Saison dans la vie d'Emmanuel *(1965;* A Season in the Life of Emmanuel *1965) for which she won both the Prix France-Québec and the Prix Médicis;* David Sterne *(1967; Eng. trans. 1973);* Le Loup *(1972;* The Wolf *1974);* Un Joualonais, sa Joualonie *(1973; published in France as* A coeur joual *1974;* St. Lawrence Blues *1974);* Pierre, la guerre du printemps 81 *(1984; revised version published in France as* Pierre *1986).*

She also wrote extensively for the theater: L'Exécution *(Montréal, Théâtre du Rideau Vert, 1968);* La Nef des sorcières *(a collective work; Montréal, Théâtre du Nouveau Monde, 1976) and has contributed several pieces for television and radio.*

Blais has been one of Québec's most influential authors since the early 1960s. She has a strong international reputation and combines elements of the literary tradition of the province of Québec with an affinity to the existentialist fiction of Western Europe and the United States. Her work reflects the emergence of a clearly identified female voice in the literature of Québec since the early 1970s.

When talking about the identity of a lesbian writer, one must consider the time in which the writer lived as well as the social and cultural circumstances proper to this writer, since outside contingencies influence how the lesbian is perceived in the context of her time, and how she perceives herself: the way each writer chooses to deal with her lesbian identity is the result of how she defines herself within her cultural background. Therefore, the question of definition is foremost in any text dealing with a lesbian author. The term "lesbian" is generally understood to mean "a woman who relates sexually and emotionally to other women" (Ponse 199). But what is "a lesbian text"?[1]

Several recent studies have been devoted to various aspects of lesbian identity and lesbian writing, and can serve as a background to explore different definitions, and to analyze the specificities of a lesbian text.[2] The main issue is that the term "lesbian" does not just suggest a sexual preference, but refers to a total identity of the person. In order to include a broad diversity of lesbian texts, I chose to adopt Lillian Faderman's definition of "lesbian":[3]

"Lesbian" describes a relationship in which two women's strongest emotions and affections are directed toward each other. Sexual contact may be a part of the relationship to a greater or lesser degree, or it may be entirely absent. By preference the two women spend most of their time together and share most aspects of their lives with each other. (17-18)

However, if the issue of defining lesbian identity has been dealt with by numerous critics, the question of how this identity is transcribed in literature remains to be explored. Defining oneself as a lesbian is obviously important for the psychological make-up of a woman and suggests a strong influence on a writer's production. Several studies dealing with various aspects of lesbian identity in literature are quite relevant to a study of Marie-Claire Blais's autobiographical fiction and her use of lesbian characters.[4] In a world dominated by heterosexist prejudices—Adrienne Rich defines heterosexism as: "a deeply ingrained prejudice, comparable to racism, sexism, and classism—a political indoctrination which must be recognized as such and which can be re-educated" (*Blood, Bread, and Poetry* 200)—it is easy to understand why lesbian writers have used (and still use) "mask, disguise, masquerade" (Russ 80) especially by means of a complex language which is veiled and obscure, in order to mask the lesbian identity. The complexity of a lesbian writer's language is analyzed by Sharon O'Brien in her study of Willa Cather's choice of male narrators entitled "'The Thing Not Named': Willa Cather as a Lesbian Writer." This study is particularly interesting in relation to Blais's own choice of male narrators or male characters in some of her fiction. This choice allows the lesbian writer to use the persona of a male narrator and to express attraction for female characters in a "safe" way. Since Blais is not an outspoken lesbian writer like Nicole Brossard, for example, an exploration of her fiction can be problematic in the context of lesbian identity, because of a distanciation from her female "self." However, the question of how lesbian identity is transcribed in the text, and how Blais uses autobiographical elements, such as her sexual identity, to transform them in fiction have never been addressed by critics of her work. This essay will explore these issues because they are essential to understand the complexity of Blais's writings and to appreciate to what extent being a lesbian influenced her strategies of self-expression, of masking and unveiling, of hiding and revealing the truth.

Despite numerous articles relating to her work, only three books have been published on Blais so far—by Philippe Stratford, Thérèse Fabi and Vincent Nadeau. They all center around the study of childhood and adolescence in Blais's work. In her earlier works, Blais presents childhood as a privileged place for creative introspection. It is worth noting that childhood represents the moment when sexual preference is not a problem, as long as the child is not confronted by the adult world, and when sexuality is expressed with the most honesty and open-mindedness. In this light, it is easy to understand why Blais chose to deal with childhood in her early fiction. Furthermore, the adolescents she presents take on another dimension in regard to the repression of homosexuality: they are mostly a-sexual and male. She rarely deals with female sexuality at all, although it is essential for women writers to express all the diversities of female sexuality. Karen Gould, in "The Censored Word and the Body Politic: Reconsidering the Fiction of Marie-Claire Blais," suggests just how important it is to reconsider the "feminine text" from the perspective of the "silenced female body" (14). Gould's analysis stresses the importance for women of expressing female sexuality, and the central role of language in the context of the dominating discourse. But, if feminine sexuality is problematic in a patriarchal context, lesbian sexuality is even more problematic, and silenced by the majority of lesbian writers themselves. In Blais's early works, the choice of male characters may be symbolic of this silence imposed on female sexuality, but it is also a sign of self-censorship. For whatever reasons, Blais distances herself doubly from the feminine. However, with "The trilogy of Pauline Archange"[5] which is written like an autobiography, she gives for the first time a central place to a female character with a first person narrator. But despite this centering on a female character, the "disembodied voice" is problematic because it reinforces the sexual oppression of women. I am particularly interested in considering Blais's autobiographical work as a "coming out" story, with its specific movements of progression punctuated by sudden changes and hesitations, and I suggest that these movements—taken together—indicate a search for a more assertive lesbian-identified voice.

Blais's stylistic patterns are characteristic of female autobiographies, as suggested by Mary Jean Green, in her excellent overview, entitled "Structures of Liberation: Female Experience and Autobiographical Form in Quebec." Green sees two major structuring principles in autobiographies written by women: a tendency to focus on relationships with others (189) and an apparent "formlessness" since women's narratives are "often not chronological and progressive but disconnected, fragmentary" (190). Such discontinuous forms tend to mirror the "fragmented, interrupted and formless nature of their [women's] lives" (190). Green also mentions Nancy K. Miller, and especially "Writing Fictions: Women's Autobiography in France,"[6] in which Miller "advocates a 'dialectical practice of reading', a 'double reading' of autobiography with fiction" (Green 191). Green studies closely the complexities of *The Manuscripts of Pauline Archange*, Blais's autobiographical fiction, and suggests the impossibility of drawing the line between "fictional fiction" and the "fictions of autobiography" (192). She states that:

> Although critics have persistently suspected that the experiences of Pauline Archange closely resemble those of the author herself as a young girl and aspiring writer in Quebec City, such an identification cannot be made with certainty. It has, indeed, been denied by the author—who is, however, known for guarding the privacy of her personal life. (192)

Green underlines an interesting use of autobiographical form by Blais, through a focus on relationships with others and, in the case of Pauline Archange, "a clear pattern of rejection of the others whose presence dominates both her life and her narrative" (198). She also suggests that this rejection of others is "a necessary prelude to the attainment of individual autonomy" (198). However, the autobiographical elements used in Pauline's fictitious story, or Blais's fictitious autobiography, start with the problematic use of the title, "manuscripts": since the author of this book is Blais and not Pauline

Archange, and since a "manuscript" refers to a piece that is not yet published, the reader is confronted with two words having a different referent, which is one of the questions raised by the "fictions of autobiography." Furthermore, the use of the name Pauline instead of Marie-Claire, for the persona of the main character of this trilogy, allows the writer to hide behind her heroine's name and forces the reader to question the truth of the events told by the young narrator. It is impossible to decide for sure whether the events presented in the trilogy are autobiographical or fictitious, based on the writer's life or invented. Such an ambiguity about the truthfulness of a text is mentioned by Sidonie Smith in her study of *A Poetics of Women's Autobiography*: "The autobiographical text becomes a narrative artifice, privileging a presence, or identity, that does not exist outside language. Given the very nature of language, embedded in the text lie alternative or deferred identities that constantly subvert any pretentions of truthfulness" (5).

In this "trilogy," Pauline's story leaves a more positive feeling about life than Blais's previous texts: Pauline will survive the pains of growing-up thanks to her discovery of writing:

> Victim or assailant, each was possessed by the bleeding world of his or her dreams. [. . I]t seemed to me, as I awoke, that this blood, spilled in unjust violence, would one day be the sap that fed my books, since no one can erase in us the marks of what we have once lived, and in feeling their presence within me, those marks, I was no longer alone . . . (*Manuscripts* 185-6)

The image of spilled blood, be it the blood of animals, children, or innocent victims of wars, recurs throughout Blais's work. But writing will allow Pauline to survive the violence surrounding her and to exist as a human being:

> If I had been given my being in some other form, perhaps I could have felt a pang of pity as I leaned down to observe a person such as myself in order to tell her story; but born into the very story I wanted to write, I aspired only to find a way out of it. What made me feel most desolate was the thought that it was such a long, such a hard business for me to live, and that in a book it would take only a few pages; yet without those few pages I was in danger of never having existed for anyone. (*Manuscripts* 105-6)

Besides survival, writing also helps the narrator to escape an unsatisfying life, by recreating it. In the third novel of this trilogy, Pauline's misery is symbolized by a reproduction of Dürer's *Melancolia*, thus bringing the pains of being to the level of art: Pauline, whose name is, after all, "Archangel," becomes a myth to herself. Although Blais rejected the autobiographical elements present in *The Manuscripts of Pauline Archange* (according to Green), in an interview with Donald Smith, she admits the presence of autobiographical elements in *A Literary Affair* (1975): "You could call it my own story, although it contains a great deal of self-criticism" (143). Mathieu Lelièvre, the main protagonist of *A Literary Affair*, is a young Québécois writer who goes to Paris and has a relationship with a flamboyant French aristocrat named Yvonne d'Argenti, a writer much older than he is, and more experienced about the facts of life: he was "armed with a Canada Council grant that made him already rich in his imagination" (11). (Blais received such a grant in 1961.) The word "imagination" is essential in this first sentence of Mathieu's story. Mathieu is impatient to see "the land he has revered since childhood" (11) and has a great many expectations and fantasies about France. He knows the country and its people through literature, especially Balzac and Proust; he is at odds with his Québécois friends because: "when his comrades spoke of revolution he would shamelessly protest that he liked only French literature, quoting Balzac and Proust and denouncing the fury of weapons" (11-12). But Mathieu is also at odds with the French people he meets, especially because, through Balzac and Proust, he has a distorted view of them. He is a young naive Balzacian hero, arriving in France to conquer Paris (or at least one woman). He has an older mistress, like Balzac's hero, Rastignac (*Le Père Goriot*), and through her, he is introduced to Parisian aristocracy, and becomes a Proustian observer of the upper-class.

A closer study of this text, replaced in the context of autobiographical fiction, suggests the presence of a lesbian relationship between the narrator and her mentor, Yvonne d'Argenti. Since humor is usually absent from Blais's texts, the presence of humor is particularly striking here: by mixing nineteenth century French literary motifs with twentieth century modern technology and mentality, Blais's descriptions of this young Québécois's reactions to France are hilarious.

If this is, indeed, Blais's "own story," it gives the reader an insight into her sense of humor about her own experiences when she discovered France and its people. It also brings out the marginal position of the Canadian toward the "real" French, and the misunderstanding common between France and Québec: attraction on the one hand, and rejection on the other hand. Furthermore, it presents a different perspective on a triangular relationship than Mary Meigs's autobiographical stories: *Lily Briscoe: A Self-Portrait* (1981) and *The Medusa Head* (1983), in which she recounts how Marie-Claire and Mary lived their *ménage à trois* with a powerful and devastating "Andrée" ("Yvonne d'Argenti"?):

> Thinking about autobiography and its pitfalls, I am tempted to tackle my own again . . . For in autobiography the seemingly audacious first person can act as a shield behind which one stands against the obsessive Other, someone loved and lost, or perhaps loved and hated . . . And by this healing action *you* becomes she, becomes closer, in fact, to the she of fiction. (7)

Mary Meigs's "tackling" of her autobiography and its process is worth mentioning in the context of this study, but a closer analysis of these two versions of the same "story" (Meigs's and Blais's) needs to be done, in order to appreciate how two writers transformed a personal situation through literature.[7] What is most important in the context of this study is how much Blais transformed her "personal" story, using a male hero or persona, for herself, and a heterosexual couple, instead of the lesbian couple that Meigs presented. This is one example of how lesbian stories can be so transformed that nothing within that story itself can indicate to the reader the presence of a lesbian relationship, unless some outside element—like the writer's own confessions[8] or an ex-lover's story—allows the reader to reconnect the threads of the "real" story.

Reading Blais's work as a "cheminement"—a slow progression—toward the expression of her self-identity brings me to consider four of her most recent texts, in which Blais deals with gender identity by alternating between characters who are male or female either in identity or in attitude, and by presenting different experiences of homosexuality. Her two clearly lesbian-identified texts, *Nights in the Underground* (1978) and *L'Ange de la solitude* (1989) were written eleven years apart. In between, Blais wrote *Deaf to the City* (1979), and *Anna's World* (1982), which both address the question of lesbian identity, and which offer a new narrative form.

All these texts present the three elements analyzed by Green in the "autobiographical fiction" of *The Manuscripts of Pauline Archange*, combined with new ones: 1) a focus on relationships with others, but also on self-growth and self-naming; 2) a "formlessness," which is only apparent, since it can reflect a rejection of patriarchal "structures" on all levels, not only social, and personal, but also linguistic; 3) an extension of the autobiographical genre, so as to blur totally what is fiction and what is reality.

In *Nights in the Underground* (1978), Blais explores women's sexual identity and explicitly deals with intimate relationships between women. She has called this text a more honest version of *A Literary Affair*,[9] but it will take her eleven years before repeating this experience. The first part of the book, which takes place in "The Underground," a bar in Montréal, presents various relationships between women. It deals more particularly with the relationship between Geneviève Aurès, a sculptor from Québec and Lali Dorman, an Austrian Jew, and then with Françoise, a middle-aged French bourgeoise.

The narrative structure is more innovative than in Blais's previous texts: for the first time, she uses a third person narration (heterodiegetic) mixed with interior monologues, which she will develop again later in *Deaf to the City* and *Anna's World*. The style is more fragmented, to mirror the various locations of the story: most of the action takes place in a bar, and Geneviève, the main character, travels back and forth between Paris and Montréal. The conversations are more syncopated, and the total absence of breaks in the phrases gives the reader a choice for rhythm.

Geneviève Aurès goes to a bar during her last days in Montréal before going back to Paris; she becomes attracted to Lali Dorman, and goes back to the bar several times to observe Lali and to get to know her. Because Lali is a secret, mysterious woman, Geneviève must reconstruct Lali's whole story based on her own observations in the bar and on what others tell her. Lali is presented as a mysterious, romantic character. Geneviève's fantasizing about Lali is parallel to the reading experience of this text, since both must deal with fragments of a story (15).

Since Lali does not like to talk about herself, even after they have become more intimate, Geneviève still receives fragmented information about Lali's past (30-32). Yet these stories represent Lali's whole being, especially when she remembers the violence in and out of her family (31-32). Their relationship does not last very long: Geneviève must return to Paris, where she lives with her boyfriend, Jean, to deal with her coming out (23). As in Blais's previous stories, memory plays a major role in this text: in Paris, Geneviève remembers Lali and the other women she met in the bar, and goes through "remembrances of things past" (38-40). She finds her strength and her self-identity through art. She is now aware that she wants to be with women (48), and shortly after, she meets an older woman, Françoise, and starts a relationship with her.

This book presents a reconsideration of traditional values and explores the friendship between the various lesbian characters in a respectful and honest light. Moreover, despite the presence of a romantic character like Lali, it does not romanticize lesbian relations: it brings forward a multi-faceted group of women, each with her own human problems.

In *Deaf to the City*, the narration alternates between Michel Agneli ("agneau" = lamb), called Mike, a terminally ill young boy and Florence, a suicidal woman in her fifties who has a close but brief bonding with Judith Langenais, a young philosophy teacher. Judith is called Lange ("l'ange" = the angel) by Mike's mother, and she tries to help suicidal persons by listening to them. She is omni-present in the thoughts of many characters, especially Florence and Mike, like a guardian angel, always by their side.

Through Florence's interior monologues, the reader gains an understanding of her reason for committing suicide. Florence cannot live any longer because she has lost desire:

> [She] asked herself if the death-agony of human beings didn't begin when they lost all desire, when like herself they no longer expected anything, confronted only with a vast wasteland on which they could walk and run. (53)

She has lost her husband, whom she loved all her life, and she cannot go on without him (57). Desire and life are connected with waiting for someone, as presented by Irène Oore in the Blaisian "cogito": "I desire therefore I am."[10] During her last day in the Hôtel des Voyageurs (ironically named, since she is getting ready for a special trip), Florence remembers fragments of her life with her husband, the boredom between them at times, his departure, and some powerful encounters with women, especially a couple of mountain climbers:

> [These women] belonged to a willful, conscious generation that made her seem insignificant; she had so little courage, while the mountain climbers feared nothing, neither man's judgement nor the mountain they already dominated with their frank gaze. (192)

In remembering, she realizes why she ignored these women: "If she had been indifferent to women, to their lives, to their particular destiny in this world for such a long time, it was because until then she'd only had eyes for her husband and had lived with him alone, for him alone" (194). Although lesbian identity is not the dominant aspect of this book, it plays an important part, since Florence seems to realize that she never reached the full potential of her life, because she was too dependent on one person and did not dare to take risks in life: "I was a society woman and deaf to everything" (176). Although death and deaf are not homophonic in French, they have a powerful connection here. The symbols associated with non-hearing, non-communication are crucial in this text: the main idea is that death is deaf to everything. Happiness is also deaf to everything, like Florence when she was with her husband, Dr. Gray. Florence remembers that "each of us has his silent death in life" (150), and that in order for her to go on with her suicide plan, she must detach herself and remain deaf to other people's pains. She must abandon Mike to his own suffering in order to go on with her planned suicide.

This story is written in one long paragraph, with interior monologues: what matters are the inner relationships, either remembered or imagined, and not the direct relationships that happen through actions, encounters, or dialogues. Since intimate contacts can often end in failure or reveal deep misunderstanding, Blais's characters compensate for this lack of communication among family members or lovers by strong connections with people met by chance and usually only briefly. In her analysis of Blais's narrative style, Viswanathan stresses the close relationship between a certain narrative mode ("focalisation multiple") and the dynamics of the story ("Echanger" 193). The numerous allusions to art in *Deaf to the City* (painting, music or writing) also serve to remind the reader that suffering is everywhere, and that artists have a special sensitivity to it.[11] Art always plays an important part in Blais's story-telling, as in Proust. Characters are often compared to a painting or a sculpture, like Mike at the beginning of this story, or they are artists themselves. But Blais's artists are not isolated in an ivory tower: they are extremely sensitive to what is going on around them. Being part of a minority has sensitized this writer to many social injustices, and she constantly refers to them in her fiction. In her interview with Donald Smith, Blais talks about her own position as a lesbian in the context of a more global struggle: "all the struggles for personal rights and the rights of minorities are extremely important. We can't hope to create a society without harmony; it's vital" (141).

The extreme sensitivity to pain and loneliness present in *Deaf to the City* continues with *Anna's World*, which centers on female characters. The French title: "Visions d'Anna" can be interpreted as Anna's visions, how she sees life for example, or as visions of other people about Anna. This story deals with both aspects of the title and intertwines the two kinds of visions. *Anna's World* is the story of a young woman, Anna, and her relationship with her mother, Raymonde, who is separated from her husband, Peter. Parallel to their story is the story of Michelle, a thirteen-year old whose parents reject their older daughter's (Liliane's) lesbianism. The two young girls, Anna and Michelle, are drifters. These young adults join the company of adolescents in distress, with whom Blais's readers are familiar.

The complex and ambiguous relationship between mother and daughter in *Anna's World* (and especially the use of silence in Blais's heroines) has been explored recently by feminist critics.[12] The mother/daughter relationship is marked by fear, distance, absence, contrasted with adoration and understanding. It seems that, despite several attempts at closeness, or communication, these women cannot fully trust each other's emotions, nor their desire to be close. There is, for example, a lot of pain in Liliane's longing for her mother's love, but Guislaine is too afraid to accept Liliane as she is. She hopes that her daughter will change, but Liliane knows that she will not change: "Guislaine, you have time to subdue all your fears, but I will not change" (170). *Anna's World* recounts "inner searches for a female self-assertion, strength, and truth—often through a return to the mother or female relationships and in one's own hesitant faltering voice expressing one's own reality" (Gould, Green, and Lewis 369-70).

On the one hand, greater options available to women today have "weakened the ties between mothers and daughters, as both search to free themselves as individuals" (Lewis 96). But women are also separated from each other in a patriarchal society that has used women as a means of exchange for male power and prestige. Women often doubt their own creative power and hide their feelings to protect themselves from open scrutiny: Michelle, Guislaine and Anna all write in secret. They are afraid of being robbed of their art, of their soul. A scene at the customs is particularly revealing. When Anna's notebooks are examined by a customs officer, Anna mentions the connection between a woman's words and her soul:

> Anna's words . . . with all their obscure, impenetrable signs, . . . and Annas body [which] was aching, she was afraid of

> being stripped bare but she would betray none of her pain
> ... let them search me, probe me, I am Anna, impenetrable.
> (*Anna* 158)

She is impenetrable because she knows that there is a very strong connection between her words and her self-identity, and she is able to assert her own strength, despite her fears.

Anna left her family in order to escape the cruelty that she sees everywhere. By coming back, she will survive, like Pauline Archange, by telling what she has seen through her obscure, unfathomable words. If telling is essential for Anna, doing is more important for Liliane, who tries to change the shape of society by her political participation in the ecological movement, and by her love for women. She is presented as a strong character, with positive goals. She sees as clearly as Anna does what is going on around her and she wants to protect the earth for her survival, because she perceives a connection between the two: "the survival of women through an intimate bonding means the survival of the earth" (Gould, Green, and Lewis 373).

There is a close parallel between *Deaf to the City* and *Anna's World* in the choice of a third person narrative structure, and the style of *Anna's World* has a powerful effect:

> The use of a third person narrative, first and second person dialogues, and a third person narrative structure even when delving into the inner thought/visions of a character effectively represents the struggle to impose oneself as central. The ensuing intellectual distancing reflects the confusion and fear of female protagonists who are searching to express women's reality in their own voices and to find support from one another. (Gould, Green, and Lewis 370)

What is particularly new here is Blais's narrative style: it is much more fragmented than in any of her previous texts, to convey the fragmented experience of her heroines. The punctuation used in *Anna's World* seems totally arbitrary. Most of the book has to do with the personal thoughts of one character or another. Many times, clues like: "thought so and so," "said so and so," are used to switch from one character to another. The fragmentation of the text "reflects the solitary visions ... of each woman and her attempts to deny and yet create a unified voice" (Gould, Green, and Lewis 373).

With her most recent book, *L'Ange de la solitude* (1989), which has not yet been translated into English, Blais wrote what can be considered a sequel to *Nights in the Underground*, by centering once again on lesbian characters. This time, most of the events occur in a commune where five women live, as if the interior monologues present in *Deaf to the City* or *Anna's World* had been a necessary step before Blais could create lesbian characters in their own surroundings.

L'Ange de la solitude (The Angel of Loneliness) is more structured than the two previous texts (*Anna's World* and *Deaf to the City*) and also more intimate. Like *Nights in the Underground*, *L'Ange de la solitude* is clearly structured in paragraphs, with titles such as 1) "Johnie's Universe," and 2) "The Threshold of Pain." The story centers around Johnie, who loves Radclyffe Hall and is writing an essay on literature from Sappho to Radclyffe Hall (21-22). This book draws on several literary traditions, such as Hall's *Well of Loneliness*, whose title is parallel to Blais's *Angel of Loneliness*, or Genet's use of feminine names for male characters, which parallels Blais's use of masculine names for some female characters. The four other women who live in the commune with Johnie have names like Gérard, l'Abeille, Polydor and Doudouline, which brings the narrator to make a connection between naming and safety: "These names belonged only to themselves. After having left the magical shelter, wouldn't they be as vulnerable and naked as these soldiers deprived of their armor of leaves, in a wood where the sly enemy could have hidden himself behind any tree?" (12) The connection between names, armor, and soldiers indicates that there is a struggle going on and that lesbians must protect themselves against hidden dangers, which brings to mind Monique Wittig's *Les Guérillères*. The women presented in *L'Ange de la solitude* are lonely and vulnerable. Some are drifters, like Gérard, but as in Blais's previous texts, salvation comes through art and also through tenderness for others.

The parallel between the way Marianne (the heterosexual woman Johnie met one summer) treats her black servant and Johnie herself, suggests a connection between racism and homophobia and demonstrates Blais's awareness of the similarities between these two kinds of oppressions. Marianne despises Johnie and "her difference which *must not* be seen" (108). Marianne also insists on hiding her affair with Johnie from her husband and her son. She is mostly a business woman, and she treats her lesbian fling like a business. This relationship with Marianne gives Johnie a "necessary shake" and because of

Marianne's rejection, she finds that her "Angel of Loneliness" had always been waiting for her in the shadow, as if to tell her:

> When will you defend your rights? You who are a soldier with no weapons, when will you cease to hide behind the leaves that protect you among the girls of the group, when will you finally be yourself, facing the world, in a splendid light? (109)

"The Sword of the Angel of Loneliness" (109) separates their bodies, as if the narrator were denouncing the false sense of security that Johnie may have found in the communal life. It seems that Johnie cannot be herself and at the same time be safe with other "girls." She must face reality, and the experience she had with Marianne forces her in that direction. Johnie reflects on the negative connotations of the label "lesbian" (the "L. word"), and realizes that "despite the most important revolution of her time, it still carries with it the same connotations of insult and [hatred] that it had during Radclyffe Hall's times" (109). This is one of the most strongly "lesbian-identified" statements that can be found in Blais's writings. The connections present here between fighting racism, sexism, and the emergence of the Gay Revolution bring a liberal agenda forward:

> Wasn't Johnie's dignity to endure the perpetuity of the Pink Triangle, on her body that had not yet been named, although one could have said that she was a lesbian or gay, wasn't her dignity to know that she still did not have a name that could be named or nameable, but that stranded among contemporaries of the Pink Triangle, her conquest of a liberation for life similar to her feeble conquest of life, had never been so threatened. (111)

In her review of "Le dernier Marie-Claire Blais," Louise Milot calls Blais's choice of male names for some female characters a kind of "gymnastique mentale"[13] and expresses her own difficulty or inability in dealing with these choices. Milot's resistance to Blais's text reflects the problem of most critics reading a lesbian-identified text, parallel to critics reading black women writers' works, as described by Alice Walker: "Critics seem usually ill-equipped to discuss and analyze the works of black women intelligently. Generally, they do not even make the attempt ... And, since black women writers are not, it would seem, very likeable—until recently they were the least willing worshippers of male supremacy—comments about them tend to be cruel" (260-61). Alice Walker's statement can be used to explore critics' reactions towards lesbian writers as well as towards black women writers. Milot does not notice the complexity of the lesbian characters presented by Blais and she states that some themes, although moving in Blais's previous texts, don't touch "us" here (25). Being touched by Blais's work might be like being touched by grace: it does not happen to everyone. As critics, we can only welcome Blais's courage in identifying herself as a lesbian writer. Her political gesture is important, and is parallel to the courage of black women artists who dare to voice the specificity of their own experience. Alice Walker stresses the loneliness of black women artists, which is parallel to what Blais faces when she identifies herself as a lesbian writer: "The writer—like the musician or painter—must be free to explore, otherwise she or he will never discover what is needed (by everyone) to be known. This means, very often, finding oneself considered 'unacceptable' by masses of people who think that the writer's obligation is not to explore or to challenge, but to second the masses' notions, whatever they are. Yet the gift of loneliness is sometimes a radical vision of society or one's people that has not previously been taken into account" (Walker 264).

"The thing not named" has come a long way. Blais has finally dared to expose herself, thus becoming at the same time more vulnerable. In her writings, she demonstrates the necessary connections between identity, community, and politics, or as Biddy Martin expresses it, the connections between "the centrality of lesbian writing" and "the emergence of a lesbian-feminist politics of experience and identity" (Martin 83). Furthermore, according to Martin, "Telling, writing, and reading autobiographical stories are linked to the perceived importance of countering representations that have rendered homosexuality invisible, perverse, aberrant, or marginal" (84).

It is important to re-evaluate Blais's work in the context of lesbian feminist literary criticism, and to understand how Blais stands out in the tradition of lesbian writers. Many aspects of Blais's work still need to be explored, but it is essential to raise some questions on the critical loss for literature (and for humanity) as a whole when the lesbian experience (or any expression of difference) is buried in silence.[14]

NOTES

1. Bonnie Zimmerman, in her very comprehensive article entitled "What has never been: An Overview of Lesbian Feminist Literary Criticism," raises important questions such as: "When is a text a 'lesbian text' or its writer a 'lesbian writer'?" and suggests that it depends on "how inclusively or exclusively we define 'lesbian'" (455).
2. Several excellent works deal with the question of lesbian identity. It is beyond the scope of this essay to offer such a critical survey, but I would like to suggest some titles for reference:

    a) Barbara Ponse, in *Identities in the Lesbian World. The Social Construction of Self* (1978), defines lesbians as "women-related women" (3), that is to say "women who call themselves lesbians (or would probably be called lesbians by others) as well as women who call themselves bisexual, 'sexual,' 'straight,' or celibate but who have sexual or emotional relationships with other women" (3). Her sociological study can be used as a reference to understand how the fact of being and/or calling oneself a lesbian can influence the style and the characters presented by a writer.

    b) In *Identity Management in Lesbian Women* (1978), Alice E. Moses deals with the impact of the lesbian label on a personal, psychological level and presents the interaction between psychological behavior and the social context in which this behavior occurs, is maintained, and changes. The goal of Moses's study on "identity management" is to answer some fundamental questions such as: "Is being a lesbian a handicap over which lesbian women consider they have little choice or is it a positive choice on their part that is very satisfying? Are there frequent management problems? How do lesbian women manage visibility issues? And how much does thinking about being identified influence risk-taking behaviors? How are the concerns of living life as a lesbian woman viewed in relation to a possible choice to live as a heterosexual woman?" (Moses ix).

    c) Susan Krieger explores the relationship between lesbian identity and the community in a review essay entitled: "Lesbian Identity and Community: Recent Social Science Literature" and suggests that "Identity is used to refer to feelings and ideas an individual has about herself" (92). She adds that we can "consider lesbianism to be a matter of total personal identity rather than primarily a sexual condition" (95) and that "the study of lesbianism began not as a study of women in relation to each other but as a study of isolated, deviant individuals" (97).

d) Mary Libertin, in "Female Friendship in Women's Verse: Toward a New Theory of Female Poetics," suggests that "A theory of female poetics must deal with the different conception women may have of society and the ensuing difference in their use of poetic devices and forms" (294). This article suggests that by using "female friendship" in criticism, "the psychosocial, psychosexual, and physiological aspects of various relationships could be shown in contrast or in interrelation" (295). However, it might be more important for feminist critics to reclaim a proper use of the term "lesbian," and to stress the reality of "lesbianism," of love between women, in order not to co-opt its very existence. Talking about "female friendship" instead of "lesbian life-style" keeps the existence of a "lesbian" experience under silence and makes it more palatable to those who wish to ignore such differences.

e) Adrienne Rich in "Compulsory Heterosexuality and Lesbian Existence," underlines how "heterosexuality has been both forcibly and subliminally imposed on women" (57) and suggests using terms like "lesbian existence" and "lesbian continuum" because for her the word "lesbianism" has "a clinical and limiting ring" (51). For Rich, "Lesbian existence suggests both the fact of the historical presence of lesbians and our continuing creation of the meaning of that existence" (51) and "lesbian continuum" includes "a range ... of woman-identified experience, not simply the fact that a woman has had or consciously desired genital sexual experience with another woman" (51). But more important is the fact that "lesbian existence has been lived ... without access to any knowledge of a tradition, a continuity, a social underpinning" (Rich 52).

3. Lilian Faderman's *Surpassing the Love of Men: Romantic Friendship and Love Between Women from the Renaissance to the Present.*

4. For example, the question raised by Joanna Russ in "To Write 'Like a Woman': Transformations of Identity in the Work of Willa Cather": "How can a lesbian novelist use her experiences and feelings, especially her sexual ones, in an era which doesn't permit her to be open about them?" (77)

5. *The Manuscripts of Pauline Archange* (translated in 1982) and which includes *Les Manuscrits de Pauline Archange* (1968) and

Vivre! Vivre! (1969), and *Dürer's Angel* (1970), a translation of *Les Apparences* (1970).

6. Miller's article is reprinted in *Life/Lines: Theorizing Women's Autobiography*, Brodzki and Schenck, eds.: 45-61.
7. Mary Meigs used the same kind of device in *Lily Briscoe*, by calling it an autobiography, since the name of the author is never mentioned. This "fictitious autobiography" is parallel to Blais's *The Manuscripts of Pauline Archange*. The connections between these two writers' literary productions might be the object of an interesting study.
8. Marie Couillard's essay entitled "Les Carnets de Marie-Claire Blais: du privé au public" suggests a more recent source of exploration. The question is not to be centered on the sexual identity of a writer, but rather to understand how sexual repression affects a writer's production, as mentioned by Joanna Russ, for example (Note 4, above).
9. Blais's interview with Donald Smith was published in English under the title: "Deliverance Through Writing."
10. Irène Oore presented this concept at the 1989 Midwest Modern Language Association Annual Meeting in Minneapolis, MN, November 2-4, 1989.
11. Among others: Münch (3, 73, 154); Lautrec and Grosz (66); Otto Dix (154); Kierkegaard (39); Dostoyevsky (75); Tolstoy (123); Bach (123); Mozart (70, 176-77); Strauss (70).
12. The relationship between mother and daughter in Blais's *Visions d'Anna* has been studied by Karen Gould, Mary Jean Green and Paula Gilbert Lewis in "Inscriptions of the Feminine: A Century of Women Writing in Quebec." Patricia Smart, in *Ecrire dans la maison du père*, goes further, by mentioning the subversive aspect of women's reconnecting with their mother through writing: "Connaître, représenter, imaginer la construction de l'identité en renouant avec le féminin-maternel est l'activité subversive commencée par la parole des filles" (334). ["To know, to represent, to imagine the construction of identity by reconnecting with femininity and motherhood is the subversive activity started by the daughters' 'prise de parole'." (My translation)].
13. Nadeau's essay published after the completion of this study reflects the same kind of difficulty.
14. Rich stresses that "the destruction of records and memorabilia and letters documenting the realities of lesbian existence must be taken very seriously as a means of keeping heterosexuality compulsory for women" ("Compulsory Heterosexuality" 52).

Therefore, whether or not they are "lesbians," feminist critics can choose to continue the traditional erasure of women's experiences by ignoring the full range of women's lives and choices, or they can decide to take an important step forward, and deal with differences. François Filiatrault, in his review of John Boswell's *Christianisme, tolérance sociale et homosexualité*, mentions the dilemma facing all critics: "On reproche aux 'gais' qui écrivent sur le sujet de ne pas être objectifs ou de vouloir justifier leur existence, tandis qu'à part les moralisateurs, les hétérosexuels n'abordent pas la question par peur de sembler 'en être'. ["'Gays' who write on the topic are criticized for not being objective or for wanting to justify their existence, whereas, apart from the moralizers, straight critics don't address the question for fear of seeming to be 'one of them'" (my translation)]. However, only through the acceptance and study of diversities can critics totally and honestly grasp the wealth of an artist's production.

WORKS CITED

Blais, Marie-Claire. *L'Ange de la solitude*. Montréal: VLB, 1989.
———. *Anna's World* (1982); trans. of *Visions d'Anna ou le vertige*. Sheila Fischman. Toronto: Lester & Orpen Dennys, 1985.
———. *Deaf to the City* (1979); trans. of *Un Sourd dans la ville*. Carol Dunlop. Woodstock, NY: Overlook, 1987.
———. *Dürer's Angel* (1970); trans. of *Les Apparences*. David Lobdell. Vancouver: Talonbooks, 1976.
———. *L'Ile*. Montréal: VLB, 1988.
———. *A Literary Affair* (1975); trans. of *Une liaison parisienne*. Sheila Fischman. Toronto: McClelland & Stewart, 1979.
———. *The Manuscripts of Pauline Archange* (1968); trans. Derek Coltman. Toronto: McClelland & Stewart, Canadian Library, 1982. [Includes *Manuscrits de Pauline Archange* (1968) and *Vivre! Vivre!* (1969)].
———. *Nights in the Underground: An Exploration of Love* (1978); trans. of *Les Nuits de l'Underground*. Ray Ellenwood. Toronto: Musson, 1979.
Brodzki, Bella and Celeste Schenck, eds. *Life/Lines: Theorizing Women's Autobiography*. Ithaca, NY: Cornell UP, 1988.

Couillard, Marie. "Les Carnets de Marie-Claire Blais: Du privé au public." *Québec Studies* 10 (Spring/Summer 1990). 1-7.

Fabi, Thérèse. *Le monde perturbé des jeunes dans l'oeuvre de Marie-Claire Blais: Sa vie, son oeuvre, la critique.* Montréal: Editions Agence d'Arc, 1973.

Faderman, Lillian. *Surpassing the Love of Men: Romantic Friendship and Love Between Women from the Renaissance to the Present.* New York: William Morrow, 1981.

Filiatrault, François. "A Review of *Christianisme, tolérance sociale et homosexualité.*" *Spirale* 58 (février 1986): 15.

Gould, Karen. "The Censored Word and the Body Politics: Reconsidering the Fiction of Marie-Claire Blais." *Journal of Popular Culture* 15.3 (Winter 1981): 14-27.

———, Mary Jean Green, and Paula Gilbert Lewis. "Inscriptions of the Feminine: A Century of Women Writing in Quebec." *American Review of Canadian Studies* 15.4 (1985): 363-88.

Green, Mary Jean. "Structures of Liberation: Female Experience and Autobiographical Form in Quebec." *Yale French Studies* 65 (1983): 124-36; rptd. in *Life/Lines*: Eds. Bella Brodzki and Celeste Schenck. 189-99.

Hall, Radclyffe. *The Well of Loneliness* (1928). New York: Pocket Books, 1950.

Jelinek, Estelle C., ed. *Women's Autobiography: Essays in Criticism.* Bloomington: Indiana UP, 1980.

Krieger, Susan. "Lesbian Identity and Community: Recent Social Science Literature." *Signs: Journal of Women in Culture and Society* 8.1 (1982): 91-108.

Kröller, Eva-Maria. "Marie-Claire Blais." *Dictionary of Literary Biography: Canadian Writers Since 1960* 53 (1986): 66-75.

Lewis, Paula Gilbert. "From Shattered Reflections to Female Bonding: Mirroring in Marie-Claire Blais's *Visions d'Anna.*" *Québec Studies* 2 (1984): 94-104.

Libertin, Mary. "Female friendship in women's verse: toward a new theory of female poetics." *Women's Studies* 9 (1982): 291-308.

Martin, Biddy. "Lesbian Identity and Autobiographical Difference[s]." In Bella Brodzki and Celeste Schenck, eds. *Life/Lines.*

Meigs, Mary. *Lily Briscoe: A Self-Portrait. An Autobiography.* Vancouver: Talonbooks, 1981.

———. *The Medusa Head.* Vancouver: Talonbooks, 1983.

Milot, Louise. "Le dernier Marie-Claire Blais." *Lettres québécoises* 55 (automne 1989): 24-25.

Moses, Alice E. *Identity Management in Lesbian Women*. New York: Praeger, 1978.
Nadeau, Vincent. *Marie-Claire Blais: Le noir et le tendre. Etude d'Une Saison dans la vie d'Emmanuel, suivi d'une bibliographie critique*. Montréal: Les Presses de l'Université de Montréal, 1974.
——. "Des Filles et du grand méchant loup: une lecture de l'*Ange de la Solitude*." *Québec Studies* 10 (Spring/Summer 1990): 45-49.
O'Brien, Sharon. "'The Thing Not Named': Willa Cather as a Lesbian Writer." *The Lesbian Issue. Essays from Signs*. Eds. Estelle B. Freedman, Barbara C. Gelpi, Susan L. Johnson, and Kathleen M. Weston. Chicago: U of Chicago P, 1985: 68-71.
Ponse, Barbara. *Identities in the Lesbian World. The Social Construction of the Self*. Westport, CT.: Greenwood, 1978.
Rich, Adrienne. "When We Dead Awaken: Writing As Re-Vision" (1971). *On Lies, Secrets, and Silences. Selected Prose 1966-1978*. New York: Norton, 1979: 33-49.
——. "Compulsory Heterosexuality and Lesbian Existence" (1980). *Blood, Bread, and Poetry. Selected Prose 1979-1985*. New York: Norton, 1986: 23-75.
Russ, Joanna. "To Write 'Like a Woman': Transformations of Identity in the Work of Willa Cather." *Historical, Literary, and Erotic Aspects of Lesbianism*. Ed. Monika Kehoe. New York: Harrington Park, 1986: 77-87.
Smart, Patricia. *Ecrire dans la maison du père. Emergence du féminin dans la tradition littéraire du Québec*. Montréal: Editions Québec/Amérique, 1988.
Smith, Donald. "Marie-Claire Blais. Deliverance Through Writing." *Interviews with Quebec and Acadian Writers*. Trans. Larry Shouldice. Toronto: Anansi, 1986; 129-45.
——. "Marie-Claire Blais ou le salut par l'écriture." *L' Ecrivain devant son oeuvre*. Montréal: Québec/Amérique, 1983. 129-46.
Smith, Sidonie. *A Poetics of Women's Autobiography. Marginality and the Fictions of Self-Representation*. Bloomington: Indiana UP, 1987.
Smith-Rosenberg, Carroll. "The Female World of Love and Ritual." *Signs: Journal of Women in Culture and Society* 1.1 (1975): 29-40.
Stratford, Philippe. *Marie-Claire Blais*. "Canadian Writers and Their Works." Toronto: Forum House, 1971.
Viswanathan, Jacqueline. "Echanger sa vie pour une autre. Focalisation multiple dans *Mrs. Dalloway* et *Le Sourd dans la ville*." *Arcadia. Zeitschrift für Vergleich* 20.2 (1985): 179-94.

Walker, Alice. *In Search of our Mothers' Gardens*. San Diego, New York: Harcourt, 1983.
Woolf, Virginia. *Mrs. Dalloway* (1925). London: Granada, 1979.
Zimmerman, Bonnie. "An Overview of Lesbian Literary Criticism." *Feminist Studies* 7.3 (Fall 1981): 451-76.

Feminist Revisions of Feminine Texts

Katherine Anne Porter's Miranda: The Agrarian Myth and Southern Womanhood

Mary Titus

During her lifetime, Katherine Anne Porter created a fictional public identity that delighted her audience's imagination. It included a revised birthdate more in keeping with her striking appearance, an exclusive, religious education in a Catholic school in New Orleans, and a genteel homelife suitable to a once wealthy, extended family still clinging to its Old Southern heritage.

As we now know, Callie Porter was born in western Texas and grew up in poverty with little formal education. Her mother died when she was two years old, her grandmother when she was nine, and the insecurity and unhappiness of her early years left her with an enduring sense of alienation, which undermined her efforts to put down physical roots or sustain emotional relationships.

Porter's restlessness and ambition brought her from newspaper work in Denver to Greenwich Village in the 1920s. From there she travelled to Mexico City as a journalist and then on to Europe, with the aid of a Guggenheim. Her nomadic lifestyle and many romantic affairs militated against sustained literary work; however, between 1920 and 1940 she produced the extraordinarily complex, perfectly crafted short fiction on which her reputation rests today. She is best known for her fiction set in Mexico, particularly "Flowering Judas," and for her ostensibly autobiographical stories about Miranda Gay, a young woman whose family heritage is deeply interwoven with myths of the antebellum South.

From approximately 1940-1960, Porter labored on a much publicized, long awaited novel, Ship of Fools. During her final years, spent mostly near Washington, D.C., she wrote little, expending her energy instead on her public identity—perhaps her greatest work of *fiction. She gathered many honors, including both the Pulitzer Prize and the National Book Award for her* Collected Stories *and was a frequent guest at the White House. When she died in 1980, she left the University of Maryland a fascinating, somewhat disorderly, and very extensive collection of manuscripts and correspondence.*

Until shortly after her death in 1980, Katherine Anne Porter was a writer known by her public myth. She was the Southern Lady, and both she and her audience celebrated her femininity, aristocracy, and roots in the romance of the Old South. Pleased to identity herself as a member of "the guilt-ridden white-pillar crowd" (*Conversations* 83) and the "grandchild of a lost War," she publicly depicted her family as "nobly unreconstructed" (*Collected Essays* 161). After Porter's death, however, an extensively researched biography debunked the romantic stories which surrounded her, revealing them as texts woven by Porter and her readers out of the strands of her autobiographical fiction and her fictive memoirs and reminiscences (Givner). As Joan Givner has argued: "In the place of Callie Porter, raised in poverty and obscurity, she created Katherine Anne Porter, an aristocratic daughter of the Old South and the descendant of a long line of distinguished statesmen" (17). Exposing the extreme deprivation of Porter's childhood in west Texas, and repeatedly revealing incidents of her infidelity to truth, Givner's biography replaced Porter's gentility with a new story of gritty poverty and struggle. Yet this portrait would have roused indignation in its subject, for over the years Porter became increasingly committed to her fictional identity, assuming it at every level from dress and speech mannerism to publicly presented values. Particularly after *Ship of Fools*, she played the Southern Lady to the hilt and seemed to believe herself the embodiment and confirmation of that cherished American role.

Throughout Porter's life the fictive "she" was a hairsbreadth away from the "I." This is particularly true in the case of her Miranda stories, which constitute the crucial texts for understanding her self-transformation. In some of her unpublished papers "I" and "Miranda" alternately identify the same subject on the same page.[1] These papers also reveal that the Miranda stories, including the short novel *Old Mortality* and the sketches which make up *The Old Order*, find their origins in Porter's labors on *Many Redeemers*, a novel she undertook in late 1932. Never completed, *Many Redeemers* represented an extraordinarily ambitious plan to retell the Porter family history in fictional form. It would cover "from about 1700 to 1918," moving from European roots to the present. Through the novel, Porter hoped to place her own life within a historical context which would give it both order and meaning. The work thus mingles personal desire and historical record, fiction and fact, or—to use Porter's terms—"legend and memory." "Legend and memory" is Porter's name for her theory connecting autobiography with fiction, which she formulated as she approached her novel. It argues that all memory inevitably becomes legend, and that all legend becomes truth. In the light of this theory, Porter could perceive her revisionary family history as her true heritage.

The Miranda stories which rose out of *Many Redeemers* are marked by the meeting of private self and cultural moment. Two specific contexts seem most essential to their formulation. As the fragments of an unpublished autobiography reveal, Porter's early childhood fed a desire for ways to gild and reorder the past. However, her attraction to the South as the stage for her personal fiction can also be credited to the influence of contemporary Agrarian ideology. In fact Porter's autobiographical fiction may be read as a gender-inflected response to the Agrarian pursuit. Reading with attention the recurring sexual violence of her autobiographical fiction, we can uncover the struggles of a woman seeking to construct a self out of a cultural myth she found both appealing and repressive. The same unresolved attraction and repulsion is inscribed in the fiction's representation of family heritage; in these stories inherited family ties simultaneously sustain and strangle. The origins and intellectual attitudes of the Agrarians need little rehearsing here. Their published work in the 1930s represents the most sophisticated articulation of that ideological cluster which surrounds the legend of antebellum plantation life. The Agrarian response to the modernization and moral upheaval accompanying WWI was a retreat to "the past," as Richard King argues, a "yearning for an organic, hierarchical order such as allegedly existed in the ante-bellum South" (51). Their ideal society represents a solidly patriarchal construct; it reverenced the white Southern family, privileging the landed gentry as inherently superior by virtue of birth, enthroning the white man, and setting the white woman up on a pedestal. Porter's ties with the Agrarian group were long and intimate. In the late 1920s, she moved into a Greenwich Village apartment building also housing Caroline Gordon. Through Gordon she met Allen Tate and the Warrens, and ten years later her fourth husband Albert Erskine, editor of The *Southern Review*. Porter found these fellow Southerners highly congenial and joined them in giving a regional definition to her generation's post WWI experience of historical and cultural dislocation. In a brief outline of *Many Redeemers* she places her personal alienation from her historical present in terms of Southern history: her generation, caught in the final throes of a dying South, is thrown from the land, old ties of place and family irrevocably broken.

> Then my own generation, born on the edge of another break-up, for the real break-up did not occur immediately after the war, but with the death of my grandmother, an old woman who almost single-handedly held the thing together until her last day. . . . I belong to the generation left stripped and homeless . . . not my father's generation . . . because they still had the land and they still had the tradition. . . . Stop with my generation on the edge of life, facing all that we did face. . . .

Like her Agrarian compatriots, Porter created a personal history in which she represented the disinherited descendent of "an aristocratic and organic order cemented by ties of family, status, [and] tradition" (King 51). Her published autobiographical essays, such as "Portrait: Old South" or "Noon Wine: The Sources" ring with phrases like "good old family," "nobly unreconstructed," or "blood-knowledge"—the chimes of the Agrarian nostalgia.

For Porter, the need to construct a "never-never land" of peaceful affluence and meaningful order was perhaps more acute than for her contemporaries. Her actual childhood left her with particularly painful memories, which gave her recurring unhappiness throughout her life (Givner 43, 45; see Titus). An unpublished fragment of autobiography, titled "Pull Dick, Pull Devil" reveals her urge to revise personal history. In it, she moves between recollections of a disorderly, increasingly impoverished childhood, and rhapsodies of orderly living. She describes her family life as emotionally chaotic; between "successive uproars, we were beaten and lectured and prayed over. . . . I realize now that all of us, from my grandmother down, were neurotics, they all seemed to live in a hornet's nest of disorder." And then, in the space of a sentence, she yields to another vision, memories of "lavender scented bed linen and thin old silver. . . . Negroes singing in the cotton field." As in Porter's public reminiscences or interviews, especially later in her life, these "memories" characteristically contain the three elements Francis Pendleton Gaines long ago designated as central to the plantation legend: a landed aristocracy, black servants, and a world resembling a golden age: the people more beautiful, life more leisurely and pastoral.[2] However, except for a few family heirlooms, and perhaps some stories from her grandmother of former prestige and security, Porter's childhood offered scant material for her depiction of home and family in either her fiction or her later fictive reminiscences. In Texas, where Porter spent her childhood, her family shared a two room log house in Indian Creek: other neighbors lived in sod huts (Givner 36-37). Whatever backbone he possessed, her father, Harrison Boone Porter, lost soon after Porter's mother died of an illness complicated by repeated pregnancies: "the family was then plunged into real grinding poverty" (Givner 45). Porter was about a year and a half old. They crowded into Porter's grandmother's house in Kyle, Texas, until her grandmother's death when Porter was eleven. Then, uprooted, they left the Texas countryside for a series of homes in San Antonio.

Reconstructing her past represented Porter's response to the instability and unhappiness of her childhood. The pattern of "Pull-Dick, Pull-Devil" reappears in many forms as she labored to cover over actual memory and confirm her ties to another, self-fabricated history. On the simplest level, she tried repeatedly and unsuccessfully to create homes which reproduced her imagined heritage; in part this explains the fact that she bought antiques and then claimed than as cherished family heirlooms (Givner 20). Of more importance is her autobiographical fiction. *Many Redeemers* represented the self-confirming text for Porter, reconstructing her heritage as an articulation of the Agrarian myth. She began the task in Europe, digging into genealogical records for aristocratic forebears, following the Southern mythographers in her attention to the purity and potency of inherited blood. Believing that appearance, intellect, and ability—in short, identity—originate in and are indelibly stamped by lineage, she undertook genealogical research as part of her work on *Many Redeemers*, trying to construct a line of descent which would connect her family back through pioneer ancestors to aristocratic European forebears. The emphasis on "blood," an integral part of the Southern myth, probably appealed to Porter for reasons other than the obsession with racial purity which marked post Civil War ideology. She imagined that her "blood" connected her to ancestors more admirable than her immediate family. As she once wrote her sister, describing her response to her father's lack of motivation and personal failure: "Sometimes I have such a horror of having had such a father it almost cripples me. Then I have to remember that I have hundreds of years of other ancestors too, really brave and firm, and I rely on them."[3]

Constructing her bloodlines, Porter was less concerned with proof of descent than with prestige, as Joan Givner has shown, and chose the most illustrious from among the Porters and Boones of history (26). She wrote Caroline Gordon that her guide in *Many Redeemers* was a truth deeper than fact; as she reconstructs history, she will "depend precisely on what I know in my blood, and in my memory, and on something that is *deeper than knowledge*."[4] These sources are most fully defined in a speech she gave to the American Women's Club of Paris in 1935. Describing her work on *Many Redeemers*, the speech anatomizes the material she drew upon while attempting to write "my own past retold in the history of my family":

> I have for this only legend, those things I have been told or that I read as a child [. . .] and my own memory of events taking place around me at the same time. And there is a third facet: my present memory and explanation to myself of my then personal life, the life of a child, which is in itself a mystery, while being living and legendary to that same child grown up.[5]

Porter's three sources can be viewed as an interactive continuum. At the farthest end lies legend, representing the past transformed and perfected into fiction. Memory extends from legend up to the present, becoming increasingly disorganized as it is more immediate. The present continually seeks to explain and so order memory, gradually transforming the furthest events into legend. Thus "the life of a child" becomes legendary "to that same child grown up."

Yet Porter's autobiographical fiction is not then the simple transformation of memory into legend; it is instead a conglomerate of extant legend, personally transformed memory, and present desire. None of these is simple or singular. As Porter goes on to define each term in "Legend and Memory," she describes thereby her creative process:

> No legend is ever true . . . the legend is that work of art which goes on in the human mind, adding to and arranging, harmonizing and rounding out, making larger or smaller than life, and holding the entire finished product in a good light and asking you to believe it. And it is true. No memory

is really faithful. It has too far to go, too many changing landscapes of the human mind and heart, to bear any sort of really trustworthy witness, except in part. So the truth in art is got by change.

Truth comes not from autobiographical fact but from transformation. The remade life, that is the life as it is transformed into fiction, is the true story. As Porter wrote Eudora Welty: "by the organic process of creation, the scattered and seemingly random events remembered through many years became fiction, that is—not a lie, really as I think you call it—but symbolic truth."[6]

The legend Porter formulated as she researched ancestors, delved into her own memory, and recalled stories of her family's past, tells of well-established, even aristocratic ancestors who endured life in a log cabin only as a temporary interim between more settled periods when their lives reproduced the world of the Old South. It is a legend shaped by the Agrarian imagination. To draw a representative selection from among the scattered, undated notes which make up much of her manuscript collection:

> It was simply true that my ancestors, crossing the Cumberland gap and going through the wilderness had carried their Latin and Greek grammars, old books of music, a piece or two of rosewood or mahogany, even an occasional tall gilded harp. They wore coonskin caps and moccasins and lived in log cabins, but only so long as they had to: their goal was land, a landed estate, with a house as much like the one they had left in Virginia or Pennsylvania as they could manage: which in turn had been as much like the one they had left in England.

The gilded harp in the log cabin is both a grand flight of fancy and an image overwhelmingly vulnerable to ridicule. Overall, the passage, like many others in Porter's published and unpublished memoirs, has close companions in the Agrarian manifestos. One might compare it to John Crowe Ransom's description of the Southern gentry in the lead essay of *I'll Take My Stand*: "They have elected to live their comparatively easy and routine lives in accordance with the tradition which they inherited, and they have consequently enjoyed a leisure, a security, and an intellectual freedom that were never the portion of pioneers" (4).

Through the process of transforming her family's history, Porter transformed herself: memory moved from legend to truth. Although she never finished *Many Redeemers*, she did create a self-embracing legend which, from this point on, progressively influenced her sense of identity. Sometime during the 1930s, Porter began to take on her public role as the aristocratic Southern Lady of letters, presenting herself as blood inheritor of the Old South. When her friend Allen Tate visited her in Paris in 1932, he noted a new, emerging personality. As he wrote John Peale Bishop, "There has been a wonderful change in her since I first knew her, even since about 1932. And I don't think it means anything good. She has become a great Personage" (Young and Hindle 172-73).

The Miranda fiction from *Many Redeemers* that Porter formulated during these years presents several characters who are similarly sustained and even ennobled by their own legends of the past. In one of the published fragments, "The Old Order," she represented her theory of "legend and memory" in the image of quilt-making. Grandmother and Nannie, both storytellers, spend hours with needles, old family finery, and "clear lemon floss," sewing family quilts. With words and thread they create a shared legend. Like Porter herself, these two women find that stitching fragments of the past into a new order provides them with a truth, an "old order" by which they can explain their present lives. Perhaps Porter's most heroic characters, Grandmother and Nannie seem more than human, possessing unwavering self-knowledge, strength, and authority. Their shared, self-made legend underlies their strong sense of identity, describing who and what and where they are, from what they and their forebears have been. Although the world that surrounds Grandmother and Nannie has changed, they remain stable, suffering no dislocation. Rather, their conversation perpetually alters and orders the present into a version of the past, incorporating it into their story. "Even the future seemed like something gone and done with when they spoke of it" (327).[7]

Porter's representation of the interaction of "legend and memory" through the image of piecing a quilt connects her theory of creative process to women's culture by employing a traditional emblem of women's writing.[8] In their collaborative work the two elderly women employ the material of women's lives, recounting marriages, births, and deaths, and stitching together fabric worn by the family women at these central events. Their "clear lemon floss" creates a beautiful and useful object from fragments of the past: the quilt suggests how the past can continue to comfort the present, passed on in a family as a thing of good use. The image, standing as Porter's sign of the creative process, suggests that the compounding of "legend and memory" was, in her mind, a particularly feminine creative process.

The self-confirming power of a personal fiction returns as a central theme in "Old Mortality." Although this short novel records only a fragment of the *Many Redeemers* project, it stands as the summation and minor accomplishment of Porter's fictional family history. Initially Amy represents the "perfect" achievement of womanhood, the family's symbol of their own past possession of perfection against which the present is measured and diminished. An "angel" or "singing angel" (176, 181), Amy sits forever posed in memory against the "bright blank heavenly blue sky" of family legend (175). Among Porter's papers gathered under the title "Old Mortality" is a typescript containing her own brief analysis of the story. It includes a discussion of the photograph with which the story opens.

> It is an imperfect photograph—doesn't really give her beauty. The children don't understand why she is thought so beautiful. Too imperfect, it doesn't give us a true picture . . . but it does give us an idea of the past.
>
> The people who had seen her and who had lived at that time had not seen her at all. The picture brought back their own youth and their own sense of reality. When they saw her as she was alive and moving and they were with her—brought back their own past and made their own lives seem real and vital.

The passage is wonderfully suggestive. It emphasizes that the photograph is an "imperfect" record, not "true"; yet it gives "an idea" of the past. That "idea" seems to be the act of recollection, which invigorates the self in the present. Twice the passage equates remembering with achieved identity: to have youth "brought back" is to attain a "sense of reality"; to have the past "brought back," is to feel one's life suddenly "real and vital." Looking at the photograph or handling heirlooms, the older family members know who and where and what they are. Speaking of Amy they become storytellers; like Grandmother and Nannie they possess a legend that explains and orders their present. As Porter states, Amy's family had never "seen her at all." The point of recollection is the self: memory creates legend, legend creates personal identity.

"Old Mortality" also suggests that legends of the past need not be beautiful to be true; they must only be believed. Porter sets the story of Amy's perfection against another version of the past, Cousin Eva's. According to Eva, Amy was "too free" and flirtatious, insensitive, "sex-ridden," and diseased (215, 216). Porter's notes indicate that Eva's story is companion rather than corrective to the family legend. "Scene on the train. Legend not exploded because the legend was true as the one who loved it told it, true as Miss Honey told it, who hated it, and true as Eva told it." Eva's version of Amy's legend represents another "symbolic truth," to use Porter's term in her letter to Eudora Welty. It arises from the wedding of legend and memory and confirms Eva's present identity: it is her ordering fiction. In her conversation with Miranda, Eva repeatedly juxtaposes herself, "I" against Amy, "she," finding herself in the opposition: "she" was ill at home; "I was sent to the hospital"; she "died"; "I came out"; "she was simply sex-ridden"; "I took to the soap box and platform when I was called upon" (215, 216). Eva finds pride and identity opposing herself to Amy; in her story she is the strong survivor and Amy is the guilty victim of the decadent past.

Cousin Eva, like all of Miranda's elders including Grandmother and Nannie, possesses a "truth," a legend of the past which sustains a present identity. At the close of "Old Mortality," when Miranda watches her father and Eva sharing family history at the train station, she sees them become more perfect and complete through the act of story-telling. They take on the ease and security of people "who occupied by right their place in the world":

> They were precisely themselves; their eyes cleared, their voices relaxed into perfect naturalness. . . . They sat back and went on talking steadily in their friendly family voices, talking about their dead. (219)

From their communion, their easy identity and sense of place arising from a shared, idealized past, Miranda is excluded. Bitterly she realizes, "It is I who have no place. . . . Where are my people and my own time." Stubbornly closing her mind "against remembering, not the past but the legend of the past, other people's memory of the past," Miranda resolves to find "the truth about what happens to me." Yet as Porter's closing appraisal of her heroine suggests, such a resolution may represent a kind of "hopefulness," but it is also "ignorance" (221). The "truth" about the self is only accessible through legend.

However, at the same time that published portions of *Many Redeemers* portray a legend of the past sustaining a present self, the same texts record Porter's personal struggle with the cultural myth with which she eventually shaped her public identity. The Agrarians reverenced the ties of family, place, and tradition, and drew deeply from the romance of the antebellum South as they constructed their ideal society. For Porter, both proved problematic. Although "The Old Order" and "Old Mortality" present legend rooted in family and place as essential to identity, they simultaneously rage against and resist these ties. Miranda's final resolutions form a litany of rejection: "She did not want any more ties with this house, she was going to leave it"; "she would have no more bonds that smothered her in love and hatred"; "I hate love, she thought, as if this were the answer, I hate loving and being loved, I hate it" (220-21). Miranda's rage echoes Porter's own, recorded many times in journals and letters. Although in the abstract she might embrace the Agrarian idealization of familial traditions, her specific experience taught her only the pain of family and memory. "The truth is, I can hardly bear to think," confess some scribbled notes, dated Mexico 1921, "And when I do, I go blind with simple anxiety and the suffering of remembrance." On June 12, 1928, she wrote her sister Gay Porter Holloway that "I have no happy memories at all to bring me there [to Texas], the first part of my life that I can bear to remember begins after I left . . . the South and went to Denver." And again to her sister on August 8, 1949:

> Very sincerely I date the beginning of my strange bad fortune since I came back from Europe, to my returning to Texas in 1936 . . . The murderous old hex of the family which I had just beaten off by main strength and had fled for fifteen years, just reached out and took me by the throat and started strangling again, just like the good old times.

The past may sustain, if it can be transformed into the "good old times" of the Old South. However, "the deathly bear trap"[9] of the Porter family would not yield easily to any form of idealization.

Porter's autobiographical fiction is marked by another conflict as well. Like the male Agrarians, she was deeply attracted to the antebellum South as a vision of a sheltered, ordered and inherited way of life. Yet as a woman she found herself profoundly alienated from that myth, for its supreme symbol, the Belle, exemplified the simultaneous idealization and control of female sexuality. The Belle's beauty and gaiety, and most of all her virginity, confirmed the beauty, gaiety, and racial purity of the white, Southern aristocracy. In this mythology, white women's sexuality was the sign of white Southern manhood and thus the focal point of a complex, repressive ideology, which rigidly defined women's place and function (see Scott, Westling, King).

Porter's stories from *Many Redeemers* are fractured by violent images of female sexuality, which tear through the smoothly woven texts of legend and memory. Beneath the surface of the smiling Belle, she saw women oppressed and destroyed by an ideology which enforced obedience to men and endorsed repeated childbearing while simultaneously denying women's sexuality. The Miranda stories share a violent imagery of defloration, suggesting Porter's recognition that for the Belle sexual intercourse represents a kind of social death. No doubt the sexual violence breaking through these stories gains impetus as well from Porter's childhood experience. Her mother's death shortly after her fifth pregnancy remained a painful and guilty memory throughout her life. We hear its echoes in Grandmother and Nannie's "grim and terrible race of procreation" (300).

"The Grave," another published fragment from *Many Redeemers*, succinctly juxtaposes the idealization and the actuality of women's sexual experience in the nineteenth century South. In the story, Miranda is just on the verge of puberty. She fantasizes about assuming the role of Belle and, for a moment, longs to "take a good cold bath, dust herself with plenty of Maria's violet talcum powder . . . put on the thinnest, most becoming dress she owned, with a big sash, and sit in a wicker chair under the trees" (365). But as she lingers, caught up in this fantasy, her brother shoots and then cuts open a pregnant rabbit, exposing in a "bloody heap" the rabbit's womb and the dead babies within. It is a violent lesson in the facts of womanhood for Miranda, a moment marked with the bloodshed that accompanies menstruation, defloration, and childbirth.

The same trail of blood runs through "Old Mortality." If superficially Amy Gay represents the perfection of the virginal, light-spirited Belle, the blood which stains her handkerchiefs when she coughs suggests the physical facts of sexuality, which she and her admirers would deny. Although she may drink "lemon and salt to stop her periods," she can never escape that bloodshed which is both symbolically fatal to her status as a Belle and potentially fatal to her as a woman (DeMouy 153). The price of winning for a woman is blood: Amy hemorrhages after "dancing all night three times in one week" (191) and Miss Lucy, Uncle Gabriel's horse, has "thick red rivulets" covering her "tender mouth and chin" after her triumph at the races (199).

A bride is a doomed woman, in "Old Mortality." Amy insists on wearing a gray wedding gown marked by a bloody splash of red feathers: "It is *my* funeral," she informs her mother; "I shall wear mourning if I like" (182). The story's imaging of the symbolic as well as the potential death accompanying marriage climaxes in Miranda's vision of "a long procession of living corpses, festering women stepping daily towards the charnel house . . . their dead faces lifted smiling" (216). The women are brides, "their corruption concealed under laces and flowers" (216). With the gay yet obedient step of the Belle, they march toward their graves.

The opposing movements of "Old Mortality," toward and against family ties, toward and against adulation of the Southern myth embodied in the Belle, come together in Miranda's final resolutions. When, at the close of the story, "her blood rebelled against the ties of blood," the two movements of the text are both implicated (220). In her urgent need to create her own "truth," she feels confined by the "legend and memory" of family members and strangled, like her creator, by the "bonds that smothered her in love and hatred" (220). At the same time she is caught within the narrow, destructive definition of her sexuality articulated in the myth of the antebellum South. As a Southern woman, Miranda is inescapably bound with the ties of blood.

Although Porter's fiction from her work on *Many Redeemers* questions the construction of gender and idealization of family ties, her public statements increasingly seemed to endorse the ideology of the Old South. Perhaps the most extreme example appears in a 1956 essay, "The Gift of Woman," which she wrote for *Woman's Home Companion*:

> Her arts are decorative and interpretive, and her gift is for being pleasing. . . . it is man that woman wishes to please. She is bride and mother; that is her destiny and things go much better if everybody accepts it without too much uproar (29).

Describing "woman," Porter describes a Southern Lady, and the subtle link between social order and women's place implicit in her words echoes any entrenched patriarchal ideology, including that of the Southern myth. Perhaps as she aged questions of sexuality became less personally threatening to her and she could embrace her role as Southern Lady without hesitation. Memory sank ever more deeply into legend, and slowly her early conflicts were covered over. The role of Southern Lady grew to be Porter's own and was enthusiastically endorsed by her admirers. Givner's biography provides ample illustrations of her dramatic self-presentation. Interviewers enjoyed describing her big hats, ropes of pearls, and gushing Southern speech, like "that of someone talking to a bird or coquetting with an old beau" (*Conversations* 78). Her appearance became the confirmation of a cherished American myth, and in her last years she grew to be a sort of public treasure. If publicly Katherine Anne Porter increasingly played the part of the Southern Lady, the texts which emerged at the start of this self-transformation radically question such a role. But as she grew into the past she had written for herself, she not only raised fewer questions about the sexual ideology which accompanied her adopted heritage, she also grew defensive about the mingling of legend and memory on which her identity was grounded. Late in life, the possession of a secure identity rooted in the South became one of her most triumphant themes. In 1969, when an interviewer asked her, "Are you sustained by your own legend?", she made clear that the word legend had become an anathema to her.

> I am sustained by my past—it's not a myth, it's history; we have the records and I know who my ancestors were and I know what they did and believed. So that this late anguish of the search for identity—of people who have no roots or no roots that they wish to acknowledge—but I know who I am and where I am and what I'm doing.[10]

Almost fifty years after her first trip to Europe, Porter forcefully denied that legend and memory were the source of a secure and sustaining identity in the present. Possessed by the legend she had labored to create throughout the thirties, she had become—from a Miranda's point of view—as blind as Nannie and Grandmother or all the storytellers in "Old Mortality" whose "hearts and imaginations [were] captivated by their past" (175).

NOTES

1. The extensive Porter manuscript collection is at the University of Maryland, College Park, Maryland. I am grateful to the special collections staff there for their kind assistance and to Isabel Bayley, Porter's literary executor, for permission to quote from Porter's unpublished papers. Here I am drawing from Porter's notes and outlines for *Many Redeemers*. Material connected with this project is primarily in the files labelled "Legend and Memory" and "Many Redeemers" at the University of Maryland; however, references to the project and some manuscripts clearly connected to it are scattered throughout Porter's papers; many are in the numerous files generically titled "Notes."
2. For an example of Porter's idyllic public memories see her 1963 interview with Barbara Johnson in *Conversations*, 78-98.
3. KAP to Gay Porter Holloway, September 20, 1952.
4. KAP to Caroline Gordon, June 9, 1935.
5. A revised version of this manuscript titled "Legend and Memory" is included in Porter's *Collected Essays* under the title "My First Speech."
6. The passage from a letter of February 20, 1956, deserves full quotation: "My God, I can compare the process only to tapping my own spinal fluid, so nearly does it come to the quick of memory, that is, numberless memories all fused together, sometimes no more tangible than dust-particles floating in a sunbeam; but the real difficulty is explaining how, by the organic process of creation, the scattered and seemingly random events remembered through many years become fiction, that is—not a lie, really as I think you call it—but symbolic truth."
7. Unless otherwise indicated, quotations from Porter's fiction are taken from *The Collected Stories*.
8. For a history of quilt-making references as textual signs of women's writing see Elaine Showalter's "Piecing and Writing."
9. "Families are deathly bear traps. The very thought of falling into the hands of mine scares the pee out of me. . . . You'd better take steps to get a little free . . . before it is everlastingly too late. . . . I would have been dead twenty five years ago if I'd stayed on." KAP to Gay Porter Holloway, December 13, 1945.
10. The typescript of this interview with Alice Denham is undated. However during the interview, Porter expresses outrage about

the footprints recently left on the moon. Her comments place the interview sometime shortly after July 21, 1969.

WORKS CITED

DeMouy, Jane Krause. *Katherine Anne Porter's Women: The Eye of Her Fiction*. Austin: U of Texas P, 1983.

Gaines, Frances Pendleton. *The Southern Plantation: A Study in the Development and Accuracy of a Tradition*. New York: Columbia UP, 1925.

Givner, Joan. *Katherine Anne Porter: A Life*. New York: Simon and Schuster, 1982.

King, Richard. *A Southern Renaissance: The Cultural Awakening of the American South, 1930-1955*. New York: Oxford UP, 1980.

Porter, Katherine Anne. *The Collected Essays and Occasional Writings of Katherine Anne Porter*, New York: Delacorte, 1970.

———. *The Collected Stories of Katherine Anne Porter*. New York: New American Library, 1965.

———. "The Gift of Woman." *Woman's Home Companion*. Dec., 1956: 29-33.

———. *Katherine Anne Porter: Conversations*. Ed. Joan Givner. Jackson: U of Mississippi P, 1987.

Scott, Anne Firor. *The Southern Lady: From Pedestal to Politics 1830-1930*. Chicago: U of Chicago P, 1970.

Showalter, Elaine. "Piecing and Writing." *The Poetics of Gender*. Ed. Nancy K. Miller. New York: Columbia UP, 1986. 222-47.

Titus, Mary. "'Mingled Sweetness and Corruption': Katherine Anne Porter's "The Fig Tree" and "The Grave." *South Atlantic Review* 53.2 (1987): 53-70.

Westling, Louise. *Sacred Groves and Ravaged Gardens*. Athens: U of Georgia P, 1985.

Young, Thomas Daniel and John J. Hindle. *The Republic of Letters in America: The Correspondence of John Peale Bishop and Allen Tate*. Louisville: UP of Kentucky, 1981. 172-73.

Gabrielle Roy's Children of My Heart *or Portrait of the Artist as a Young Woman*

Agnès Whitfield

Born in Manitoba (Canada) in 1909, Gabrielle Roy lived most of her adult life in Québec. In 1947, she won France's coveted Prix Fémina for her first, and perhaps best-known novel, The Tin Flute, *a touching study of working-class Montréal. Her subsequent works reflect a continued concern with social questions:* The Cashier (1954), The Hidden Mountain *(1961),* Windflower *(1970); and an increasing preoccupation with more personal and autobiographical matters:* Where Nests the Water Hen *(1950),* Street of Riches *(1955),* The Road Past Altamont *(1966),* Enchanted Summer *(1972),* Garden in the Wind *(1975),* Children of My Heart *(1977). A posthumous autobiography,* Enchantment and Sorrow *was published in 1984, a year after her death. Gabrielle Roy is generally considered to be one of Québec's greatest writers.*

Despite her compelling denunciation of the social and economic exploitation of French-Canadian, immigrant and native women, Gabrielle Roy (1909-1983) has generally been considered a traditionalist on women's issues, or at best, a "feminist humanist" (Lewis, *Literary Vision* 77). However unjust their fate, it would seem, her female characters nonetheless extol those virtues of traditional femininity, gentle resignation and tender altruism, exemplified by Roseanna Lacasse, the touching *mater dolorosa* of Roy's best-known novel, *Bonheur d'occasion*. Recently, however, scholars have begun to question the critical myths which underlie this conventional, albeit paradoxical, interpretation of Roy's portrayal of the female condition.[1] Feminist readings of her novels, such as Patricia Smart's thoughtful analysis of *Bonheur d'occasion* (197-234) are (dis)covering the darker side of what Phyllis Grosskurth once disparagingly called Roy's "mother's-eye view of the world" (7).

The author's posthumous autobiography, *La Détresse et l'enchantement*, has lent impetus to this reappraisal. In *her* story, Gabrielle Roy was independent and adventurous, with a passion for freedom and travel which contrasts sharply with the traditional vision of women ascribed to her as a writer. In the light of recent feminist research, such a self-portrait of the artist as young woman has called for a more sensitive de-coding of the tensions and ambiguities in Gabrielle Roy's fiction. As Shirley Foster writes in an article on early twentieth-century American women novelists, not without relevance to highly traditional French Canada, female writers have often been compelled by external ideological pressures to use "artistic devices which voice their unease without obviously challenging literary or sexual conventions" (154). Tensions or ambiguities can also arise in their writing, pursues Foster, from "their awareness of the complex and often contradictory nature of female aspiration" (154). Hence the difficulty in de-coding such texts whose narrative and thematic structures often at once disguise and reveal an implicit criticism of patriarchy.

Gabrielle Roy's problematic portrayal of the artist is a case in point, confirming Patricia Spacks's affirmation that "relatively few women have asserted themselves unambiguously as shaping artists in the act of writing about themselves" (181). Roy addresses the theme of the artist most explicitly in her novel, *La Montagne secrète*, through the reflections of a male painter, Pierre Cadorai, whose life is consumed by his aesthetic quest. This choice of a male hero is already revealing, for, in her autobiographical fiction, such as *La Route d'Altamont*, *Rue Deschambault* and *Ces enfants de ma vie* (*Children of My Heart*), which deals with her own childhood and early experiences as a teacher in Manitoba, the aesthetic quest and related questions of artistic identity and expression are treated obliquely. Not surprisingly, critical studies of Gabrielle Roy's aesthetic vision usually focus on *La Montagne secrète* or use this book as a model,[2] while the feminist implications of her autobiographical fiction, generally under-rated in comparison with her other works,[3] have not been fully explored.

Considered one of Roy's most "passionate and troubling" books (Marcotte 17, our translation), *Children of My Heart* is also, in this respect, one of her most problematic. Certainly, Roy's earlier autobiographical works, *Rue Deschambault* and *La Route d'Altamont*, are more clearly introspective, more easily identifiable as "spiritual biographies of the narrator, on the road toward self-discovery and self-acceptance" (Lewis, *Literary Vision* 17). In contrast, the very title of *Children of My Heart* announces a displacement of focus away from the artist's self to "those" children, as the original French title reads, whom she will be remembering, although the possessive adjective affirms what Philippe Lejeune has called the "autobiographical pact" (15) between author, narrator and protagonist, and discretely retains possession of the artist's "heart," or "life" in French.

This subtle juxtaposition of self and others is mirrored throughout *Children of My Heart* in the understated relationship between the narrator and her story. Although the first sentence of the novel, "When I think back, as I often do these days, to my years as a young teacher . . . "(9), firmly identifies the narration as retrospective, the narrator's priority seems, on an initial reading, to lie not with her own present but with the events and people of her past. In fact, so infrequent, at times, are the explicit references to the narrator's present self that much of the text could almost be read as a third-person narrative about the experiences of the narrator's youthful self, a young school teacher in Manitoba, and her first pupils.

That such a narrative structure has indeed appeared somewhat ambiguous or inconsistent is reflected in the critical response to *Children of My Heart*. In particular, critics have had difficulty in determining the volume's *genre*. For some, it is merely a collection of "short stories about children" (Riddick 20, our translation), a "series of fictionalized reminiscences" (Keywan 73), but "not a novel, as its publishers claim" (Abley 56). For others, the thematic links between chapters and the use of the first-person narrator are sufficient to ensure the artistic unity of the novelistic form, but only at the expense of autobiography. "If at first glance, the signature and the use of the first-person allow the reader to identify the teacher with a real person called Gabrielle Roy," writes Gilles Marcotte, "we are soon convinced of the irrelevance of this association. The narrator is a full-fledged character" (17, our translation). For still other critics, *Children of My Heart* inhabits a formal no-man's land, presenting "the typical admixture of autobiography to short stories" (Hesse 82).

However, such resistance to categorization, as Estelle Jelinek has pointed out, is a frequent characteristic of women's autobiographical writing (17). In this case, it is as much the relational nature as the form of Roy's vision which is problematic. Yet, Roy's focus on the other also places her firmly within the female autobiographical tradition. Women seem to require another self both to define and to represent their own identity. As Mary Mason has argued, "The self-discovery of female identity seems to acknowledge this real presence and recognition of another consciousness and the disclosure of female self is linked to the identification of some 'other'" (22). While this role is often played by the writer's spouse or mother, women also write to or about their children.[4] In this context, then, the children Roy describes are to be analyzed not so much as subjects worthy of representation in themselves, although such may they be, but as part of the subtle narrative technique by which the author defines her own self in relation to an "other." It is the fundamentally relational duality of the title which must be respected, rather than some perceived, or pre-conceived, priority of focus.

Significantly, a similar identity/alterity dynamic also underlies the first part of *La Détresse et l'enchantement*, which deals with the same early teaching experiences described in *Children of My Heart*. Read co-extensively, these two texts constitute an almost perfect foil one for the other. Roy's autobiography focuses almost exclusively on the female others in her life, her sisters and especially her aging mother; the author's father, who died while she was at Teacher's College, is at best a shadowy figure. In contrast, *Children of My Heart* is essentially structured around male others, children, for the most part, but also their fathers. Although a discrete but important maternal presence is retained, this is accomplished through the representation of the children's families rather than by an analysis of the narrator's relationship with her own mother.

Also revealing is the fact that both texts end with a departure. While this may appear purely coincidental in the case of Roy's autobiography, the author's teaching career culminating indeed with her departure for Paris, Roy's decision to end the first part of her autobiography with this event is nonetheless the result as much of artistic choice as anecdotal veracity. The corresponding structure of *Children of My Heart* is an even more obvious artistic construct, as it has been adopted at the expense of chronological order. In each book, furthermore, similar anecdotal details reinforce the intense emotional charge of the departure for both narrators: a train station, a busy send-off by numerous friends and colleagues, the presentation of a cherished gift by a favorite young male friend, a last descriptive zoom on a beloved face, that of Médéric, the narrator's young friend, in *Children of My Heart*, that of Roy's mother in *La Détresse et l'enchantement*. Undoubtedly, it is this last detail which is the most significant, through its evocation of the intense and ambivalent emotions experienced by both narrators. Both texts can thus be seen to highlight relation and separation, and to posit the importance, for Gabrielle Roy, of the search at once for intimacy and autonomy.

Why this search should be problematic and what consequences this might have for Gabrielle Roy's conception of the artist as woman can be clarified through a more detailed analysis of the narrative structure of her fictional autobiography.[5] Not unlike Lillian Hellman's *Pentimento*, *Children of My Heart* is presented as a series of portraits, although, in Roy's book, each 'cameo' tells a similar story, that of the discovery of a young boy's gift, whether artistic or expressive. In the first chapter, "Vincento," Gabrielle Roy describes little Vincento's stormy arrival at school and his acceptance of his new fate when he, in turn with all the other pupils, learns how to draw his house on the blackboard. In "L'Enfant de Noël" (The Christmas Child), Clair, a meticulous writer, suffers in silence until he too finds a way, despite his family's poverty, to offer his beloved teacher a gift. In "L'Alouette" (The Lark), Nil discovers that his beautiful voice can bring pleasure to the elderly and ill. In "Demetrioff," the last of the recalcitrant Demetrioff children is transformed by his marvelous talent for calligraphy. André, the hero of "La Maison gardée" (Guarding the House), offers the gift of protection to his mother, bed-ridden through a difficult pregnancy while her husband is away lumbering. The last and most complex story of the book, "De la truite dans l'eau glacée" (Trout in Ice Water), relates the ambiguous relationship between the narrator and a young adolescent, Médéric, who give to each other the gift of knowledge, she by initiating him to the pleasure of reading, and he, by introducing her to the beauty of nature.

Explicitly, then, the book describes a formative experience in the lives of six boys who, through the expression of an artistic or emotional gift, each achieve a measure of self-discovery and self-realization. The narrator herself underlines the importance of this theme of male identity by her frequent comparisons and references to manhood. "I had the class of the very smallest," she writes in the initial story, "It was their first step into an unknown world" (9). In "The Christmas Child," she implicitly links a young boy's emotional response to that of the adult male: "I found out that it could be harder to change the mind of a loving child than that of a grown man armed with all his strength" (19). The large Demetrioff clan of boys, all in the "very mould" (59-60) of their father, offers a perfect step-by-step image of the transformation from boy to man: "There are two or three bigger ones hanging on in the Brothers' classes," the narrator remembers one of her colleagues' remark, "Put one of the little ones beside them and it's the same face but not quite as tough" (56-57). In "Guarding the House," little André is described as "sitting astride his chair like a man, his hands joined behind the chair-back" (104). In the last story, the narrator catches her pupil at the verge of manhood: "I had never yet seen so clearly the transitory linkage between child and man, which lasts until the one takes over" (161).

Nowhere, even in the tone of such comments, does the narrator appear to doubt the nature of "manhood." If the toughness of the Demetrioff clan is subtly criticized, it is not perceived as deviant. Nor does the narrator feel compelled to clarify her observations for the reader to whom she thus attributes a similar security of definition. At this level of interpretation, *Children of My Heart* appears to echo *The Hidden Mountain* in its explicit portrayal of the development of the male child and, particularly, in his realization as an artist. For each of the stories, as Réjean Robidoux has pointed out, "can and should also be read as a symbolic discourse on writing" ("Gabrielle Roy" 21, our translation). Inscribed in the shadows of this explicit text, the nature of the narrator's own identity as female and writer is represented not as a quest but as a question, defined only by its apparent absence.

However, a de-coding of the implicit structures of the text offers a more complex, almost contrapuntal, interplay of sexual identity. On the one hand, the gender patterns and relationships which underlie the creative gift discovered by each boy paradoxically reveal an empowerment of a matriarchal perception of creativity, rather than the confirmation of a patriarchal model suggested by the explicit structure of the text. On the other hand, modifications in the chronological presentation of her experiences enable Gabrielle Roy to explore the unspoken question of the text and to explain, to some degree, the problematic nature of self-realization for the artist as young woman.

Significantly, in his process of self-discovery, each male child comes to distance himself from or to redefine in more positive terms the traditional patriarchal role. Artistic self-expression and affirmation of identity thus imply a new, and more independent, relationship with a paternal figure. "Glued to his father's side" (12), Vincento must physically detach himself from the latter, in order to take his place for the first time in a classroom. By their gift, Clair and André, who both live in single-parent homes, assume, in part, a positive version of the role of their absent father. André does this literally, by doing the heavy farm work which would normally fall on his father, willing, but obliged by economic necessity to absent himself from the home in winter; Clair achieves the same effect symbolically by offering his gift to his teacher on behalf of "his mother and [him]self" (32), as the perfect "gentleman" (26) able to accept the discursive responsibility rejected by his wayward father. Through their expressive gift, little Demetrioff and Médéric find a new identity for themselves outside the tyrannical role model offered to them by their fathers and whose tracks they initially seemed destined to follow.

This distancing from the repressive patriarch is all the more revealing in that it is accompanied by a validation of the maternal tradition. With the exception of little Demetrioff, "impelled to write by generations long past" (71), all the boys receive their artistic or emotional vocation from their mothers. It is Nil's mother who teaches him to sing and who transmits to her son her touching love for her lost Ukraine; Nil's father, curiously, is never mentioned in the story. Clair's affection for his teacher replicates his mother's love and self-sacrifice for him. Indeed, the fine linen handkerchief, a *woman's* work of art, which he gives to his teacher was originally a gift his mother received from one of the women she cleaned house for. The maternal gift of nurturing and recognizing the other which André extends to his mother stems from the latter's willing acceptance of the sacrifices necessary to avoid miscarriage of her un-born child, and is reflected, in turn, in André's love for his younger brother. As André describes how helpful Emile can be, writes Roy, "A flash of intense pride, almost of maternal joy, lit the depths of his worried eyes" (95). Like his "deep violet" eyes "full of sad dreams beneath . . . long, dark lashes" (144), Médéric's intense love for nature and freedom, so attractive to his teacher, has been inherited from his Indian Mother.

Even more significant, in this respect, is the very nature of the artistic expression achieved by each boy. Gabrielle Roy, herself, refers to a "gift" (157). Furthermore, the expression or realization of this gift, understood here in the sense of vocation, itself implies another, more concrete, act of giving, this time by the boy to those to whom he expresses his talent. Through his singing, Nil brings "joy" (52) to the lives of the sick and elderly. Demetrioff the Last magically transforms the brutal Demetrioff senior into a proud father:

> With his little shiny eyes [the latter] stared us down, forcing us to witness that . . . Demetrioff the Last knew how to write. What the letters stood for perhaps mattered no more to him than to his son. The gift of being able to trace them was marvellous in itself. (75)

In his turn, Médéric gives his teacher his own particular form of going-away present, "an enormous bouquet of field flowers, light as a butterfly, barely holding together its fragile stems with their awkward grace" (170-171).

Indeed, Médéric's bouquet, which haunts the last scene of the book, draws together in one compelling image the different strands which each chapter adds to Roy's decidedly matriarchal conception of the artistic "gift." A tender collection of wild flowers, "a simple strand of grass tied around it like a ribbon" (171), Médéric's bouquet offers a particularly feminine reconciliation of art with nature. Rather than conquer or master nature, the young man's artistic act has been to achieve a new arrangement and a completeness of the wild flowers for which he has "search[ed] the underbrush since dawn . . . so that not the smallest flower of this tender season would be missing from his offering" (171). Roy thus situates her own vision of creativity within the female tradition of the bountiful and beautiful garden,[6] extended here to nature in its entirety.

More importantly, at once an aesthetic object and an affective "offering" (171), Médéric's bouquet provides an explicit synthesis of art and affect, whose equivalence, but not identity, is emphasized structurally throughout the text, by the juxtaposition, from one chapter to another, of the artistic and the emotional gift. In *Children of My Heart*, then, the artistic act is one of expression and communication (giving),[7] rather than Promethean conquest, thus reflecting the difference between "the basic feminine sense of self [as] connected to the world," as Nancy Chodorow had argued, and "the basic masculine sense of self [as] separate" (169). Artistic realization, suggests Roy, offers a possible solution to the feminine need to reconcile connection with the other and expression of the self, intimacy and autonomy.

Almost paradoxically, then, the role of the male other in relation to which Gabrielle Roy has chosen to define her own self as artist in *Children of My Heart* would appear essentially to validate, albeit implicitly, a female creative model. But such an interpretation of the "other" can provide only a partial answer to the unspoken question of the text, the apparent "void of the [female] self" (Moglen 52). Certainly, by their very insistence on androgynous traits,[8] each of Roy's 'Portraits of the artist as young man' at once re(plays) and dis(plays) the problematic representation of the female subject in the patriarchal tradition. What remains troubling, however, is that Roy appears to achieve this dis(closure) of patriarchy's negative inscription of the artist as young woman only by maintaining her own self-effacement from the text. It is only, literally *through* the "other," that her identity as female artist can be expressed.

To resolve, or to confirm, this contradiction, in other words, to situate the limits of Roy's implicit critique of patriarchy, it is necessary to examine another textual strategy used by the author. As André Brochu ("Ces enfants" 40) and Réjean Robidoux ("Gabrielle Roy" 21) have pointed out, in relation to her own experience, Gabrielle Roy has reversed the chronological order of her portraits. The city school for boys for which the narrator leaves at the end of the book is, in fact, the setting for the volume's first chapters. The most obvious effect of this change is to underscore the linear development of the male child, who is seen as progressing from small boy in "Vincento" to adolescent in "Trout in Ice Water"; by the same logic, the narrator, who becomes younger, in her memory, as the pupils she remembers grow older, is represented as regressing in time.

Curiously, while this insistence on the forward-looking and linear trajectory of the male character can be seen to reinforce the negative inscription of the absent female quest for identity, the text itself implies no parallel path to womanhood. Instead, the narrator's own displacement as female is represented as endlessly circular.[9] For even her departure at the end of the text serves only to bring her back, once again, if not to childhood, at least to adolescence. Structurally, it is this last, and most touching story of the text, where both male and female trajectories meet in the romantic attachment between fourteen-year-old Médéric and his eighteen-year-old teacher, which the text offers as the key to the problematic identity of the artist as young woman.

Traditionally, critics have interpreted this adventure, and the teacher's departure which, superficially at least, marks its closure, as the difficult "initiatory rite" (Robidoux, "Gabrielle Roy" 21, our translation) between childhood and adulthood, the "painful birth into the adult world" (Riddick 21, our translation). "It is this actual process of maturing that Gabrielle Roy views as the most tragic aspect of childhood," concludes Paula Gilbert Lewis, "Youth is fresh and spontaneous, but it is also fragile and vulnerable precisely because it is temporary" (*Literary Vision* 39-40). The relationship itself is thus perceived as necessarily platonic and fleeting, for both the young teacher and Médéric must ultimately pursue their separate paths. Furthermore, it is precisely because of this inevitable separation that the romantic adventure is read, metaphorically, as a step toward the self-realization of the artist. The latter must accept to "live less," concludes Robidoux, in order to "write more" ("Gabrielle Roy" 21, our translation); the artist as portrayed in Roy's fiction, argues François Ricard, must "continually renounce his [sic] relationships with others" in order to create (*Gabrielle Roy* 108, our translation).

Such readings of the last chapter of *Children of My Heart* clearly reflect certain patriarchal premisses, namely a restrictive view of sexuality, which excludes by definition even the possibility of a sexual relationship between the young teacher and Médéric, and an implicit perception of art as essentially autonomous and individualistic. However, the circular structure of the narrator's own trajectory renders this insistence on separation problematic; the reader is led, instead, to ask what precisely in the relationship between the narrator's young self and Médéric compels the former to return to what is obviously a formative experience for her, and why she is at once unable to explore it completely, or relinquish its emotional hold.

On initial reading, "Trout in Ice Water" calls forth indeed several sexual stereotypes. From his first day in school, Médéric assumes all the physical attributes of the swaggering young buck. He himself chooses when to come, "taking me by surprise," writes the narrator, "—just his style" (112). His arrival is sudden, spectacular and disruptive of the narrator's authority:

> The class was paying no attention to me. Big and small, they all had their eyes rivetted far across the prairie on a white spot that was rapidly approaching. The white spot became a horse with a black mane. Soon I could make out, crouching over the neck of his mount, a young rider who with wild gestures was urging his fiery steed, already flat-out, to greater efforts. On the back of his head he wore an immense cowboy hat. (112)

Drawing out her description, the narrator follows Médéric's every gesture, from his "one leap" (112) to dismount, to his deliberate swagger, calculated "to increase the suspense he knew he had created" (112) as "finally, his big hat pushed down over his eyes, he arrived in the doorway" (112-113) in the stereotypical, provocatively male pose of the cowboy:

> There he stood, in high-heeled boots with Mexican designs, his legs apart, his hands deep in the pockets of his fringed pants, a studded belt around his hips. He took stock of us

with an eye in which there was disdain and commiseration for the prisoners we were. (113)

In contrast to Médéric's masculine vitality, the narrator's attitude appears passive and uncertain, conventionally feminine: "what could I do?" she writes, "He was easily a head taller than I and no doubt at least that far ahead of me in other aspects of life" (114). But while the narrator thus implies a recognition of Médéric's sexual authority, she does not succumb to her "own helplessness" (114). Gabrielle Pascal has suggested that it is the narrator's reliance on her professional authority as teacher which enables her to maintain her independence in her relationship with Médéric, while at the same time satisfying certain "romantic" needs (59). Certainly, the relationship is firmly set within the social restrictions of the pedagogical situation. The narrator, herself, acknowledges that she is aware of the role she is expected to play as teacher, by invoking, in Médéric's presence, the visit of "the school inspector . . . the priest . . . or just somebody from the school board" (115).

However, it is precisely such references to patriarchal authority or expectations which make the narrator's own subterranean but consistent insistence on equality all the more subversive. Sometimes direct, sometimes more subtle, this personal discourse serves to undermine the patriarchal values the text appears to accept. Roy starts the chapter by describing the village gossip concerning Médéric:

> They told me he'd held "the last teacher" at bay at the point of his jack-knife when she'd wanted to take the ruler to him. . . . There wasn't one who didn't predict that there'd be war between us. (111)

But this public (patriarchal) perception of the school teacher's authority is followed immediately by a private (anti-patriarchal) revision of the same martial image: "And in fact it was to be war . . . a mysterious war in which we confronted each other unarmed, each of us equally at a loss" (111).

This same preoccupation with equality and reciprocity, or more precisely, love without conquest, returns throughout the chapter in numerous small descriptive details. "Waiting for [her] heart to settle down," the narrator discovers that Médéric "was just as troubled" (115). She speaks to him not from her desk but from his:

> Unconsciously I just have noticed that when I stood beside this lanky adolescent I seemed slight and small, and imagined that I lost stature and authority in his eyes. On the other hand, if I had him come to me at my desk it was he, thin and awkward, leaning over to follow the lesson, who lost in prestige. (118)

The excursion on horseback to the Babcock Hills where the two young people stroke the "trout in ice water" mentioned in the title, leads to two particularly revealing images of equality.

The first replays the initial dynamic vision of Médéric on horseback, joined now by the narrator herself:

> Even today when that memory returns, my soul swells with contentment and happiness. What is it about the view from a certain height that fills us with such elation? . . . What I believe to be certain is that I had never seen the prairie so awesome in all its breadth, its fullness, its noble sadness, its transfigured beauty, as I did that morning from the saddle with Médéric, our two horses standing side by side. (130)

In the second image, the two young people, now "face to face," literally *speak* to each other their spiritual and sensual pleasure:

> The sparkle in his eyes showed his pleasure at feeling a wild thing tame at his fingertips. On opposite sides of the spring, face to face, we described our experiences which were so identical that the same happy smile came to our lips.
> "Have you got one, mamzelle?"
> "Yes, I think so . . . "
> "Is he staying? Does he let you touch him?"
> "Yes, yes, he does!" (133)

Rich in symbolism, the language of this scene mimics a sexual and emotional coming together which, through the "inexplicable abandon" (134) of the trout, transcends difference in a mutually affirming ("Yes, yes") identity of pleasure.

Situated beyond the physical limits, in both senses of the word, of patriarchal society, this experience proves impossible for the narrator to pursue. The rest of the chapter focuses on Rodrigue Eymard, the father of Médéric, the tyrannical and repressive patriarch *par excellence*, who re-interprets his son's adventure in conformity with his own "calculating" (142) and exploitative vision of sexuality as possession. It is only as she returns, literally and symbolically, to the village in a snow storm after a visit to the paternal domain, that the narrator, evoking, for the first time an image of unfulfilled love, re-imagines her relationship with Médéric in, revealingly, a mirror image:

> Suddenly, beside my own face appeared that of Médéric who had come closer without knowing that the glass reflected him as well. He leaned toward me, perhaps to see if I was sleeping. As I neither moved nor spoke he may have thought I was dozing. My eyes half closed, I watched him in the mirror of the lantern where, borne on drifting snow, our two faces passed, blurred like an old wedding photo. (151)

Significantly, although the narrator accepts the abandonment of her relationship with Médéric required by society's norms, she nonetheless continues to confront patriarchal values by engaging in a struggle with Rodrigue Eymard over the education of Médéric. Will Médéric return to "his old violence" (158), "exposed only to his father's influence" (159), or "Would I win out in the end?" (159) asks the narrator. It is to this latter question that the bouquet Médéric offers the narrator in the last touching scene of the story brings a positive response. A compelling image of matriarchal creativity, Médéric's offering also represents, within the interpersonal dynamic of the text, an explicit reaffirmation of the young man's adherence to the narrator's feminine values of mutual nurturing.

Clearly, then, it is the sexual inscription of the artist as young woman within the confines of patriarchy, which Gabrielle Roy exposes as the ultimate obstacle to the reconciliation of intimacy and autonomy, and the cause of the problematic self-realization of the female artist. Roy thus joins many other woman writers for whom, as Patricia Spacks has argued, "the puzzle of how power relates to love in a woman's experience is central to the dilemma of woman as artist" (160). What distinguishes Roy's approach, however, is her implicit affirmation of the need to transcend the representation of this dilemma as a "conflict between the yearning for artistic expression and the desire for relationship" (Spacks 166). For the circular structure of the text serves not only to underscore how the patriarchal framework itself prevents the resolution of this dilemma but also expresses Gabrielle Roy's profound adherence to a matriarchal vision of sexuality. Furthermore, as Médéric's touching bouquet so eloquently reveals, it is firmly within this matriarchal conception of mutually nurturing sexuality that the author also situates her vision of artistic realization. In this sense, her "tireless return to childhood" (Robidoux, "Gabrielle Roy" 21, our translation), which many critics have perceived as a sentimental and nostalgic longing for the lost innocence of youth, can also, and should be, read as an irrepressible desire to reactualize the Golden Age of matriarchy.[10]

As a woman writing in a male-dominated society, Roy has displayed the fundamental dilemma of the artist as young woman in the shadows of her text, through a juxtaposition of dream and reality, private and public discourse. The implicit structures of the text expose the contradictions of the latter while at the same time validating the legitimacy of the former. Tracing the female process of self-realization initially *through* the other, Roy ultimately dis(closes) the possible reconciliation of artistic and personal identity *with*, or more precisely, *beside* the other, within a matriarchal social construct. Finally, then, it is this fundamentally anti-patriarchal re-vision of the portrait of the artist as young woman which renders *Children of My Heart* so "passionate and troubling" (Marcotte 17).

NOTES

1. Some idea of the diversity of such attempts can be obtained from the following: Bourbonnais; Courchesne; Grace; Lewis, "Trois générations"; Smart; and Whitfield.
2. Some examples of this approach can be found in the following: Friand; Lewis, *Literary Vision*; Morency; Ricard, *Gabrielle Roy*; Robidoux, "Le roman"; and Socken.
3. François Ricard suggests that Gabrielle Roy was herself aware of this critical tendency to undervalue her autobiographical fiction ("La Métamorphose" 441-456).
4. Examples and analysis of this phenomenon can be found in the following: Jelinek, Mason and Reimer.
5. In the English translation, Alan Brown has eliminated the title of each story, and reorganized the book into three "Parts," keeping however the same order of the stories. Accordingly, the narrative analysis which follows is based on the original text and the translations provided for the French section titles are my own.

6. A more complete analysis of this tradition can be found in the garden theme in Walker, *In Search of Our Mothers' Gardens*.
7. Hesse also touches on this aspect of Gabrielle Roy's conception of art as "being synonymous with commitment" (62), but fails to link this with gender.
8. The androgynous nature of the traits Roy attributes to her pupils has been pointed out by Courchesne who also examines in detail the power relationships between the young teacher and the male-ordered world of her pupils.
9. This structural insistence on the circular motive in *Children of My Heart* is replicated in other texts by Gabrielle Roy, in the circular spatial patterns associated with female characters (Brochu, "Thèmes et structures").
10. On this topic a more complete discussion is provided by Walker, *The Woman's Encyclopedia* (690-691).

WORKS CITED

Abley, M. "Less is More." *Maclean's* 12 March 1979, 56.

Bourbonnais, N. "Gabrielle Roy: la représentation du corps féminin." *Voix et Images* 40 (1988): 72-89.

Brochu, A. "Thèmes et structures de *Bonheur d'occasion*." *Ecrits du Canada français* XX (1966): 163-208.

———. "Ces enfants de ma vie." *Livres et Auteurs québécois* (1977): 40.

Chodorow, N. *The Reproduction of Mothering: Psychoanalysis and the Sociology of Gender*. Berkeley, Los Angeles, London: U of California P, 1978.

Courchesne, M. "Matriarcat ou patriarcat: rapports de force dans *Ces Enfants de ma vie*." *Actes du Colloque inter-universitaire des jeunes chercheur(e)s en littérature québécoise*. Québec: CRELIQ, 1989. n. pag.

Foster, S. "The Open Cage: Freedom, Marriage and the Heroine in Early Twentieth-Century American Women's Novels." *Women's Writing: A Challenge to Theory*. Ed. M. Monteith. Sussex: Harvester, New York: St. Martin's, 1986. 154-174.

Friand, B. "Gabrielle Roy's *The Hidden Mountain*: A Poetic Expression of Existential Thought." *Malahat Review* 52 (1979): 77-85.

Grace, S. E. "Urban/Rural Codes in Roy, Laurence, and Atwood." *Women Writers and the City*. Ed. S. M. Squier. Knoxville: U of Tennessee P, 1984. 193-209.

Grosskurth, P. "Gabrielle Roy and the Silken Noose." *Canadian Literature* 42 (1969): 6-13.

Hesse, M.G. *Gabrielle Roy*. Boston: Twayne, 1984.

Jelinek, E., ed. *Women's Autobiography: Essays in Criticism*. Bloomington, London: Indiana UP, 1980.

Keywan, Z. "Straight From the Heart." *The Gazette* 10 March 1979, 73.

Lejeune, Ph. *Le Pacte autobiographique*. Paris: Editions du Seuil, 1975.

Lewis, P. G. *The Literary Vision of Gabrielle Roy: An Analysis of Her Works*. Birmingham, Alabama and Lawrence, Kansas: Summa Publications, 1984.

——. "Trois générations de femmes: le reflet fille-mère dans quelques nouvelles de Gabrielle Roy." *Voix et Images* X.3 (1985): 165-176.

Marcotte, G. "Gabrielle Roy et l'institutrice passionnée." *Le Devoir* 24 September 1977, 17.

Mason, M.G. "The Other Voice." *Life/Lines: Theorizing Women's Autobiography*. Ed. B. Brodzki and C. Schenck. Ithaca and London: Cornell UP, 1988. 19-44.

Moglen, H. *Charlotte Brontë: The Self Conceived*. New York: W.W. Norton, 1976.

Morency, J. *Un Roman du regard:* La Montagne secrète *de Gabrielle Roy*. Québec: CRELIQ, 1986.

Pascal, G. "La Femme dans l'oeuvre de Gabrielle Roy." *Revue de l'Université d'Ottawa* 50.1 (1980): 55-61.

Reimer, G.T. "Revisions of Labour in Margaret Oliphant's Autobiography." *Life/Lines: Theorizing Women's Autobiography*. Ed. B. Brodzki and C. Schenck. Ithaca and London: Cornell UP, 1988. 203-220.

Ricard, F. *Gabrielle Roy*. Montréal: Fides, 1975.

——. "La Métamorphose" d'un écrivain. Essai biographique." *Etudes littéraires* XVII.3 (1984): 441-456.

Riddick, T.V. "Gabrielle Roy dans la plénitude de son art." *Le Devoir* 27 Oct. 1977, 20.

Robidoux, R., "Le roman et la recherche du sens de la vie, Vocation: écrivain." *Mélanges de civilisation canadienne-française offerts au professeur Paul Wyczynski*. Ed. P. Savard, Ottawa: Edition de l'Université d'Ottawa, 1974. 225-235.

———. "Gabrielle Roy, La merveille du retour à la source," *Le Droit* 20 May 1978, 21.

Roy, G. *Bonheur d'occasion*. Montréal: Société des Editions Pascal, 1945.

———. *Ces enfants de ma vie*. Montréal: Stanké, 1977.

———. *Children of My Heart*. Trans. Alan Brown. Toronto: McClelland and Stewart, 1979.

———. *La Détresse et l'enchantement*. Montréal: Boréal Express, 1984.

———. *La Montagne secrète*. Montréal: Beauchemin, 1961.

———. *La Route d'Altamont*. Montréal: Editions HMH, 1966.

———. *Rue Deschambault*. Montréal: Beauchemin, 1955.

Smart, P. *Ecrire dans la Maison du père. L'Emergence du féminin dans la tradition littéraire du Québec*. Montréal: Editions Québec/Amérique, 1988.

Socken, P. "Art and the Artist in Gabrielle Roy's Works." *Revue de l'Université d'Ottawa* 45.3 (1975): 344-350.

Spacks, P.A.M. *The Female Imagination*. New York: Alfred A. Knopf, 1975.

Walker, A. *In Search of Our Mothers' Gardens*. New York: Harcourt, 1983.

Walker, B. *The Woman's Encyclopedia of Myths and Secrets*. San Francisco: Harper, 1983.

Whitfield, A. "Gabrielle Roy as Feminist: Re-reading the Critical Myths." *Canadian Literature*. Forthcoming.

Personal Texts and Historical Contexts

The Kaleidoscopic Vision: Autobiographical Inscription in the Works of Tatyana Mamonova

Sharon Hileman and Ann K. Johnson

Born in 1943, Tatyana Mamonova was trained as a pharmacist. Her real interests, however, were writing poetry and drawing. She worked as a reviewer and translator for Aurora, *a Soviet youth magazine, and was the only woman whose work was included in the first exhibition of Soviet nonconformist painters.*

Dissatisfied with the status and position of women in the U.S.S.R., Mamonova and other dissident women compiled and distributed an underground publication, Women and Russia: An Almanac to Women about Women, *which addressed the problems confronting Soviet women. All of these women were forced into exile eventually; Mamonova, with her husband and son, left the Soviet Union in 1980 and sought asylum in the West. She is currently Writer-in-Residence at Hartford College for Women in Connecticut.*

During 1981 and 1982 Mamonova made speaking tours of Britain and the United States to publicize the problems of Soviet women and call for an International Feminist Organization. In addition to editing Women and Russia: Feminist Writings from the Soviet Union *(1984), Mamonova has recently published a collection of her essays,* Russian Women's Studies: Essays on Sexism in Soviet Culture *(1988). At the same time she continues to write both poetry and short stories.*

We know that women writers are marginalized in patriarchal cultures so that they speak and write as outsiders, generating critiques of the dominant culture and its discourse. Simultaneously, as a result of their shared marginal status, women writers begin to create conventions and a discourse of their own, a women's culture that then counters and subverts the hegemonic aspirations of the patriarchy.

Women writers of autobiography, for instance, may create decentered, nonlinear narratives that do not rely on crisis resolution for plot structure. Rejecting the models of Augustine and Rousseau, a writer like Gertrude Stein postulates an entirely new approach to autobiography. Her title—*The Autobiography of Alice B. Toklas*—indicates that the story of Gertrude Stein will be told indirectly; the inside will be approached from the outside. Nor does Stein move chronologically through the events of her life. She writes around events, causing them to exist in narrative past, present, and future: "All that was very much later and now to go back again to the beginning" (60). Telescoping time and self, Stein writes the plural, continuous prose we now call *écriture féminine*.[1] Sidonie Smith in *A Poetics of Women's Autobiography* explains that the subject position from which a woman speaks may be "outside time, plural, fluid, bisexual, de-centered, and nonegocentric" (58). In other words, the concept of individualistic and representative self which informs male autobiography is not necessarily present in female autobiography.

Some theorists believe that all women's autobiographies are written in terms of "other," whether that other is constituted by a single individual or a collective. Ann Bradstreet's autobiographical writings, for example, create a self defined through its relationship with family as well as its membership in an entire spiritual community.[2]

Women writers of autobiographical fiction may appropriate the subject positions and narrative strategies of women autobiographers, and they can also be expected to place their narrator/protagonists in stories that deny traditional readers' expectations. As Rachel DuPlessis indicates, " A writer expresses dissent from an ideological formation by attacking elements of narrative that repeat, sustain, or embody the values and attitudes in question" (34). One of these elements in western literature, since the development of the novel, has been the role of the heterosexual love plot as the narrative motor that propels the text. Clearly, there are other relationships that are crucial in women's lives, which we might expect the woman writer of autobiographical fiction to foreground. Homosocial bonds, homosexual relationships, interfamilial groupings and regroupings, as well as the tempering of the individual by the collective are all possible sites of such stories. Furthermore, the woman writer of autobiographical short stories may construct a series of competing or complementary stories about herself, so that the relationship of one self to another self becomes the primary locus of interest.

Still another dimension must be added to this theoretical framework when the woman writer inhabits and critiques a totalitarian patriarchal culture. In such a society she is doubly marginalized, writing as a woman and a dissident, identifiable and silenceable if her voice becomes too threatening.

The Soviet Union has dealt with its contemporary dissident women writers in a variety of easily imagined ways: arrests, interrogations by the KGB, threats against friends and family, labor camp and prison sentences, forced exile, and evidently even murder. Many of the dissident Soviet women who in 1979 wrote and distributed the first contemporary feminist *samizdat* (underground publication), *Women and Russia: An Almanac to Women about Women,* no longer live in the USSR. Five are in exile in the West; another was killed in an automobile accident in Leningrad in 1983 (an action of the KGB, some speculate).[3]

Tatyana Mamonova was the editor of this Soviet feminist publication, which contained women's creative work and discussions of social issues affecting women. In the *Introduction to Women and Russia: Feminist Writings from the Soviet Union,* published in the United States in 1984, Mamonova tells the story of the *Almanac*: why it needed to be distributed, how the KGB threatened her with arrest if a second issue were published, and how even dissident men were so threatened by women's issues that they would not support the feminists. Mamonova points out that patriarchal traditions still predominate in most Soviet families, and while girls may be told they are equal to boys, they grow up to discover that "a woman is expected to have children, be an outstanding worker, take responsibility for the home, and, despite everything, still be beautiful" (xx).

Although women make up half of the Soviet Union's population, they constitute only twenty-five percent of the membership in the Communist Party. Women perform most of the heavy, unskilled labor in the USSR and usually have "dead-end jobs" with little hope for promotion (Holt 263). Many Soviet women are doctors, but this profession pays little in Russia; it is the male administrators of medical clinics who are well-paid (*Women and Russia* xviii).

Nor are support services and facilities available for Soviet women. They must spend hours in queues in order to shop, they have difficulty finding day care even if they qualify for it through their "official" positions, they receive little state support as single mothers, and they have virtually no access to sex education and birth control devices. Consequently, abortion clinics have become what Mamonova calls "production lines," where numerous abortions are done simultaneously, without anesthetics. Maternity wards are not much better. In a major Leningrad clinic women may be denied all contact with their husbands, denied anesthetics, and denied opportunities to shower (Mamonova, *Women and Russia* xix).

Life can be much harder for the Soviet woman than for many of her American counterparts. Nonetheless, Robin Morgan, an American feminist who interviewed and then wrote an article about four of the Soviet women émigrés, emphasized the similarities she saw in Russian and American women's lives. Morgan concluded that regardless of democratic or totalitarian political structure, both kinds of governments, "while claiming major ideological distinction from one another, share a similar patriarchal indifference to and suppression of their female citizens" (49).

Tatyana Mamonova, in addition to being a political writer and speaker who addresses the patriarchy's indifference to and suppression of women, is also the author of approximately seventy short stories, many of which employ an autobiographical "I" as narrator and protagonist. These stories tend to be brief (2-3 pages), fragmented, and self-contained. They end without closure, often seeming to stop rather than actually end. Protagonists are women on journeys; women who have been dispossessed; women who look to other women for support. As protagonists and characters tell about places they have been and people they have known, a kaleidoscopic vision is created. Structured through the reality and metaphor of journey, narratives unfold in which one locale gives way to another, one language is displaced by another, one type of relationship yields to another.

Mamonova's stories, in fact, illustrate a variety of the subject positions Smith has attributed to women autobiographers and develop several of the counterplots to heterosexual love that DuPlessis has sketched. Since Mamonova also writes from the position and perspective of the doubly marginalized, we believe a study of her stories will substantiate Smith's claim that during times of destabilization women are "able to promote their own vision of empowering selfhood" (174).

Mamonova inscribes the self within its fictions in four recurring ways: through metonymic and metaphoric depictions of relations to others, by pluralizing and de-centering the subject, and by foregrounding an autonomous subject. Metonymic stories are often recognizable by their titles: in "Tjan," "Ashir Bibi," "Betsy," and "Rosa," a first-person narrator provides developed, realistic characterizations of the eponymous protagonists and shows how bonds are formed between self and other. In metaphoric stories, on the other hand, "others" are usually nameless and become the means through which the narrator/protagonist can recapture a past feeling or state of being. Titles for these stories suggest both allegorical readings—"Youth," "Life," "All Roads Lead to Rome"—and symbolic possibilities—"Up and Down," "Departure." The third technique Mamonova employs is a vacating of the subject position. The first-person narrator remains in the story, but other characters are allowed to give their own first-person accounts—tell their own stories. Often these are stories of Russian village women, women from the provinces whose discourse would not usually find any means of written expression. Finally, as Mamonova writes the stories of emigration and life in the West, a very different form of self-inscription appears. Instead of the self defined in some ways through its relations with others, there is now an autonomous narrator/protagonist. Hinted at in "Kleine" and fully realized in "Morning" and "Cities," this figure is powerfully self-actualizing and filled with exuberance. By looking at some of these stories more closely, we will be able to see how each technique is given form.

Metonymy is the trope associated with realistic fiction such as the nineteenth-century novel. It originates in the perception of similarities rather than differences; art that is "like" whatever it represents or which chronicles events that correspond to historical or actual occurrences is considered metonymic. But artists who create metonymic rather than metaphoric depictions may be projecting alternative social structures rather than describing those that already exist.

Mamonova's stories that fall into this category consistently focus on the relationship between the narrator and another woman, creating numerous versions of a woman-defined identity. The first-person narrator and her friend Olga in "The Novgorod Nun" are young women, probably in their late teens, who have been friends since childhood and now sketch together. Since Olga is studying architecture, the two women journey to the Russian town of Novgorod to sketch the ancient architecture. Thwarting our expectations of young Soviet women's behavior, they rent a room at a convent and attend church services at the adjoining cathedral. The narrator goes on to describe the "mesmerizing" voice of a nun who sings in the choir, a voice that incorporates the "soul of Russia," "leading me from the twentieth century back into the depths of time."[4] Both Olga and the narrator are deeply moved as they return to their convent cell and decide to share its one narrow bed rather than unfold a cot which has also been provided. "Inadvertently touching one another" while lying in this bed, the two women discuss the nun and the remarkable feelings she has evoked in them. The narrator would even ask the nun to lie down with them if she entered the room since a person with such a voice must "know . . . life's secrets." Then the story concludes as the narrator feels Olga quiver and also feels her tears.

Although this last part of the narrative is infused with eroticism, the story is not presenting a homosexual relationship so much as strong homosocial bonding. The suggestion is that expanded female bonding, which would occur if the nun could be invited into the women's bed, would result in expanded knowledge, knowledge that goes beyond the boundaries of the individual and beyond the limits of time. Such powerful women's knowledge, which the narrator suggests can be intuited and shared by women, is as threatening to patriarchal culture as is the concept of female bonding. (This is one reason the Soviet Union takes severe action against homosexuals: women suspected of being lesbians are incarcerated in mental institutions.) By hinting at homosexually accessed power and depicting a religious community and its rituals, "The Novgorod Nun" posits two major challenges to Soviet ideology and hegemony.

However, Mamonova and by extension her first-person narrator are products of dual discourse: the language and conventions of the dominant culture constantly try to reassert themselves in the marginalized critiques voiced by women. Another of Mamonova's metonymically rendered stories, "Tjan," illustrates the difficulty a woman has negotiating between the poles of tradition and opposition that mark both discourse and behavior.

Like "The Novgorod Nun," the story "Tjan" describes a journeying first-person protagonist, the place she visits, and the people she meets there. In this story the narrator is a Leningrad journalist who has made a twelve-hour flight to Kamchatka (an outlying Russian province) to visit a friend. Here she meets Tjan, an Itelman village girl who has come to Kamchatka to take a meteorology exam. The narrator accepts an invitation from Tjan to visit her small village, where Tjan's mother hospitably prepares delicacies for her, and Tjan even dresses her in Itelman native costume. The following day the narrator accompanies Tjan to the meteorological station, which is located a considerable distance from the village and must be reached by walking. During the trip the narrator becomes terrified at the prospect of crossing a mountain stream whose only bridge is a large log. She cannot proceed until Tjan comes back, takes her by the hand, and helps her cross.

This bonding is soon dissevered, though, because the narrator is incapable of sustaining her relationship with Tjan. At the meteorological station she finds the supervisor is "a white woman, a Russian," with whom she can discuss mutual interests. During this dialogue, the Russian woman ignores Tjan unless speaking to her "as an official to an underling." The narrator indicates she now shares the Russian's perspective by noting that "my little Itelman friend" observed and resented such treatment. As they return to the village, Tjan hurries on ahead, causing the narrator to fear abandonment; although she is able to rejoin Tjan, when they reach the mountain stream, the narrator must now cross the log bridge alone.

The narrator has been torn by contradictory impulses in this story and acknowledges the dilemma as she asks Tjan, "How should I have reacted to the questions of that woman?" Instead of any female bonding, the three women characters are estranged from one another at the end of the story, physically and emotionally. The wedge has been driven by "that woman," an embodiment of the dominant Russian culture's patriarchal values: privileging, disdaining, and "other"-denying. But the point to be stressed here is that the narrator was willingly drawn to the Russian supervisor as a person who shared her own interests and cosmopolitan background. To embrace the known is usually the safest option, especially if one must confront physical peril by choosing an alternative. The ending to this story indicates that such peril no longer exists if one chooses correctly: the narrator can walk across the log bridge by herself because she no longer invests it with the power to instill fear, no longer sees it as an obstacle that women can overcome only if they unite. Yet the problem of women's relations to one another remains as unresolved in this story as the question Mamonova's narrator poses. How to respond to the claims and attractions of a culture that ultimately excludes one is the problem of how to negotiate a place for oneself in that culture and its discourse. Answers are not always forthcoming; sometimes one can present only the dialogue that sets forth the problem.

If Mamonova's metonymic stories raise questions about how the self responds to issues emerging from the public sphere, her metaphorically rendered stories seem to deal more directly with the private sphere. In these stories the "other" is absent, so the narrator is more of a writer evoking the past than a protagonist participating in a series of ongoing actions. An absent, nameless other is often addressed as "you" in these stories, almost as the recipient of a letter would be addressed. Settings are either unelaborated (resulting in apparent interior monologue in "Up and Down") or so idyllically evoked that they become mythopoeic. "Youth" describes a Moscow countryside in terms that make it sound like the Garden of Eden.

These are stories of loss—loss of friends, lovers, and the self of one's youth. But the stories do not chronicle the events that precede or explain the loss. "Departure" begins "You went away to another continent," but we are never told why, never told whether the absence is temporary or permanent, never told the name of this departed other. (An English translation does not even indicate the sex of the individual.)

Instead, the story focuses on the narrator's loneliness and depression. Alone, this narrator/protagonist scarcely seems to have an identity. No mention is made of her profession, and her only action in the story is to walk along the corridor and into the room that has been abandoned. This room was originally an attic, and the narrator believes it is becoming one again, even though the possessions and furniture of its former inhabitant were left behind in the hurried departure. Both the room and the narrator seem to shrink in upon themselves, unable to sustain identities that were conferred by the absent other.

In contrast to the depression and ennui of "Departure," the mood evoked in "Up and Down" is one of pleasant recollection and enjoyable musing. Here the narrator again recalls an absent, nameless other and the life she shared with that person. But in this story, both people have vocations—"You were a poet; I was an artist"—as well as fluid identities: "Sometimes we exchanged roles." The narrator also reveals the metaphorical fluidity of this story's title. At one point in her recollection "up and down" describes the "waves of life" which she and her partner thought would wash them up on a high bank of success. Later she mentions that they always lived in either the attics or cellars of the houses they rented and briefly notes the advantages of each. Near the end of the story she uses "heaven" and "hell" to suggest the extremes traversed during the relationship.

These sorts of stories, because they seem to emerge directly from the memory of the narrator, may reflect more of a private self than the metonymically portrayed stories. Yet an author always stands behind the narrator and the story itself, making narrative choices which may not be as significant as we like to think. A Soviet dissident author knows that all writing is "public" writing in the sense that it can be confiscated, read, and willfully misread at any time. When to write is to defy, the very act of writing transforms private contents into public statements. One may write as if one is creating an image of a private self, but the very idea of privacy in totalitarian culture is always a fiction, always an impossibility.

Mamonova may also be illustrating the public nature of her fiction when she vacates the subject position of first-person narrator and allows other speakers to assume it. These stories can have a dialogic form, so that some interaction occurs between the displaced narrator and the central narrator/protagonist. Or the story may plunge immediately into a first-person narrative account, with only a few concluding sentences to indicate the presence of a frame narrative. In either case, independent voices tell stories of their speakers' experiences, and the narrator in whom Mamonova inscribes herself becomes an audience. The narrator/author, then, is united with readers in the enterprise of listening. Audience is absorbed into the story, investing the fiction with still another type of plurality.

In her essays on sexism in the Soviet Union, published as *Russian Women's Studies: Essays on Sexism in Soviet Culture*, Mamonova employs some of the same techniques for including audience that appear in these stories. The essays also tend to be brief, suggesting an author's unwillingness to monopolize, and almost inviting reader (or listener) response. Many of these essays were originally oral presentations at feminist conferences where Mamonova had been asked to speak. Successive short essays, dealing with a wide range of subjects, are like conversations, where one topic displaces another as different speakers pursue the tangents that interest them most. Like conversationalists, speakers in prose fiction contribute accretional and disjunctive elements in such an exchange.

The Mamonova-narrator and her travelling companion in "The Native from the Northern Shores" listen to the woman who has become the protagonist/narrator tell about her children, her own childhood, her nomadic travels, her husband's work, and the hardships that she has experienced. The stories are punctuated by descriptive commentary from the Mamonova-narrator, who chronicles the woman's actions and interprets her emotions: "She put the guitar down. Sadness overcame her. It was as though memories had taken hold of her and led her out of our cabin on the boat." The Mamonova-narrator does not speak during the story; she is a recipient, one who listens to the woman's songs and stories and accepts the candy that the woman repeatedly offers. "Warmth" and "cozy" are words the Mamonova-narrator uses to describe the sensations created by this woman who has dominated the narrative.

Clearly, the Mamonova-narrator is content sharing her narrative space. As the story concludes, the woman storyteller leaves the boat's cabin, but the Mamonova-narrator's final comments reevoke her presence. In this way the narrative frame functions to keep the woman from the northern shore in its center.

A very different technique is used in the story "At the Border." No narrative frame is provided: the story begins with a direct first-person account. Only when the narrator mentions that her husband is in the border patrol service is it clear that this speaker is not the Mamonova-narrator. The woman tells a story about mistaken identity. She has reported a "suspicious person" to the authorities because he asked her the location of the border, but the next day she is told the person was a peasant who did not want to cross the border accidentally.

After concluding this story, the narrator immediately begins another one about a woman from the same border area. Again the issue is a question of identity: this woman had embezzled from a bank, served a two-year prison term, and then been helped to escape on the condition that she become a spy. However, the village people, by observing her suspicious behavior, determined that she was not the person she appeared to be.

As the story concludes, three statements are made by the Mamonova-narrator. First she describes the storyteller's appearance, then she provides the story's setting by mentioning the province their train has just crossed, and finally she observes, "What you don't hear on these long Siberian travels!" These few remarks almost seem to be an afterthought of the author. Distancing is made more pronounced by the use of "you" in the last sentence, an oddly impersonal pronoun here that suggests anyone, not just the narrator, could be the storyteller's audience. In this way Mamonova seemingly withdraws the autobiographical self from the narrative. As a result, the Mamonova-narrator avoids complicity with stories that portray women as dupes of the dominant culture and one of its favorite games, politics.

Both of the stories in "At the Border" are about women who make mistakes and are either laughed at or exposed. These are not stories like "Tjan" where the narrator reveals her own ambivalences about paternal culture. Instead, they show the negative operations of the culture and women's powerless positions within it. The woman storyteller explains how "boring" it is to sit at home while her husband is on patrol; the woman spy has no real choice: whether she is literally in prison or practicing espionage, she is not her own person.

Mamonova positions herself outside this story because there is no inviting warmth at the border as there was in the boat's cabin with the woman from the northern shores. Paternal concerns create borders, whose purpose is to exclude, whereas a woman-defined culture, as Mamonova depicts it, emanates from sharing and the desire to include. The stories of women in both spheres need to be told, and by altering the way she inscribes herself as audience in each story, Mamonova can comment on women's lives while remaining silent.

In Mamonova's last type of story, she uses her first-person narrator as a foregrounded subject who can make forthright statements. Because Mamonova writes these stories in the West, she is no longer marginalized in the same way she was in the Soviet Union. The change is reflected in the concerns of the narrator.

A story like "Cities" has a first-person narrator who is a business person, although she would prefer to be working as an artist, painting. After flying to Detroit, she has waited over an hour for a cab and is "exhausted from the heat, dust, and endless bustle." The narrator begins a dialogue with herself, asking, "What are they all doing there with their suitcases? What could they have seen in Detroit's dirt? . . . Why am I here?" Unlike the earlier stories where the narrator defined herself through the presence, absence, or voices of others, she here experiences a direct confrontation with self only. There still are other antagonists, represented by the smog-filled, polluted city and its alienated inhabitants and visitors. Nevertheless, the focus in this story is the narrator's ability to resolve her dilemma and act on a decision. As the story ends, she refuses to placate clients any longer.

A very different city and situation are evoked in the story "Morning." Here the narrator describes autumn in an unnamed New England city where there are "golden rays of sunrise," "red, yellow, ochre" trees, and "fresh clean air." She goes out into this "veritable Festival of Nature" to jog, and, in a story written entirely in the present tense, tells of the happiness and exuberance she feels. There is no dialogue, even with self, in this story because the narrator seems to be perfectly content. The kinds of conflict that appeared in earlier stories have vanished, giving way to a celebratory, almost idyllic mood. Some of the narrator's same joy in nature was portrayed in "Youth," but that story emphasized the loss of both a companion and a former self. Written in the past tense, "Youth" was an obvious product of the narrator's memory, which may explain its tone.

"Morning," however, tries to create a sense of immediacy, a rendering of life as it is being lived. Of course, there is always disjunction in autobiographical writing since the self that writes is different from the self that experiences. But autobiographical fiction provides more options for depicting self than does pure autobiography. Thus, Mamonova is not bound by the retrospective vision of the autobiographer and can write a story in the present tense. The result is an emphasis on process, specifically the continuous process involved in the making of a self. Wanting to show a self that expresses "life in formation," Mamonova follows a tradition established by Russian women autobiographers (Heldt 65), even though her forms of autobiographical self-inscription are not traditional.

"Morning" may seem to be the most private of Mamonova's stories, but like all her other stories it is part of a public record of experiences, a record of being a twentieth-century Soviet woman in a particular place at a particular time.[5] Nor can it be simply classified as émigré literature. Mamonova does not even consider herself an émigrée, perhaps because such a label seems to limit identity to loss. Instead of focusing on loss and the past, Mamonova accumulates new experiences, creating an identity that is international and cross-cultural.

For instance, as an international writer interweaving past and present selves, Mamonova fashions an American story written in Russian, "Stroll along the Hudson River Bank." The first-person narrator, seeking respite from the heat and humidity, walks along the river, observing urban American culture. The result is an interesting linguistic phenomenon: terms like "Hudson River," "Dunkin Donuts," "Burger King," "McDonald's," "rap music," "break dance," "yuppie," and "Trade World Center" are simply transliterated into the Cyrillic with no attempt at translation or explanation.

A cross-cultural perspective appears in another way in the story "Euphoria." Set in San Francisco, the story portrays a concerned woman psychiatrist and her attempts to treat her patient. It is highly unlikely that Mamonova could have depicted a Soviet psychiatrist in the same way since Soviet mental health workers and institutions are often enlisted in the cause of political repression. As this story indicates, Mamonova's work takes form not only as a result of changes in locale but also because of cultural differences that are incorporated into her fiction.

Only by reading a collection of such an author's work can we develop a sense of the autobiographical self within it. To read many of Mamonova's short stories is to experience immediate engagement and disengagement. Since there is continuous displacement of characters, settings, cultures, and even the first-person narrator, readers may experience confusion and disorientation. Yet numerous and various displacements have formed the writing self behind the stories, so Mamonova is only using fictional form as a correlative of lived experience. The result is a series of powerful, provocative stories, not surprising, perhaps, from someone the KGB always labeled *agent provocateur*.

NOTES

1. Many of the ideas about autobiography expressed in this paper are informed by studies and discussions from an NEH-sponsored Summer Seminar for College Teachers, "Forms of Autobiography," directed by James Olney, 1988, which Sharon Hileman attended.
2. In "The Other Voice: Autobiographies of Women Writers," Mary Mason speculates that there are four types of women's autobiography, all written in terms of "other," and she specifically relates Anne Bradstreet's autobiographical writings to a "collective other."
3. In addition to Tatyana Mamonova, other Soviet women in exile include Yuliya Voznesenskaya, Natalya Malakovskaya, Tatyana Goricheva and Sofia Sokolova. All were arrested in 1980 and given the choice of going to prison or accepting a ticket to the West. Their stories are told in greater detail by Alix Holt in "The First Soviet Feminists" and Robin Morgan in "The First Feminist Exiles from the USSR." Kari Unksova was killed in a "strange traffic accident" two weeks before her forced departure from the USSR in 1983, according to Bosiljka Stevanovic and Vladimir Wertsman (436).
4. Mamonova is currently seeking a publisher for her collection of stories, which is now available only in typescript.
5. Elizabeth Fox-Genovese ascribes a similar function to black women's autobiographies, which she characterizes as "the historical experience of being black and female in a specific society at a specific moment" (65).

WORKS CITED

DuPlessis, Rachel Blau. *Writing beyond the Ending: Narrative Strategies of Twentieth-Century Women Writers*. Bloomington: Indiana UP, 1985.

Fox-Genovese, Elizabeth. "My Statue, My Self: Autobiographical Writings of Afro-American Women." *The Private Self: Theory and Practice of Women's Autobiographical Writings*. Ed. Shari Benstock. Chapel Hill: U of North Carolina P, 1988. 63-89.

Heldt, Barbara. *Terrible Perfection: Women and Russian Literature*. Bloomington: Indiana UP, 1987.

Holt, Alix. "The First Soviet Feminists." *Soviet Sisterhood*. Ed. Barbara Holland. Bloomington: Indiana UP, 1985. 237-265.

Mamonova, Tatyana. *Russian Women's Studies: Essays on Sexism in Soviet Culture*. N.Y.: Pergamon, 1988.

——. *Women and Russia: Feminist Writings from the Soviet Union*. Boston: Beacon, 1984.

Mason, Mary. "The Other Voice: Autobiographies of Women Writers." *Autobiography: Essays Theoretical and Critical*. Ed. James Olney. Princeton: Princeton UP, 1980.

Morgan, Robin. "The First Feminist Exiles from the U.S.S.R." *MS* 9 (November 1980): 49+.

Smith, Sidonie. *A Poetics of Women's Autobiography: Marginality and the Fictions of Self-Representation*. Bloomington: Indiana UP, 1987.

Stein, Gertrude. *The Autobiography of Alice B. Toklas*. N.Y.: Random, 1960.

Stevanovic, Bosiljka and Vladimir Wartsman. *Free Voices in Russian Literature, 1950s to 1980s: A Bibliographical Aid*. N.Y.: Russica, 1987.

A Never-Ending Autobiography: The Fiction of Carmen Martín Gaite

Concha Alborg

Carmen Martín Gaite is one of Spain's best known writers of the "posguerra" generation (after the Civil War). In 1983 her prize winning novel El cuarto de atrás (The Back Room) was translated by Columbia University Press in their Twentieth-Century Continental Fiction Series. Her reputation has grown steadily since her first novel Entre visillos (Through the Curtains) was published in 1958, itself awarded the prestigious Nadal Prize. To this date Martín Gaite has written five novels, two novellas, fifteen short stories, some poems, and children's books, in addition to her important essays on literary criticism and feminist issues. In 1988 she was awarded Spain's most important distinction, the Príncipe de Asturias prize, for her accomplishments as a writer whose novels bridge the socio-realism of the mid century with more intimate contemporary literature.

Recently a great deal of attention has been given to the autobiographical form, even if all this attention has failed to produce a consensus. Theoreticians like James Olney have dedicated complete volumes to the definition of autobiography, which can be as simple as: " . . . a point of view on the writer's own past life" (42), to the complex considerations of historical, psychological, philosophical and cosmological factors that, using his term, shape "the metaphors of self." Janet Varner Gunn, among others, has pointed out that the new trend is to shift the critic's interest from "bio" to "auto" or from life to self (3); in other words, less consideration is given to the biographical details than to the development of the inner self. This tendency is also evident in autobiographical fiction which requires some deliberations in its own right.

For critics like John Pilling the fact that an author's life is part of his or her novels doesn't obscure the genre of autobiography, but rather defines it (1-2). Along with this is a characteristic significant change from past to present which catalyzes the writing process (116-117). For Philippe Lejeune the difference between an autobiography and an autobiographical novel has to do with what he calls the "autobiographical pact" which refers to the agreement to tell the truth between the author and the reader. Without this pact, even the use of the author's proper name can be ambivalent if only initials are used, for example, or if the name is disguised by a play on words in such a way that the reader doesn't always know right away if one is reading autobiography or "autofiction" (9-25). It is also possible, according to the theory of Robert Elbaz, to define autobiography and fiction as the same genre because they both are fictions: " . . . they are both appropriations of selfhood through fictive voices" (198). William Spengemann argues that fiction is "the only true autobiography" (137) while he states that the more criticism is done in autobiography, the more its boundaries expand (XII).

When it comes to women's autobiography the theoretical implications are broader yet, since one has to consider the whole issue of feminist writing. Sidonie Smith argues that "males represent experiences of self, others, space, and time in individualistic, objective, and distant ways, while females represent experiences in relatively interpersonal, subjective, immediate ways" (13). Elizabeth Wilson defines women's autobiographies as "fragmented" (182) and Norine Voss characterizes them as "disjointed" (221); both basing their findings on the traditional assumption that women's lives take others into account while men are more focused on their own experience. Domna C. Stanton, who also notices this discontinuity, goes so far as to create a new term, "autogynography," to describe women's autobiography (3-20).

The poetics of autobiography by women in Spain is yet to be written. Randolph Pope in his comprehensive study of Spanish autobiography up to the Eighteenth Century includes two women: Leonor López de Córdoba (also in Domna Stanton's book), who happens to be the first Spanish autobiographer, and Santa Teresa de Jesús, better known for her mystic importance. In contemporary Spain autobiography written by women is virtually nonexistent. During Franco's time the genre all but disappeared due to the risk of exposing anyone's life to the scrutiny of a strict censorship; this lack, then, can be considered as a generational handicap. Memoirs did start to flourish in the years of democracy, with Juan Goytisolo's scathing *Coto vedado* for example, but women have remained surprisingly silent, with the notable exception of Elena Soriano's *Testimonio materno*, which deals explicitly with her son's tragic death and only marginally with her own life.

Surprisingly, however, many of the novels written by women during the "posguerra" (the postwar years, 1939-1975) were deemed to be autobiographical and often they were unjustly scorned by the critics for this tendency.[1] Juan Luis Alborg, for example, judges that Carmen Laforet "needs her own life experiences to provide the essential fictional material" (I:134), but, at the same time, criticizes Mercedes Salisachs when she deals with an unfamiliar situation (II:391). The same critic, however, praises José Luis Castillo Puche for his first hand knowledge, "reality lived from the inside," in his novels (I:292) and doesn't object to Jesús Fernández Santos's autobiographical fiction (II:373-382).

Carmen Martín Gaite who admittedly writes autobiographical fiction has miraculously escaped critical censure due to her obvious talent of combining imagination and personal experience. Although critics like Manuel Durán have correctly pointed out that Martín Gaite is the author of "one book" (234, 238)—the one of her life—no one has questioned either her originality or her creativity. Each of her novels, and her essays as well, expertly combine elements of her personal life, her poetics, and her thoughts in a different manner even when her reader can discern "life lines" which are repeated and are, therefore, unmistakably her own.

Characteristically, Martín Gaite writes freely in her novels not only about her adolescence when she was studying in the Institute of Salamanca, but also about the years of the Civil War. Childhood is very important to her from a literary point of view because that is where her memory lies (Gazarian 26). This is the case of *Entre visillos* (Through the Curtains 1958), and again in *El cuarto de atrás*, (1978; *The Back Room* 1983). In the latter she also speaks at length about her life as a writer and her literary creation. However candid she may appear to be about herself, she clearly concealed many other aspects of her biography, mainly those that have to do with her relationship with men, including her marriage to and separation from Rafael Sánchez Ferlosio (a well-known writer himself), or any other features that would deal with her sexuality and femininity, such as pregnancy and childbirth. Despite the fact that Eulalia, the protagonist of *Retahílas* (*Yarns* 1974) was recently separated, like herself, the biographical details are absent, for the most part, from this novel. It seems as if Martín Gaite is consciously using what Lejeune has called the "soft pedal" in his article "Autobiography in the Third Person" (28-29). That is to say that the author has contracted to do this: "I write myself by silencing myself. I would only have to raise my foot to increase the volume" (29).

It could be argued that Martín Gaite has chosen to repress this aspect of her personality due to the climate of repression which prevailed in Franco's Spain. Interestingly enough, however, when she recreates her life after 1975 as she did in *The Back Room*, she has "raised her foot" to incorporate the explicit socio-political criticism which was missing from the earlier works, but has remained equally coy in reference to her personal life. Nancy K. Miller, when she explores women's autobiography in France, has observed a similar phenomenon noting that "autobiology is not the subtext of autobiography" (51). It seems as if many of the writers were "mothers by accident of nature, writers by design" (53).[2]

This situation closely parallels that of Martín Gaite when we analyze the autobiographical strategies in her fiction. Despite the personal references between her characters and herself, what she has truly exposed in her novels is her literary persona, not the woman in French feminist terms[3]—which should not be so surprising considering that Martín Gaite doesn't consider herself a feminist. In other words, she writes her intellectual autobiography through her fiction and more than her biographical data, it's her voice, her ideas, and her conception of life that comes forth.

I propose, therefore, to explore the three novels already mentioned, *Entre visillos*, *Retahílas*, and *The Back Room*[4] in relation to some of her essays that are intrinsically related to them, mainly *Usos amorosos de la posguerra española* (Romantic Rituals in the Postwar Era 1987), *La búsqueda de interlocutor y otras búsquedas* (The Search for an Interlocutor and Other Searches 1973), *Desde la ventana* (From the Window 1987), and *El cuento de nunca acabar* (The Never Ending Tale 1983).

Natalia, the protagonist of *Entre visillos*, and Carmen Martín Gaite have many traits in common: they both lived in the provincial city of Salamanca while studying in the more progressive "Instituto" despite the fact that they could afford a sheltered private school. They both have sisters (the author has only one), and they also share a studious, reflective personality.[5] Most importantly, they felt stifled by the oppressive social codes which prescribed the proper conduct for young women (232-233): to be very adept in the social graces, barely interested in intellectual pursuits and committed to marry "a good catch" that would insure an equally protected and boring existence for generations to come. Natalia, and by her own admission Martín Gaite, is more interested in pursuing an education in Madrid than in dancing and gossiping in the social circles.[6]

Natalia is the prototype of what Martín Gaite has described in her essay *Desde la ventana* as "La chica rara" ("The Oddball"), basing her comments on another protagonist, Andrea of *Nada* by Carmen Laforet.[7] "This paradigm of a woman," she tells us, "which in one way or another questions the 'normalcy' of the amorous and domestic conduct that society orders to obey, is going to be repeated with some variations in other women's texts like those of Ana María Matute, Dolores Medio and myself" (99). The most significant trait of this "oddball" is her nonconformist attitude that makes her rebel against the family ties that bind her to the interior of her house, forcing her to look through the curtains.[8] Natalia is not alone in her dreams of escape. Elvira, another character in this novel, can also be labeled a "chica rara" (*Desde la ventana* 100), even if she gives up her ambitions to be an artist and ends up marrying the proverbial hometown boy. In some ways *Entre visillos* is a generational autobiography due to its focus on a group of adolescents caught in the restrictions of their particular time and space.[9]

According to Martín Gaite's essay, often the "chica rara" finds someone outside her generational group to help her escape her surroundings (104-105). Natalia listens to her older teacher, Pablo Klein, about pursuing her studies even if she is supposed to relinquish her goals in deference to her older's sister most pressing problems. Despite the obvious identification of Natalia with Martín Gaite, it has been pointed out that Pablo is the author's mask-presumptive.[10] He is the same age as the author when she wrote this novel and, like her, he comes back to Salamanca as an observer to view and comment on the town of their youth (50). In fact, the incorporation of Pablo as an alter-ego makes a lot of sense because this dichotomy between the remembrances of the past and the I of the present is one of the characteristics of the autobiographical genre (Pilling 116-117), and being a male he could be freer than a female protagonist. Another trait is the awareness of the self which is explicitly developed in Natalia's first person diary, which alternates with the third person objective narrator.

Appropriately *Entre visillos* is dedicated to Carmen Martín Gaite's older sister with this telling note: "For my sister Anita, who rolled down the stairs with her first evening gown, and she laughed, seated on the landing." Anita, like her sister, doesn't take society's strict rules to heart; it may be pointed out that she lives in Madrid and has never married.

The final distinction of the novels with a "chica rara" for a protagonist is the lack of a happy ending, because "in life there are no happy endings" (*Desde la ventana* 108). Natalia sees Pablo and her sister leave on the same train while she waits her turn to escape to Madrid; like she told her father: " . . . if I have to be a resigned and reasonable woman, I'd rather not live" (233).

It can be said that *Entre visillos* is a fictionalized account of Martín Gaite's essay *Usos amorosos de la posguerra española* published thirty years later which the author started to write, she tells us in *The Back Room*, on the day of Franco's funeral. If in the novel she adhered to the objective point of view of the socio-realistic literature written in the fifties in Spain and to its strict censorship, in the essay she was able to fill in the explicit criticism of the Franco regime that governed the people—the women in particular—depriving them of their basic freedoms.[11] Martín Gaite pulls no punches, for example, when it comes to exposing the antifeminism of the "Sección Femenina de Falange" ("Falangist Feminine Section") created by Pilar Primo de Rivera, the sister of José Antonio Primo de Rivera, the Falangist leader (56-62). Many other incidents, spiced up with personal anecdotes corroborate the fact that *Entre visillos* is autobiographical, since they are reminiscent of her novel: the eternal search for a husband (chapter II), the "niña topolino" (trend-setter girl) which is a portrait of Gertru in the novel (79-81), the same trivial language (86), the studies in the Instituto (92), the evening strolls in the main square (184), the engagement party (207) and so on.

But despite its title which promises us the "romantic ways" of the Spaniards in the postwar era, and despite the lack of censorship when it was published in the eighties and the freedom of the essay genre, Martín Gaite still refrains from telling the complete story about the sexual mores of those years. Except for the brief mention of the prostitutes (102-106) she does not include practices that could be considered offensive. Having lived in Spain in the fifties I can attest to the members of the clergy who had their own children (calling them "nephews") and lovers ("aunts") or the maids who often became the "señoritos'" (the sons of the man of the house) first sexual experience; if they got pregnant, they quickly disappeared to marry the unsuspecting boyfriend in their hometown. A well-known practice, absent from this essay as well, is the so-called "estar de Rodríguez" (to be like a Rodríguez) which meant that the mother was away at the shore or the mountains with the children and the father had a girlfriend for the summer in the city.

These examples aside, it is hard to see how Martín Gaite could deny that she is a feminist, while most of this essay denounces the double standard between men and women by pointing out the inequities of the situation. *Desde la ventana* is feminist as well in its attempt to give an overview of the Spanish literature written by women.[12] But *Retahílas* is perhaps Martín Gaite's most engaging novel in feminist terms for its portrayal of love and marriage. Interestingly enough, although this novel seems to be the least autobiographical of the ones we study here, the author affirms that it is the one into which she has put the most passion and that it is her favorite novel.[13] As Spengemann has pointed out, what makes novels autobiographical is "not their inclusion of biographical materials but their efforts to discover, through fictive action, some ground upon which conflicting aspects of the writer's own nature might be reconciled in a complete being" (132).

Retahílas is structured as a conversation between Eulalia and her nephew, Germán. During an entire evening, while they await the death of the elderly matriarch, their words weave back and forth (in alternate chapters) like yarns being woven in a loom. Given the fact that Eulalia, like Martín Gaite, had recently separated from her husband, it would be tempting to try to make a comparison between the two in personal terms, but the biographical information is characteristically missing. This is all that Martín Gaite shares with the reader in her sketch: "Since the autumn of 1970 I have lived alone with my daughter Marta in the same house on Doctor Esquerdo, which for seventeen years I had shared with Rafael. Our separation was amicable, and we continue to see each other frequently. He comes here whenever he likes" (Brown 32). We know equally little about Eulalia's breakup in the novel, other than that she still cares for him (133).

If we look, however, in another of Martín Gaite's essays, *La búsqueda de interlocutor,* we can establish a correlation between her voice and the discourse of Eulalia in *Retahílas*.[14] In this essay the author defines her well known passion for conversation: " . . . any search for esteem, for identity, for affirmation or for confrontation with the world is reduced, definitely, to a search for an interlocutor" (8). And Eulalia praises the power of the spoken word (87) urging her nephew to listen attentively so "she won't lose her interlocutor" (100). Just as Pablo Klein could be interpreted as an alter ego of the author in *Entre visillos*, so can Germán be a "good mirror," or a reflection, for the author in this novel. In "The Bad Mirrors," the first essay of *La búsqueda de interlocutor*, she defines a "bad mirror" as the one "that can neither look nor read other than what has already been seen and read by others," while a "good mirror" would welcome its images "without subjecting it to interpretations, like virgin territory" (17). Germán, like Eulalia (and therefore Carmen), expresses the same ideas about dialogue: " . . . to be able to speak was to love each other" for always associated "the idea of love with conversation" (162). In some ways the dialogues between Germán and Eulalia, in Lejeune's terms, are like "fictive" characters in an autobiography suited for this type of "polemical literature" ("Autobiography" 44).

Germán, however, differs from Eulalia in his opinion about marriage. While he wants to get married, she did not want to in her youth: "There were my rebel years, I couldn't stand this house, nor engagements, nor marriages, nor anything that would imply a commitment" (108), even if the freedom that she has without her husband weighs heavy on her (135). Freedom is another theme that Martín Gaite discusses in the essay we are studying. In "Las mujeres liberadas" ("The Liberated Women") she warns about the dangers of the so-called liberation from marriage that can turn out to be a loss of binding ties (130). Eulalia, likewise, regrets that she didn't have children (213). The heart of the matter is that one has to decide between being free and alone or committed with its risks (131).[15] This ambivalent attitude about marriage and freedom coupled with the author's proclamation can be seen as antifeminist, yet Carmen Martín Gaite has done a great deal to fight the male/female stereotypes both in her essays and her fiction.[16] In my opinion what she objects to is not the concept of women's rights, but the radical manifestations and noisy demonstrations associated with the term "feminism" in Spain to this day.[17] She refers to this attitude with words like "pancartas," "clamores," "protestas," "gritos exasperados," "codazos," "agresividad" ("posters," "screams," "protests," "exasperated screeches," "aggression") that in her view are the arms of the liberated women (126). Likewise, Eulalia complains in *Retahílas* about her state of "enraged feminism" (145). Phyllis Zatlin has pointed out that often the male characters are the best champions of women's right to self-identity in Martín Gaite's fiction ("Feminist Authors" 332). While this is true of Germán, it is even more evident with the man in black of *The Back Room*.

On a stormy night this enigmatic character comes to visit Carmen, who is herself the protagonist of the novel, in order to interview her about her work. While they engage in lively conversation a stack of paper on Martín Gaite's desk grows unexplainedly. At the end, she wakes up with the arrival of her daughter only to find the mysterious visitor gone and the manuscript for *The Back Room* completed. Clearly we can see in this novel characteristics which remind the reader of Martín Gaite's earlier works, fulfilling through the use of repetition and memory, by Michael Sprinker's definition, some of the most crucial considerations for autobiography (329). Like *Retahílas* this novel takes place in one night, and it is mostly a dialogue between a man and a woman focusing on the author's ideas about communication. Like *Entre visillos* and *Usos amorosos* it explores in depth the postwar years while Carmen lived in Salamanca (although some wonderful new adventures are added here, like the one in Burgos looking for her father's repossessed car, 104-11). At the same time the man in black is related to Pablo and Germán because, like them, he can be defined as an alter ego, or the Jungian's "animus" of the author.[18] Nevertheless, he is markedly original.

In "El hombre musa" ("Man as Muse") in *Desde la ventana*, Martín Gaite examines the "empty mold" (78) that the traditional woman muse has played in Spanish literature. For her it is engaging to transpose "the concept of muse, symbolized by a pale young woman with a distant look, with an unknown and disquieting man that spurs the feminine imagination like a motor" (83). Obviously, this is the role played by the man in black in *The Back Room* as he discusses Martín Gaite's early fiction and inspires her to break the writer's block that she admittedly was suffering at the beginning of the novel. Her intention with this role reversal can be deemed feminist as well: "In this sense, it proposes a subversion of the conventionally admitted relations between men and women" (34).

Martín Gaite goes on to say that women, and we must assume that she speaks for herself, would rather be appreciated as intellectual interlocutors than as amorous partners (85). Despite this affirmation in the essay, in *The Back Room* there is a sexual tension between Carmen and the man which never develops into an encounter (perhaps because the man's girlfriend calls, arousing Carmen's suspicions).[19] Martín Gaite is, however, totally candid when answering the interviewer's questions about her previous novels and the essay that she was writing (*Usos amorosos*). It is as if she needs to hide in her fiction to be able to talk freely about her works since she repeatedly stated in "real life" interviews that she is incapable of analyzing her own books.[20]

There is no need to explore here the diverse autobiographical aspects of this novel that have already been studied: Catherine Bellver mentions the impact of the Spanish Civil War on the young Carmen; Linda Levine has focused on Martín Gaite as an "artist" paying attention to her parody of the "novela rosa" ("melodramatic novel"); Joan Brown examines the socio-political implications and its fantastic elements; and Claude Chauchadis explores the meaning of games in this so called "autobiographie fantastique" (340), concluding that autobiography itself is just another game for Martín Gaite. There is, however, one facet of Carmen's personality that had remained hidden from her fiction until the publication of The Back Room which has to do with the present of her life and not with her memory of the past like the others mentioned, and that is her identity as a mother.[21]

Her daughter Marta is a character in The Back Room; she comes in the house after a late evening out, to find her mother asleep on her bed. She is the one who brings Carmen back to the reality of everyday life with the details of her outing, while at the same time, she corroborates the visit by the man when she sees two drinking glasses in the sitting room and the little gold box that he had left. According to Estelle Jelinek, a subject which is often omitted from women's autobiographies are siblings, children, mates, and romantic attachments (11), while parents are more likely to be dealt with (12). Carmen Martín Gaite, as we have seen, has done so in her fiction; even in her short autobiographical sketch (Brown), it is true that her father and mother are treated more extensively than her daughter (who is only mentioned) or than her first born child, Miguel, who died when he was one year old.

When we turn to El cuento de nunca acabar (The Never Ending Tale), Martín Gaite's most comprehensive essay, we do find, however, many references to motherhood. Often matters of child rearing are discussed: the child's first knowledge of language ["La obligación y la devoción" ("Obligation and Devotion")], children's games ["Reflexiones en el parque" ("Reflections in the Park")], children's love of stories ["La Cenicienta" ("Cinderella")] and a number of other aspects of a youngster's education. In one of the many beautiful images that fill the book, children are like mirrors because they "pick up punctually whatever is reflected on them: images, short stories, expressions, scenes, and they keep it all" (319). But, undoubtedly, the most moving facet of the whole essay, and one that sheds some light on Carmen's personality, is her love for her daughter. Marta, even as a young child, appears concerned about her mother's writing—which can be seen in *The Back Room* as well (205-206)—and it is she who gives her the "cuadernos para todo" ("catch-all notebooks") where the notations that make up this whole essay are recorded. For the reader who knows Martín Gaite's biography, the incorporation of the tender relationship between mother and daughter—particularly evident in "Ruptura de relaciones" ("The Breakup")—is doubly moving as Marta suffered an untimely death at the age of twenty-nine in 1985.

El cuento de nunca acabar fills in other gaps that are also an intrinsic part of *The Back Room*. There is, for example, extensive scrutiny of literary theory, narrative techniques and the writing process. In some ways this essay (written between 1973-1982) has served as a workroom for *The Back Room*, for example, when Martín Gaite describes what is for her the optimal creative time which coincides with the genesis of the novel: "it usually comes in summer nights, like today's, when this total sensation that makes me recuperate remnants of my childhood and youth entangled with those of others' childhood and youth that have been told here ... comes over me" (48). Love, suggested in its subtitle, "Apuntes sobre la narración, el amor y la mentira" ("Notes on Narration, Love and Lies"), could have also been another missing link, but, as we have repeatedly seen in the works of Martín Gaite, it is nearly absent there too. There are only a few pages (377-380) out of more than four hundred that make up the book that deal with love, and those are of a rhetorical nature without any personal references.[22] But it is in *The Back Room*, after all, where we can read her most candid thoughts about love: "My failures in love have always stemmed from that, from the fear that someone may leave me at a loss for words, reduced to the naked power of my gaze or my body. . . . And the men I liked, the ones who perhaps liked me too, took up with some other girl" (182).[23] However, as we know, the man in black and Carmen don't get together either. It seems only fitting that it is he who urges her to write: "Of a great story of love and mystery that you don't dare tell ... " (197).

It could be concluded, then, that, given Martín Gaite's ambivalent position on feminism, she has chosen to silence herself on matters of sexuality, motherhood, and relationships (typically considered female), for fear of being read as a woman and not as a writer. Miller has addressed this self-consciousness in women's autobiographical writing in France; like her counterparts, it can be said of Martín Gaite that "The historical truth of a woman writer's life lies in the reader's grasp of her intratext: the body of her writing and not the writing of her body" (61).

The writing of autobiography implies an unfinished project since, if the author is still living, there can be, presumably, more pages to be written. Certainly for Martín Gaite, autobiography is a never-ending undertaking because she has chosen to tell and retell from different perspectives—in fiction as well as in essays—some of her life experiences, but, most of all, her convictions, and her expertise as a writer. Hers is an intellectual autobiography with emphasis on the "auto" and not on the "bio." Martín Gaite will certainly continue to impress her readers with her creativity and originality, yet it is unlikely that she will fill in the silences that she has so closely kept.[24]

NOTES

1. Margaret E.W. Jones points out the tendency to autobiographical fiction as a generational characteristic (125). Traditionally, in any literature, one of the most common objections to autobiographical fiction is that it is too easy. See Avrom Fleishman's *Figures of Autobiography* (191).
2. Men, as well, don't reveal painful or intimate memoirs, and their sexual encounters also tend to be absent (Jelineck 10).
3. Sidonie Smith argues that the language of *l'écriture féminine*, or the textual representation of female sexuality is yet to be inscribed in autobiographies in any literature as women don't write themselves in anything other than the phallologocentric *écriture* of Western culture (18).
4. I use the English title of this last novel because it has been translated by Helen R. Lane. The other two and the essays have not been translated as of this date. Except for *The Back Room*, when I'll make use of Lane's edition, all the other translations are mine and the pages in parentheses correlate to the Spanish originals.
5. For Carmen Martín Gaite's autobiographical information I refer the reader to the useful, and beautiful as well, autobiographical sketch that she wrote for Joan Brown's book. It is translated into English (20-34) and included as an appendix in its Spanish original (193-206).
6. Lynn Talbot studies *Entre visillos* through the archetypal patterns which show the demands that society places on women and their desire to break those molds. The bibliography on Carmen Martín

Gaite is quite extensive, for two updated references see the one in Brown's book (181-192) and the very complete one by Isabel M. Roger.

7. *Nada* by Carmen Laforet was the winner of the first Nadal prize (1944)—won also by *Entre visillos* in 1957—and one of the most significant novels of the whole postwar generation.
8. For in-depth studies of Martín Gaite's social criticism see Joan Lipman Brown's article "The Nonconformist Character as Social Critic in the Novels of Carmen Martín Gaite" and "Carmen Martín Gaite as a Social Critic" by Catherine G. Bellver. I'd like to point out that the title of the novel *Through the Curtains* and of the essay *From the Window* are obviously related. For Martín Gaite a woman at the window symbolizes a thirst for freedom and independence, hence the first chapter of this book, entitled "Mirando a través de la ventana" ("Looking Through the Window"), deals with the early women in Spanish literature.
9. María Dolores Albiac Blanco utilizes the term "generational autobiography" in her essay on Ramón Pérez de Ayala.
10. In "A Splice of Life: Carmen Martín Gaite's *Entre visillos*," John W. Kronik (53), also points out the self awareness of the first person diary (54).
11. Joan Brown in her article "One Autobiography, Twice Told," writes about the relationship between *Entre visillos* and *The Back Room* which deals, in part, with the same years.
12. See Phyllis Zatlin Boring's article where she points out Martín Gaite's feminist views as they are reflected through the characters of her fiction. See also by the same author "Divorce in the Contemporary Spanish Novel," and Linda Gould Levine's "The Censored Sex."
13. In an interview with Hector Medina (192, 193). For some information about language and its representation in this novel see the articles of Gonzalo Navajas and Emma Martinell.
14. Marcia Welles states that "Martín Gaite's 'theory of interlocution' is put into practice, so to speak, in *Retahílas*" (201); other critics have also come to the same conclusion (Brown, "The Nonconformist" 173).
15. Curiously enough Carmen Martín Gaite dedicated her book *Usos amorosos del dieciocho en España* (Romantic Rituals of the Eighteenth Century in Spain) to her husband, two years after their separation, with these words: "For Rafael, who taught me how to inhabit solitude and not to be a wife."

16. See "The Decoding and Encoding of Sex Roles in Carmen Martín Gaite's *Retahílas*" by Elizabeth Ordóñez.
17. María Campo Alange, a contemporary Spanish playwright, makes a similar statement in an interview in *Estreno* (14).
18. These are terms used by Julian Palley and Blas Matamoros (598). Kathleen M. Glenn sees him as an incarnation of the devil; Jean Alsina (332) relates the man in black to Macanaz, the historical figure and subject of Martín Gaite's essay. The bibliography on this novel, by far the most studied of the author, is very extensive. There are five articles with this one in *From Fiction to Metafiction: Essays in Honor of Carmen Martín Gaite*.
19. See pages 29, 32, 93, 122, 138, 166, 190 and 199 for diverse hints of intimacy (their fingers touch, her head lies on his shoulder...etc) that maintain the suspense.
20. She says as much in "Retahíla con nieve en Nueva York" ("Loose Thread with Snow in New York") the introductory essay that she wrote for the volume *From Fiction to Metafiction*.
21. *Retahílas* is dedicated to her daughter Marta and *Usos amorosos* has this inscription: "For all Spanish women, between fifty and sixty years of age, who do not understand their children. And for their children, who don't understand them."
22. In *Revista de Estudios Hispánicos* there was an interesting study in which Randolph Pope, Amy Kaminsky, Andrew Bush and Ruth El Saffar wrote an ongoing critical dialogue about *El cuento de nunca acabar*.
23. There is another tell-tale remark by Martín Gaite in *The Back Room*: "I preferred to ask questions. Allusions to sex scared me, they were impossible to grasp and of ambiguous gender, like butterflies" (192). None of her characters' sexual experiences are ever described either.
24. I had a chance to discuss this article after it was written in its present form with Carmen Martín Gaite (August, 1989). She insisted that she has no intention of revealing the aspects of her personality that she has so far concealed. She has no interest whatsoever in doing so.

WORKS CITED

Albiac Blanco, María Dolores. "Autobiografía personal y autobiografía generacional en la obra de Ramón Pérez de Ayala." *L'Autobiographie en Espagne.* 181-201.

Alborg, Juan Luis. *Hora actual de la novela española*, 1,2. Madrid: Taurus, 1958, 1962.

Alsina, Jean, Claude Chauchadis, Michéle Ramond. "Approches d'une autobiographie féminine: *El cuarto de atrás* de Carmen Martín Gaite. *L'Autobiographie en Espagne.* 323-352.

L'Autobiographie en Espagne. Actes du IIe Colloque International de la Baume-Les-Aix. 23-25 mai 1981. Aix-en-Provence: Universite de Provence, 1982.

Autobiography: Essays Theoretical and Critical. Ed. James Olney. Princeton: Princeton UP, 1980.

Bellver, Catherine. "Carmen Martín Gaite as a Social Critic." *Letras Femeninas* 6 (1980): 3-16.

———. "War as Rite of Passage in *El cuarto de atrás*." *Letras Femeninas* 12 (1986): 69-77.

Brown, Joan Lipman. "A Fantastic Memoir: Technique and History in *El cuarto de atrás*." *Anales de la Literatura Española Contemporánea* 6 (1981): 13-20.

———. "The Nonconformist Character as Social Critic in the Novels of Carmen Martín Gaite." *Kentucky Romance Quarterly* 28 (1981): 165-176.

———. "One Autobiography, Twice Told: Martín Gaite's *Entre visillos* and *El cuarto de atrás*." *Hispanic Journal* 7 (1986): 37-47.

———. *Secrets from* The Back Room: *the Fiction of Carmen Martín Gaite.* University, Mississippi: Romance Monographs, 1987.

Durán, Manuel. "Carmen Martín Gaite, *Retahílas, El cuarto de atrás*, y el diálogo sin fin." *Revista Iberoamericana* 116-117 (1981): 233-240.

Elbaz, Robert. "Autobiography, Ideology, and Genre Theory." *Orbis Litterarum* 38 (1983): 187-204.

"Encuesta: ¿Por qué no estrenan las mujeres en España?" *Estreno* 10 (1984): 13-25.

The Female Autograph: Theory and Practice of Autobiography from the Twentieth Century. Ed. Domna C. Stanton. Chicago: The U of Chicago P, 1987.

Fleishman, Avrom. *Figures of Autobiography: The Language of Self-Writing in Victorian and Modern England*. Berkeley: U of California P, 1983.

From Fiction to Metafiction: Essays in Honor of Carmen Martín Gaite. Eds. Mirella Servodidio and Marcia L. Welles. Lincoln: Society of Spanish and Spanish-American Studies, 1983.

Gazarian Gautier, Marie-Lise. "Conversación con Carmen Martín Gaite en Nueva York." *From Fiction to Metafiction*. 25-33.

Goytisolo, Juan. *Coto Vedado*. Barcelona: Seix Barral, 1985.

Gunn, Janet Varner. *Autobiography: Toward a Poetics of Experience*. Philadelphia: U of Pennsylvania P, 1982.

Jelinek, Estelle C. "Women's Autobiography and the Male Tradition" in *Women's Autobiography: Essays in Criticism*. Bloomington: Indiana UP, 1980.

Jones, Margaret E. W. "Del compromiso al egoísmo: la metamorfosis de la protagonista en la novelística femenina de posguerra." *Novelistas Femeninas de la Posguerra*. Ed. Janet W. Pérez. Madrid: José Porrua, 1983: 125-134.

Kronik, John W. "A Splice of Life: Carmen Martín Gaite's *Entre visillos*." *From Fiction to Metafiction*. 49-60.

Laforet, Carmen. *Nada*. Barcelona: Destino, 1978.

Lejeune, Philippe. "Autobiography in the Third Person." *New Literary History* 9 (1977): 27-50.

———. "Le Pacte Autobiographique (Bis)." *L'Autobiographie en Espagne*. 7-25.

Levine, Linda Gould. "Carmen Martín Gaite's *El cuarto de atrás*: A Portrait of the Artist as a Woman." *From Fiction to Metafiction*. 161-172.

———. "The Censored Sex. Women as Author and Character in Franco's Spain." *Women in Hispanic Literature. Icons and Fallen Idols*. Ed. Beth Miller. Berkeley: U of California P, 1983: 289-315.

Life/Lines: Theorizing Women's Autobiography. Eds. Bella Brodzki and Celeste Schenck. Ithaca: Cornell UP, 1988.

Martín Gaite, Carmen. *The Back Room*. Trans. Helen R. Lane. New York: Columbia UP, 1983.

———. *La búsqueda de interlocutor y otras búsquedas*. Barcelona: Destino, 1982.

———. *El cuarto de atrás*. Barcelona: Destino, 1982.

———. *El cuento de nunca acabar. Apuntes sobre la narración, el amor y la mentira*. Madrid: Trieste, 1983.

———. *Desde la ventana*. Madrid: Espasa Calpe, 1987.

——. *Entre visillos*. 7th ed. Barcelona: Destino, 1978.
——. *El proceso de Macanaz. Historia de un empapelamiento*. Madrid: Editorial Moneda y Crédito, 1970.
——. "Retahíla con nieve en Nueva York (Para mi madre in memoriam)." *From Fiction to Metafiction*. 19-25
——. *Retahílas*. 2nd ed. Barcelona: Destino, 1979.
——. *Usos amorosos del dieciocho en España*. Barcelona: Anagrama, 1988.
——. *Usos amorosos de la postguerra española*. Barcelona: Anagrama, 1987.
Martinell Gifre, Emma. "Un aspecto de la técnica presentativa de C. Martín Gaite en *Retahílas*." *Archivum* 31-32 (1981-1982): 463-479.
Medina, Héctor. "Conversación con Carmen Martín Gaite." *Anales de la Literatura Española Contemporánea* 8 (1983): 183-194.
Miller, Nancy K. "Writing Fictions: Women's Autobiography in France." *Life/Lines*. 45-61.
Navajas, Gonzalo. "El diálogo y el yo en *Retahílas* de Carmen Martín Gaite." *Teoría y práctica de la novela española posmoderna*. Barcelona: Edicions del Mall. 1987. 43-58.
Olney, James. *Metaphors of Self: The Meaning of Autobiography*. Princeton: Princeton UP, 1972.
Ordóñez, Elizabeth. "The Decoding and Encoding of Sex Roles in Carmen Martín Gaite's *Retahílas*." *Kentucky Romance Quarterly* 27 (1980): 237-244.
Palley, Julian. "El interlocutor soñado de *El cuarto de atrás* de Carmen Martín Gaite." *Insula* 499-500 (1988): 50.
Pilling, John. *Autobiography and Imagination: Studies in Self-Scrutiny*. London: Routledge, 1981.
Pope, Randolph D. *La autobiografía española hasta Torres Villarroel*. Frankfurt: Peter Lang, 1974.
——, Amy Kaminsky, Andrew Bush and Ruth El Saffar. "*El cuento de nunca acabar*. A critical Dialogue." *Revista de Estudios Hispánicos* 22 (1988): 107-134.
Roger, Isabel M. "Carmen Martín Gaite: una trayectoria novelística y su bibliografía." *Anales de la Literatura Española Contemporánea* 13 (1988): 293-317.
Smith, Sidonie. *A Poetics of Women's Autobiography of Self-Representation*. Bloomington: Indiana UP, 1987.
Soriano, Elena. *Testimonio materno*. Barcelona: Plaza y Janes, 1986.
Spengemann, William C. *The Forms of Autobiography*. New Haven: Yale UP, 1980.

Sprinker, Michael. "Fictions of the Self: The End of Autobiography." *Autobiography. Essays Theoretical and Critical*. 320-342.

Talbot, Lynn K. "Female Archetypes in Carmen Martín Gaite's *Entre visillos*." *Anales de la Literatura Española Contemporánea* 12 (1987): 79-94.

Voss, Norine. "'Saying the Unsayable': An Introduction to Women's Autobiography." *Gender Studies. New Directions in Feminist Criticism*. Ed. Judith Spector. Bowling Green: Bowling Green State U Popular P, 1986.

Welles, Marcia L. "Carmen Martín Gaite: Fiction as Desire." *From Fiction to Metafiction*. 197-207.

Wilson, Elizabeth. "Mirror Writing: An Autobiography." *Feminist Literary Theory. A Reader*. Ed. Mary Eagleton. Oxford: Basil Blackwell, 1986. 181-184.

Zatlin Boring, Phyllis. "Carmen Martín Gaite Feminist Author." *Revista de Estudios Hispánicos* 11 (1977): 323-338.

———. "Divorce in the Contemporary Spanish Novel." *Perspectivas de la novela*. Ed. Alva V. Ebersole. Valencia: Albatros, 1979. 115-122.

The Difficulty of Saying "I": Reassembling a Self in Christa Wolf's Autobiographical Fiction

Kathleen L. Komar

Born March 18, 1929, in Landsberg on the Warthe (now the Polish town of Gorzów Wielkopolski), German Democratic Republic author Christa Wolf has become the dominant voice of German literature (East or West) today. She has been awarded the Arts Prize of the city of Halle (1961), the Heinrich Mann Prize of the Academy of Arts of the GDR (1963), the Theodor Fontane Prize of Potsdam (1973), and the Georg Büchner Prize of the German Academy for Language and Literature (1980) among others.

A dedicated socialist who has been active in the politics as well as the literature of the GDR, Wolf has always dared to protest the ills of the East German society in which she so firmly believes. She has also criticized the patriarchal and military complexes of both East and West. Growing up during World War II, fleeing the approaching Russian troops in 1945, and helping to build a new socialist state after the war, Wolf remains an active author and independent thinker who was among the first to write about personal involvement during the war years without creating false anti-fascist heroes. She studied German literature in Jena and Leipzig from 1949-53, and later worked as a research assistant to the German Writers' Union and as an editor for major journals and publishing houses.

Wolf's early works Moskauer Novelle *(1961; Moscow Novella)* and Der geteilte Himmel *(1963; Divided Heaven 1965)* could be described as "Socialist Realism" as it was prescribed by the aesthetic committees of the GDR. In 1968 in Nachdenken über Christa T. *(The Quest for Christa T. 1970)* Wolf created her own version of "realism," which acknowledged the individual's need to develop a stable self even within a socialist society, and which brought her into conflict with GDR *cultural functionaries. In* Kindheitsmuster *(1976;* Patterns of Childhood *1980), Wolf explored the Nazi era and the childhood of those who grew up under Hitler. In* Kein Ort. Nirgends *(1979;* No Place on Earth *1982) Wolf examined the lives of two figures of German Romanticism; in her* Kassandra *(1983;* Cassandra *1984) she rewrites the life of the famous prophetess of Troy. In her most recent work* Störfall: Nachrichten eines Tages *(1987;* Accident: A Day's News *1989) Wolf analyzes the repercussions of the Chernobyl nuclear accident.*

Always a voice of social conscience, Wolf has also come to be a strong advocate of women's rights and abilities. Married to writer and scholar Gerhard Wolf, she currently lives outside of East Berlin.

When the narrator of Christa Wolf's *Kindheitsmuster* (*Patterns of Childhood*),[1] decides to relate her childhood years in the third person rather than the first person one would traditionally expect of an autobiography, she reproduces the gesture of Wolf herself who displaces her own childhood memories into the fictional text by authoring *Patterns of Childhood*. Wolf's most autobiographically fictional text thus produces a structure of narrative Chinese boxes in which the dilemma of the author in conceiving and writing the text is reproduced identically within the novel. *Patterns of Childhood* therefore not only reflects Wolf's life, but the very process of her writing. This embedding of the author's existential and aesthetic predicaments within the fictional text plays a major role in Wolf's *Nachdenken über Christa T.* (*The Quest for Christa T.*)[2] and *Störfall: Nachrichten eines Tages* (*Accident: A Day's News*) as well as in *Patterns of Childhood*. Taken together, these three texts form a continuous autobiographical fictional narrative that reveals Wolf's attempts to come to terms with defining the self in literature.

Early in *Patterns of Childhood*, the narrator must choose between the disturbing objectification of third person narration or silence: "to remain speechless, or else to live in the third person. The first is impossible, the second uncanny" (*A Model Childhood* 3).[3] She cannot face the participation of her earlier, childhood self in the Nazi era. "Words, phrases, whole chains of thought that could call them [the memories that the narrator wants to avoid] forth, don't let them come up. . . . Because it is unbearable to think the tiny word 'I' in connection with the word 'Auschwitz.' 'I' in the past conditional: I would have. I might have. I could have. Done it. Obeyed orders" (*A Model Childhood* 230).[4] Ironically, the narrator did not participate directly in the fighting or in the death camps; she led a typical ill-informed, middle-class life in which one believes in country and tries to fit into the social whole. But the narrator is quite conscious of the deceptive speed with which East Germany disposed of the war as no longer its problem since the war resulted from the capitalist, imperialist economy of the west. The narrator knows that the mentality that produced the Holocaust is not limited to the boundaries of West Germany nor to the period of World War II. Her reflections recall the past for a whole generation of Germans, East and West, who grew up during the war years. Not old enough to be directly responsible for the war, those born in the mid to late 1920s nonetheless shoulder the burden of memory and self-examination after Hitler's fall. Christa Wolf takes up that burden in *Patterns of Childhood*.

The trauma associated with having grown up during the Hitler era makes it impossible for the narrator to connect her current self, living in the German Democratic Republic of the early 1970s, with the intelligent and fragile child being molded during the Nazi period. Wolf herself explains the process by which she came to the final form of the text:

> I have a series of beginnings for *Patterns of Childhood* that were narrated in first person, as simple remembrance. I then gave that up. One reason was that this child wasn't narratable for me in the first person, because I was no longer she. I couldn't identify with her. Perhaps that is characteristic on the whole for adults in relationship to themselves as a child. In my case it was particularly significant, because this childhood in Germany really was completely foreign to the adult I had become. Repression and the desire not to know were also naturally a part of it, but I wanted precisely to know now. In spite of that, I didn't succeed in calling this child "I." There was also a psychological barrier there—it couldn't be explained by aesthetics only. ("Documentation: Christa Wolf" 95. Translation mine.)

The narrated self thus becomes the third-person "Nelly Jordan" while the narrator ruminates on current events in a second-person form that implicates the reader too in its reflections and responsibility. This formal complicity of the reader is particularly important for the generation of Christa Wolf's peers who shared her fate of being too young to have affected World War II, but old enough to have absorbed the lesson that fascism offered. The fictional text thus becomes not just a personal autobiography but also a generational one.

In many ways Christa Wolf makes the same decision of self-objectification regarding the Nazi era that shaped her youth as her narrator does. One of the earliest of the GDR writers to confront personal involvement in World War II,[5] Wolf breaks the taboo against acknowledging the wide-spread fascist sentiment among many of her peers and elders. She is relentlessly honest in doing so. Alexander Stephan comments on Wolf's unparalleled realism in *Patterns of Childhood* as he asserts that her text easily outstrips those of GDR writers Anna Seghers, Franz Fühmann and Hermann Kant in coming to grips with the past (123). Wolf undermines the image of socialist heroes bravely resisting the Nazis to depict many who supported Nazi rule and many who were indifferent or cowed into conformity (such as Nelly Jordan's father).[6] Wolf herself comments on the general fictional material about this period during a reading from the manuscript of *Patterns of Childhood* in 1975:

> It bothers me a bit that many of our books about this period end with heroes who rapidly change, with heroes who actually come to rather significant and correct political and human insights already during the fascist period. I don't want to dispute any author's experience. But my experience was different. I have experienced that it took a very long time before tiny insights at first and then later deeper changes were possible. ("Diskussion mit Christa Wolf" 861. Translation mine.)

Christa Wolf is certainly not out to create heroes in her own reminiscences—and certainly not to cast her main character as one. She fully acknowledges that as a child Nelly is much like her peers, and that they are all caught up in the same desires to be good children and good Germans. The patterning that shapes Nelly's and Wolf's childhood made possible the anesthetized lack of response of Germany under Hitler. But Wolf's decision to cast her memories in a fictionalized autobiographical format gives her a distance from which to be ruthlessly honest and clear-sighted about what pressures shaped her and her peers' childhoods and adolescent years in Germany during World War II.

Patterns of Childhood is temporally two stories—or rather three. It is the story of the child Nelly who is growing up in a middle-class family during the years of Hitler's rise and fall. She learns early on from her own childhood experiences that one is often punished unjustly and rewarded undeservedly. Nelly experiences the rising national sentiment in favor of the *Führer*. Like the other girls her age, she joins youth groups such as the *Bund deutscher Mädchen*, and has a crush on a "patriotic," disciplined, and enthusiastically Nazi teacher, Juliane Strauch. She is vaguely aware of the purchase of a candy factory by her uncle for what seems a very cheap price and of the flight of its former Jewish owner. She realizes that her mentally deficient aunt disappears into the governmental machinery. She lives through *Kristallnacht*, the destruction of the synagogues, and feels a momentary sympathy for the Jews but nevertheless has been taught to fear them as the inferior other. And finally, Nelly and her family are uprooted as they must flee the advancing Russian troops. This first level covers roughly the early 1930s to 1947.

The second two temporal levels take place in the early 1970s. The second level begins with the narrator's two-day return visit in 1971 to her once German hometown, now part of Poland; the third level continues between 1972 and 1975 as the narrator attempts to emplot her childhood and its ramifications while realizing that much has *not* changed in human attitudes and consciousness as the political events of the 1970s demonstrate to her. This narrator is constantly aware not only of her childhood, but of her contemporary environment and its problems. She realizes that the GDR has not become the Utopian society she had hoped for. She records also the aggressions of the western powers in various third-world countries. She attempts to come to terms with both her past and her present and to help her daughter Lenka to understand some of those patterns of childhood that shaped the lives of her generation.

While the narrator decides to treat Nelly Jordan's childhood in third person, her own reflections on the past and on contemporary events in the GDR and the world are cast in second person. The rupture of consciousness figured by this splitting forms the underlying tension of the text. The real "plot" of *Patterns of Childhood* is the reintegration of the self of the narrator. The narrator realizes that her story will come to a successful end only when she can reintegrate and reunify the community of selves she has created in writing the text—that is, only when she can reconstruct herself as a whole being. This unification is symbolized by the convergence of the third-person passages "about" the young Nelly and the second-person passages of the narrator's self-address into the closing unified first person of the final page of the text. In fact, Wolf defines her tale as precisely the tracing of this convergence:

> The final point would be reached when the second and the third person were to meet again in the first or, better still, were to meet with the first person. When it would no longer have to be "you" and "she" but a candid, unreserved "I." It seemed very doubtful to you whether you could reach this point at all, whether the road you've taken would ever lead to it. *(A Model Childhood 349)*[7]

Although she is not sure that her task of personal reintegration is possible, the narrator continues to seek a newly defined community of selves who can be united into a single but multidimensional subject.[8] Wolf's closing page is characteristically multivalent. She does, finally, succeed in using the first person in her text, but it is a first person who must admit uncertainty. To the ultimate question of the closure of her tale, "And the past, which can still split the first person into the second and the third—has its hegemony been broken? Will the voices be still?" the narrator must answer for the first time *in the first person*, "Ich weiß es nicht" (I don't know). *(A Model Childhood* 406).[9] But even the admission of ambivalence from a reintegrated community of selves may signal a redefinition of the concept of the female subject and the way in which she defines herself. This construction of a community of selves carries over to Wolf's *Kassandra (Cassandra)*[10] where Cassandra seeks, and finally finds, a "we" in her search for self, and to the process of reestablishing the many selves of Christa T. The notion of a communal self gives contemporary women writers an option to the singular, isolated, (male) consciousness celebrated for so long in the western tradition. But community in this feminist sense is not mere group conformity; it must protect and sustain difference rather than absorbing or eradicating it.

By taking such a relentlessly honest look at her past and at World War II as her formative years in *Patterns of Childhood*, Wolf points up the fact that even normally positive values such as the desire for community can be used negatively. Nelly's strong desire to belong to her community allows her to invest so much energy and emotion in a fascist state. We cannot unthinkingly adopt a politically defined community without running the risk of ending up with a Nazi state. Wolf doesn't simply seek the warm feeling of belonging in her works. She realizes that Nelly's desire for belonging and love helps to trap her. Nelly realizes that being loved and obeying are one and the same;[11] and obedience leads her to deny the "other." Wolf strongly suggests that we must be able to recognize the "other" as different but equally valuable to have a positive community. In her childhood Nelly intuitively empathizes with Jews or with playmates who are different, but she is taught by society not to recognize the other as equal to oneself. The narrator does not want this lesson passed on to her own daughter who seems much more open and receptive to difference than Nelly was at her age and who serves to some extent as a foil for the narrator.[12] Wolf wants a newly constituted community of responsible individuals who see themselves as the subjects of history and not as its objects. Such a personal and communal reassessment of our role as active subjects calls into question the function of each member of society in creating what we think of as history. Demanding such a reassessment not just for post-war Germany but for all of us in the nuclear age is an important cultural critique.

While Wolf is obviously not identical to her narrator in *Patterns of Childhood*, they share enough details of experience to label the text an autobiographical fiction.[13] Both Wolf and her narrator come from L. (Landsberg an der Warthe) and return to the town long after the war when it has become the Polish city of G. (Gorzów Wielkopolski).[14] This return visit in 1971 triggers the painful process of coming to grips with the past ("Vergangenheitsbewältigung") that the writing of the text *Patterns of Childhood* records. Both Wolf and Nelly Jordan flee the approaching Russian troops in 1945; both serve as secretary to the mayor in the local principality. Both Wolf and Nelly Jordan recover from a mild case of lung disease in a sanatorium. Both Wolf and her narrator have a daughter to whom they must try to explain their involvement during the Nazi era, and both have husbands whose advice they value.

The fact that Wolf's husband is the scholar, writer Gerhard Wolf while the narrator's is abbreviated as H., and that Wolf's daughters are named Annette and Katrin (*Patterns of Childhood* is dedicated to them) while the narrator's is named Lenka, on the other hand, help to substantiate Wolf's ingenuous disclaimer that precedes the text:

> All characters in this book are the invention of the narrator. None is identical with any person living or dead. Neither do any of the described episodes coincide with actual events.
>
> Anyone believing that he detects a similarity between a character in the narrative and either himself or anyone else should consider the strange lack of individuality in the

behavior of many contemporaries. Generally recognizable behavior patterns should be blamed on circumstances. C.W.[15]

Wolf thus carefully and ironically complicates our reading of the text and our ability to disentangle reality and "fiction," autobiography and novel. She implies both that her text is a uniquely devised fiction and that it is exemplary of her generation and unavoidably "real." But even more curiously, Wolf claims that the characters are invented not by the author ("Verfasserin") as we would expect in such a disavowal, but by the narrator—who is herself a fictional character. If we read "Erzählerin" (narrator) as "she who narrates," it becomes even more impossible to disentangle the narrator and the author, the fictional teller and the "real" writer of the book.

Wolf used this same strategy of confusion in a discussion of her earlier novel *The Quest for Christa T.* In a 1968 essay entitled "Selbstinterview"[16] (Self-interview), Wolf indicates that she wrote Christa T. from a very subjective impulse, because someone very close to her died, and she could not accept the death. Writing about it was a means of protecting herself. Wolf claims to delve into the early life of this friend and to use documentary material such as diaries, letters, sketches of Christa T. which were made available to her. But to the question of whether she was writing a posthumous biography, she answers:

> That's what I thought at first. Later I noticed that the object of my story was not or did not remain so specifically her, Christa T. Suddenly I stood facing myself, I hadn't anticipated that. The relationship between "us"—Christa T. and the I-narrator—forced itself into the center: the difference of character and their points of contiguity, the tensions between "us" and their dissolution, or the lack of dissolution. ("Selbstinterview" 51-52)

The comment indicates the closeness of Wolf herself to both her character and her narrator in *Christa T.*; this novel could be read as a chronological sequel (although it is published earlier) to the fictional autobiography *Patterns of Childhood* since it covers the postwar years up to the 1960s. (In fact, Christa T. even appears briefly in the later novel.[17]) Wolf makes it difficult to disentangle the lives of her character, her narrator and herself. And yet she does not concede their identity either. She continues in the same essay:

> Question: At any rate you admit that two authentic characters emerge: Christa T. and an "I."
> Answer: Have I admitted that? You would be right if in the end both characters were not invented.... ("Selbstinterview" 52)

The constant interplay between reality and fiction, self and narrator breaks down the boundaries between the two and puts them on an equal footing. Just as the narrator of *Christa T.* is forced to invent certain scenes in order to produce a "true" and verisimilar text, Wolf mixes fiction and reality in order to produce a realism of "subjective authenticity." By "subjective authenticity" Wolf suggests a kind of writing in which the author is intimately involved with her material rather than maintaining an ironic distance from it, a mode of composition in which an author comes to terms with the reality around her and which reflects that very process, a method of writing that respects no traditional literary boundaries and that cannot keep reality and fiction artificially separated.[18]

Much is at stake in this conscious confusion of fiction and reality. By conflating the experiences of author and narrator without allowing them to be identified as the same, Wolf calls into question the whole separation of fiction and reality (a challenging of the boundaries between different kinds of knowledge that the Romantics were fond of in their day, and feminists in ours). The narrated life, whether fictitious or "real" must be emplotted in order to be conveyed. The act of emplotment itself forms a major focus of the narration.

The difficulty of coming to tell a life, the difficulty of saying "I" (as Wolf herself puts it in *Christa T.*), looms large in Wolf's *Patterns of Childhood* as well as *Christa T.* The narrator's first memory of Nelly in *Patterns of Childhood*, for example, is the three-year-old child who experiences the surprise of separateness in her first consciousness of "Ich" (I) as distinct from others—and particularly as distinct from mother to whom she will never again be able to tell "everything."[19] Christa T.'s difficulty in saying "I" recurs[20] as she finds it hard to locate a specific self-definition that will include all the various selves that she in fact is. Christa T.'s preference for the third person in her own writing seems an attractive option to the narrator who comments, "I understand the secret of the third person, who is there without being tangible and who, when circumstances favor her, can bring down more reality upon herself than the first person: The difficulty of saying 'I'" (*The Quest for Christa T.* 170).[21] But the third person seems a questionable solution[22] as it merely allows one part of the self to turn another part into an object. This produces the same uncanny result that the narrator of *Patterns of Childhood* experiences. The solution, perhaps, to the isolated self is the obvious yet complex notion of community. The difficulty of saying "I" could be countered not by saying "she," but "we."

For Wolf's three-year-old Nelly, saying "I" represents a separation of self from environment. Wolf implies that the privileged state of unity usually ascribed to childhood in literature is lost very early. Nelly's saying "I" is a fragmentation rather than a unification, a disjoining that must be mended by reestablishment of the self within a legitimate community. The difficulty of saying "I" for Wolf thus seems twofold. First, one must find the discrete self that is so often lost to categories and labels. Second, however, one must give this unencumbered, individual self that has escaped externally imposed role definitions a new potential for development by reintegration into a meaningful community.

The act of remembering helps to create this new community.[23] Remembering in *Patterns of Childhood* is an act of uniting with another—in this case with another self, the young child being molded by her environment who is then reevaluated and literally re-membered, reassembled by the older and more experienced narrator some twenty-seven years later. What begins as thought within an isolated individual self thus rapidly becomes an activity of a community of selves which are being reassembled in the act of recording the memories. In *Christa T.* too, the act of remembering is a communal activity that involves many minds recalling Christa's past and reassembling her being.

Christa T. realizes the significance of community as she endlessly searches for meaningful integration into her society. The cautious reemergence of the "I" of the narrator in the last page of *Patterns of Childhood* reflects the same movement to create a "subject" based on experience of community. Wolf recognizes the need to generalize and universalize personal experience before a "self" can be established. Only after her process of re-membering, literally reassembling her self, can her narrator in *Patterns of Childhood* struggle to achieve a first-person voice as the text closes.

In Wolf's 1987 text *Accident: A Day's News*, her narrator possesses a stronger and more independent first-person voice. Clearly the same voice that narrated *Patterns of Childhood* (the same recounting of dislocating her brother's arm, for example, and the guilt it entailed as well as their both suffering typhus), the narrator now emerges less guardedly, less distanced from self and from reader.

Although *Accident*, like *Christa T.* and *Patterns of Childhood*, is prefaced with the assertion that all its characters are inventions of Christa Wolf, the voice of the narrative more clearly rings with Wolf's own essayistic tones than any of her earlier texts. In fact, as Anna Kuhn suggests (212), the book might as easily be considered an essay as a fictional narrative. No longer objectified or hidden behind a pseudonym, the narrator of *Accident* is clearly the thinking and autonomous subject of her tale.

The precarious convergence of third and second person only fleetingly attained at the end of *Patterns of Childhood* stabilizes into a consistent first-person narration. Second person is reserved primarily for discussions with absent loves—the narrator's brother and husband. The first-person narrator of *Accident* is even willing to reveal her own short-comings and human foibles. Having just recalled her own close relationship to her brother and their shared childhood fairy tales, for example, the narrator nonetheless resents having other sibling loves called to her attention. The young man who comes to the narrator's farm seeking his infant sister's grave from World War II angers the narrator because he impinges upon her idyllic retreat. Having come to grips with her own past in *Patterns of Childhood*, the narrator now seeks sanctuary from the burden of other people's memories—perhaps because the present itself has become such a burden. This is a more personally candid voice than Wolf reveals in her earlier texts.

Accident examines the repercussions of the Chernobyl disaster; for instance, the first-person narrator realizes that everyday words like "cloud" take on an unavoidable new meaning after the nuclear accident. Even poetic formulations such as "Oh sky, radiant azure" (O Himmel, strahlender Azur) become as contaminated as the ground of northern and eastern Europe. Many of the social and political problems that are implied in *Patterns of Childhood* are stated outright in *Accident*. The reasons for saying too little too late, for suppressing protest are painfully familiar—fear, uncertainty, lack of hope or deceptive hopes. The narrator of *Accident* examines why we so tacitly allow the technological progress that threatens to destroy us just as the reader cannot help wondering at the same time why so many tacitly allowed the technology and destruction of the war. The relationship between killing and inventing seems unbreakable in either war or peace time. The narrator envisions scientists as their own laboratory rats, driven to push the button of technological progress endlessly, regardless of the consequences.

The narrator moves constantly between the sober recognition of the deadly dangers modern technology has produced (the irony of nuclear destruction in peacetime) and the dampening needs of everyday life, to eat, to work, which induce us to deny or forget the nuclear dangers we have unleashed. Wolf's 1983 narrative *Cassandra* opposes war and its dehumanization; *Accident* opposes modern peacetime technology gone awry like the cancer cells that threaten the life of the narrator's brother. The utopian impulse to produce boundless, inexhaustible energy for all has led rather to nuclear contamination for all. Not the bomb but the local power plant emerges as a deadly threat that renders so much in life meaningless. The narrator attends to quotidian chores—gardening, grocery shopping, collecting the mail, listening to radio and television, reading[24]—as she reflects on the new sense of imminent mortality that Chernobyl produces. Obedience, even to one's own self-imposed duties, becomes absurd. Goals, she realizes, are suddenly all deprived of their sense. And what is left to define the self when all goals are removed?

This extended monologue becomes a dialogue, however, as the narrator communicates telepathically with her brother (who accompanied her on her return to the hometown in *Patterns of Childhood*) who is undergoing a brain operation. The narrator's responses to her brother's imagined or remembered comments makes the text dialogic as does the chorus of voices from the past (grandfather, grandmother and her admonitions not to waste food) and the present (the narrator's two daughters as well as various neighbors and an elderly Jewish psychologist). The narrator even speaks to various plants in her garden as nature itself joins in the dialogue. What we would expect to remain a monologic text, a single self ruminating, thus becomes dialogic and communal. Even the attempt to shut out other people's memories and pains becomes a record of inescapable community when it is preserved in the narrative. The boundaries of the individual self and consciousness are extended into a community of selves all of whom are part of the narrating "I."

The narrating "I" itself becomes more closely than ever connected with the author. Very much in Wolf's own voice, Wolf's narrator realizes that the writing self, the author, must struggle to shine through the unavoidable socially encoded lines of the text in order to escape being trapped in a language already encoded by patriarchy and technology. She must be personally present in her narrative in order to be a voice of protest. Quoting from an English text by the emigré Jewish psychologist Charlotte Wolff, the narrator then reflects on her own authentic self:

> [in English in the text] "We are forced to use our multiple personalities like players acting different plays. We have to hide our authentic Self under a mask, and act a part in order to come to terms with a stereotyped social code." [end English] Is it so? It is so. While writing, brother—because you asked—, we have more and more to play the role of the writing person and ourselves at the same time, in that we fall out of the role, rip off the masks, let our authentic self shine through—behind lines which, whether we want it that way or not, follow the social code. We are mostly blind in the face of this process. A day such as this, paradoxical in its repercussions, forces us, forces me, to turn the personal outward, to overcome the resistance.[25]

The global danger and imminence of mortality produced by Chernobyl makes the melding of the writing self, the narrating self and the narrated self even more crucial. Wolf's concept of "subjective Authenticity" becomes a moral imperative to reveal the authorial self in the text, to reject the arbitrary literary historical demand that fiction and non-fiction, novel and autobiography, be carefully segregated in a naive opposition of imagination and fact. In a world threatened with "peaceful" nuclear destruction, all forms of comprehension are indispensable; Wolf's narratives make us realize that the relationship between fact and fiction is more complex—and more complicit—than we had previously imagined. Under the pressure of that realization, Christa Wolf assembles the most coherent and multivalent self of her writing career. Whether *Accident* is autobiography, essay or novel, it presents a self who has indeed turned the personal outward while she has absorbed the external—the events and people of her world—into an expanded "I" which is a communal as well as personal voice.

NOTES

1. Christa Wolf's *Kindheitsmuster* was originally translated as *A Model Childhood*. When the book was issued as a paperback in

1984, the title was revised (wisely, I think) to *Patterns of Childhood*. The German implies both translations, but the "Model Childhood" must be read somewhat ironically. I will refer to the English translation as *Patterns of Childhood* since I believe it to be a much better title. I will be quoting, however, from the original hard-back edition which is titled *A Model Childhood*.
2. The English title unfortunately loses the sense of thinking back over the character; instead, it implies a more future oriented process.
3. Since the page limitations of this book do not allow me to quote the passages in German in their entirety, I will provide the page references to the German editions for the reader's reference. For this quotation, see *Kindheitsmuster* 9.
4. *Kindheitsmuster* 215.
5. A number of other authors such as Hermann Kant, Franz Fühmann, Erich Loest and Heiner Müller also begin to write about their memories of the Nazi experience around the years that Wolf publishes *Patterns of Childhood*. For an extended discussion of the presentation of the Nazi period in the GDR, see Patricia Herminghouse, "Vergangenheit als Problem der Gegenwart: Zur Darstellung des Faschismus in der neueren DDR-Literatur," in *Literatur der DDR in den 70er Jahren*.
6. Some GDR critics, such as Annemarie Auer in "Gegenerinnerung," *Sinn und Form* 29 (1977), 847-78, fault Wolf's book for not acknowledging those who worked for the defeat of the Nazis and helped to create a social revolution in East Germany.
7. The German seems even clearer on the issue of the merging of the second and third person. Wolf writes: "Der Endpunkt wäre erreicht, wenn zweite und dritte Person wieder in der ersten zusammenträfen, mehr noch: zusammenfielen. Wo nicht mehr 'du' und 'sie'—wo unverhohlen 'ich' gesagt werden müßte. Es kam dir sehr fraglich vor, ob du diesen Punkt erreichen könntest, ob der Weg, den du eingeschlagen hast, überhaupt dorthin führt. *Kindheitsmuster* 322.
8. Julia Kristeva shares Wolf's attraction to the notion of a communal self. When asked to write an autobiographical sketch for *The Female Autograph*, Kristeva responded by writing in first person plural. She explains:

> What follows, then, will be an autobiography in the first person plural, a "we" of complicity, friendship, love. . . . What the "I" loses in delegating itself to the group is

partially regained in the metamorphoses of the "we." It is by transforming itself, by changing itself totally that the collective image, the group portrait, proves it is a momentarily fixed passion. To speak of "us" is not an analysis, it is a history that analyzes itself. But isn't any autobiography, even if it doesn't involve "us," a desire to make a collective public image exist, for "you," for "us"? (219-220)

Christa Wolf, I think, would certainly answer "yes." She would also agree with the transformative power—both psychological and political—of writing the communal self.
9. *Kindheitsmuster* 377-78.
10. The "Frankfurter Poetik-Vorlesungen" which precede the narrative of *Kassandra* in its original form were published as a separate volume, *Voraussetzungen einer Erzählung: Kassandra*, by Luchterhand also in 1983. The English translation rejoins the narrative to the essays but puts the narrative first rather than having it follow the essays as it originally did.
11. "Gehorchen und Geliebtwerden ein und dasselbe ist." *Kindheitsmuster* 20; *A Model Childhood* 14-15.
12. A number of critics comment on the narrator's daughter Lenka as a foil to the narrator. See Annemarie Auer, "Gegenerinnerung" 869-70; Sigrid Bock, "Christa Wolf: *Kindheitsmuster*" 127; Judith Ryan, *The Uncompleted Past: Postwar German Novels and the Third Reich* (Detroit: Wayne State UP, 1983) 152-53; Marie-Luise Linn, "Doppelte Kindheit—Zur Interpretation von Christa Wolfs *Kindheitsmuster*" 52-66; and David Dollenmayer, "Generational Patterns in Christa Wolf's *Kindheitsmuster*" 229-34.
13. Anna Kuhn suggests in her introduction to *Christa Wolf's Utopian Vision: from Marxism to Feminism* (18) that "all of Christa Wolf's writing is ultimately autobiographical." While I think this assertion might be a bit sweeping or that perhaps it could be said of all engaged authors, I do agree with Kuhn that Wolf constantly attempts to erode the distinctions between reality and fiction.
14. A number of sources could be consulted for the biographical details on Wolf's life. Alexander Stephan's *Christa Wolf* provides an extremely helpful table of dates of important events in Wolf's life. And, very recently, Therese Hörnigk's *Christa Wolf* offers the most detailed account to date of Wolf's biography.
15. *Kindheitsmuster*, unnumbered prefacing page.

16. All translations from this essay are my own.
17. I am not entirely convinced that one should simply declare the narrators of *Christa T.* and *Patterns of Childhood* to be the same person as Anna Kuhn does in her excellent study *Christa Wolf's Utopian Vision* or as Robert K. Shirer does in his *Difficulties of Saying "I": The Narrator as Protagonist in Christa Wolf's "Kindheitsmuster" and Uwe Johnson's "Jahrestage"* (69). I believe that the narratives are indeed continuations of the same story and that the same narrative consciousness permeates them (as it does *Accident*), but the story is of an entire generation. If Nelly Jordan were the specific narrator of *Christa T.*, it would seem to me that Christa T. would figure more prominently in Nelly's childhood than the one-line mention she receives in *Patterns of Childhood*. The two novels do, however, function similarly to much of Faulkner's work in which the same central narrative and problems recur through different emplotments.
18. For an extended discussion of Wolf's term "subjektive Authentizität," see her "Subjektive Authentizität: Gespräch mit Hans Kaufmann," particularly 322-25.
19. "Yes: to be rid of your own soul, to be able to look your mother in the eye as she sits on the edge of your bed in the evening, wanting to know if you have told her everything: But you must tell me everything. To lie brazenly: Everything, yes! When you know deep down: not everything, not ever again. Because that's impossible" (*A Model Childhood* 14). For the German, see *Kindheitsmuster* 19.
20. See, for example, *Nachdenken über Christa T.* 173 or *The Quest for Christa T.* 174.
21. *Nachdenken über Christa T.* 168.
22. Jeanette Clausen in her essay,"The Difficulty of Saying 'I' as Theme and Narrative Technique in the works of Christa Wolf," argues that the use of "she" rather than "I" is a clearer indication of the gender of the person being identified and therefore functions as a resistance to being drowned in a general first-person designation that is in reality defined by the patriarchy. Katherina von Hammerstein in her perceptive article, "Warum nicht Christian T.? Christa Wolf zur Frauenfrage, Untersuchung an einem frühen Beispiel: *Nachdenken über Christa T.*," pursues Clausen's assertion with a particular regard for Wolf's feminist versus gender-inclusively humanitarian concerns. I would maintain, however, that the use of third person in *Patterns of Childhood* belies this idea since Nelly (who is always spoken of

in third person) is clearly seen from a distance as a character now foreign to the narrator as Wolf's own comments suggest. The narrator of *Patterns of Childhood* sees the third person as a necessary evil that will allow her to speak at all about the traumatic experiences of World War II. Even in *Christa T.*, the narrator uses a familiar second-person form to address the now departed Christa as well as a first-person plural to indicate a bond with her. The narrator thus discovers that community and interpersonal contact may outweigh any supposed advantages to the third-person form.

23. For discussion of memory and its role in Wolf's works, see Kathleen L. Komar, "The Communal Self: Re-Membering Female Identity in the Works of Christa Wolf and Monique Wittig" forthcoming.
24. The narrator reads Joseph Conrad's *Heart of Darkness* and points out that the "cruising yawl" upon which Marlowe embarks on his remembrances is named "Nelly" *(Störfall* 116). One cannot help but think of Wolf's own Nelly Jordan and to remark that both Conrad's Nellie and Wolf's Nelly form the site upon which two very complex narratives of remembrance play themselves out. When Wolf mentions Conrad's *Heart of Darkness* in her 1987 text *Accident*, she claims to be reading it for the first time in 1986 (whereas *Patterns of Childhood* appeared in 1976), but the accidental discovery of Conrad's *Heart of Darkness* on the occasion of the Chernobyl incident seems too good to be true. In any case, one is led to speculate on the relationship between the two Nellies.
25. *Störfall* 92. The German is perhaps even clearer. It reads: "We are forced to use our multiple personalities like players acting different plays. We have to hide our authentic Self under a mask, and act a part in order to come to terms with a stereotyped social code." Ist es so? So ist es. Schreibend, Bruder—weil du gefragt hast—, haben wir mehr und mehr die Rolle des Schreibenden zu spielen und uns zugleich, indem wir aus der Rolle fallen, die Masken abzureißen, unser authentisches Selbst hervorschimmern zu lassen—hinter Zeilen, die, ob wir es wollen oder nicht, dem sozialen Code folgen. Diesem Vorgang gegenüber sind wir meistens blind. Ein Tag wie dieser, paradox in seinen Auswirkungen, zwingt uns, zwingt mich, Persönliches nach außen zu kehren, das Widerstreben zu überwinden."

WORKS CITED

Auer, Annemarie. "Gegenerinnerung." *Sinn und Form* 29 (1977): 847-78.

Bock, Sigrid. "Christa Wolf: *Kindheitsmuster*." *Weimarer Beiträge* 23 (1977): 102-30.

Clausen, Jeanette. "The Difficulty of Saying 'I' as Theme and Narrative Technique in the works of Christa Wolf." *Amsterdamer Beiträge zur neueren Germanistik* 10 (1980): 319-33.

Dollenmayer, David. "Generational Patterns in Christa Wolf's *Kindheitsmuster*." *German Life and Letters*. 33 (1986): 229-34.

Hammerstein, Katherina von. "Warum nicht Christian T.? Christa Wolf zur Frauenfrage, Untersuchung an einem frühen Beispiel: *Nachdenken über Christa T.*" *New German Review* 3 (1987): 17-29.

Herminghouse, Patricia. "Vergangenheit als Problem der Gegenwart: Zur Darstellung des Faschismus in der neueren DDR-Literatur." *Literatur der DDR in den 70er Jahren*. Eds. Peter Uwe Hohendahl and Patricia Herminghouse. Frankfurt am Main: Suhrkamp, 1983. 259-94.

Hörnigk, Therese. *Christa Wolf*. Göttingen: Steidl Verlag, 1989.

Komar, Kathleen L. "The Communal Self: Re-Membering Female Identity in the Works of Christa Wolf and Monique Wittig" forthcoming in *Comparative Literature*.

Kristeva, Julia. "My Memory's Hyperbole." Trans. Athena Viscusi. *The Female Autograph*. Ed. Domna C. Stanton. Chicago: The U of Chicago P, 1984. 219-35.

Kuhn, Anna. *Christa Wolf's Utopian Vision: from Marxism to Feminism*. Cambridge: Cambridge UP, 1988.

Linn, Marie-Luise. "Doppelte Kindheit—Zur Interpretation von Christa Wolfs *Kindheitsmuster*." *Der Deutschunterricht* 30 (1978): 52-66.

Ryan, Judith. *The Uncompleted Past: Postwar German Novels and the Third Reich*. Detroit: Wayne State UP, 1983.

Shirer, Robert K. Difficulties of Saying "I": The Narrator as Protagonist in Christa Wolf's "Kindheitsmuster" and Uwe Johnson's "Jahrestage." New York: Lang, 1988.

Stephan, Alexander. *Christa Wolf*. München: Beck, 1987 (revised and extended edition).

Wolf, Christa. *Accident: A Day's News*. Trans. Heike Schwarzbauer and Rick Takvorian. New York: Farrar, Straus & Giroux, 1989.

———. *Cassandra: A Novel and Four Essays*. Trans. Jan Van Heurck. New York: Farrar, Straus & Giroux, 1984.

———. "Diskussion mit Christa Wolf." *Sinn und Form* 28 (1976): 861-88.

———. "Documentation: Christa Wolf." *The German Quarterly* 57.1 (1984): 91-115.

———. *Kassandra*. Darmstadt und Neuwied: Hermann Luchterhand Verlag, 1983.

———. *Kindheitsmuster*. Darmstadt und Neuwied: Hermann Luchterhand Verlag, 1979. Originally published by Aufbau-Verlag, Berlin und Weimar, 1976.

———. *A Model Childhood*. Trans. Ursula Molinaro and Hedwig Rappolt. New York: Farrar, Straus & Giroux, 1980. Title revised to *Patterns of Childhood* in 1984.

———. *Nachdenken über Christa T.* Darmstadt und Neuwied: Hermann Luchterhand Verlag, 1969. Originally published by Mitteldeutscher Verlag, Halle, 1968.

———. *The Quest for Christa T.* Trans. Christopher Middleton. New York: Farrar, Straus and Giroux, 1970.

———. "Selbstinterview." *Lesen und Schreiben. Neue Sammlung*. Darmstadt und Neuwied: Luchterhand, 1980: 51-55.

———. *Störfall: Nachrichten eines Tages*. Darmstadt und Neuwied: Luchterhand, 1987.

———. "Subjektive Authentizität: Gespräch mit Hans Kaufmann." *Die Dimension des Autors: Essays und Aufsätze, Reden und Gespräche*. Band II. Berlin und Weimar: Aufbau-Verlag, 1986:317-49.

———. *Voraussetzungen einer Erzählung: Kassandra*. Darmstadt und Neuwied: Hermann Luchterhand Verlag, 1983.

Ideology and Self-Representation: The Case of Israeli Women Writers

Yael S. Feldman

Before Shulamit Lapid's novel (discussed in this collection) was published, she was, at the age of forty-seven, a rather obscure author of several collections of short stories (1969, 1974, 1979) and one book for children (1971). Only one of her earliest stories, "The Order of the Garter" (1969), harbored an unmistakably feminist protest, contemporary in its setting. With her first novel, Gei Oni *(1982) this protest was displaced to the 1880s, illustrating the typical Israeli ambivalence about feminism. By her own admission, Lapid does not consider herself a feminist, but she has been limiting herself to "women's subjects." Except for one novel (1984) all her subsequent work features female protagonists. While her first play, "Abandoned Property" (1987), explored the psychological dynamics between mother and daughters in a broken family on the margins of the social system (and her second play is entitled "Surrogate Mother," 1990), her recent novel,* Local Paper *(1989), features a lower middle-class woman journalist in a contemporary provincial town. Thirty years old and single, Lisa is a throwback to the turn-of-the-century detective spinster of English literature. In this popular quasi detective story Lapid does what she has not dared to do in* Gei Oni; *she imagines a female character more common in contemporary America than in Israel: an unmarried woman who is proud of her work ethic, of her "professionalism," and whose priorities are "working" and "being in love."*
Lapid herself, a former chair of the Israeli Writers' Association, is a happily married mother, who has described herself in a recent interview as "small, delicate, and becoming more and more aggressive" at her "ripe fifty-four" . . . (See the Summer 1989 issue of Lilith, *where a translation of her story "The Bed" is also published 19-22).*

"All the men will be coming from wars now," said Professor Barzel. "They'll all have learned to fight. The country will change again. Everything will become more professional, the fighting too. The individual won't count any more, only the stupid plural. The plural is always stupid . . . "
"And what will be then, Elias?" asked Hulda worriedly.
"We will be then," said Elias, so quietly that they couldn't be sure they had heard right. "For better or worse, we will be."
A City of Many Days
Shulamith Hareven, 1972

The binary opposition anxiously projected into the future in this dialogue is age-old and universal—the individual vs. the collective, or the personal vs. the social. Yet what gives this almost stock opposition a particular twist is its clearly defined cultural and historical grounding—the experience of the protagonists of the Israeli novel *A City of Many Days* (1972), in which Shulamith Hareven reconstructs life in Jerusalem under the British mandate, before and during World War II. It is against the background of the polyphony of voices of that period that the author "worriedly" constructs the forthcoming replacement of the "first person singular" by the "first person plural," of the voice of the private self by that of the communal self. This is not an existential or otherwise symbolic construction. Rather, it is a fictional reconstruction of a very palpable, historically anchored reality—the notorious *WE* of the *Palmach*, the 1948 generation that spearheaded the struggle for Israeli independence ("we are everywhere the first/we, we, the Palmach . . . ," as their song proudly announced).

By having her characters both ascribe the creation of this group self to the circumstance of the historical moment (war and national strife) and grieve the loss of the voice of the individual, Hareven demonstrates some of the tensions underlying Israeli society from its very inception. Situated as it is a few pages before the end of the narrative (197-8), this dialogue functions as an interpreting sign, almost as a closure. It retrospectively highlights the cultural code underpinning this novel—the uneasy existence of the personal and the psychological within a society of collective persuasion.[1]

This inherent ambivalence is not unique to Hareven's narrative. Rather, it is characteristic of a whole range of contemporary Israeli novels that come very close to introspection and self-analysis, but exhibit ambivalence when approaching the "forbidden zone." This is particularly true of a group of fictional autobiographies that I have elsewhere suggested to treat as a *modality* rather than a genre, thereby cutting across issues of presentation (fictional vs. factual) or formal features (first vs. third person narration) (Feldman, "Gender In/Difference":193). As a rule, novels classified in this category are not the paradigmatic first book of a budding artist, nor are they the recollection in tranquility of old age. Rather, these are the products of writers in their mid-career who try to make sense of their life and art by constructing a real or fictive "self" whose life-story they tell in retrospect, as viewed from the vantage point of the present, of the narrating moment.[2]

If there is anything outstanding about these constructions, it is their by-and-large challenge of some basic tenets of "classical" (often nicknamed "metaphysical") theory of autobiography. Not that these fictional autobiographies are highly post-modernist: Generally, their "subjects" are not threatened by Lacan's "alienation through language," nor by Derrida's "decentering" (see Mehlman, Sturrock, summarized in Feldman, "New Psychoanalytic Models"). Rather, what impinges on these personal narratives is the pressure of socio-political realities, condensed into particular historical moments. While this pressure, often in the shape of an ideological crisis, is the moving force behind the need to construct a self and fix it in language, it is also what undermines any attempt to live up to the ideals of western autobiography—autonomy, privacy and individualism.

To the extent that these life-stories collapse the conventional opposition between the individual and the communal, the private and the public, they exhibit a certain "pull towards ideology," an impulse that Janet Gunn sees as a "threat" to experiential autobiography:

> The pull towards ideology is all the more difficult for autobiography to resist because the ideological impulse has so much in common with the autobiographical impulse. Both arise from . . . a need for acknowledging a meaningful orientation in a world; . . . and both represent an effort to take hold of something in the process of vanishing or disintegrating. (1982:119-120)

Whether or not this pull towards ideology is conceived as a threat or a blessing is, of course, a matter of one's politico-cultural conviction. The interesting question, however, is precisely under what conditions the ideological impulse does compete with or take over the psychologically oriented autobiography. Gunn does not ask this question, possibly because she treats exclusively the tradition of Western autobiography. For it is in recent theories of female (and non-Western) autobiography that a redefinition of the genre has been tacitly taking shape.

Corroborating the claims of certain strands in gender psychology (Rowbotham, Chodorow, Gilligan), these theorists see the female subject as relational rather than autonomous. They claim that woman's identity—in life and on paper—is mediated through "others," that her "self" is communal and collective rather than purely individual (see Blackburn, Mason, Friedman, Watson and part II of Brodzki and Schenck [Colonized Subjects]). If this observation is correct it opens up a two-fold hornet's nest: 1. Is the gender difference we observe "essentialist" or "culturalist," constitutional or acquired? and 2. What is the effect of this difference on the presuppositions of "classical" Western autobiography (as defined, say, by Gusdorf, Olney, Lejeune, Spengemann, Jay, Eakin et al.)?

That these questions are directly related to the post-structuralist debate over the "subject" is no doubt clear. If gender difference can be shown to be culturally/historically/ideologically determined, then the historicity of the subject in general should be similarly understood. And if features of the "female subject" can be found in male autobiographies (as Germaine Brée has recently claimed for Leiris and Barthes), and vice versa, then perhaps some of our most cherished concepts should be reconsidered.

To this theoretical debate Israeli autobiographies may add a new dimension, for they problematize not only conventional oppositions deemed inherent to the genre, but also some popularly accepted gender distinctions. Surprisingly, there is a clear correspondence between certain aspects of the so-called typical female autobiography and contemporary Israeli fictional autobiographies; and unless all Israeli autobiographers are women, this fact alone should cast grave doubts on essentialist definitions of gender, both within and without the genre. On the other hand, the same fact should encourage culturalist approaches to gender, as it demonstrates how gender boundaries may be crossed given the pressure of similar sociocultural conditions (see Cohen, Seidenberg).

And this is not the whole picture. Paradoxically, there is hardly a woman among the Israeli (fictional) autobiographers I have in mind. This absence is doubly surprising in view of the intimately autobiographical Hebrew prose written by women at the beginning of the century (see Berlowitz). In this they did not differ, of course, from their sister autobiographers in English, and perhaps the world over (see Jelinek, Smith, Benstock). But this resemblance is only superficial, pertaining to non-canonic texts. For unlike the English tradition, the Hebrew canon has featured a long list of women-poets but no women-novelists. Until the last decade Hebrew prose was mostly the domain of male writers. The few women who excelled in fiction mostly wrote short stories and novellas, mainly in the lyrical-impressionistic mode (e.g. Devorah Baron, 1887-1956).

Does this mean that we have come full circle to bedrock gender differences? I suspect not. Rather, as early as the turn of the century women were cast in a well-defined role by the arbiters of the renaissance of Hebrew:

> Only women are capable of reviving Hebrew—this old, forgotten, dry and hard language—by permeating it with emotion, tenderness, suppleness and subtlety. . . .

This generous—as well as limiting—evaluation was offered in 1897 by Eliezer Ben-Yehuda, the first propagator of spoken Hebrew; and it is not easy to determine today which was more effective—the encouragement or the limitation. For although a number of women graced Ben-Yehuda's journals (including his wife, whose real field was chemistry!), not one of them left her mark on the canon of Hebrew literature. Predictably, the breakthrough of women into the canon took place—two decades later—in poetry, where it was easier to accommodate the stereotypic ideal cut out for them by their male patrons (cf. Miron 1989).[3]

It took more than half a century for the old barriers to begin crumbling. And it was only in the last two decades that a number of women made the shift from short stories to novels, some of which are of almost epic proportions. Until very recently, however, none of these narratives came close to the fictional autobiography, even in its "arrested" form, as found among Israeli male writers.[4] I would nevertheless argue that at least some of these novels are nothing less than "masked autobiographies," reflecting—in different degrees of displacement—their authors' struggles with the question of the female subject.

I first suspected that this was the case when I saw the term "feminist" on the jacket of *Gei Oni*, a "historical" novel published in 1982, whose narrated time is the early 1880s. The transparent anachronism of the usage set me on the detective trail.[5] I soon discovered a pattern: In several recent novels by Israeli women, contemporary concerns are projected onto "liberated" heroines of another time or another place. In fact, one can point to a process of regression in the choice of historical settings, from Jerusalem of the 1920s and 30s in *A City of Many Days* (1972, quoted in our epigraph)—a period the author, Shulamith Hareven, could not have experienced directly, since she arrived in Palestine as a child only in 1940)—through Palestine of 1882 in Shulamit Lapid's *Gei Oni* (1982), to the vaguely and poetically defined European past (seventeenth century) in Amalia Kahana-Carmon's novella "The Bridge of the Green Duck" (in *Up in Montifer*, 1984). However, this regression is counterbalanced by a diametrically opposite *progression* in the "feminist" consciousness of the protagonists of these novels. As a group, they move from traditional gender roles in a patriarchal society to a utopian new womanhood, paradoxically projected back into the historico-mythical past.

If this analysis is correct, then Hebrew literature is still at the stage that Carolyn Heilbrun charted out about a decade ago in *Reinventing Womanhood*:

> Women are only recently taking up autobiography in the attempt to show themselves . . . (though the autobiographies are often in the form of novels). (1979:134)

But why should this be so? Why should contemporary Israeli women be incapable of facing their personal selves directly? Moreover, why can't they, to quote Heilbrun again, "imagine women characters with even the autonomy they themselves have achieved" (1979:71)? Why isn't one of these *Bildungsromane* cast in the mold of the *Künstlerroman*? And why isn't there even one "portrait of an artist" among these novels of development? Is it because of the precariousness of their writers' self-image as "artists"? Or is it because this aspect of their recently gained autonomy is subsumed by more communal—and perhaps more basic—concerns and achievements?

The answer is "yes," I am afraid, to both questions. The first will take us back to woman's problematic place in the Jewish tradition, which by and large excludes her from participating in man's public roles (see Heschel et al.). The second "yes," on the other hand, will highlight the *cross-gender* correspondence apparent in the Israeli corpus; for just like their male counterparts, the three novels of development mentioned above are motivated by socio-political pressures and are organized around major historical events. The latter function as the pivotal moments in the heroines' "voyages in" (cf. Abel et al.) thereby embedding their subjective experience within a larger, collective order.

By way of demonstrating my claim, I offer an analysis of the second of these books, the highly popular historical novel, *Gei Oni* (1982). The fascination of this novel partially stems from the unprecedented manner in which it engages issues of gender and ideology. One must add, however, that this is done by a displacement to the nineteenth century, to the beginning of the Zionist movement and the modern-time resettlement of the Land of Israel.

Stylistically, this is not a novel of great sophistication. Written in a rather coarse realistic style, it is crowded with dialogues and interior monologues that are barely distinguishable; the third-person narration weaves its way through a maze of "relationships" that could easily rival those of any Hollywood or TV romantic melodrama. Nothing is implied here, not even the characters' most intimate reflections. Thoughts, emotions, ideology and popular psychology, are all evenly spread out, lit by the strong flashlight of the authorial voice, as if illuminated by the bright Israeli sun.

Yet despite its limitations (and perhaps because of them—the book is often classified as a novel for young readers), *Gei Oni* caught the imagination of Israeli readership. In the first place, it played right into the wave of nostalgia that swept the country in the 80s, when the first centenary of the earliest Jewish *Aliya* (immigration) to Palestine was celebrated. Indeed, Shulamit Lapid—until then a rather obscure short story writer (1969, 1974, 1979), but since then a prolific novelist and dramatist—wrote her first novel *in anticipation* of 1982. In that year the Galilean settlement Rosh Pinah, whose earlier name had been Gei Oni, celebrated one hundred years of its existence. Judging by the reception the book enjoyed, the timing was right; readers exhibited great hunger for the richly documented panorama of that distant past, filtered as it was through a fictional prism.

This was not the only reason, however. Readers were no doubt responding to the novelty of being introduced to a "serious" historical reconstruction through the eyes and mind of Fanya—a young Russian immigrant who joins Gei Oni in the opening scene, and remains the central consciousness through which the narrative is focalized to the end of the novel.

But why should this be considered such a novelty? Wasn't the pioneer movement, indeed, the Zionist ethos in general, supposed to have promoted the equality of women? In fact, wasn't "the woman question" one of the basic issues debated—and deemed solved—by the early communes and kibbutzim (see Margalit, 1971)? The answer is "yes," of course, to all of the above; but only as long as we remember to add the qualifier—"in theory." For what recent research has shown is that in practice, neither the early settlers nor the second wave of immigrants at the turn of the century had transcended the patriarchal norms of their home communities in Europe (see Izraeli, Bernstein and Hazelton). And as Shulamit Lapid herself has recounted (oral communication, 1984), she could find no historical model for her heroine in the archival records of Gei Oni, later named Rosh Pinah.[6]

As the jacket of the book states, the names of those "giant women" who were part and parcel of the early settlement wave "are absent from history books because the records of the saviors of the motherland list only men." Even among the figures of the second *aliya*, Lapid could make use only of one exceptional personality—Manya Shochat (1879-1959).[7] Fanya had to be invented, then: a woman who "did not know she was a feminist," but whom the contemporary reader recognizes as such, as the jacket of the book clearly attests.

We are in a better position now to appreciate the source of the great appeal that *Gei Oni* exerted on its readership. The book was a bold attempt to do justice to the founding mothers, to rectify by fiction the wrongs of (male-dominated) history. And it was no small challenge. For how does one create a narrative frame that would authentically preserve the patriarchal way of life of the 1880s, while at the same time would accommodate a fictive protagonist whose own norms would satisfy contemporary "feminist" expectations?

The solution came in the form of a collage, welding together two novelistic genres—the first-settlers epic and the romantic melodrama. On one level, *Gei Oni* is a typical settlement drama, almost a western ("The Wild East," as one of its reviewers labelled it; see Oryan; and cf. Har'el), realistically depicting the struggles against all odds of the small Galilean group in the early 1880s. The chief antagonist of this plot is nature itself, the mythical mother earth. In this story she is no welcoming bride; as we join the narrative she has been holding back her gifts for two consecutive years. Severe draught has chased away most of the pioneers, leaving behind just a few tenacious and idealistic families, including that of Yehi'el, the male protagonist of the novel.

On another level, this is a typically euphoric "heroine's text," as defined by Nancy Miller. It is a predictable love story whose models are not only the canonic texts adored by the protagonist (*Anna Karenina*, which had just "arrived" from Russia, and books by Jane Austen, Fanya's favorite; see 161), but also popular romances à la

Rudolf Valentino which Shulamit Lapid herself ridiculed in one of her journalistic forays (see Lapid 1975). Despite her ridicule, Lapid utilizes the popular genre with great dexterity: Fanya is the self-conscious budding young woman, who struggles to preserve her independent spirit while falling in love with her enigmatic "dark prince." The latter, for his part, is "handsome like the prince of Wales" (34, 69, 85), "wise like king Solomon" (117), and the envy of all women. Predictably, he is also proud, reticent and distant—the very qualities Lapid has enumerated in her brief article ("preferably, a widower/divorcé/bachelor, thirty years old, tanned, dark hair, a sneering look . . . ")—which means, of course, that although he falls in love with Fanya's looks the moment he sees her, he keeps the secret to himself. Since neither the reader nor Fanya gets to know the truth before half the story is over, a chain of romantic misunderstandings and jealousies constitute the better part of the plot. To add insult to injury, there are echoes of Daphne du Maurier's *Rebecca*: Fanya is "welcomed" to her "prince's" abode by the picture of his deceased wife, whose two sisters are conveniently present to evoke her beauty and otherworldly qualities whenever they can—all of which naturally makes the dénouement that much sweeter.

But before we get there, a question arises: Haven't we wandered too far afield from "founding mothers" and "inadvertent feminism," as I have elsewhere called it (1985)? Can the conventions of the romance, of the heroine's euphoric text, which Lapid herself declared "obsolete," indulge a fighting, independent spirit à la Manya Shochat? —Hardly, of course. Lapid could not have sustained her model *and* satisfy her feminist quest had she kept the model intact. Nor could she write a true historical novel (fully omniscient narration, authorial perspective into general historical processes) while staying as close to Fanya's consciousness as she did (more about this below). She resolved this problem, however, by splicing the two models together just at their respective points of cracking. In other words, the meeting ground between them is that of deviation, where their generic conventions are violated. As we shall soon see, it is from the intersection of two *frustrated* genres that a new model emerges, one that generously accommodates contemporary expectations.

To begin with, Fanya's romance deviates from its imputed model in one crucial detail—its dénouement does not coincide with the closure of the novel. Nor does it lead to a proposal or an engagement. For all this typical "heroine's text" takes place *within* the boundaries of a marriage. And our two protagonists are atypical as well: Fanya is not only an orphan, as suggested by Lapid in the above quoted piece ("an English orphan, preferably penniless"); she is a sixteen-year-old survivor of a Russian pogrom (the infamous Ukrainian pogroms of 1881-2 that are credited with inspiring the first wave of immigration to Palestine), who finds refuge in the Promised Land, accompanied by an old uncle, a deranged brother, and a baby—the initially unwanted fruit of her rape in that pogrom. Yehi'el, who happens to see her upon her arrival in Jaffa, is a twenty-six-year-old widower and a father of two, one of the few courageous souls still left in the nearly desolate Gei Oni.

As the narrative opens, we are privileged to Fanya's reflections after a hasty betrothal in Jaffa. While Yehi'el's motives are not disclosed, it soon becomes clear that for Fanya this is not just a marriage of convenience, but also a marriage of appearances. Upon arrival in Gei Oni she insists on separate sleeping arrangements—a rather unexpected turn within the conventions of the romance, but a perfectly plausible step for a psychologically conceived character, who is still smarting from her traumatic past. The attentive reader will notice, however, a structural and symbolic analogy in this otherwise realistically motivated action. It is not only the human bride who denies her husband her favors; with the draught continuing, the fertilization of mother earth is also prevented.

There is a perfect symmetry, then, between the two plots—the psychological and the mythic, the romantic and the historical. In both of them the male principle is initially defeated and no consummation is possible. This symmetry does not escape Yehi'el himself, who, unaware of Fanya's trauma, reacts to her refusal by saying: "When you change your mind, let me know. I ask for favors only from the land (=earth) (45)." To get the story rolling again both female protagonists must give in. It is against the background of the long-awaited rains (117, 121, 123)—a pioneers' version of the notorious Romantic storm?—that the passionate (and confessional) reunion between Fanya and Yehi'el finally takes place (119-128), and the euphoric plot seems to have reached its happy ending.

But not quite. For in the second part of the narrative, the settlement plot comes back with a vengeance, leaning down heavily on the delicate balance of the new romantic attachment. The Galilee, or mother earth (or perhaps the pioneering quest itself) "pressures" the human subjects of this story, limiting their freedom of choice and forcing them into its mold. But unlike her predecessors, Lapid is not willing to accept the verdict of the historical moment, of the Zionist "dream of redemption, burning like fire in the bones" (103-4, 144, 175). She does not have Fanya "skip over her own self," as did Sarah in *A City of Many Days* (cf. Feldman, "Feminism under Siege"), but rather lets her develop her female subjectivity despite and against the pressures of the collective vision, with all its tragic consequences. By so doing, Lapid has unwittingly blended her two models into a third one, a *Bildungsroman* which may be rather fanciful for the 1880s, but is totally satisfying to readers one hundred years later.

I have elsewhere suggested to name this new model after Erich Neumann's analysis of *Amor and Psyche*, namely, "The Psychic Development of the Feminine" (1952). The heuristic convenience of this choice stems from the story's origins, as Neumann brilliantly shows, in the myth of the "Great Mother," the archetypal mother earth. It is this archetype that has nourished all myths—old and young—of a return to the motherland, Zionism not excluded. And it is this nexus of images and metaphors that has been recently questioned, in the attempt to explain the problematic place of woman in the Zionist ethos.

Only a few years before the publication of *Gei Oni*, psychologist Lesley Hazelton deconstructed the familiar Zionist image of sons-lovers returning to motherland/earth "to build and be rebuilt in her" (notice the effect of Hebrew's genderized grammar: "land" as well as city, country, state, are all grammatically feminine in Hebrew!). She did this by a literal, almost *ad absurdum* analysis of the psychoanalytic ramifications of this language:

> But while Zion played Jocasta to the male pioneers' Oedipus, where was the Agamemnon to the women pioneers' Electra? What value could all this libidinous attraction have for them? What archetypal images could it arouse in a woman's mind? What role was there for women in this scenario of sons and fathers fertilizing the motherland? (1977:93)

As startling as this query is on first reading, it loses some of its persuasive power once we recognize one small oversight: Except in songs, has Zion ever played Jocasta to her returning sons? *Was* she a welcoming bride? Or has she been mostly an earlier Jungian archetype—"The Great Mother"?

The difference is crucial. In the primitive myth the female figure had not yet undergone what Neumann calls "the process of secondary personalization"; she had not yet functioned as a human representation, but as an "impersonal blind principle of fertility" (*The Origins*). In fact, this is the *negative* aspect of the "great mother," the scary

"Terrible Mother" that Neumann has unearthed in the ancient myths and fertility rituals. In these myths the male had more to lose than to gain, for the impregnation of the female principle was achieved only through the perennial death of her "consort," her son/lover/savior, later incarnated in the myths of Tamuz, Osiris and Dionysus.

We can now return to the plot of *Gei Oni* and discern that its scenario does not support Hazelton's feminist worries. Here it is not "Electra" who is excluded from the game, but rather "Oedipus." The deep structure of the historical plot is therefore not a Freudian triade, but an earlier, Neumannesque diade, that of the Terrible Mother and her doomed consort. In Yehi'el's failure to conquer mother-earth (he eventually dies of malaria), primitive fertility myths play themselves out once more. The essence of myth, we are reminded, is endless repetition. Standing alone, then, the settlement script would have come to an impasse, if not for its dynamic intersection with the second plot, the heroine's text.

In this text, Yehi'el is a "passive accomplice" in Fanya's long and often bewildered search for her own identity as a woman and an autonomous individuum. As in the myth of Amor and Psyche, the main psychological thrust of our story is the liberation of the female protagonist from the yoke of the social norms imposed on her by Aphrodite-like representatives of the community. "Psyche's act of rebellion," says Neumann in his interpretation of *Amor and Psyche* (the Hebrew translation of which appeared just in 1981!), "signals the end of the mythic era. From now on it is the era of human love, when the human soul knowingly undertakes all fateful decisions for its own life" (60).

It is interesting to note that Neumann speaks about the maturity of the human soul in general. That this process is symbolized for him precisely in the process of individuation of the feminine principle, should come as no surprise. After all, it is the latter that has to liberate itself from the blind collective principle of fertility and veer toward the "light"–the archetypal symbol of masculine consciousness in Neumann's (and others') conceptual system (68). Although this genderized reading has its problems (particularly for feminist critics; see Heilbrun, Edwards, Ferguson), it can readily accommodate the *Bildung* plot of our story. Fanya "develops" from a scathed teenager who acts under duress and runs away at her first experience of pain and frustration, to a mature woman who stays on, out of conscious choice, to realize the pioneering dream of her dead husband-lover.

Predictably, Fanya achieves her independence by a process of individuation in which she transcends the norms dictated to her by mother-figures who try to teach her "her natural place" (117, 144, 175, 234). Like Psyche, she reaches maturity after a series of tasks which she undertakes in order to save her husband and home from the devastation wrought by mother nature. We find her breaking into the male-dominated world of commerce, of political discussion, even of armed self-defence. At the same time, she does not deny her femininity (cf. Psyche's care to preserve her beauty), her *difference* from the male world surrounding her: the fun of light-hearted chat, of good romantic novels, of some child-like pranks (104, 144, 175). Her personal code is defined, then, as the freedom to choose the best of the two worlds, to move freely from one to the other (cf. Kamuf). This heroine fully embodies cross-gender equality as she shuttles between home and "world," Gei Oni and Jaffa, taking care of husband and children and trading, gypsy-like, on the road.

As for Yehi'el, he turns out to be just as exceptional. Although he does not fully approve of Fanya's "androgynous" tendencies, he does not stand in her way, which is more than can be said of any of his peers (109, 172-3, 188, 236). The result is a virtual reversal of conventional gender-roles (with Yehi'el staying close to home and Fanya going into the world), and more importantly—the transformation of Fanya from a child-bride into a mature wife-companion, fully aware of her choices, sexual as well as social.

It is only natural, then, that as the novel comes to a close and Yehi'el succumbs to exhaustion and malaria, the reader is ready to embrace Fanya's *Bildung* as a necessary training for her ultimate task—the perpetuation of the historico-mythical quest. But in an ironic twist of Hazelton's critique, Fanya, although ready to undertake the role, perceives it as something alien, not her own script:

> Shall she sell their home? Driving Yehi'el out of his dream? This home and this land were the purpose of his life. Once again fate has decreed that she realized others' dreams. Has she ever had her own dreams? But perhaps everyone is like this? Everyone realizes someone else's dream? (256)

Is this a "feminist" protest, lamenting the lot of women in general? Or is this a specific charge against the androcentric Zionist dream? And who is the "everyone" of the final questions: Women? All people?— The lines seem to blur here, leaving the reader with a sense of an unfocused grievance. For what is read throughout the novel as a critique of a male-engendered ideology ("Her father's dream of rebirth has turned into sacred insanity which now consumes her youthful years, her life" (102, and cf.142, 194, 202-3, 226), now takes on an existential turn, possibly hiding behind "the human condition."

We may be witnessing here an attempt (prevalent in women's life writing, as recently demonstrated by Heilbrun in *Writing A Woman's Life,*) to rationalize away the justified rage against a social system, that in the guise of a new ideology has reinscribed traditional double standards toward women. More often than not, Fanya's feelings remain unexpressed. Typically, her frustration and hurt are reported to the reader ("Fanya wanted to scream: And I? And I?, but she kept silent," 176, and cf. 105, 144, 164, 187, 217), but they always remain confined within the seething turmoil of her narrated inner monologues. When they are actually verbalized, it is only in the framework of private female discourse. Fanya may have penetrated male *praxis*, but not its *public discourse*. The prevailing ideology remains untouched by her feminist critique. In the final analysis, Fanya's quest for selfhood inscribes itself only as a comment on the margins of an androcentric system.

We should not be surprised, then, that Lapid does not give her heroine the chance to try and make it on her own. In the last page, the plot of the romance prevails. Sasha, an old acquaintance, himself a survivor of the Ukrainian pogroms, reappears, asking permission "to help and be helped" (cf. the Zionist quest "to build and be rebuilt"). With this new beginning, the novel reverts to its two original models: the historical and the romantic. Subjective experience is embedded again in Jewish collectivity, symbolized throughout the story by the legendary Phoenix ("This is what we Jews do. Start all over again. Again. And again. And again."), only to be taken over by an old/new romance closure:

> . . . "I need you, Fanya! Will you allow me to help you?"
> Fanya looked at him wondering. Then she thought that if he hugged her, her head would barely reach his shoulder. And then her eyes filled with tears. (266)

What right do we have to claim this quasi-historical quasi-feminist romance as a masked autobiography?—Obviously, there could be no biographical ties between the author, our contemporary, and the pioneers of a century ago.[8] But at the same time the authorial intention is quite transparent: to project into the historical past feminist concerns and expectations that present-day Israeli reality cannot satisfy. This intention grows suspiciously palpable when we consider a peculiar technical aspect of the novel. Although it is told in a straightforward "third-person" narration, information is mostly limited to that which is available to the heroine. Fanya is not only the protagonist of the action, but also its point of focalization. Her inner world is too close to that of the narrator (to the exclusion of all other figural perspectives), to do justice to the narration of a *historical* novel. This lack of (ironic or other) distance, as well as the narrator's narrow point of view, undermines the work's claim to be a historical novel. It generates the impression that the development of the heroine's consciousness is a projection of a contemporary *Bildungsroman* or spiritual autobiography, masqueraded as a more acceptable genre. Lapid had obviously felt that Israeli society of the early 1980s would accept a "feminist" identity as a historical projection, but would find it difficult to digest as a realistic proposition for the here and now.

Working within the conventions of the popular romance, Lapid (who is herself a happily married mother and a former Chair of the Israeli Writers' Association) uses the historical and ideological materials as a setting against which her protagonists reach toward their optimal development. She does not subject her own premises about gender to a serious scrutiny ("motherhood," for example, is never really problematized: Fanya just weaves it into her busy schedule, although it is never clear how); nor does she indulge in a psychological exploration of her characters. She is content to follow their present entanglements to their happy endings without delving into the larger questions posed by the issues she has dramatized.

The exploration of some of these questions is the domain of the third of our "quasi-autobiographies," Amalia Kahana-Carmon's novella, *The Bridge of the Green Duck* (1984). Unlike our first two cases this is not an author's first novel. It is also the first story we encounter that uses first-person narration, thus coming very close to an autobiographic modality. Saying this, we should emphasize that the author took every precaution to distance herself and the reader from the potential intimacy implied by an autobiographic discourse. Using the most arcane Hebrew style, she fashioned an ostensible female voice of the seventeenth century, telling of life in exile and captivity within a heavily androcentric society.

In this highly stylized novella, set in the romantically distant European past, gender antagonism is metaphorized by Jewish-gentile relationship, and female existential captivity is embedded in Jewish exile. Furthermore, the personal story takes on allegorical dimensions so that the "woman question" becomes a paradigm of a general issue —the problem of the "other":

"Gentiles and Jews, they are like men and women," my father always said. "Why," I once asked. "Only because of preconceived judgments. Of each side: about oneself; about the other, too," my father smiled. "Each side has its own picture," my father used to say. "Its image of the other. Therefore, when addressing someone from the other side, to the image and not to the person one would speak." (116)

The implications of this double embedding are too complex to be probed here (see Feldman, "The Other"). Suffice it to say, by way of summarizing, that the female subjectivity emerging from this highly conceptualized narrative goes way beyond cross-gender equality. Unlike her predecessors, this protagonist's growth is wholly determined by her object-relations with *male* models, whose ostensible autonomy—the ideal usually attributed to an accomplished male identity—is the promised goal beckoning the heroine beyond the closure of the text. Lack of space does not allow us to elaborate the meaning of this position in the context of Kahana-Carmon's own oeuvre or that of her peer writers. It is clear, however, that she consciously struggles against the tradition of the "feminist romance," of which *Gei Oni* is a prime example, and to which most of her own work definitely belongs. But it is just as obvious that for Israeli women writers this battle against stereotyped gender perceptions has been carried out mostly in the guise of mythical projections, while their self representation has been rarely accomplished without the help of a national-collective overlayer.[9] As such, the Israeli corpus of quasi-autobiographies readily supports both a cultural definition of gender and a historically determined understanding of the subject.

NOTES

1. Although the intriguing history of the reception of modern psychology by Israeli culture has yet to be written, it is clear that almost from the beginning Zionist ideology and Freudian psychology were locked in an uneasy coexistence. The tension between these two competing solutions to the Jewish malaise— both products of turn-of-the-century Vienna—has been recently traced back to the pioneers of the 1920s who tried, although not very successfully, to reconcile the two (see Feldman, "Zionism").

Later historical developments (e.g. World War II, the Holocaust, the War of Independence and the continuous state of siege in which Israel has found itself since its establishment in 1948) strengthened the national and collective identity of the young state, at the expense of Freudian or other modes of personal introspection practiced in the West. Recently, however, Israeli writers have begun to question and problematize this state of affairs by appropriating the "forbidden" luxury for their literary critique of ideology. For a detailed analysis see my "Back to Vienna," as well as my forthcoming *Freudianism and its Discontents in Hebrew Literature*.
2. Obvious examples of this genre are novels by Shahar, Bartov, and Oz, which are discussed in Feldman, "Gender In/Difference."
3. It was also easier to write verse without the training in classical Hebrew traditionally reserved only for males. It is no coincidence that the first modern Hebrew prose writer, Devorah Baron, had been raised "as a son," that is—instructed in the sacred sources—by her father who was a rabbi; and see Govrin.
4. This is not to say that these narratives do not use autobiographic materials—e.g. Noami Fraenkel, Rachel Eitan, Amalia Kahana-Carmon, Dalia Ravikovitch, Hedda Boshes, Yehudit Hendel—but rather that they do not take the *shape* of autobiographic retrospection.
5. In the Oxford Dictionary, composed between 1884 and 1928, "feminism" gets the briefest treatment of all female-related entries—"The qualities of females"—and it is accompanied by the qualifier "Rare."
6. Literature does not score much higher on this point, the few exceptions [e.g. Alper, Shamir] notwithstanding. Israeli literature has been good in inscribing women's victimization, as shown by Esther Fuchs, although I am not sure I share her enthusiasm for this project.
7. Shochat's fascinating biography, *Before Golda*, told by Rachel Yanait Ben-Zvi, was recently released in translation (Biblio Press, 1988), as was a documentary film based on it.
8. Except, perhaps, in the fact that Lapid was born in Rumania (1935), the native country of some of the settlers in Rosh Pinah.
9. For a recent exception that both epitomizes and transcends the genre described here see Ruth Almog's 1987 novel *Dangling Roots*. And see my forthcoming "Inventing One's Own Life: From Feminism to Post-Feminism in Israeli Literature."

WORKS CITED

Abel, Elizabeth, Marianne Hirsch, and Elizabeth Langland, eds. *The Voyage In: Fictions of Female Development*. UP of New England, 1983.

Alper, Rivka. *Hamitnahalim baHar*. [The Settlers of the Mountain]. Tel Aviv: Am Oved, 1962.

Bartov, Hanoch. *Shel mi atta, yeled?* Tel Aviv: Am oved, 1970. *Whose Little Boy are You?* Tr. Hillel Halkin. JPS, Philadelphia, 1978.

Benstock, Shari, ed. *The Private Self: Theory and Practice of Women's Autobiographical Writings*. Chapel Hill: North Carolina P, 1988.

Berlowitz, Yaffa. "The Literature of the Early Pioneer Women." *Proza*, 66-67 (July, 1983):31-33 (Hebrew).

Bernstein, Devorah. "The Status and Organization of Urban Working Women in the 20s and 30s." *Katedra* 34 (1988): 115-144. (Hebrew).

———. "The Women Workers' Movement in Pre-State Israel, 1919-1939." *Signs* 12:3 (1987): 454-470.

Blackburn, Regina. "In Search of the Black Female Self." in *Women's Autobiography*. Ed. Estelle C. Jelinek. Bloomington: Indiana UP, 1980. 133-148.

Brée, Germaine. "Autogynography." *Studies in Autobiography*. Ed. James Olney. New York: Oxford UP, 1988: 171-179.

Brodzki, Bella and Celeste Schenck, eds. *Life/Lines: Theorizing Women's Autobiography*. Ithaca: Cornell UP, 1988.

Chodorow, Nancy. *The Reproduction of Mothering: Psychoanalysis and the Sociology of Gender*. Berkeley: California UP, 1978.

Cohen, Mabel Blake. "Personal Identity and Sexual Identity." *Psychoanalysis and Women*. Ed. Jean Baker Miller. New York: Penguin, 1973. 156-182.

Edwards, Lee. "The Labors of Psyche: Towards a Theory of Female Heroes." *Critical Inquiry* 6 (1979): 33-49.

Eakin, Paul John. *Fictions in Autobiography: Studies in the Art of Self Invention*. Princeton: Princeton UP, 1985.

Feldman, Yael. "Back to Vienna: Zionism on the Literary Couch." *Vision Confronts Reality*. Eds. Ruth Kozodoy, David Sidorsky, Kalman Sultanik. London & Toronto: Associated University Presses, 1989. 310-335. Reprinted in *Tikkun* (November 1979): 31-34; 91-96.

———. "Feminism under Siege: The Vicarious Selves of Israeli Women Writers." *Prooftexts* 10:3 (1990): 1-22.

———. *Freudianism & Its Discontents in Hebrew Literature.* (Forthcoming).

———. "Gender In/Difference in Contemporary Hebrew Fictional Autobiographies." *Biography: An Interdisciplinary Quarterly* 11:3 (Summer 1988): 189-209. Reprinted in *Sex, Love, & Signs: European Journal for Semiotic Studies* 1:3 (1989): 435-456.

———. "Inadvertent Feminism: The Image of Frontier Women in Contemporary Israeli Fiction." *Modern Hebrew Literature* 10:3-4 (1985):34-37.

———. "New Psychoanalytic Models for Theory of Comparative Study of Autobiography." *Toward a Theory of Comparative Literature.* Ed. Mario J. Valdes. New York: Peter Lang, 1989. 125-133.

———. The 'Other Within' in Contemporary Israeli Fiction." *Middle East Review* 25:1 (Fall 1989): 47-53.

———. "Zionism—Neurosis or cure? The 'Historical' Drama of Y. Sobol." *Prooftexts* 7:2 (May 1987): 145-162.

Ferguson, Mary Anne. "The Female Novel of Development and the Myth of Psyche." *The Voyage In: Fictions of Female Development.* Eds. Abel et al., 228-243.

Friedman, Susan Stanford. "Theories of Autobiography and Fictions of the Self in H. D.'s Canon." M.L.A. Conference, NY, 1983. (Forthcoming in Thomas R. Smith, ed. *Self-Representations.*)

Fuchs, Esther. *Israeli Mythogenies.* Albany: SUNY P, 1987.

Gilligan, Carol. *In a Different Voice.* Cambridge: Harvard, 1982.

Govrin, Nurit. *Devorah Baron: The First Half.* Jerusalem: Bialik Institute, 1988. (Hebrew).

Gunn, Janet Varner. *Autobiography: Towards a Poetics of Experience.* Philadelphia: U of Pennsylvania P, 1982.

Gusdorf, Georges. "Conditions and Limits of Autobiography." *Autobiography.* Ed. James Olney. 1980. 28-48.

Har'el, Shlomo. "Around the Settlement—Between Myth and Historicism." *Between History and Literature.* Tel Aviv: Tel Aviv UP, 1983. 134-150. (Hebrew).

Hareven, Shulamith. *Ir Yamim Rabim.* Tel Aviv: Am Oved, 1972. *City of Many Days.* Tr. Hillel Halkin. Garden City, N.Y., 1977.

Hazelton, Lesley. *Israeli Women: The Reality behind the Myth.* New York, 1977.

Heilbrun, Carolyn G. *Reinventing Womanhood.* New York: Norton, 1979.

———. *Writing a Woman's Life.* New York: Norton, 1988.

Heschel, Susannah, ed. *On Being a Jewish Feminist.* New York: Schocken, 1983.

Izraeli, Dafna. "The Working Women Movement in Palestine from its Inception to 1929." *Katedra* 32 (1984): 109-140.

———. "The Zionist Women's Movement in Palestine, 1911-1927: A Sociological Analysis." *Signs* 7:1 (1981): 87-114.

Jay, Paul. *Being in the Text*. Ithaca & London: Cornell UP, 1984.

Jelinek, Estelle C. *Women's Autobiography*. Bloomington: Indiana UP, 1980. 1-20.

Kahana-Carmon, Amalia. "The Bridge of the Green Duck." *LeMala beMontifer* (Up on Montifer). Tel Aviv: Siman Kria and Hakibutz Hameuchad, 1984. 59-184.

Lapid, Shulamit. *Gei Oni*. Jerusalem: Keter, 1982.

———. "The Popular Romantic Novel." *Ma'ariv* 17.10.1975. (Hebrew).

Lejeune, Philippe. *On Autobiography*. Tr. Katherine Leary. Minneapolis: U of Minnesota P, 1989.

Margalit, Elkana. *Hashomer hatza'ir—From a Youngsters' Commune to Revolutionary Marxism*. Tel Aviv: Tel Aviv UP, 1971. (Hebrew)

Mason, Mary G. "The Other Voice: Autobiographies of Women Writers." *Autobiography*. Ed. James Olney. 207-235.

Mehlman, Jeffrey. *A Structural Study of Autobiography*. Ithaca: Cornell, 1974.

Miller, Nancy. *The Heroine's Text*. New York: Columbia UP, 1980.

Miron, Dan. "Founding Mothers, Step Sisters: On the Emergence of Women Poets in Hebrew." *Alpayim* 1 (1989): 29-58. (Hebrew).

Neumann, Erich. *Amor & Psyche: The Psychic Development of the Feminine*. Princeton: Princeton UP, 1952.

Olney, James, ed. *Autobiography: Essays Theoretical and Critical*. Princeton: Princeton UP, 1980.

———. *Metaphors of Self: The Meaning of Autobiography*. Princeton: Princeton UP, 1972.

———. *Studies in Autobiography*. New York: Oxford UP, 1988.

Oryan, Yehudit. "The Wild East." *Yediot Aharonot* (16.4. 1982): 22, 26. (Hebrew).

Oz, Amos. *Har HaEtza HaRa'ah*. 1976. *The Hill of Evil Council*. Tr. Nicholas de Lange. New York, 1978.

Rowbotham, Sheila. *Woman's Consciousness, Man's World*. London: Penguin, 1973.

Seidenberg, Robert. "Is Anatomy Destiny?" in *Psychoanalysis and Women*, ed. Jean Baker Miller, Penguin, 1973: 306-29.

Shahar, David. *Heichal hakelim hashvurim*. 1967-1986. *The Palace of Shattered Vessels*. Tr. Dalya Bilu. Boston, 1975.

Shamir, Moshe. *Yona meHatzer Zarah*. [A Foreign Dove]. Tel Aviv, 1975.

——. *Hinumat Kalah*. [The Bridal Veil]. Tel Aviv, 1984.
Smith, Sidonie. *A Poetics of Women's Autobiography*. Bloomington: Indiana UP, 1987.
Spengemann, W. C. *The Forms of Autobiography*. New Haven and London: Yale UP, 1980.
Sturrock, John. "The New Model Autobiography." *M.L.H.* 9 (1977): 51-63.
Watson, Julia. "Shadowed Presence: Modern Women Writers' Autobiographies and the Other." *Studies in Autobiography*. Ed. James Olney. 180-189.

Notes on Contributors

Cora Agatucci teaches writing, literature, and women's studies at Central Oregon Community College. She is currently working on articles on student autobiographical writing and the nineteenth-century reception of Victorian women novelists.

Concha Alborg is the author of *Temas y técnicas en la narrativa de Jesús Fernández Santos* and has published several articles on contemporary novelists from Spain. Currently she teaches at Saint Joseph's University in Philadelphia.

Keith Byerman, Associate Professor of English at Indiana State University, is the author of *Fingering the Jagged Grain: Tradition and Form in Recent Black Fiction* and co-author of *Alice Walker: An Annotated Bibliography.*

Yael S. Feldman is author of *Modernism and Cultural Transfer* (1986, HUCP) and co-editor of *Approaches to Teaching the Hebrew Bible as Literature* (1989, MLAP). She teaches Hebrew and Comparative Literature at NYU and has published extensively on Israeli drama and fiction.

Miriam Fuchs, who teaches at the University of Hawaii, has published articles on Djuna Barnes, Marguerite Young, and other contemporary writers. She co-edited with Ellen Friedman *Breaking the Sequence: Women's Experimental Fiction* (Princeton UP, 1989) and the Fall 1989 issue of *Review of Contemporary Fiction* on the writing of Kathy Acker, Christine Brooke-Rose, and Marguerite Young.

Donald C. Goellnicht is the author of *The Poet-Physician: Keats and Medical Science,* as well as essays on English Romanticism and on Asian American writing. He teaches English at McMaster University in Canada.

Colette T. Hall, Associate Professor of French at Ursinus College, has published several articles on Violette Leduc, Marie Cardinal and French feminist theory.

Sharon Hileman is Associate Professor of English at Sul Ross State University and has written several articles on women's autobiographical fiction and letter-writing. Currently she is compiling a regional collection of women's archival material.

Molly Hite is Associate Professor of English at Cornell University. Her most recent book is *The Other Side of the Story: Structures and Strategies of Contemporary Feminist Narrative* (Cornell UP, 1989).

Ann Johnson is completing her dissertation at the University of Denver on "Urban Ghetto Riots 1964-70: Comparative Soviet and American Press Coverage." She has taught comparative women's history and written articles for Women's Studies International Forum, Colorado Women's Studies, and the Southwest Institute for Research on Women.

Kathleen L. Komar is the author of *Transcending Angels: Rainer Maria Rilke's "Duino Elegies"* (1987) and *Pattern and Chaos: Multilinear Novels by Dos Passos, Faulkner, Döblin, and Koeppen* (1983) as well as numerous articles on nineteenth and twentieth century German and American authors. She is currently working on a book on contemporary feminist re-visions of the women of the Trojan War.

Jacquelyn Y. McLendon is Assistant Professor of African-American Literature at Amherst College with a special interest in women writers of the Harlem Renaissance. She has articles forthcoming on Gwendolyn Brooks and Nella Larsen and is currently working on a full-length study of Nella Larsen and Jessie Fauset.

Janice Morgan is an Assistant Professor of French at Murray State University. She has published articles on Marguerite Duras and on French film.

Janine Ricouart is Assistant Professor of French at George Mason University. She has published several articles on Simone de Beauvoir, Marie-Claire Blais, Marguerite Duras, and Madeleine Monette. Her forthcoming book entitled *Ecriture féminine et violence: Une étude de Marguerite Duras*, will be published by Summa. She is currently pursuing her research on lesbian representation in literature and film from France and Québec.

Flora H. Schiminovich teaches Spanish and Latin American Literature at Barnard College, Columbia University. She is the author of *La obra de Macedonio Fernández: una lectura surrealista* (Madrid: Pliegos, 1986), as well as many articles on Latin American literature. She is working on a book on Latin American women writers.

Catherine Slawy-Sutton is Assistant Professor of French at Davidson College. She has written on various aspects of Colette's works. Her research interests also include contemporary French women writers and feminist theory.

Mary Titus has published several articles on Southern women writers and is currently at work on *Katherine Anne Porter: Modernism and the Southern Lady*. She is an Assistant Professor of American Literature at St. Olaf College.

Agnès Whitfield, Associate Professor of translation at York University in Canada, is the author of *Le Je(u) illocutoire*, a study of form and protest in the contemporary first-person novel in Québec, as well as numerous essays on twentieth-century Québec fiction.